D1557882

CUSTER

CUSTER

THE MAKING OF A YOUNG GENERAL

Edward G. Longacre

Skyhorse Publishing

Skyhorse Publishing books may be purchased in bulk at special discounts for sales promotion, corporate gifts, fund-raising, or educational purposes. Special editions can also be created to specifications. For details, contact the Special Sales Department, Skyhorse Publishing, 307 West 36th Street, 11th Floor, New York, NY 10018 or info@skyhorsepublishing.com.

Skyhorse® and Skyhorse Publishing® are registered trademarks of Skyhorse Publishing, Inc.®, a Delaware corporation.

Visit our website at www.skyhorsepublishing.com.

10 9 8 7 6 5 4 3 2 1

Library of Congress Cataloging-in-Publication Data is available on file.

Cover design by Rain Saukas
Cover photo credit: National Archives

Print ISBN: 978-1-5107-3319-0
Ebook ISBN: 978-1-5107-3320-6

Printed in the United States of America.

for
David and Heidi
Andy and Pam

Contents

Introduction

Military historians find it curious—some find it disconcerting—that the general public assumes that George Armstrong Custer's sole claim to a place in the national memory is the untimely fate that befell him and 262 officers and men of the 7th United States Cavalry plus scouts and civilians in southeastern Montana Territory on a June day in 1876. Many students of history, even those who consider themselves well-acquainted with the salient events of America's past, fail to realize that Custer's celebrity predated by more than a dozen years his encounter with the Lakota Sioux and Cheyenne at the Little Bighorn. In fact, the nationwide attention Custer garnered while defending the Union dwarfed the notoriety that followed him on the post-Civil War frontier. From mid-1863 until the spring of 1865 Custer was known in all sections of the war-torn nation as the quintessential "boy general"—at twenty-three, the youngest officer in the volunteer army with a star on his shoulders. His exploits on campaign and in battle received major attention in newspapers throughout the North while his portrait regularly graced the pages of the nation's most widely read publications.

Although Custer's fame may have antedated his exploits as an Indian fighter, published works that concentrate on his Civil War service are few, and even fewer capture the essence of his rise to renown. Almost all Custer biographies cover the entire range of his military career and devote a disparate amount of attention to his campaigns against Native Americans. Devoid of the glory and the quasi-chivalric character of his battles against the forces of the Confederacy, Custer's campaigns in the West generated controversy, criticism, and, in the minds of millions of Americans then and since, infamy.

Twenty years ago I made a limited effort to characterize the Civil War Custer in a book about the Michigan Cavalry Brigade of the Army of the Potomac, the command he led to fame in Pennsylvania, Maryland, and Virginia from 1863 to 1865. The present study, which focuses on Custer himself, covers the years leading up to his attainment of star rank as well as his first three months in command, during which he developed the tactics and style of leadership that would propel him through the rest of the war. That epoch saw a young general rise on the strength of his merits and potential to attain the success that escaped many another leader who enjoyed advantages of maturity and field experience denied to him. A projected second volume will cover the remainder of Custer's Civil War service and his controversial stint in Texas during the early months of Reconstruction.

The current book has two principal goals. It attempts to identify and correct the myths, misconceptions, and misinterpretations that have distorted readers' impressions of the soldier and the man. The scrutiny of dubious historical analysis extends beyond Custer's field operations to include his youth and upbringing, his professional education, his service as a staff officer to a host of powerful superiors, and his courtship of Elizabeth Clift Bacon of Monroe, Michigan. The work also seeks to add depth to the Custer narrative by providing a substantial amount of detail on aspects of his life and career that have received relatively brief attention from historians, biographers, and the compilers of the *Official Records of the Union and Confederate Armies*. For this reason I quote at greater length than any other chronicler Custer's wartime letters to family and friends, in order to relate his prewar and wartime service as much as possible through his own eyes and in his own words. In almost every instance his writings are rendered verbatim except for the inclusion of essential punctuation, thus correcting a stylistic lapse that Custer never managed to overcome.

Acknowledgments

When I began researching this study in the fall of 2015 the first librarian or archivist to provided assistance was Charmaine Wawrzyniec, curator of the Custer collection at the Ellis Library and Reference Center in Monroe, Michigan. Over the intervening months Charmaine furnished me with Custer documents including battle and campaign reports, some hitherto unknown, and she graciously answered a myriad of questions about Custer's life on and off the battlefield. Through her I reestablished contact with a longtime Custer collector, researcher, and historian, the Reverend Vincent A. Heier of Robertsville, Missouri, who generously took time from his duties as a reserve priest of the Diocese of Saint Louis to provide books, articles, and various other sources pertinent to my research. These included typed transcriptions and summaries of dozens of letters written by Custer, members of his family, and numerous other relatives, friends, and army comrades.

Others who provided material assistance include Susan Lintelmann of the United States Military Academy Library, from whom I obtained copies of Custer correspondence from West Point's vast collection of Civil War manuscripts. Her colleague Susan Mauldin-Ware of the U.S.M.A. Archives provided access to Custer's notoriously lengthy cadet disciplinary log. At the Little Bighorn Battlefield National Monument in Montana I was aided by Cindy Hogan, who at my behest diligently searched the vast collection of documents in the Elizabeth Bacon Custer Collection. Caitlyn Riehle and Nicholas Speth of the Monroe County Historical Museum and Archives obtained for me copies of letters in the George Armstrong Custer and Lawrence A. Frost collections. At the U.S. Army Heritage and Education Center, Carlisle Barracks, Pennsylvania, Rich Baker and Marlea Leljedal made available copies of letters and diaries by members of Custer's Wolverine Brigade. In Cadiz, Ohio, I obtained information and photographs pertaining to the Custer family with the help of Dr. Scott Pendleton, president of the Harrison County Historical Society, and Susan Adams, president of the Harrison County Genealogical Society. Sandra Trenholm of New York's Gilder Lehrman Institute of American

History provided background on dispatches carried by Custer during the Antietam Campaign. Brian Moose of the L. Tom Perry Special Collections at Brigham Young University, Provo, Utah, helped me obtain copies of Custer's prewar correspondence with his friend John Chamberlain.

Various private individuals also rendered assistance. Robert F. O'Neill relayed copies of numerous documents gleaned from the files of the National Archives, the Library of Congress, and the Burton Historical Collection at the Detroit Public Library, supplementing my own research in those institutions. Bob also lent assistance and offered advice on a wide range of Custer-related topics, generously answering the many questions I sent his way, more than a few of which required considerable time on his part. Clark B. ("Bud") Hall helped me understand the dynamics of battles in which Custer took part, especially Second Brandy Station. Paul Davis obtained for me a copy of the wartime diary of Brevet Major Charles H. Safford of the 5th Michigan Cavalry. Greg Biggs shared his knowledge of the Confederate flags captured or acquired by Custer. John W. Leland directed me to eyewitness accounts of some of Custer's post-Gettysburg operations.

For the excellent maps that grace this book I thank Paul Dangel of Berwyn, Pennsylvania, with whom I have collaborated profitably for more than twenty years. Jay Cassell and Veronica Alvarado of Skyhorse Publishing were uniformly helpful and encouraging. My granddaughter, LeAnn Hamilton, helped locate relevant illustrations and made them suitable for reproduction. I cannot adequately thank my wife, Melody Ann Longacre, without whose support in a variety of research and editorial capacities this book could not have been written.

It should go without saying that none of the individuals mentioned above is responsible for the themes, interpretations, or conclusions of the author.

Chapter I

Impulsive Youth

Conflicting stories, as well as inconsistent or missing records, complicate understanding many aspects of Custer's life and career, beginning with his birth. It is generally accepted that George Armstrong Custer was born in the village of New Rumley in rural Harrison County, Ohio, on December 5, 1839. Supposedly he came into the world in the lower-right room of a two-story log house built a quarter-century earlier by James G. Ward, Custer's maternal grandfather. Other sources dispute these details. A persistent legend claims that the house in New Rumley was heavily damaged by a fire that broke out a few weeks before Custer was born. This had occurred on a wintery day when a blacksmith's bellows was moved too close to the rear corner of the house in an effort to shield it from the falling snow. The fire forced the unborn child's parents, Emmanuel Henry Custer and Maria Ward Kirkpatrick Custer, to vacate the premises until the damage could be repaired.

The dwelling was rebuilt in the first decade of the twentieth century on the corner of Liberty and Main Streets in New Rumley, the site of a heroic-sized statue of Custer erected in 1932. Two years earlier, in anticipation of the need to clear ground for an adjoining memorial park, the remodeled, privately owned house had been moved about a hundred yards down the street from its former location. A little more than five decades after his death Custer's birth-place had become, in a sense, a casualty of his fame.[1]

But was New Rumley in fact his hometown? According to Custer historian John M. Carroll, the possibility exists that the future general was not born in the village, although not far from it. "One popular legend," Carroll writes, "is that the actual site of the Custer home was really in West Liberty, and that New Rumley actually abutted West Liberty, but not for nearly 100 yards down the main street . . . away from the Custer home." Unable to disprove this bit of oral history, Carroll admits that the claim lacks a firm foundation but observes that "all legends have a basis in fact."

A "more reasonable conjecture," according to Carroll, is that Custer was born in the village of Scio, some three miles west of New Rumley. This inference is based on the possibility that the fire that may have driven the Custers from their home forced them to take up residence on a farmstead known locally as the Gotshall Farm. If this was where Maria Custer gave birth to her son George, as Carroll suggests, the conclusion is that "the General was, again, technically not born in New Rumley, though the family soon returned to the newly repaired home" it had been forced to leave.[2]

Regardless of the dwelling where he was born, George Custer boasted a lengthy and colorful lineage that in this country stretched at least as far back as the mid-eighteenth century. According to some sources the family had Hessian roots, suggesting that the first "Kuster" to reach American soil fought with the British in the Revolutionary War, but diligent research by members of the family in the British war records effectively disproved this story. In fact George Armstrong Custer's great-grandfather, Emmanuel Custer, a native of Maryland, is known to have served as a noncommissioned officer in the colonial militia. The family was also linked to the history of the early colonies through Emmanuel's father, Paul Custer, who married a cousin of the mother of George Washington. Thus, as Harrison County historian L. Milton Ronsheim proudly noted in his 1929 biography of Armstrong Custer, the latter "was not only from Colonial stock, but also of the same blood which produced the Father of the Nation."[3]

In 1782, when the couple was living in Berks County, Pennsylvania, Emmanuel's wife Maria gave birth to their first child, John. Their son, Armstrong Custer's grandfather, grew up in Maryland, where his parents had returned after having moved to Ohio and living for an indeterminate period in Harrison County. By his early twenties John, then married to the former Catherine Valentine, had sired the first of seven children, one of whom was named George Washington Custer.

John and Catherine's first son, Emmanuel Henry Custer, was born in Cresaptown, Maryland, on December 10, 1806. As a young man Emmanuel followed his grandparents' westward migration, eventually settling in New Rumley. There he plied the blacksmith's trade, a needful occupation that must have been much in demand since, as Ronsheim notes, "he was the only smith for miles around." His new community, which sprawled along the stagecoach route between Steubenville and points northwest, was a Custer family establishment, having been laid out in 1813 by Emmanuel's uncle Jacob. By the time

Emmanuel Custer settled there the rechristened village had grown to accommodate two dozen families, almost five times as many as when Rumley Town was plotted.[4]

At first, Emmanuel made a success of his business, not only because it was an integral part of the local economy, but because he was industrious, affable, well-versed on the issues of the day and something of an orator. Even before Andrew Jackson claimed the White House in 1828, the eastern-born smithy had become an ardent Democrat, ready to engage those of opposing political persuasions in spirited discussion. As one of George Custer's more recent biographers observes, Emmanuel "relished such debates, and in his loud voice held forth, with each point perhaps emphasized by the clang of hammer on anvil."

Years later the smithy's daughter-in-law, Elizabeth Bacon Custer—who, according to her friend and literary executor Marguerite Merington, had been "brought up to believe that salvation was reserved exclusively for Republicans"—asked Emmanuel, the son of a devout Whig, how he could have transferred his allegiance to the Democratic Party. She received a curious reply: "As a boy I was greatly stirred by a character, a veteran of the Revolution, also of the War of 1812, who used to come around piping war tunes on a fife. A Democrat, he professed himself. And then I made up my mind that if that was the side a man could come out on, after two wars, that would be the side for me." Emmanuel's explanation may not have been wholly credible especially given his witty response to another question Libbie Custer posed to him during the same conversation: did it not shake his faith in his party to know that a majority of America's clergymen were Republicans? "Father Custer," a nominal Presbyterian who after his second marriage had converted to Methodism (as had the formerly Lutheran Maria Custer), replied that the ministers' political preference did not weaken his belief in the party of Jackson, "but it does shake my faith in their religion."[5]

As this conversation suggests, even as a young man Emmanuel Custer was not of an unrelievedly serious turn of mind; friends and neighbors found him cheerful and fun-loving, with an affinity for games and friendly competition. He would bequeath his light-hearted personality to his children, especially, it would seem, his first surviving son.

*   *   *

During his first four years in Harrison County Emmanuel remained a bachelor, but in August 1828 he wed Matilda Viers, daughter of the local justice of the peace. Two years later, having moved to a house on the village's main street adjacent to Emmanuel's shop, the couple became the parents of a daughter who died early in the following year but was followed over the next two years by two healthy sons. Tragedy, however, repeated itself in the summer of 1834 with the sudden death of Matilda.

Grieving but determined to make his family circle whole again, the blacksmith remained single for less than two years. During that period he met and grew close to Maria Ward Kirkpatrick. Maria had been a resident of New Rumley for twenty years, having settled there at age nine with her tavern-operator parents, James and Catherine Ward, and three siblings. In January 1823 fifteen-year-old Maria had married twenty-seven-year-old Israel R. Kirkpatrick, a New Rumley storekeeper. Despite the disparity in their ages the union appears to have been a happy one—the couple reared two children—though apparently they never operated the tavern that Maria's father had run (conspicuously unsuccessfully) until his death in 1824.

In 1835, the same year that Emmanuel Custer's wife died, Israel Kirkpatrick passed away. Harrison County historian Charles Wallace writes that at that time "there were only about ten dozen people living in New Rumley and family tragedies were shared by the whole tiny community. The Custers and Kirkpatricks mourned for one another and Emmanuel and Maria, old friends in a small village, were impelled by a common sorrow to draw closer." The shared grief that bonded the two, and the need to provide for motherless and fatherless offspring, culminated in their marriage on February 23, 1836. Rather than reside in Emmanuel's home, the couple settled in the log house that James Ward had built.

For the next two years the same tragedies that had inflicted so much suffering on Emmanuel and Maria stalked the new couple. In the summer of 1839 John Custer, Emmanuel's last-born child with his first wife, died at age two. Then, in cruel succession, Emmanuel and Maria lost their first two children. Understandably, a family friend would describe Maria at this point in her life as a woman who "showed a high degree of refinement, with a twinge of sadness resting upon her countenance." When she became pregnant again in spring 1839, the Custers prayed for a happier outcome while silently dreading the heartbreak of another empty cradle.

The couple was relieved and overjoyed when, three weeks before Christmas, Maria gave birth to a healthy son whom they named George Armstrong, supposedly after his grandly named uncle. According to a local story, however, he received his name from the family's pastor, who prayed over Maria when it was feared that she and the child would both die during delivery. The boy was known to his family as Armstrong and, more frequently, as "Autie," the two-year-old's lisping pronunciation of his middle name.[6]

From birth Autie was hearty and energetic, with a fair complexion, "dancing blue eyes," and reddish-yellow hair that curled over his brow in striking fashion. By all accounts he inherited not only his father's blond appearance but also his cheerful, boisterous nature and his love of games and friendly competition. Contrasting moods suggested other parental acquisitions. Historian Wallace notes that George's maternal grandfather was known for a volatile temperament that occasionally landed him in trouble with the law. Not only had James Ward been fined for practices relating to his tavern keeping, but he had also been hauled into court more than once for harassing neighbors. Wallace adds that while Maria appears to have been spared her father's dark side, "some of her children, especially George Custer, inherited an ample share of it."[7]

Over the next twelve years, Emmanuel and Maria provided their first surviving son with four siblings: brothers Nevin, Thomas, and Boston, and sister Margaret, born, respectively, in July 1842, March 1845, October 1848, and January 1852, Margaret's birth coming one month after her father's forty-fifth birthday. While Thomas and Boston grew up, like Autie, hale and hearty, possessed of considerable energy and physical strength if not an especially powerful build, Nevin from childhood was slight to the point of frailty. It was noted that the gentleness with which the family treated him was fully shared by his older brother, a trait "unusual for one who had occupied first place in a family for so long."[8]

Nevin's physique would prevent him from becoming the only Custer brother not to serve with the army in any capacity. The others, especially Autie, grew up in a quasi-military atmosphere that had much to do with their ancestors' service in past wars and Emmanuel's enlistment in a local militia unit, the New Rumley Guards. Even as a child George learned to be stoical in trying circumstances, enduring suffering in soldierly fashion. When a toothache sent him to a local doctor for an extraction, his father reminded him that although discomfort would follow he "must be a good soldier." The admonition had its effect; although the boy's mouth and jaw throbbed, he shed no tears.[9]

Although Maria Custer dressed her first-born in a miniature soldier's uniform and armed him with a toy musket or sword, some who knew the family well claimed that Autie's parents did not encourage his military aspirations.

Yet at least one historian observes that Custer's apparent life-long affinity for the soldier's life owed to his growing up "in a military atmosphere which he loved so well." If so, his predilection ran to mounted service, for as the son of a blacksmith he developed an early love for horses and a zest for riding. By his teens, he had become an accomplished equestrian.

Some biographers have suggested that a pro-military environment was more or less the national norm during the boy's formative years. In fact, until the mid-1840s, America, steeped in English history and Jeffersonian preferences for a small, carefully monitored military establishment, was anything but a bastion of soldierly influence. Over the half-decade leading to the commencement of war with Mexico in the spring of 1846, the nation's military manpower numbers dropped every year except one. During the same period professional military education experienced a steep decline, one indication being that between 1843 and 1847 the average size of the incoming cadet class of the United States Military Academy at West Point decreased by more than 30 percent. The Mexican-American conflict reversed this trend but only for the duration of the conflict, which effectively ended with the capture of Mexico City in September 1847. The fortified capital fell to regular and volunteer troops led by Commanding General Winfield Scott, from childhood one of Autie Custer's most revered heroes.[10]

Whether or not the boy's soldierly ambitions received parental support, he grew up in a family whose loving nature he deeply appreciated. His vibrant father and quietly doting mother saw to it that, although money was never easy to come by, Autie, his siblings, and their half-siblings enjoyed as many material resources and as much intellectual stimulation and emotional support as any children could reasonably expect. In later life Maria recalled that "I was not fortunate enough to have wealth to make [our] home beautiful, always my desire. So I tried to fill the empty space with little acts of kindness." Sometimes it was simply a matter of serving a meal that the children liked: "It was my greatest pleasure to get it for them."[11]

Parental care extended to the children's religious upbringing. Autie and his brothers habitually resisted accompanying their parents to church. In later life he was never affiliated with a particular religion. Even so, his parents ensured that during his most impressionable years he never lacked exposure to moral or ethical instruction. Despite the boy's studied indifference toward theology, for a time Emmanuel entertained the notion that Autie would become a minister—supposedly a scholarship was waiting for him at a Methodist-affiliated college in Meadville, Pennsylvania. But Autie remained opposed, and a tuition-free education went to a more suitable applicant.[12]

He never forgot the guiding hands that shaped his early years or the care and sense of security he enjoyed when part of the family circle. When years later Emmanuel Custer expressed regret that he had not been able to do more for his son materially, Armstrong assured him that "I never wanted for anything necessary. You and Mother instilled in me principles of industry, self-reliance, honesty. You taught me the value of temperate habits, the difference between right and wrong. I look back on the days spent under the home-roof as a period of pure happiness, and I feel thankful for such noble parents." Some biographers have suggested that nostalgia clouded Custer's memory; they point to his dubious claim to having learned the benefits of self-discipline and "temperate habits." In truth, despite occasionally backsliding, Custer did adopt and maintain temperate habits at least in his use of alcohol and tobacco. To be sure, industry and self-reliance were traits he never lacked at any period of his later life, and to attribute them to parental oversight seems fully justified.[13]

Some characteristics are especially identifiable as having been passed on to him by Emmanuel and Maria Custer. Undoubtedly through his mother's influence he developed hygienic habits seemingly unusual for his era. In later life his wife would remark, with quiet amusement, how often he washed his hands and that he never failed to brush his teeth after eating. Not only did he reflect his father's military and political attitudes, but he also grew up loving competitive games—those he could play on terra firma, since he never professed to enjoy swimming or boating.[14]

He also participated in his share of youthful deviltry. Even as a young man playing jokes and pranks never failed to delight him. Nevin Custer wrote that his brother "always had to have something going" in the way of amusement. The second son would recall an especially outlandish prank that Cadet Custer pulled on returning home during his only West Point furlough. Learning that Nevin was cultivating the soil in the family's wheat field, Autie told their mother that he intended to "scare Nev." Donning a hoopskirt, a shaker bonnet, and one of Maria's dresses, he "came up to the field and leaned on the fence with his head resting on his arm" and struck a coquettish pose. At first Nevin took the onlooker for a comely lass he had never laid eyes on before; when he finally recognized his brother he was so flabbergasted he nearly dropped the reins and allowed the plow horse to run off.[15]

At times Autie would enlist other family members in his merriment. Once he challenged his father to a footrace, betting that he could give Emmanuel a substantial head start and still beat him. "Well," Nevin recalled, "father took the barter and I was to hold the money and the first one out got the money. I went up bout ten rods to see that everything was all right, and when they came [running] I was to grab father and hold him until Autie caught up. You may guess who got the money." Nevin added: "That was the Custer [brand of humor] . . . they can't help it, it is born in them . . . to want to have somebody in hot water" at all times.[16]

*   *   *

At age six George Armstrong Custer received his first exposure to formal education in the local district schools. In line with the common-school system of the day, he was placed in a cramped log schoolhouse alongside students of various ages and sizes. Milton Ronsheim writes that "it was typical of the old one-room schools, with desks around the walls. Probably sixty pupils attended at this time, and among the teachers were a Mr. Ford and a Mr. Burns. Schools lasted but a few short months."[17]

That was still too long for Autie Custer, who from the first proved an indifferent student, although his love of reading (novels, not textbooks) and flashes of native intelligence impressed his teachers. He would do the work expected of him without going beyond the basic requirements while showing a decided preference for recess. In the schoolyard he could engage in the rough-and-tumble games he excelled at, such as "catcher" and hide-and-seek, with an occasional game of town ball, a precursor of baseball then coming into some semblance of formalized play in other, more settled parts of the country. As a classmate remembered, Autie indulged a perhaps-natural tendency to boss around the younger pupils, who came to regard him as their leader outside the classroom.[18]

When he was seven the Custer family circle suffered a notable breach when his half-sister, twenty-one-year-old Lydia Ann Kirkpatrick, left home to settle in southeastern Michigan. Of his several inherited siblings, the boy had always felt most closely attached to his mother's oldest daughter. The depth of his affection was such that Autie considered her a second mother. Others too spoke of her gentle nature and air of refinement; upon meeting her for the first time in the winter of 1864, Custer's fiancée Libbie described the then-thirty-nine-year-old

Ann (as she was known in the family) as "such a lady," whose charm and graciousness put all around her, even strangers, at ease. Thus the boy was shaken and saddened when in the fall of 1846 Ann announced her pending marriage to David Reed of Monroe, a New Rumley native whose family and Emmanuel Custer's may have been linked by an earlier marriage.[19]

The Custers appear to have had a prior connection with Monroe, Michigan, where the young couple settled. According to a nineteenth-century history of Monroe County, in May 1842 Emmanuel and his wife along with Autie and his half brothers and sisters (Maria was then seven months pregnant with Nevin) had moved to Monroe where they rented a farm. Reasons for the resettlement remain obscure, but the family's time in the Wolverine State proved to be both brief and unfortunate. When horse thieves ravaged the family's stable it took six months for Father Custer to recoup the loss, whereupon he, Maria, and the children returned to New Rumley. Ann and David were married there on December 1, 1846, and six years would pass before Autie could reunite with the half-sister.[20]

In the spring of 1849, Emmanuel Custer, for unknown reasons, gave up the blacksmith's trade to try his hand at farming. For the second time in seven years he uprooted his family, this time moving it to North Township, some seven miles out in the country. Charles Wallace describes the change of profession and scenery as somewhat puzzling given that the eighty-acre farmstead Emmanuel purchased lacked uniformly fertile soil. The farmhouse was "a plain log building located in a dark damp valley far from the main roads. At best the farm was only a subsistence enterprise because it was too small to properly maintain a family of nine. Nevertheless the Custers worked their little farm faithfully for a decade and apparently they never regretted the move from New Rumley."[21]

In his new home young George was introduced to the everyday drudgery of farm work, which he shared with his brothers and half-brothers, David and John Kirkpatrick. At an early period he firmly and irrevocably decided that husbandry was not the life for him, and when he left home to enter West Point and an entirely different profession, he never looked back on his life on the farm except perhaps with a shudder.

The dreaded prospect of being shackled to the soil may have influenced him to pay greater attention to his schooling, which resumed soon after the family resettled. The farmstead straddled the boundary line between North and Rumley Townships, permitting the Custer children to attend the schools of either community. Emmanuel chose to send Autie and his brothers to the Creal School, a decade-old country institution located on a ridge about a mile and half north of neighboring Scio. As he had in the district school he first attended, the boy proved to be anything but a brilliant student though again he displayed indications that, had he applied himself, he might have excelled in at least some of his studies. One of his classmates (perhaps prompted by a charitable memory) recalled Custer as "an apt scholar" as well as "a leader among the boys, mischievous and full of practical jokes." To be sure, he consistently outshone some of the other pupils including brother Nevin who, it was observed, was slow to master "his numbers" as applied to the science of weights and measures.[22]

As before, Autie clearly preferred the schoolyard to the schoolroom, ball playing to textbook recitation. Another fellow student, Richard M. Vorhees, later an Ohio appellate judge, wrote that throughout the school year Custer "was a leader in sports, by nature manly, exuberant, enthusiastic. . . ." The boy was also beginning to show signs—until then unnoticed, overlooked, or forgiven—of impulsiveness, especially when challenging others who got crossways of him. At Creal he was frequently involved in rough play and involved in several bouts with other pupils.[23]

George's impulsiveness sometimes morphed into the kind of reckless behavior that, if it did not appear to worry his parents, alarmed his teachers. The following conversation, which took place later in his educational career, could also have occurred at Creal, where the boy was made to answer for more than his share of transgressions. It testifies not only to his increasing tendency to act rashly, without regard to consequences but also to his unwillingness to reform:

> **George:** "I know I was wrong, but I could not help it."
> **Teacher:** "Could not help it?"
> **George:** "No Sir. I wanted to do it."
> **Teacher:** "But could you not restrain your impulses?"
> **George:** "Don't know Sir—never tried."
> **Teacher:** "But don't you think you ought to try?"
> **George:** "What if I could? But I don't feel like trying."[24]

It was at Creal that he began to socialize actively with groups of children his own age. Early on he decided that male companionship was preferable to the company of girls, in contrast to the forwardness he had shown toward the other sex at an earlier age. One of his cousins, Mary Custer of Scio, recalled accompanying her physician father on a visit to the Custer blacksmith shop where she was told to "go and meet my cousins. I went over into the yard where two small boys were playing, the larger of whom had light golden hair, and was dressed in a striped calico shirt. When the boys saw me coming, the large one who was my cousin Autie, came up to me [and] when I told him that I was his cousin Mary . . . he replied, 'Well if you are my cousin I guess I ought to kiss you,' which he forthwith proceeded to do, somewhat to my surprise, as I was not used to boy playmates and even at that tender age did not know whether it was just the proper thing to do even between cousins." Mary related the incident because she considered it "indicative of the impulsive nature of the General even when a boy. . . ."[25]

Over time the boisterous youngster with the blue eyes, strawberry-blond hair, and freckles would discover that girls found him attractive. But although somewhat attuned to the feminine mind through his close relations with his sister and half-sister, until his mid-teens he paid girls scant attention, showing a degree of shyness not unnatural in a boy his age.

* * *

By the time he was twelve Autie had completed the normal period of study for common-school students of his time. His parents were undecided as to whether he should continue his education. Aware that their son, though intelligent and precocious, had no great love for book learning, they agreed to apprentice him to a cabinetmaker in the Harrison County seat of Cadiz, fifteen miles from New Rumley. The experiment proved a disaster. Turning a foot lathe and stocking bins with oak, maple, and cherry wood failed to stir Autie's interest or engage his imagination, and he came to hate the tedious and mind-numbingly repetitive work. The misery-drenched letters he sent his family finally persuaded Emmanuel to bring him home.[26]

As had his unhappy experience at farming, Autie's brief exposure to employment outside the home made him reconsider acquiring an advanced education. Perhaps reluctantly, his parents approved of his intentions. They could have sent him to the high school in Cadiz, but it charged a steep tuition. Therefore they paid heed when Lydia Ann, who had been begging them to send Autie to her, wrote that educational facilities in Monroe were abundant, of high quality, and less costly than those in Harrison County. After some hesita-tion, Autie's parents agreed to allow him to live with the Reeds for the duration of the then-current semester. And so in the summer or fall of 1852 father and son made the long journey to southeastern Michigan, which would be Autie's home off and on for the next two and a half years.

Autie was overjoyed to be reunited with the surrogate mother he cherished and fit comfortably into the Reed household. When not in the classroom he seemed to enjoy helping his half-sister with some of the same chores he had detested back home. When Ann was otherwise occupied, he cared for her chil-dren, including her oldest, Henry Armstrong ("Autie") Reed, whom she had named for her brother and of whom the older Armstrong was very fond. As a lover of horses, he would have happily assisted David Reed with his livery busi-ness. According to his first biographer, while living in Monroe the youngster consistently showed "extreme gentleness and kindness of heart. To her [Ann] he was the most docile of boys, obeying her slightest wish the moment it was expressed. He was exceedingly tender-hearted also; so much so that he could never bear even to see a chicken killed; and the sight of suffering of any kind completely unnerved him."[27]

But he was less than thrilled when the Reeds entered him in the New Dublin School and later in the Stebbins Academy. The latter institution, whose student body consisted exclusively of boys and young men, may have served to deepen the shyness he continued to show around females. One day while walking home from Stebbins he was hailed by a little girl swinging on the gate of her family's picket fence. Her greeting of "Hello you Custer boy!" seemed to startle them both, and she immediately fled inside the house. The impul-sive stranger was eight-year-old Elizabeth Clift Bacon, daughter of one of the community's most prominent residents, Monroe County Circuit Court Judge Daniel S. Bacon, a leader in local Republican circles. Quite possibly Autie never expected to speak to the girl again; if so, one doubts he regretted the prospect.[28]

At Stebbins the new pupil displayed the same indifference toward his studies as he had back home in Ohio. His preference for adventure fiction over the works of Plato or Homer continued. Even so, the academy's name-sake detected ability in the boy, whose gifts included a talent for rhetoric and composition.[29]

In early 1855, with the academy having closed its doors, sixteen-year-old George bid his second family goodbye and returned to Harrison County. Back on the Custer farm, his educational career apparently at an end, he was faced with determining how he would spend the balance of his teenage years, and the years beyond. The dull and strenuous chores he took up only exacerbated his restlessness. As Charles Wallace puts it, "he had never learned a craft, not even that of a blacksmith although he had lived near a forge much of his life. And though he had resided on a farm, he was certainly no farmer. . . . The only tool he possessed was between the ears, and the sole marketable commodity was the knowledge he had stored there."[30]

Although he had drifted through his school years, the recent graduate wondered if he had learned enough from those who had taught him at Creal and Stebbins to emulate their manners and methods, and at least entertain—perhaps even educate—a classroom. In some circles teaching was considered a career for those who lacked talent or ambition, but what other choice did he have? At this time Ohio's common-school system was undergoing an expansion and improvement program that made the profession at least marginally more attractive; one result was a statewide shortage of teachers, and qualification standards were low. Moreover, most teachers at the grade school level were as young as he was, many even younger. A majority were recent graduates of schools such as Stebbins and therefore only a few years older than the children they sought to instruct. Often they pored over the same textbooks as their pupils, trying to stay one or two lessons ahead of them.

Thus it was that Armstrong Custer, perhaps the least likely candidate for such a position, applied for a teaching job at the Beech Point District School in Athens Township and was duly hired for the summer 1855 session. The distance from New Rumley—almost a hundred miles—meant that he had to board with a local family named McCoy. Thus he returned to the Custer farm only during vacation periods—his first extended separation from the homes he had known in Harrison County and Monroe. But there were advantages to his situation. He did well enough at the job to maintain self-respect and he considered himself more than adequately compensated. He never forgot the satisfaction he experienced or the surprise and gratification on his mother's face when during his first visit home he deposited in her lap his first earnings—twenty-six dollars.[31]

It was at Beech Point that Armstrong began to hone the social skills that would make him attractive to peers of both sexes. He no longer considered girls inconvenient distractions from thoughts or deeds of greater importance but rather as sometimes-fascinating creatures worth cultivating. He began to attend the dances and parties thrown by families with children at the local schools and also the vocal competitions known as "singing schools" or "singing bees" that had become popular with the young set of the area. At those gatherings he mingled freely with girls his own age, with some of whom he actively flirted.

His growing popularity with the ladies engendered jealousy among male acquaintances who lacked his good looks and outgoing personality. One of these was Joseph Dickerson, with whom he roomed in the McCoy home. One snowy winter's day the two friends drove a bobsled to pick up a group of girls heading for a singing bee. So many piled into the sled that Dickerson was made to ride one of the horses. The weather made his situation disagreeable enough, but the thought of his friend snuggling with the girls in the rear was maddening. On the way back the riding arrangements remained unchanged. At a sharp bend in the road Dickerson purposely drove the horses into a snow bank, tipping the sled over and "spilling its fair contents with Custer, into a heap in the deep snow." No one was hurt and apparently no hard feelings resulted.[32]

Armstrong was not all fun and flirtation. Whether or not he became a truly proficient educator, he proved popular with his pupils. However, he left the position not long after he started, and decided to put the money he had made at Beech Point towards his own education, this time at the collegiate level. Before year's end he enrolled at the newly established McNeely Normal School at Hopedale, Harrison County. Throughout the ensuing year he attended the school "off and on" while teaching common-school pupils on the side. In March 1856, upon the close of the winter term at McNeely, he took the examination for a teaching certificate, which was granted him on March 28, the first of three he obtained over the next three months.

In April he returned to McNeely for the spring session, lodging in a student cottage on the campus. That June he was graduated from the school at commencement exercises attended by Mary Custer. She would remark on her cousin's pleasing looks, his well-cut clothes, and the confident way he moved among the assembled guests. Mary also noted his evident regret at having to leave an institution that had become a home to him though he had lived there for less than half a year.[33]

From McNeely Armstrong returned to teaching at the local elementary schools, this time in Cadiz Township. During the summer of 1856 and through the following winter he was employed at a school in District Number 5, about four miles from the county seat. There he rented a room in the home of Alexander Holland, situated close to the school grounds. Over time he grew close to his host family, especially nineteen-year-old Mary Jane Holland, known to her friends as "Mollie." Pretty and vivacious, she seems to have caught his eye, and his imagination, from their first meeting. At some point she became the object of Armstrong's first romantic indulgence.[34]

Mollie Holland may have assumed a place in his thoughts, but a quickly developing plan threatened to crowd her out, at least temporarily. By mid-December 1856 he was writing Ann Reed about his current job, which paid thirty dollars per session, an increase of two dollars over his former position and four dollars more than he had made at Beech Point. The salary may have been satisfactory, but now he had determined to quit the profession. Furthering his childhood preference, he intended to embark on a military career. To make a success of that career he planned to seek entrance to West Point via application to the local congressman, John A. Bingham.

He informed Ann that he had shared his intentions with his parents, with mixed results: "Mother is much opposed to me going there but Father and David [Kirkpatrick] are in favor of it very much. I think it is the best place that I could go." At least from a monetary standpoint the move made sense. Not only would the Academy provide him with a finished education, throughout the five-year course he would be paid every month as much as he now made during one session at the district school. To bolster his argument he relayed a rumor that an acquaintance from Cadiz, who had been graduated from West Point in 1840, had accumulated more than two hundred thousand dollars over the course of his army service. If the future cooperated, Armstrong Custer could do at least as well for himself as Captain John McNutt.[35]

Having made up his mind as to his future course, the would-be soldier could only hope that those he depended on to advance the plans he had so ambitiously laid out—starting with Congressman Bingham—came through for him.

Chapter II

Immortality at West Point

One of the most vexing conundrums relating to Custer's early life concerns the manner in which he received his appointment to the Military Academy. There is no dispute that it was offered him by his local congressman, John A. Bingham of Cadiz. But because politics, both at the local and federal level, played a major role in awarding entrée into such a prestigious, tuition-free institution, for generations many historians have assumed that Custer's appointment came about through irregular channels. There appears to be no basis for this claim, but it has taken on a life of its own since Custer biographers introduced it in the 1950s.

The political angle has seduced many otherwise scrupulous historians into accepting the claim as fact. It is true that at the time of Custer's appointment John Bingham was a rising leader of the moderate wing of the Republican Party (after the Civil War he would align with the radical faction and in 1866 would draft the equal protection clause of the Fourteenth Amendment). However, Custer's family, and the young man himself, had proven themselves to be staunch Democrats. In the years prior to his son's attempt to enter West Point Emmanuel Custer had served prominently on the Democratic Central Committee of Harrison County. During the campaign of 1856, when the Republicans put forth their first presidential candidate, John C. Frémont, the elder Custer strenuously promoted his Democratic opponent James Buchanan, who would gain the White House in November 1856.[1]

While Emmanuel chaired several Democratic meetings in and around New Rumley, his son, along with some like-minded friends, attended the local Buchanan rallies. It is assumed that he was on hand for one such gathering, held early in August on the McNeely School grounds in Hopedale. The rally attracted much attention because some of the younger attendees came dressed as "border ruffians," with reference to the high-profile unrest then plaguing the Kansas Territory, where bands of abolitionists and proslavery advocates were clashing on a regular basis. Not only did the ruffians come out in support of their candidate; they also played the role of hecklers at opposing rallies. In mid-September young Custer turned up at a Republican meeting in Cadiz at which Congressman Bingham spoke. Dressed in ruffian fashion, "his coat wrong side out and wearing a stove pipe hat," he became an unwanted participant in the parade of Frémont supporters that preceded the speechifying. Supposedly shouts and catcalls from the "motley crew of vagabonds" (as one reporter called them) made it difficult for Bingham and the other orators to be heard.[2]

How a staunch Republican could have awarded a coveted office to the son of an avowed opponent, especially when Bingham presumably had other, more politically acceptable, candidates vying for his favor, has long puzzled historians. Over time a consensus has emerged that Custer got his appointment not on merit but through the machinations of the father of Mollie Holland, Custer's first love. It seems that Alexander Holland learned, through the interception of letters from Custer, that the couple had spent much time together out of sight of her parents. This infuriated Dr. Holland, who did not appreciate his boarder's advances toward his daughter. More likely, he did not regard Mollie's lover as a fit candidate for a son-in-law. The Holland family may not have ranked significantly higher than the Custers on the social scale, but as far as suitors went Mollie could do better—much better—than a feckless, underachieving schoolteacher, especially one of suspect political principles.[3]

Holland, like his friend John Bingham, was an ardent Republican who regarded Democrats, especially those who posed as brutish bullies, with disdain. Thus he confronted the object of his ire and kicked him out of his home. He was livid when Custer promptly took up residence with a neighbor and continued to see Mollie on the sly. Realizing that a long-term solution was necessary to end the relationship, Holland supposedly visited his friend and asked him, as a personal favor, to do his best to send Custer off to the Hudson highlands. Because a West Point cadet could not marry, for five years he would stay single while pursuing a military education far apart from Mollie; surely the romance would not survive such a lengthy separation. According to one avid proponent of this theory, Charles Wallace, from Bingham's point of view, "Armstrong was then little more than a persistent constituent of the wrong political persuasion. Sending him to West Point at the request of an old party friend was an expedient that might even turn a small profit at the next election. Thus a little political favor was exchanged in Cadiz and George Armstrong Custer was recommended to the U.S. Military Academy."[4]

This story has not only been accepted as fact by latter-day chroniclers, but it has also repeatedly been stated as such, without qualification or caveat. Unlike the alternative account of Custer's place of birth, the quid pro quo involving Holland and Bingham has never been accorded the status of local legend; it has been treated as gospel truth even by discerning historians and biographers. Yet none of these writers offers any evidence to support the claim. Readers who search their source citations find only references to Custer's attempts at lyric poetry, which include the following:

> To Mary
> I've seen and kissed that crimson lip
> With honied smiles o'erflowing.
> Enchanted watched the opening rose,
> Upon thy soft cheek glowing.
>
> Dear Mary, they eyes may prove less blue;
> Thy beauty fade tomorrow.
> But Oh, my heart can ne'er forget
> Thy parting look of sorrow.[5]

This ode to young love and others similar in form and content have been authenticated as composed by George Armstrong Custer, and they physically exist in the collections of the library of Yale University. But there is no document of any kind—at least none that those who repeat the tale of Custer's backdoor appointment to West Point have unearthed—that mentions the Holland-Bingham agreement, let alone provides details of its formulation. Sources on the subject are conspicuously missing from the citations of every biography from Jay Monaghan's 1959 biography (apparently the first account of Custer's life to mention Holland's machinations) and T. J. Stiles's study of Custer's physical, emotional, and psychological lives, published fifty-six years later.[6]

The theory that Custer did not receive his appointment through his own achievements and potential encounters opposition from some well-established facts. Admittedly, Bingham, had he served as a means of barring an amorous swain from the family of a prospective father-in-law, would never have acknowledged the action especially after Custer became a household name in the North and he became a tragic hero to millions of his countrymen. Even so, the congressman never so much as suggested that he favored Custer's candidacy for any reason other than the favorable impression the young man made on him.

Custer's initial effort to gain Bingham's support took the form of a letter sent from his classroom at the normal school in Hopedale on May 27, 1856. It was a simple inquiry for information about the West Point application process, something he could not obtain in his present position. In this letter Custer declared his interest in attending the military academy, claimed that "my age and tastes would be in accordance with its requirements," and offered to provide "testimonials of moral character" from Dr. McNeely. In conclusion, "I would also say that I have the consent of my parents in the course which I have in view."[7]

It seems doubtful that Custer was seeking entrance to the next Academy class, which would begin its studies only six weeks after he wrote the congressman. In any case, when he replied on June 4 Bingham informed his correspondent that the appointment for the Class of 1861 had already been made. Discouraging to Custer's ambitions was the accompanying news that an applicant for appointment to the following class, a young man from Jefferson County, had been identified. Even so, Bingham enclosed the information Custer had sought, which the young man seems to have regarded as a gesture of encouragement.

On the eleventh Custer wrote again, thanking the congressman for his favor and stressing how well he met the qualifications for an appointment to the Class of '62: "In all the points specified I would come under the requirements set forth in your communication, being about seventeen years of age, above the medium height [five-foot-eight] and of remarkably strong constitution and vigorous frame. If that young man from Jeff. County of whom you spoke does not push the matter, or if you hear of any other vacancy, I should be glad to hear from you."[8]

Instead of waiting to hear again from Bingham, Custer "pushed the matter" in a way that showed his resolve to become a West Point cadet. That fall, when teaching in Cadiz Township—a job Charles Wallace suggests he took because the school was within walking distance of Bingham's home—he sought out the congressman for a face-to-face meeting. He had told Mary Custer of his intention to do so; she recalled that although he hoped it would further his candidacy "he expressed a doubt as to whether the Judge [Bingham] would consider him, for Uncle Emmanuel was a very ardent and radical Democrat, and he was afraid that politics might enter into the judge's decision." Realizing that Bingham was probably well aware of his family's political leanings, Custer decided to acknowledge them. Even so, as he saw it, the meeting went well. "When he came back in the evening," Mary wrote, "he told us . . . how nicely he [Bingham] had treated him and was very enthusiastic over his possibility at being recommended by the Judge for the appointment. . . ."[9]

It appears that Custer's enthusiasm was not misplaced. Representative Bingham took the measure of his visitor, liked what he saw and heard, and was struck by the young man's determination. In fact, even before meeting him, Bingham had judged him to be a worthy applicant to the most respected military institution in the land. According to Marguerite Merington, Bingham wrote of having "received a letter, a real boy's letter, that captivated me . . . Written in a boyish hand, but firmly, legibly, it told me that the writer—a 'Democratic boy,' that I might be under no misapprehension—wanted to be a soldier. . . . Struck by its originality, I replied at once."[10]

In the end, candor and creativity won out over political disabilities, although Custer had to put in another eight months of toil in a profession he did not favor before a letter reached him granting him a West Point appointment. By then gentle but persistent persuasion by her family had overcome Maria Custer's initial objection to her son's career choice, and Emmanuel had agreed to secure a loan against the farm to cover the Academy's two-hundred-dollar admission fee.[11]

There is nothing in the record to suggest that Congressman Bingham manipulated Custer's selection as a personal favor to a friend. Although mid-nineteenth century American politics was a bare-knuckle contest that gave no quarter and spared few combatants, the crossing of political lines in the awarding of government preferment was not an unheard-of occurrence. To be sure, it was sufficiently uncommon to attract public notice. Early in the Civil War, by which time Custer was an up-and-coming staff officer in the Army of the Potomac, the editor of a Democratic newspaper in Steubenville, Ohio, lauded Bingham for "the disinterested and honorable course which he followed to Geo. A. Custer. He deserves much of the credit for giving to the Stars and Stripes a defender who could never turn his back to a friend or an enemy."[12]

It is possible that external circumstances played a role in Custer's success. Perhaps for one reason or another the applicant from Jefferson County had rejected the appointment, if in fact it had been offered to him. Perhaps, as Custer hoped, his presumed rival had not promoted himself as strongly as he himself had, or the fellow had reconsidered his career path. Or perhaps Bingham had been tickled by the irony of granting the son of a prominent political opponent an opportunity that in the normal course of events would have gone to an avowed Republican. We are not privy to the range of motivations that may have driven Bingham's decision, but a clandestine bargain to rid a local father of his daughter's unpropitious but oversexed suitor does not appear to be one of them.

*   *   *

Custer's trip to West Point began at the train station at Scio in late May of 1857, where he started off to the well-wishes of family members and friends. The journey consumed a week or more by rail, canal boat, and stagecoach across the Allegheny Mountains, and again by train to New York City, from whose port he took a ship up the North River toward his final destination. He set foot on the West Point wharf shortly before the June 20 entrance examinations— perfunctory physical and mental affairs required of all incoming cadets, or "plebes." After a few weeks of being tutored by upperclassmen in the rudiments of soldiering, Custer and his classmates were introduced to the routine of the annual summer encampment, conducted on the grounds that adjoined the ruins of the Revolutionary War-era stronghold of Fort Clinton, well beyond the turreted, slate-grey walls of the academic campus. The duties demanded of the new cadets were many and rigorous, but their life in camp was enlivened by balls held every Monday, Wednesday, and Friday evening. As Custer explained in a letter to a hometown friend, these functions were attended by "the visitors who spend the summer here, [and] the music cannot be surpassed as we pride ourselves on possessing the finest band in the U.S."[13]

In this Spartan environment, made up of rows of tents almost wholly lacking in furnishings, Cadet Custer mingled with the several dozen other members of the West Point Class of 1862. They included youngsters from twenty-five states and territories and the District of Columbia plus eleven who had received presidential ("at-large") appointments. Each incoming plebe had pledged himself to a course of study that, since 1854, took five years to complete. For the first fifty-two years of the institution's existence the course had been four years long, but over the past three decades, the Academy's board of visitors and numerous army officers had recommended broadening the curriculum, which they considered top-heavy with mathematics, science, and engineering courses, to add such worthy disciplines as English grammar, Spanish, geography, and history.

The new program also placed greater emphasis on military tactics (the Academy had long been viewed as a school of civil and military engineering rather than a tactical training ground). Secretary of War Jefferson Davis had accepted the recommendations and with the support of Brevet Lieutenant Colonel Robert E. Lee, the Academy's superintendent, had ordered the addition of a fifth school year to accommodate the critics. In October 1858, during Custer's second (or fourth-class) year, Davis's successor, John B. Floyd, would return the term of study to its original length, only to change his mind six months later, apparently under pressure from now-Senator Davis, chairman of the Senate Military Affairs Committee, and reinstate the five-year course. Floyd's decision incurred the vocal displeasure of the cadets, who, as Custer would write in his unfinished memoirs, were "anxious to render their detention at the Academy as brief as possible." In the end, however, they need not have remonstrated; by the spring of 1861, with civil war imminent, four years would be all that was asked of them.[14]

From the earliest days of his first encampment Custer learned the harsh lessons of Academy life, which included repetitive drill, rigorous tactical instruction, and strict discipline. Fifth-class-year cadets learned the functions of the lowest-ranking soldiers. From privates they would move up the ladder of relative rank until schooled in the duties of line officers during their final year of study. From 5:30 a.m. till 5 p.m. they digested the fundamentals of infantry, artillery, and cavalry tactics, along with more exotic lessons in fencing and bayonet practice. Guard duty and fatigue details were everyday chores, and the cadets were frequently turned out for parades and inspections. In later years Custer and his classmates would spend a part of their summer in the Academy's ordnance laboratory constructing various types of munitions.

During his first summer Custer also encountered the time-honored tradition of hazing, sometimes referred to as "deviling," an initiation rite through which upperclassmen strove to make life miserable and, if possible, humiliating to the lower classes over whom they asserted a certain degree of authority. Historians have noted that although sometimes excessive, inordinately devilish, and deliberately cruel, the forms of hazing bestowed on Custer and the other "animals" usually took the form of practical jokes, elaborate pranks, and efforts at imposing discipline such as forcing the freshmen to polish the boots, sweep the floors, and clean the muskets of their seniors. As one West Point chronicler notes, "on balance the hazing of the antebellum period probably did more good than evil. In the first place, it identified the most obvious misfits, those psychologically incapable of adjusting to discipline. Secondly, the practice helped create a close-knit band of plebe brothers, united against the upper classes, thus solidifying at an early stage the class spirit so dear to West Pointers."[15]

Especially during his plebe year, Custer was the target of much hazing. One of the most memorable incidents occurred even before he donned his uniform of cadet gray. As his brother Nevin related, during breakfast on the day after he reached the Point "he was helped to a plate of gravy and when no one was looking . . . one big potato came square on his plate and the gravy [splashed] all over his black clothes. He never said a word; that was the way they broke in newcomers."[16]

Custer's ability to tolerate such treatment without resentment or recrimination made him popular even with some of the upperclassmen who occasionally tormented him. Emmanuel Custer's son was jovial, fun-loving, and open to friendship. According to one of his classmates at the McNeely School, "Custer was what he appeared. There was nothing hidden in his nature. He was kind and generous to his friends, bitter and implacable towards his enemies."[17]

Fortunately, most of those who came to know him at the Academy became his friends, many for life. During Custer's fourth-class year he shared quarters with Tully McCrea of Ohio. McCrea spoke for a majority of those who knew him when he described his roommate as "a whole-souled generous friend" with "a hearty smile" and "a penchant for oddity" that made him a ringleader of many escapades, most of them frowned upon by Academy officials. Another fellow Ohioan, Morris Schaff, would write that "West Point has had many a character to deal with, but it may be a question whether it ever had a cadet so exuberant, one who cared so little for its serious attempts to elevate and burnish . . . . And yet we all loved him. . . ." In his memoir of West Point life, written almost fifty years after his graduation, Schaff, one of several underclassmen whom Custer, once in a position of some seniority, took under his wing, rhapsodized about "his nature, so full of those streams that rise, so to speak, among the high hills of our being. I have in mind his joyousness, his attachment to the friends of his youth, and his never-ending delight in talking about his old home. . . ."[18]

The galaxy of friends Custer acquired at West Point encompassed many Northern-born cadets, including those from cities with whom a small-town son of the Midwest might not seem to have much in common. These included not only classmates of moderate scholastic ability or ambition, among whom he was always numbered, but those who ranked high on the list of achievement and merit including New Yorker Patrick H. O'Rorke, who would graduate at the head of Custer's class, and Henry A. Du Pont of Delaware, the first-place graduate in the class that left the Academy one month before Custer's. Other Northerners with whom he developed close ties included several who would serve with him in the Union cavalry including H. Judson Kilpatrick of New Jersey, Wesley Merritt of New York, and James Harrison Wilson of Illinois. New Jersey-born cadet Alexander Cummings McWhorter Pennington would command a horse artillery battery under Custer during the latter's formative months in brigade command. Fellow Midwesterners with whom he was closely associated, in addition to McCrea and Schaff, included Leroy S. Elbert of Iowa, George A. Woodruff of Michigan, and Wisconsin-born Alonzo H. Cushing.

A somewhat larger circle of friends hailed from the South. Although war was four years away when he entered the Academy, sectional lines were already being drawn, and not many friendships straddled those lines. Toward the end of his tenure at West Point, a war of sorts, restricted to some extent by regulations and strictly imposed discipline but very intense and increasingly bitter, was dividing the cadet corps, underclassmen from both sections eyeing each other with suspicion and resentment.

Yet throughout his years on the Hudson Custer, perhaps more than any other native Northerner in the Class of 1862, maintained the high regard of his Southern-born classmates. Hailing from a state watered by the Ohio River, the historical dividing line between the sections, he was geographically as well as politically acceptable to his Southern-born comrades. As an avowed Democrat who had no strong feelings on the slavery question already dominating the national political discourse, he was viewed as sharing Southern interests. Above all, he was no abolitionist, a term, as he recalled, that was considered "one of opprobrium, and the cadet who had the courage to avow himself an abolitionist must be prepared to face the social frowns of the great majority of his comrades and at times to defend his opinions by his physical strength and mettle."[19]

Thanks to his nonthreatening convictions he moved easily among the Southerners, and in fact lobbied successfully to be assigned, throughout his term at the Academy, to a company of cadets predominated by the sons of Dixie. By official policy, the four companies that comprised the Academy's infantry battalion were filled according to the cadets' heights—the taller ones in Companies A and D, the shorter fellows in Companies B and C, so as to present a uniform appearance while in formation. In practice, however, the units were divided along sectional lines, with the Northern-born and Southern-born cadets jockeying for positions in those companies in which classmates native to the same region predominated.[20]

Custer would have felt comfortable in any of these organizations, but his preference for companions who hailed from the slave states was clear and consistent. His closest friends included those from virtually every Southern state. Among his own class he was particularly close to George Owen Watts of Kentucky, John "Gimlet" Lea of Mississippi, and Pierce Manning Butler Young of Georgia. Upperclassmen friends included Stephen Dodson Ramseur of North Carolina (Class of 1860) and, from the Class of 1861, John Pelham of Alabama and the Virginia-born and Texas-reared Thomas Lafayette Rosser. His roommate during his second year at the Point, Lafayette Lane, was the scion of a Southern-sympathizing family from Oregon, then a territory and one year later a newly admitted state. With these and other Southern-born classmates he would remain close throughout the war that lay ahead. During pauses in military operations, he would occasionally enter Confederate lines under a flag of truce to renew acquaintances with old friends still garbed in cadet-like gray.[21]

* * *

Once summer encampment ended, West Point's academic year got underway. Custer and his mates moved into sparsely furnished quarters in the institution's three-story stone barracks. They took their meals at the cadet mess hall, where they digested a steady diet of meat, bread, and potatoes, the quality of which Morris Schaff described as "abominable." They attended classes in the main academic building, known simply as "the Academy," a multipurpose facility three stories tall with a large open floor on the ground level that in the winter months served as a riding hall. Plebes and upperclassmen alike pored over their textbooks in their cramped (twelve-foot-square), gas-lit rooms, some of which were shared by as many as three other cadets, or in the quieter confines of the Academy's library and observatory, a Tudor Gothic complex constructed in 1841 under the direction of one of the institution's most influential superintendents, Major Richard Delafield. They underwent exercises in the tactics of all the service branches on the Academy's commodious parade ground, along whose northwestern edge sat three sets of duplexes housing the heads of the academic departments and the newly erected dean's quarters.[22]

Amid these somber and imposing surroundings one would suppose Cadet Custer buckled down to the task of gaining an education that would make his professors and later his military superiors proud. In in this effort, however— except for brief flashes of intellectual acumen such as he had displayed to his teachers in Ohio—he failed signally. He wanted it that way. While determined to graduate and gain a commission in the army, he was set on enjoying as much fun as possible amid the quasi-monastic setting he now inhabited. He informed one of the many fellow Ohioans in the cadet battalion, Peter Smith Michie of the Class of 1863, that there were only two notable positions in any class—the man at its head and the one at its foot. He did not care to strive to gain the first distinction—it involved too much work and ran counter to his free-spirited nature—and so he put his energy and imagination into becoming the "immortal," the man most at risk of being declared academically deficient and vulnerable to dismissal.[23]

It would be a delicate balancing act to perform well enough in the class-room and on the parade ground to get by while squeezing the maximum amount of enjoyment from the experience. This was especially the case due to the frequency and seeming capriciousness with which school officials handed out demerits (or "skins") for a wide variety of offenses, the weight of which had a direct bearing on a cadet's class standing. But Custer was determined to exploit the loopholes in the system as no one before him, and he was ever alert to those who would deny him his fun. As Cadet Michie recalled, "he never saw an adjutant in full uniform that he did not suspect that he was the object of his search for the purpose of being placed under arrest, and to have five minutes more freedom he would cut and run for it, to delay if possible the well-known formula: 'Sir, you are hereby placed in arrest and confined to quarters, by direction of the superintendent'."[24]

His dedication to this goal and the persistence with which he pursued it gained the results he desired. At the close of his fifth-class year he ranked fifty-eighth out of sixty-eight cadets. Thereafter his class standing plummeted to fifty-ninth out of sixty class members at the end of the 1859 class year, fifty-seven out of fifty-seven in 1860, and thirty-fourth of thirty-four in the Class of 1861, which had been pared down by the loss of Southern-born cadets who had opted to join the military forces of the Confederacy prior to graduation.

The grades he received in the various subjects taught in the classroom and on the drill plain mirrored the downward spiral of his class standing. When his plebe year ended he ranked fifty-seventh among his classmates in mathematics, the core subject of the Academy curriculum, and fifty-seventh in English grammar, then a part of the course in ethics. The following year he attained the same rank in math, fell to fifty-eighth in English, and placed fifty-fifth in his mastery of French, the international language of military affairs.

At the close of his third-class year, July 1860, he stood fifty-seventh in philosophy (a combination of physics, mechanics, and astronomy), fifty-third in French, and fifty-sixth in Spanish. His only marginally acceptable ranking was in military drawing, one of the few subjects in which he seemed to take a real interest and displayed some talent. His standing continued to slide during the remainder of his time at the Point.[25]

In his final year at the Academy Custer and his fellows were at last instructed in the tactics of the several combat arms of the army and introduced to coursework in strategy, grand tactics, and military organization. The Ohioan placed thirty-first in artillery practice, thirty-third in infantry tactics, and an astonishing forty-fourth in cavalry tactics, despite excelling in equitation. During one riding lesson he made the highest jump on record with the exception of Ulysses S. Grant's legendary performance aboard a powerfully built sorrel name York seven years earlier.[26]

It is difficult to reconcile Custer's standing in cavalry instruction and the success he would achieve in that arm, unless he made a determined effort to underperform. It is likewise strange that he fared so poorly in English since he appears to have had a facility for composition. The only surviving example is an essay he submitted during his fourth-class year to Second Lieutenant Frederick Lynn Childs, his instructor in ethics. Ironically, considering Custer's future relations with Native Americans, it comprises a sympathetic portrait of a noble savage unbowed in the face of looming extinction.[27]

Custer's literary tastes continued to run to the adventure novels he devoured in his youth. His interest in the ways of the Indian propelled him into borrowing from the Academy's sixteen-thousand-volume library the *Leatherstocking Tales* of James Fennimore Cooper. His sympathetic attitude towards the culture of the Old South was bolstered by John Pendleton Kennedy's *Swallow Barn*, which glorified plantation life, Southern chivalry, and the mutually beneficial relationship between master and slave. According to Custer's biographer Jay

Monaghan, however, his interest in out-of-class readings ended abruptly early in his second year at the Academy when he borrowed his last book—another Southern romance, *Eutaw*, by William Gilmore Simms.[28]

Perhaps he felt he no longer had the time for pleasure reading given the demands of his courses and the need to stay academically eligible. It was very nearly a losing effort. Mathematics, taught daily to sections of from ten to twelve cadets by the austere and exacting Professor Albert E. Church, presented one of the greatest hurdles to his quest to maintain the Academy's equivalent of the gentleman's C (or perhaps more accurately, the poor man's D), but somehow he managed it.

His ability to master French as taught by the "courteous and conscientious but not overly demanding" Hyacinth A. Agnel, was not appreciably greater. In later years Libbie Custer was fond of telling how George was instructed by Agnel to translate upon first reading a text that began *Léopold duc d' Autriche, se mettit sur les plaines*. His rendering of the phrase was memorable: "Leopold, duck and ostrich. . . ." He fared no better in Spanish, a course he took daily for four months during his third-class year. So anxious was the clever cadet to quit the domain of Patrice de Janon, who headed the newly created Department of Spanish, he once asked the good professor to render "class dismissed" in his native tongue. Upon doing so, Janon watched open-mouthed as every cadet rose and followed Custer out of the room.[29]

There appears to be no account of Custer's relations with the star member of the Academy's faculty, Dennis Hart Mahan, professor of engineering. Many historians believe that a generation of military officers, including hundreds who fought for Union and Confederacy, developed their concepts of strategy and tactics from Mahan's teachings. Contradictory evidence suggests that Mahan's influence on his pupils was primarily in the area of military engineering, with particular emphasis on the construction and maintenance of permanent and field fortifications. His teachings on tactical matters were limited to a six-lesson (nine-hour) course, "The Science of War," sandwiched between his lectures on fieldworks and military drawing. Custer, given his interest in what he later called "glorious war," undoubtedly paid more attention to this segment of Mahan's course—which covered tables of organization and equipment, reconnaissance and outpost duties, the precepts of attack and defense, "together with the elements of grand tactics and strategy"—than the heavily technical elements of civil engineering, including such unexciting topics as architecture and stonecutting.[30]

It is impossible to determine if the tactics Custer employed during his active-duty career derived from his studies under Mahan. Since he so frequently improvised in response to enemy threats, it is tempting to speculate that very little of what he learned in a classroom contributed to his success as a general officer of cavalry. And yet he did not see it that way. After his death his widow confided to her nephew, Brice C. W. Custer, that her husband had been "most concerned about rumors that he was reckless in the Civil War in charging an enemy without evident tactical planning." He had emphasized to Libbie that "he never went into battle without reviewing beforehand all he'd learned about tactics, and the strategy of the Confederate commanders, some of whom had been his West Point classmates."[31]

*   *   *

Custer's scholastic struggles were legendary among his classmates. As one remarked, his fearlessness in action came as no surprise to anyone who had observed him "walking up with calm deliberation to the head of the section-room to face the instructors with the confession that he knew nothing of his lesson." He was just as fearless in his determination to have the time of his life regardless of the consequences. Stories of his escapades and encounters with disapproving superiors enlivened the humdrum lives of generations of cadets.[32]

He lacked the authority to impose his will on anyone during his plebe year, when he was constantly hazed, accused of every possible transgression against the Academy's arcane code of conduct, and addressed by a number of derisive nicknames, most of them relating to his distinctive appearance: "Fanny" and "Curly" for his long, flowing locks and pinkish complexion, and "Cinnamon" for the heavily-scented hair oil he favored. [33]

Once he shed his animal status and became a "yearling," he began to administer to others the same treatment he had received over the preceding year. Naturally creative and perhaps somewhat diabolical, he hazed the new plebes with obvious relish. Some of his efforts to distress or discombobulate were of low intensity, such as when he dumped the contents of a box of coat buttons on the heads of lowerclassmen passing by the room he shared with Cadet McCrea; the latter forever remembered "the bewildered plebes as they passed the window . . . and Custer's merry laugh at the look of astonishment" on their faces.[34]

The prankster repeatedly hazed Jasper Myers of the Class of 1862, whose gnarly beard made Custer declare, as Morris Schaff wrote, "that he ought to go right back home and send his son,—he evidently had made a mistake, he said; it was his boy that the government meant should have the appointment and not the old man." [35]

Most of Custer's pranks demanded greater physical exertion and achieved more dramatic results. During his second summer encampment, while serving as cadet officer of the guard, he hauled sleeping fifth-classmen out of their tents with a clothesline fastened to their ankles, then dragged them to a remote tract known as Hangman's Hollow. There he and other upperclassmen whose antics he inspired and shaped would threaten their quaking victims with hideous forms of torture—none of which was ever carried out. [36]

One of his favorite diversions was the midnight raid, which targeted the barracks rooms of underclassmen. On one such foray he and a like-minded classmate collected clothes from the rooms of short plebes, tossed them into the rooms of tall classmates, then stole and strewed the latter's clothing on the short fellows' floors. Being time- and labor-intensive, these expeditions did not always escape the attention of the authorities. Midway through one such escapade, as a fellow yearling recalled, "the gleam of a dark lantern in the hall just below us, warned us that [an officer was] on our trail. Custer, who was in front of me, dropped his load of clothes on him, and I followed suit; Custer jumped over the ballustrade [sic], and escaped downstairs before the victim could get out of the tangle." His almost uncanny ability to avoid detection and punishment may have been the first manifestation of "Custer's luck," a trait that would define him up to the moment he met Crazy Horse and Gall on the Little Bighorn.

At this early stage of his career Custer's luck was not inviolate. It deserted him when he and another upperclassman pulled a particularly elaborate prank during a summer encampment: the "official visit of the Great Highan-Ki-dank." This was the name given to "a combination of two yearlings—a tall strong one, on whose shoulders was mounted a lanky yearling, holding a six foot pole horizontally in front of him, from which depended a sheet, completely screening the double personality. When this thing suddenly appeared, in the darkness of night and in answer to the challenge of the sentinel [it replied in a] stentorian voice, 'The Great Highan-Ki-dank and Friends,' then the upper part of the dual monster dismounted, and made a rush at the sentinel, who fled . . . calling frantically for the Corporal of the Guard."

Due to the ensuing commotion Custer and his co-conspirator failed to escape detection. Hauled before a disciplinary board, they were found guilty of conduct unbecoming to the cadet corps and sentenced to several weeks' confinement in a guard tent. The offenders found the punishment "very obnoxious, as we had to turn out in ranks every time the guard was paraded during the night, which was sometimes twice an hour."[37]

Custer may have ridden hard on the unfortunates who happened to cross his path, but few took lasting offense; most, including Cadet Myers, literally laughed off Custer's antics. Over time, in fact, his victims decided that his treatment of them amounted to nothing more than "boyish—but harmless— frolics." A half-century later one who had repeatedly been hazed by Custer, Colonel Elias V. Andruss, recalled that his tormentor "was beyond a doubt the most popular man in his class, and even the 'plebes' deemed it an honor and a pleasure to be 'deviled' by him!"[38]

*   *   *

During his first two years at the Academy Custer may have indulged in "lighthearted" play, but in the summer of 1859, around the time he went home on the single furlough a cadet was permitted during his schooling, his behavior seems to have taken a sharp turn toward dissipation. He had long avoided some of the more popular vices such as tobacco products, on one occasion declaring that "nothing could induce me to use tobacco either by smoking or chewing as I consider it a filthy, if not unhealthy, practice." It was a stance he would maintain for the rest of his life, but when visitors were caught smoking in his quarters it was he who incurred demerits for it.[39]

Toward the end of his fourth-class year, he appears to have acquired a decided taste for alcohol. While some chroniclers maintain that he never drank while at West Point and on few occasions thereafter, numerous anecdotes attest to his accompanying thirsty classmates on a pilgrimage to Benny Havens's Tavern, a noted den of cadet debauchery about three miles from the Academy grounds. In his memoirs he fondly recalled his trips to Benny's, which he managed by outsmarting the officers who made inspection rounds every evening at 10 p.m. After bed check Custer and his friends would place dummies under their covers, don the pieces of civilian attire they had last worn before they entered the Academy, and slip out into the darkness where they either evaded the sentinels pacing outside their barracks or bribed them to look the other way.

Benny Havens's customers would spend hours availing themselves of forbidden hospitality that encompassed not only wines and whiskey but also home-cooked meals, occasional live entertainment, and the company of comely serving-girls that included Benny's three daughters. As Custer admitted, the tavern "possessed stronger attractions than the study and demonstration of a problem in Euclid or the prosy discussion of some abstract proposition of moral science."[40]

At least one biographer claims that Custer, along with his friend Tom Rosser, devised a way to pursue their carousing during school hours. When off Academy grounds on a mounted exercise, the two would pass to the rear of the column and once beyond sight of the instructor fall out to visit either Benny Havens's or some other watering hole along the route, where they would dally until the column returned and bring up its rear on the way home. It is possible that, like other cadets, Custer sometimes secreted bottles of alcohol in his barracks room. However, drinking was an offense that courted instant dismissal; if he did imbibe on Academy grounds he was clever enough or lucky enough to get away with it.[41]

During this period he also indulged at least once, and probably more often, in sexual activity. Some biographers relate the names of young women Custer may have maneuvered into bed during the brief leaves cadets were able to obtain for various reasons. Tully McCrea affirmed that being a handsome fellow, Custer "is a very successful ladies' man. Nor does he care an iota how many of the fair ones break their hearts for him." McCrea heard a rumor that Custer had become engaged to a young woman from the West Point area named Mariah, though "I do not believe it . . . [and] hope that there is no foundation in the report." Yet the object of Custer's romantic dreams—and apparently also his libidinous inclinations—remained Mary Holland, who despite her father's disapproval had kept in touch with her so-called "Bachelor Boy" during his first two years on the Hudson.[42]

While Mollie's correspondence has been lost to history, a few of his letters to her remain. In one dated November 1858, he reported himself "as full of mischief as ever." Six weeks later he asked if he could see her during his summer furlough and begged her to "tell what plan you can make up so that we can have that great 'sleep' . . . do not put me off by saying that you cannot think of any but tell me some one and another thing." Her reply must have been to his satisfaction, for it seems likely that at some point during his two-month leave—part of which he spent with his family in Harrison County and the remainder with the Reeds in Monroe—he visited her outside the Holland home. If so, the reunion may have turned out badly, for it marked the last time they would be together.[43]

Perhaps as a result, he sought solace in the arms of another woman, for when he returned to the Academy in late August, he was suffering from a sexually transmitted disease. Historians suggest that he contracted gonorrhea as a result of a visit to a prostitute, probably during his stopover in Manhattan. The condition, common to many cadets returning from furlough, placed him in the post hospital where, as he wrote, he was "detained" during the beginning of the fall term. It has been suggested that the infection, which resisted effective treatment during this era, persisted to the point of rendering him permanently sterile. Certainly it affected his class work, putting him "behind in [my] studies" at a critical time in his education. If his romance with Dr. Holland's daughter had not already ended, it did not survive this crisis in his life.[44]

*   .*   *

During his third- and second-class years, Custer's behavior became more troubling, his offenses against the code of conduct more extreme. One of his most celebrated exploits involved the theft of a persistently loud rooster—the cause of worsening sleep deprivation—belonging to a tactical officer, Lieutenant Henry Douglas, whose residence adjoined Custer's barracks.[45]

During this period Custer appears to have engaged in fights with more than one of his classmates. If one of his Civil War subordinates can be believed, he engaged in physical altercations with at least two cadet noncommissioned officers and handily won both bouts. Another escapade with serious repercussions, had he been caught, is mentioned by Merington: "He and a comrade one day swam the Hudson, clothes tied to head. A banquet was being held in the James home on the opposite shore. The swimmers did not sit with the guests, but they did full justice to the delectable courses, served to them in the stable by a conniving butler."[46]

His boldest and most serious offense—but, again, one that failed to land him in serious trouble—involved the theft of a professor's notes and questions prior to the fall-term examinations of January 1861. On this occasion Custer's habitual indifference toward passing a course despite being unprepared had deserted him. He and almost three dozen classmates had been declared deficient in at least one of their courses and faced reexamination. He was so worried he might fail the retest that he sneaked into the instructor's room at the West Point Hotel when the latter was absent.

His desperate stratagem failed. As Tully McCrea wrote in a letter home, Custer "found the book in which the list of subjects was and was in the act of copying them when he heard somebody coming. He knew that it would not do to get caught in a private room at the Hotel, so he tore the leaf out of the book and left as soon as possible. . . . In doing so he spoiled everything." As soon as the instructor discovered the theft he changed all the subjects, "and the risk and trouble was all for nothing." McCrea did not, however, berate his classmate, instead declaring that Custer ought to have stolen the entire book, copied it in his quarters, and found a way to return it before it turned up missing: "This might have been done by bribing one of the servants at the Hotel."[47]

It may be supposed that Custer's crime incurred severe punishment, but his uncanny luck held. He was arrested and threatened with dismissal, but three weeks later—to McCrea's astonishment, and probably also his own—he was released. One factor in his favor was that he had not been the only thief in his class. Several other cadets had obtained advance copies of the French and rhetoric exams; some passed them undetected, but others were caught and subjected to some form of discipline.

The severity of Custer's offense was, in fact, a matter of debate. As James L. Morrison, Jr., notes, "Contrary to later views at West Point, cheating was not considered a serious breach of morality in the antebellum era, and detection did not bring expulsion at the hands of officers or fellow cadets." Nor did his subsequent performance before the examining board where Custer found himself required to answer a different list of questions than those he had stolen. Not surprisingly, he failed miserably, but his survival was ensured when the Office of Secretary of War Joseph Holt, to whom his case was appealed, ruled that he could continue with the course despite his demonstrated ignorance of the subject.[48]

Cadet McCrea was now tiring of his former roommate's antics. He believed that before graduation came around, Custer's transgressions would catch up to him and he would be banished to civilian life. As the Ohioan wrote in a letter to his sweetheart, "he is too clever for his own good."[49]

* * *

Most sources state that during his time at the Academy Custer incurred a total of 812 demerits for more than 450 offenses, although a glance at his delinquency log makes the actual number appear to fall just short of 900. The nature and relative severity of his infractions deserve some scrutiny. He accumulated 436 skins during his first two years, 455 during his third- and second-class years. The numbers may have been close to even but, on the whole, the offenses he committed between September 1859 and June 1861 were of a more serious nature. His earlier transgressions, most of which cost him one or two demerits, were school-boyish: late for inspection, laughing and talking in class, and other such small infractions. His later offenses, a greater percentage of which cost him more points, included talking back to an instructor, defacing government property (writing on the walls of his room and vandalizing his tent), and the like.[50]

Given the effect on his standing, little wonder that he finished at the foot of his class. He would have fared even worse had dozens of skins not been expunged from the rolls. This was accomplished by performing punishment tours, or "extras": four-hour stints of additional guard duty, performed on sixty-six Saturdays, each erasing one demerit. The ameliorative effects enabled him to avoid crossing the hundred-point limit per semester that could trigger immediate expulsion.[51]

To his credit, he never complained about the penalties he accumulated or bemoaned his inability to avoid them. He was capable of moderating his behavior when necessary to avoid extreme consequences, as during the three-month period in 1859–60 when he received not a single demerit. At bottom, he viewed the Academy's tracking of cadet misbehavior as a commendable effort to instill discipline; he simply did not consider the practice beneficial to him. And although he refused to play by its rules, he maintained a deep affection for his school and an appreciation of its core values. As he wrote his half-sister in June of 1858, "I would not leave this place for any amount of money, for I would rather have a good education and no money than a fortune and be ignorant."[52]

Nor was he above self-criticism. He went so far as to advise lowerclassmen, if they wished to advance their careers, to avoid his example of dissipation and error. One day he was found lying in the grass in the shadow of the guard tent to which he had been consigned. In that posture he was approached by a fresh-faced lad assigned to guard the prisoner. Custer languidly looked up and spoke thus: "Plebe, see the disgrace that has befallen your predecessor, all for neglecting duty, devilling plebes, bucking regulations etc. Take warning from this horrible example before you. Stick to your books, obey regulations, and graduate [at] the head of your class." Sagacious advice indeed, and the youngster paid heed. Cadet Milton B. Adams would graduate fifth his class and make a distinguished record as an officer in the Army Corps of Engineers.[53]

*   *   *

Custer's scholastic performance may have been marred by extraordinary misconduct, but he had a few challengers for the title of worst disciplinary record in West Point history. Then, too, as some historians have pointed out, he might well have placed higher had all cadets who entered the Academy with him in the summer of 1857 remained to graduate. According to John M. Carroll, around two dozen of those who dropped out for various reasons including academic deficiency could have finished behind him. He became the designated immortal "because of a decimated class and not necessarily because of an earned academic standing."[54]

George Armstrong Custer was determined to gain a commission in the Army and he wanted to wring from his schooling the maximum amount of pleasure consistent with that determination. It took some doing, but he attained both goals, proving beyond doubt that there was more than one way to forge a successful career at the United States Military Academy.

Chapter III

To the Field of Battle

At West Point the guns of war were heard, and felt, years before they began firing—faintly at first and then with a pulsing insistence that portended disaster. Well before Custer and his classmates matriculated, political tensions had been building in reaction to events that had turned the sectional divide into a yawning abyss, including the Missouri Compromise of 1820, the nullification movement in South Carolina twelve years later (that almost ignited civil war three decades before Fort Sumter) and, more recently, the Compromise of 1850 and the Kansas-Nebraska Act of 1854. These measures, intended to halt or at least forestall the drive toward disunion, ran afoul of another law—that of unintended consequences. Thanks to the tunnel vision and intransigence of the county's lawmakers, by Custer's last year at the Academy war had become inevitable.

Custer did not find it strange that a crisis was brewing on the Hudson just as it was elsewhere in the fractured nation. As he observed in his unfinished memoirs,

> as each congressional district and territory of the United States had a representative in Congress, so each had its representatives at the Military Academy. And there was no phase of the great political questions of the times, particularly the agitation of the slavery question as discussed and maintained by the various agitators in Congress, but found its exponents among the cadets. In fact the latter as a rule reflected the political sentiments of the particular member who represented in Congress the locality from which the cadet happened to hail. Of course there were exceptions to this rule, but in the absence of any clearly formed political sentiment or belief of his own, it seemed to be the fashion, if nothing more, that each particular cadet should adopt the declared views and opinions of his representative in Congress.[1]

Custer failed to mention that he himself was an exception to the rule he cited. John Bingham, the man responsible for his acceptance at West Point and thus his subsequent military career, was an avowed opponent of the extension of slavery into the territories. Custer was far apart from his back-home benefactor on the slavery question. It was not a matter of no "clearly formed political sentiment" on his part, for he had consistently favored the efforts of Democratic leaders to oppose restrictions on slavery's expansion anywhere in the country, and he was sympathetic to the interests of the Southern bloc of the party for which Custer's father professed undying loyalty. As Stiles has written, Emmanuel Custer "held dear the Jacksonian ideals of individualism and equality. But the individuals and equals he had in mind were all white men. This was a general truth in American politics, but a particular truth about him."[2]

In April 1860, toward the close of his third year at the Academy, Cadet Custer explained his political credo in letters to a friend from New Rumley, John Chamberlain, a supporter of the Republican Party. He did so in the wake of recent events that had accelerated the drive to disunion, one of the most inflammatory being the October raid of the militant abolitionist John Brown on the federal arsenal at Harpers Ferry, Virginia, with the intention of inciting a slave uprising. Chamberlain may not have regarded Brown as a martyr but Custer suspected that he was a supporter of Senator William Henry Seward of New York, a frontrunner for the Republican presidential nomination, who in a celebrated speech eighteen months earlier had warned the people of the North and South of an "irrepressible conflict" taking shape in their midst. If so, Custer felt sorry for his friend, "for in case he gets the nomination at Chicago he will most assuredly suffer defeat next fall." The party that claimed the Custer family's loyalty "is sure to come out victorious in the next national contest," whoever won its nomination at the Democratic convention to be held in late April at Charleston, South Carolina.[3]

Upon hearing back from Chamberlain, Custer wrote again, giving a passionate defense of Democratic principles and a charitable view of the party's infighting that had caused the Charleston convention to adjourn after the delegates could not agree on a candidate. Although both blocs would later hold additional conventions of their own, Custer was certain they "will be united in nominating a sound national & conservative man . . . who by advocating *equal rights* to the citizens of every section of our republic will put down and defeat" any Republican nominee. In a later passage he identified those whom he believed deserved but had been denied equal rights under the law: "The South has insult after insult heaped upon her but when such acts as the John Brown raid at Harpers Ferry are committed and such writings as the Helper book [*The Impending Crisis of the South*, a celebrated anti-slavery screed by apostate Southerner Hinton Rowan Helper] circulated, all of which emanates from the Republican Party they determine no longer to submit to such aggression but demand that northern abolitionists shall not interfere with their constitutional rights. . . ."[4]

Custer may have been an advocate of state rights and an apologist for slavery, but he was no clairvoyant. In closing his letter, he insisted that "it will be demonstrated next fall that the appeal has not been made in vain but will result in the utter defeat of the Republicans. . . ." Six months after he wrote, Abraham Lincoln won the presidency by defeating the two candidates put forth by the hopelessly divided Democrats, Stephen A. Douglas of Illinois and John C. Breckinridge of Kentucky, as well as John Bell, standard-bearer of the middle-of-the-road Constitutional Union Party.

The election of a "black Republican," even one whose stance on the slavery question appeared ambiguous—while strongly opposed its extension into the western territories, Lincoln supported gradual, compensated emancipation and the colonization of freed slaves to Africa—told every cadet with a modicum of political perception that life at West Point would never be the same. Four days after Lincoln's victory Custer wrote Ann Reed that "I fear there will be much trouble. Several of the Southern states and perhaps all of them will withdraw from the Union in a few days, and it is highly probable that war will be the result. All the [Southern] cadets here have determined to resign and go home as soon as their states leave the Union."

The portents were certainly ominous. As Custer wrote, "no one can calmly contemplate the result of a war between the North and the South. Brother would be arrayed against brother, father against son. The country would be impoverished." Yet he held out hope that a shooting war was avoidable. Although the union would be broken, perhaps beyond repair, "it is probable however that the Southern States or at least a portion of them will leave peaceably and thus save us the spectacle of one portion of [the] country in arms against then other. I sincerely hope we may be spared this sorrow. . . ."[5]

*   *   *

The effect of Lincoln's election was quickly felt on both the national and local levels. "Fire-eating" South Carolina, which had threatened to leave the Union once before to protest tariff rates considered ruinous to Southern agriculture, seceded on December 20, and sister states made preparations to follow her lead. At West Point, Lincoln was hanged in effigy outside the cadet barracks (just as John Brown had been a year earlier) although the crude figure was so quickly removed that few students or faculty members laid eyes on it.[6]

From this point on, the fissures in the cadet corps widened and deepened. For months, if not years, fights had broken out between representatives of both sections, the most famous being a bloody confrontation between Wade Gibbes of South Carolina and the abolitionist Emory Upton. In the wake of Lincoln's triumph verbal and physical confrontations became an even more prevalent feature of cadet life.[7]

Custer, being politically acceptable to his Southern classmates, is not known to have participated in any of these sectional brawls. But as 1861 dawned and a parade of Southern states followed South Carolina out of the Union, his support of Southern rights may have begun to loosen. On occasion his sense of friendship, always strong and lasting, seems to have trumped his political inclinations. When his buddy, the soft-spoken and affable Ohioan Morris Schaff, was threatened with a beating by a "very aggressive" Southerner, Custer, in company with "Deacon" Elbert, told him: "If he lays a hand on you, Morris, we'll maul the earth with him."[8]

Still, he tried to hang on to his Southern friends to the last. Shortly after the election he had a conversation with "a gallant" fellow from Georgia, Pierce Young. Without preamble, Young turned toward his classmate and in "a half jocular, half earnest manner," uttered words that Cadet Custer never forgot: "Custer, my boy, we're going to have war. It's no use talking. . . . Now let me prophecy what will happen to you and me. You will go home, and your abolition governor will probably make you a colonel of a cavalry regiment. I will go down to Georgia, and ask Governor [Joseph E.] Brown to give me a cavalry regiment. And who knows but we may move against each other during the war."

Young went on to predict that, better armed and equipped, Custer's side would probably prevail in the early skirmishes, but "we'll get the best of the fight in the end, because we will fight for a principle, a cause, while you will fight only to perpetuate the abuse of power." Custer wrote that although at the time neither of them put stock in "this boyish prediction," in some regards Young—who in less than three years would rise, as his friend would, to general officer of cavalry and who would heavily engage Custer's forces on more than one battlefield—was remarkable prescient.[9]

Two events during the late winter and early spring of 1861 would complete the implosion of the cadet corps while showing Custer the path he must take through the debris field. On February 22, Washington's birthday, dueling demonstrations broke out in the wake of the Academy band playing the national airs during the evening ceremony known as tattoo. As the bandsmen paraded across the West Point Plain toward what served as an unofficial dividing line between the predominately Northern and Southern wings of the cadet barracks, they boomed out "The Star-Spangled Banner." From the windows of their quarters a large group of Northerners greeted the music with unauthorized cheering. "I believe it was begun at our window by Custer," wrote Morris Schaff, "for it took a man of his courage and heedlessness openly to violate the regulations." Immediately afterward the inhabitants of the Southern wing, led by Custer's friend Tom Rosser, broke into applause for their homeland, followed by choruses of "Dixie." The contest went on until Rosser and his comrades were overwhelmed by the swelling voices of their more numerous competitors.[10]

On April 12, six weeks after Lincoln's inaugural, the dam burst, sweeping away all efforts at maintaining collegiality. On that morning South Carolina forces under Brigadier General Gustave Toutant Beauregard—who had spent an incongruous five days in January as West Point's superintendent—bombarded the federal garrison of Fort Sumter in Charleston Harbor, and war was no longer a subject for debate. The departure of the Southern-born or -reared cadets increased dramatically. At the time, however, Custer entertained no hard feelings against his Southern brethren; as he told a Northern cadet who resented the mass exodus, "I'm going to stick to the Union but I refuse to hold the slightest bitterness against any Southern cadet or Southern army officer who resigns and follows the fortunes of his home State."[11]

He went so far as to salute some members of his class during their leave-taking. Another understanding Northerner, Elias Andruss, would write that "there seemed to be an irresistible belief among them [the Southerners] that it would not be *chivalric* but *cowardly* not to join their States in Secession. So strong was this sentiment, that boys of Northern parentage, though born at Southern posts where their fathers were serving as army officers, were imbued with this same spirit." Between November 1860 and December 1861, 173 cadets would resign from the Academy to avoid fighting against fellow Southerners. Five others who resigned were born in the North but had been admitted to the Academy from Southern congressional districts.[12]

Even as the "Southrons" departed, Academy staff members were called to duty in Washington. A battery of light artillery, which had trained the cadets in gunnery tactics, was dispatched to the capital under Captain Charles Griffin, a future major general in the volunteer service. Rumors sprang up that all remaining cadets would be assigned to active duty with the army, perhaps in advance of graduation. As their professors told them, even incompletely educated officers were needed to muster-in and drill the thousands of volunteers soon to be rushing to enlistment stations across the region.[13]

The prospect of an early escape from the "detention" of the Academy had a definite allure for Custer, but the circumstances of his release bothered him greatly. Two days before Beauregard's guns started in Custer had written Ann Reed that "I have scarcely thought of anything else" but the outbreak of a general conflict, which he correctly believed would occur in less than a week. He realized that when it came "it will be beyond the power of human foresight to predict when and where it will terminate or what will be the consequences."[14]

One possible consequence was that he and his classmates would not be permitted to graduate at all. Even so, he had no objection to serving his country as best he could, in accord with the oath of allegiance to the federal government he had taken upon entering the Academy. He was fully aware that his stance would pit him—quite possibly in mortal combat—against the Southern-born cadets whose friendship and values he continued to cherish, but his political allegiances had been irreparably torn. He was heading off to war for a principle and there was no turning back. When Custer's half-sister wrote that she hoped he would not have to take part in the conflict, he did not share her feelings: "In times like this, we should discard all private and personal desires and consider nothing but the prosperity and welfare of our country." Having been educated and trained at the government's expense, he would be guilty of "the basest ingratitude" should he somehow find a way to avoid the fighting that lay ahead.

He had already written to Ohio's Republican governor, William Dennison, to offer his services in case the War Department authorized regular army officers to transfer to the volunteer service for the duration of the conflict, an action in accordance with law "in time of war." Custer's motivation was a combination of patriotism and self-interest: "I would prefer serving with the troops of my native state, besides I could get a much higher office as in the regular army I would be a Lieutenant but in the volunteers I could be certain of being at least a Captain and probably higher." Dennison welcomed Custer's overture but sent a stock response, one he must have given to many another Buckeye eager for high rank and authority in the state's forces. Custer quoted the governor as proud "of such noble offers from her sons and she knew how bravely they would battle in the field for the honor of their flag and their state and in the meantime to accept his sincerest thanks for my gallant tender."[15]

* * *

In the wake of Fort Sumter, the forty-five remaining members of the Class of 1861 were ordered to report to the War Department for assignment. By early June some of them were already heavily involved in the fighting; on the tenth, Judson Kilpatrick became the first regular army officer to be wounded in action during an engagement at Big Bethel on the Virginia Peninsula. When the Class of 1862 formally sought War Department permission to be graduated early as well, its request was granted and commencement was scheduled for June 24. Although weeks of intensified study was required of the petitioners, Custer numbered among those completing their education on a high note, having been informed of his commissioning in the arm of his choice, the 2nd United States Cavalry.[16]

Custer managed to pass the final battery of tests. For once, despite all the distractions besetting him, he had found the time and the will to study diligently. Then, almost at the last minute, his prospects for leaving West Point with a degree and a commission appeared to vaporize. On June 29, while awaiting orders to join his outfit, he committed an offense that not only saddled him with the maximum number of demerits—five—but resulted in his court-martial, with dismissal from the Academy a real possibility.

He was on summer encampment duty that evening when a hazing incident escalated into a fistfight between a plebe and his principal antagonist. A raucous crowd gathered, cheering on the contestants. Custer effectively joined them; instead of halting the fight at once, "the instincts of the boy prevailed over the obligations of the officer of the guard," and he pushed back the spectators to provide the room for a fair fight. Two Academy officers, attracted to the commotion and being advised of Custer's involvement in it, reported him for failing to suppress the fight. The next day he was summoned to the tent of the commandant of cadets, Lieutenant Colonel John F. Reynolds, who sent him to his quarters in arrest. As Custer noted, "the facts of the case were reported to Washington, on formal charges and specifications, and a court-martial asked for to determine the degree of my punishment."[17]

Custer's situation appeared dire, but in the end his luck—the luck that had seen him through so many scrapes before—held yet again. On July 5, two weeks after his classmates departed the Academy for points south Custer went on trial, charged with neglect of duty and conduct prejudicial to good order and military discipline. To the formal charges and specifications he plead guilty "as a matter of course."[18]

Initially the proceedings appeared to go in his favor. Cadets William Ludlow and Peter Ryerson testified that their confrontation amounted to no more than a scuffle, an opinion endorsed not only by Custer in a four-page statement he entered in his own defense but also by one of the officers who came on the scene as the fight broke up and who effectively served as a character witness for the accused. A week after the proceedings began, however, no verdict had been rendered by the nine-officer panel and Custer was still under arrest, unable to join his classmates at the headquarters of the army.[19]

In his statement he had essentially thrown himself on the mercy of the court, admitting his offense but minimizing its severity and begging the tribunal to consider his conduct in the context of his complete record at West Point. Since he was fully aware of the scent that record gave off, his defense reeked of abject desperation. His heartfelt statement of misery over the timing of his offense may have served him best: his inability to follow his classmates to war "surpassed in a hundred fold the punishment" that would have been meted out in peacetime. Genuine anguish poured from his closing statement, in which he bemoaned "the detention and mortification which it has already occasioned me and the torturing suspension I must experience before I hear the findings of this Court. . . ."[20]

In the end his emotional plea, plus the obvious value of every educated officer in that time of crisis, helped persuaded the court to extend leniency. In mid-July, it found him guilty on both charges but only set his punishment as an official reprimand. Custer later learned that some of his classmates already in Washington had attempted to intercede in his behalf—"fortunately," he recalled, "some of them had influential friends here." One of these friends, apparently, was Congressman Bingham, who, having heard of Custer's predicament, is supposed to have persuaded War Department officials to go easy on him, although the details of his intercession remain unknown.[21]

Whatever the extent of outside intervention, the result of greatest import for Custer was the order he received by telegraph relieving him from arrest and directing him to report to the office of the Adjutant General of the Army.

According to Custer historian Lawrence Frost, the accused never learned of the court's decision, and so his narrow escape did not bother him afterward. By the morning of July 18 he was pacing the deck of a Hudson River steamer striving to catch up with other members of the second West Point Class of 1861. Every one may have ranked higher than he on the scholastic scale, but he was determined that none would outperform him once the bullets began to fly.[22]

* * *

He reached New York City that afternoon, where he delayed his long-deferred journey enough to dress the part of the young officer. Assisted by the salesmen and tailors at the local branch of Horstmann's, a Philadelphia-based military-furnishings firm, he donned the uniform of a second lieutenant of cavalry, completing his ensemble with the addition of "sabre, revolver, sash, spurs, etc." Once suitably attired, he took the evening train to Washington, sharing coach space with hundreds of other officers and men bound for the seat of war. He never forgot the outpouring of war enthusiasm he witnessed over the next several hours. The journey was one of fits and starts, the train stopping at depot after depot and on occasion shunted onto the siding to allow engines hauling military cargo of greater priority to take the lead.

At virtually every stop crowds of civilians gathered around the cars, cheering them on their way, some proffering refreshments to passengers. The manifest support of the citizenry for the effort to save the Union impressed Custer and inflated his pride: "Their enthusiasm knew no bounds; they received us with cheers and cheered us in parting. It was no unusual sight, on leaving a station surrounded by these loyal people, to see matrons and maidens embracing and kissing with patriotic fervor the men, entire strangers to them, whom they saw hastening to the defense of the nation." He was, of course, one of them.[23]

While Custer's train crawled southward on overburdened rails, the war that had just begun was about to explode into bloody combat. Even before the skirmish at Big Bethel, would-be warriors from almost every Southern state had been gathering in upper Virginia to await the anticipated advance of their enemy. Almost thirty thousand of them—the majority garbed in some semblance of a uniform—had hunkered down behind an imperfect line of field works below a creek called Bull Run and north of a rail depot, Manassas Junction, where they had come under the command of the Fort Sumter hero G. T. Beauregard.

Barely twenty-five miles to the northeast, Washington teemed with thirty-five-thousand semi-organized recruits who had spent the last few weeks drilling under the bemused supervision of Brigadier General Irvin McDowell, the senior leader of volunteers to hail from Custer's native state. Editors and politicians across the North had been clamoring for a quick, decisive movement on the Confederate capital at Richmond. The path to that objective lay through Beauregard's lines, and McDowell, against his better judgment, had nerved himself to make the movement.

The Military Academy was well represented among the principal antagonists: both Beauregard and McDowell were graduates of the Class of 1838. While the former had served as the Academy's superintendent in the last days of peace, for four years prior to the war in Mexico the latter had held the equally responsible position of Academy adjutant. Dozens of other West Pointers, most of them wearing officers' insignia, with a few dropouts serving as humble soldiers, would add their knowledge and training to the ignorant armies about to clash by day on Sunday, July 21.[24]

Just after daylight on the twentieth Custer reached Washington, which he found abuzz with news of an impending clash near Manassas. According to his memoirs he went directly from the depot to a boarding house at F and Fourteenth Streets where some of his classmates had taken rooms. He found that all but one had left in response to orders; the remaining cadet was a former roommate, James P. Parker of Missouri. Parker had failed to graduate, having been deemed "academically deficient" in his final semester, though he had received a commission. He had recently tendered his resignation and consequently had been dismissed from the service, enabling him to join the ranks of the Confederacy.[25]

The bleary-eyed Missourian told Custer that McDowell's army, which had left Washington four days earlier, had already encountered Beauregard's forces in preliminary skirmishing and that a full-scale battle was probably hours away. The news made Custer realize that the two friends were about to go their separate ways. He recalled that "we had eaten day by day at the same table, had struggled together in the effort to master the same problems of study; we had marched by each other's side year after year, elbow to elbow, when engaged in the duties of drill, parade, etc., and had shared our blankets with each other when learning the requirements of camp life. Henceforth this was all to be thrust from our memory as far as possible. . . ." The jolt of parting with comrades who held opposing political views was something he would experience time and again over the next four years, and the sensation of loss and sorrow would never diminish.

From the boarding house Custer walked the three blocks to the War Department building, where he reported to the office of the adjutant general of the army "as my instructions directed me to do." What transpired in that building we know only through Custer's own account which, though somewhat overly dramatic and self-serving, has come to be accepted as fact. He notes, credibly enough, that he was much impressed by "the number of officials I saw and the numerous messengers to be seen flitting from room to room, bearing immense numbers of huge-looking envelopes. The entire department had an air of busy occupation that, taken in connection with the important military events then daily transpiring and hourly expected, and contrasted with then hum-drum life I had but lately led as a cadet, added to the bewilderment I naturally felt." With perhaps less verisimilitude, he claims that upon being checked in by the desk officer, he was casually asked if he would care to be presented to Brevet Lieutenant General Winfield Scott, commanding general of the army, "to which of course, I joyfully assented."[26]

A private audience with the most famous soldier of his era was the dream of many a senior career officer; that such an opportunity should be granted to a spanking-new second lieutenant who had yet to serve in the field was the honor of a lifetime. In fact Scott, who affected an avuncular attitude toward young officers, on many occasions had invited them into his office for casual conversation, though usually in a group setting. The respect and affection the seventy-five-year-old general commanded among the students and graduates of West Point—an institution he had not attended but whose steadfast patron he had become—was intense and enduring. William Woods Averell of the Class of 1855, then a subaltern in the Regiment of Mounted Rifles and later a brevet major general of volunteer cavalry, recalled that Scott, "with his immense proportions and impressive manner inspired us with feeling of genuine veneration almost amounting to awe. . . Neither did the thought exist that he would not always be the Commander in Chief."[27]

Custer followed his escort into Scott's office, where he found the general seated at a table covered with maps and documents easily identifiable as war-related. Scott had been in conference with political officials—Custer thought he recognized Republican Senator James W. Grimes of Iowa among the eminent group. The adjutant introduced the visitor as "Lieutenant Custer of the Second Cavalry; he has just reported from West Point, and I did not know but that you might have some special orders to give him." As Custer recalled the upshot, Scott shook his hand most cordially and said, "Well, my young friend,

I am glad to welcome you to the service at this critical time. Our country has need of the strong arms of all her loyal sons in this emergency." Upon inquiring into Custer's background, Scott added: "We have had the assistance of quite a number of you young men from the Academy, drilling volunteers, etc. Now what can I do for you? Would you prefer to be ordered to General Mansfield [Brigadier General Joseph K. F. Mansfield, commander of the military department of Washington] to aid in this work, or is it your desire for something more active?"

Almost staggered by the thought that the nation's greatest soldier would ask his active-duty preference, Scott's visitor "ventured to stammer out that I earnestly desired to be ordered to at once join my company, then with General McDowell." To this Scott replied: "A very commendable resolution, young man," and he directed the adjutant general to issue orders to that effect. Scott then inquired if Custer had provided himself with a horse. The younger man replied that he had not. The general expressed regret, explaining that procuring one at this juncture would be a nigh-impossible task—the army had swept the capital clean of all serviceable mounts. However, should Custer find one he was to report back to the War Department at seven that night: "I desire to send some dispatches to General McDowell, and you can be the bearer of them. You are not afraid of a night ride, are you?" Custer was not—to be assigned to carry communiqués from the leader of the army to the leader of its largest fighting force was another honor he doubted he was worthy of, but he saluted smartly, left Scott's office, and went in search of transportation.

Over the next several hours Custer made the rounds of the city's livery stables but found not a single available mount. The realization that "I was not to be able to take advantage of the splendid opportunity for distinction opened before me" pushed him toward despair until, strictly by chance, he met an enlisted man who had pulled duty at West Point while Custer was there. The man had reached the capital weeks earlier as a member of Captain Griffin's battery. The unit, now Company D of the newly organized 5th United States Artillery, a component of McDowell's Army of Northeastern Virginia, was stationed at Centreville, about six miles northeast of Manassas Junction. Griffin had sent the soldier back to the capital to retrieve a battery horse that had been left behind on the morning of July 16 when the entire Federal force marched out of the city.

Custer seized the opportunity thus presented, persuading the man to delay his return until after 7 p.m.—not a difficult decision when the Commanding

General was in need of this particular horse. When Custer returned bearing the documents that had been handed him, he recognized the prized animal as "Wellington," whom he had ridden many times during equitation practice at the Academy. The familiarity between horse and rider seemed a good omen, and Custer and his unnamed companion set off for Centreville on a hopeful note.

The euphoric feeling survived long after the mounted men crossed Long Bridge and plunged into the Virginia darkness. "The hours of night flew quickly past," Custer remembered, "engrossed as my mind was with the excitement and serious novelty of the occasion as well as occasionally diverted by the conversation of my companion." The news he conveyed included details of a skirmish between elements of the opposing armies two days earlier at a Bull Run crossing called Blackburn's Ford.[28]

Neither Custer nor his informant knew it, but the fighting of the eighteenth, while limited to less than 10 percent of McDowell's and Beauregard's forces, would have a major effect on the larger battle to come. The unexpected encounter had resulted from a supposedly limited advance toward the Confederate right flank that prematurely disclosed McDowell's intention to strike in that sector with a much larger force. Convinced he must now attack the far left of the Bull Run defenses, McDowell had committed himself to a multicolumn offensive in that direction via a wide turning-movement. The complicated plan, while tactically sound, would tax the energy and acumen of his citizen-soldiers, hampering their ability to coordinate operations and mount diversionary movements. From Custer's perspective, however, the meeting-engagement of July 18 had come at just the right time. Because it compelled him to revamp his strategy, a task that took two days, McDowell would not be ready to launch his assault until Lieutenant Custer was on hand to take part in it.[29]

* * *

Custer and his riding partner did not reach Centreville, the army's staging area, until between 2 and 3 a.m. on the morning of the twenty-first. To get there Wellington had been forced to pick his way in the dark along roads filled with volunteer troops, many of them lying prone or supine to catch a few final minutes of sleep. That so many were off their feet portended trouble for the Army of Northeastern Virginia. As Custer would later learn, by half past two the movement toward the Confederate left ought to have been well begun. Aware that it would take hours to complete, McDowell wished it to take place in darkness so as to increase the advantage of surprise. But the first column to move out had done so slowly and clumsily, miscues to be expected of green troops. Behind this force, which would make a diversion to hold the enemy's attention, the two divisions that were to cross Bull Run and attack Beauregard's left flank were unavoidably late hitting the road.[30]

Despite the corporate dawdling, Custer was aware that combat was imminent. Upon handing General Scott's dispatches to one of McDowell's staff officers, he learned that the entire army was under arms and would strike as soon as it got into its assigned positions. Over a hastily prepared breakfast consisting of coffee, a small steak, and cornbread, he picked up additional details of McDowell's promising but complex strategy. He appreciated being privy to the great plan in which he would play a role, but he was delighted to have been provided with a meal, even one so meager. Had he known "that I was not to have an opportunity to taste food during the next thirty hours, I should have appreciated the opportunity I then enjoyed even more highly."[31]

Custer learned that the majority of the small force of cavalry attached to McDowell's command—seven companies of regulars under Major Innis Newton Palmer of his own regiment—had been assigned to one of the assault forces, the division of Brigadier General David Hunter (one company of the 2nd United States Dragoons would be attached to the division of Colonel Samuel P. Heintzelman, in Hunter's rear). Because Hunter's column was so slow to get moving, his horsemen, though saddled and in column, had yet to leave Centreville. As soon as he finished eating, Custer rode out to find them—presumably upon Wellington, whom he appears somehow to have detached from Griffin's battery.[32]

Upon reaching his destination he reported to First Lieutenant Thomas Drummond, commanding Custer's troop, Company G of the 2nd Cavalry. Drummond greeted him warmly and introduced him to the other officers. Most were strangers to Custer and in the pre-dawn darkness they remained so even after salutes and handshakes had been exchanged. Probably not to his surprise, Custer found he was the junior officer among all present, although another recently commissioned second lieutenant—Leicester Walker, also of Ohio, who had been appointed from civil life—was senior to him by only six weeks. As he would soon discover, Walker was disposed to defer to him, a

West Pointer, in matters of tactics and leadership, a situation that appealed to Custer's ego but upon which he resolved not to presume.[33]

By 4:30 a.m., Hunter's column and the troopers assigned to cover its front, flank, and rear were finally in motion. As the spearhead of McDowell's offensive, it moved out the Warrenton Turnpike leading southwestward from Centreville, and by 6 a.m. it veered north, plunging through what Custer called "an immense forest" and heading for a crossing of Bull Run at Sudley Ford. Along this roundabout route, the going was frustratingly slow, partially the result of troops unused to hard marching and also due to mistakes by a local guide who for fear of exposing the division's movements led it so far to the north that he doubled the time it took to reach its destination. Well before then, a signal gun that was supposed to trigger the grand assault had begun firing. Nothing was going according to plan or schedule, and for all the precautions Hunter had taken, the Rebel left was becoming aware of the magnitude and direction of the Union threat.[34]

The stop-start progress of the turning movement was a vexing experience for young men going into their first battle, Lieutenant Custer among them. But once the ford at Sudley Springs was reached and crossed sometime after nine, action heated up, making them forget the rigor and tedium of the march thus far. Along the stream the entire column was halted, allowing the infantry to rest before the enemy was encountered and permitting the cavalry's horses to drink.

Close to 10 a.m. Hunter's infantry and artillery finally advanced to open the battle. Soon the air was filled with the crack of musketry as the vanguard of the column, the brigade of Colonel Ambrose E. Burnside, became engaged with a much smaller force under Major Nathan G. Evans. But while the foot soldiers surged forward, the cavalry was held in place. Custer and his colleagues sat their horses, trying to gauge the progress of the fight not only by sound but through the reports of soldiers drifting back from the front, many of them disabled by wounds.

The horsemen could only wonder when their superiors would decide how—or if—to employ them. Much of the rapidly expanding battlefield was hilly and heavily wooded, terrain considered too rough for mounted maneuvering. At this early stage of the conflict commanders on both sides, lacking an understanding of cavalry's missions and capabilities, were reluctant to use it in its primary role as scouts and guides for the infantry. Instead, with few exceptions throughout this day, the horse soldiers would be relegated to a secondary role in support of artillery units.

This became clear only after one of General McDowell's staff officers galloped up on a lathered horse with orders that Major Palmer should ford the run and top the ridge beyond. Once on the high ground his command was to support a battery going into position in the northwest quadrant of the intersection of the Warrenton Turnpike and the north-south-running Sudley Road. Improbably enough, the artillery unit was Charles Griffin's, staffed by the officers and enlisted men who had followed him from West Point to Washington. Griffin, like Palmer, had been attached to the brigade originally headed by Colonel Andrew Porter but now led by the latter's favorite subordinate, Lieutenant Averell of the Regiment of Mounted Rifles (Porter had moved up to division command to replace Colonel Hunter, who had been wounded by a rifle ball). The anomalous arrangement notwithstanding, Averell would command the brigade through the rest of the fight.

Saluting the message-bearer, Innis Palmer ordered the mounted battalion forward at a rapid clip. Custer recalled that "as we ascended the crest I saw Griffin with his battery galloping into position. The enemy had discovered him, and their artillery had opened fire upon him, but the shots were aimed so high the balls passed overhead. . . . I remember well the strange hissing and extremely vicious sound of the first cannon shot I heard as it whirled through the air." He had heard that sound before, many times, during artillery practice at the Academy, "but a man listens with changed interest when the direction of the balls is toward instead of away from him."[35]

In his report of the battle Griffin noted that during this early phase of the fighting his battery changed position several times, at one point advancing about two hundred yards toward the Rebel right, where Evans's small force had been reinforced by the brigades of Brigadier General Barnard Bee and Colonel Francis S. Bartow. At first Palmer's troopers were stationed well in rear of the battery, at the foot of a crest upon which Griffin was maneuvering. Here the horsemen were shielded from the enemy's fire, but then came word that the enemy was preparing to charge the battery and that Palmer must repel the assault.

Custer understood that a mounted charge was imminent, and the realization shook him: "When it is remembered that but three days before I had quitted West Point as a schoolboy, and as yet had never ridden at anything more dangerous or terrible than a three-foot hurdle, or tried my sabre upon anything more animated or combative than a leather-head stuffed with tan bark, it may be imagined that my mind was more or less given to anxious thoughts as we ascended the slope of the hill in front of us." Conscious that he was under the gaze of colleagues more experienced than he, Custer prayed that he would perform capably enough to win their approval.[36]

He was abruptly shaken from his reverie by Lieutenant Walker who, riding beside him up the hill, asked: "Custer, what weapon are you going to use in the charge?" The options were saber and pistol; both men carried one of each. Either weapon would have served well in close-quarters fighting, but Custer, perhaps given his schoolboy literary tastes, opted for the sword, which he drew from its scabbard "and rode forward as if totally unconcerned." At once his companion followed suit, but before their respective platoons plunged to the attack Custer began having second thoughts. To wield the saber required its bearer to move so close to an opponent as to become an inviting target. He therefore decided to replace it with the revolver, the use of which enabled a man to "select his own time and distance."

Sheathing his sword, he drew the handgun and poised it opposite his shoulder—movements copied by Lieutenant Walker. Only minutes later, as Major Palmer took position at the head of the column, Custer changed his mind again: it might be difficult, if not impossible, to fire accurately from the saddle; then, too, should he get caught up in the excitement of the charge he might fire off every cartridge, "by which time in all probability we would be in the midst of our enemies, and slashing right and left at each other; in which case a sabre would be of much greater value and service than an empty revolver. This seemed convincing, so much so that my revolver found its way again to its holster, and the sabre was again at my shoulder. Again did Walker, as if in pantomime, follow my example."

Custer's succession of second-guesses ended when the crest was reached, where instead of encountering musketry the horsemen were subjected to "hot artillery fire." The column recoiled briefly, then under the direction of the major and his subordinates, steadied itself. Custer was especially impressed by the conduct of one officer who rode to the head of his company where he called out, in a calm and resolute voice, "Now, men, do your duty." Custer was shocked to learn that a few days after the battle the man resigned his commission to join the ranks of the army he had been about to assail.[37]

Custer's exercise in selecting the proper weaponry for a mounted assault went for naught. Just as the column prepared to go forward and weather a storm of shot and shell, it was directed to retire to the base of the hill. It had been determined that no attack on Griffin's guns was imminent, and so the order to charge in their support had been countermanded.

Back in its sheltered position, the cavalry, safe from immediate harm, was reduced to the role of spectator. From the top of a ridge close to the line of their advancing infantry, Custer had an unimpeded view of the events that ensued. When, late in the morning, the line held by Evans, Bee, and Bartow broke under the attacks of Porter and Heintzelman—a combined total of 13,500 troops and twenty-four cannons—the tide appeared to turn irreversibly in the Federals' favor.

The outmanned Confederates were compelled to seek refuge atop a long and broad elevation known as Henry Hill. There they were reinforced by a body of stout-fighting infantry under Brigadier General Thomas J. Jackson, soon to be known as the "Stonewall Brigade." In mid-afternoon, Jackson's men and other hastily gathered supports halted the Union advance, in the process savaging the attackers. Their victims included the men of Griffin's battery, who through a misguided order to advance up the heights within range of Confederate riles suffered the loss of all but one of its guns as well as twenty-seven men killed, wounded, or missing, and fifty horses shot down in their traces. No supporting attack by seven companies of cavalry would have prevented the damage done to Griffin or to the infantry units that had attempted to seize Henry Hill.[38]

Moments before the now-reinforced enemy launched a counterattack, Lieutenants Custer and Walker were congratulating themselves on a glorious victory in the process of being won. Suddenly they spied a long line of men advancing through a patch of woods toward the rear of the Union battle line: "It never occurred to either of us that the troops we then saw could be any but some of our reinforcements making their way to the front. Before doubts could arise we saw the Confederate flag floating over a portion of the line just emerging from the timber." Then a battery opened on Custer's part of the field, and he heard the dreaded cry: "We're flanked! We're flanked!"

After that, all was commotion and confusion. Having fought gamely but futilely for seven hours under a merciless sun without sufficient water, covered in dust, sweat, and blood, the Army of Northeastern Virginia had had enough. So began a general retreat, slowly at first but then rapidly and haphazardly as panic spread through the ranks. "No pen or description," wrote Custer, "can give anything like a correct idea of the rout and demoralization that followed. Officers and men joined in one vast crowd, abandoning, except in isolated instances, all attempts to preserve their organizations."

As the retreat gained momentum, he began to appreciate how badly the cavalry had been used in the fight—a failing not only of McDowell and his lieutenants but one shared by their opponents: "A moderate force of good cavalry at that moment could have secured to the Confederates nearly every man and gun that crossed Bull Run in the early morning." But the horsemen available to Beauregard and his recently arrived superior, General Joseph E. Johnston, were just as few as those in Union blue. The only force of any size that had been brought into the fight was the Virginia regiment of Lieutenant Colonel James Ewell Brown ("Jeb") Stuart, later designated the 1st Virginia and to become the most celebrated mounted outfit in either army. Stuart's participation had been limited to attacking two of the infantry regiments that had failed to sweep the Stonewall Brigade off Henry Hill. The Virginians had ridden roughshod over the already-retreating Yankees, inflicting casualties and panic until halted and turned back by the single unit of Federal horsemen to see even a modicum of action this day, the company of Captain Albert V. Colburn.[39]

McDowell did, however, assign his cavalry one important mission, though too late to salvage victory: protect the army's rear during the retreat. In company with a two-gun section of a battery commanded by Captain Richard Arnold, Custer and his compatriots gave a creditable account of themselves, fending off pursuit by elements of Rebel infantry and cavalry. At the crossing of Bull Run, Stuart's men strained to land a finishing blow, but salvos from Arnold's guns persuaded them to back off. Soon afterward, from concern that other, more combative forces might be closing in, Major Palmer received orders to push on to Centreville "in order to save my command." The rapid movement failed, however, to save Arnold's cannons, which had to be abandoned near the debris-blocked bridge where Cub Run crossed the Warrenton Pike.[40]

Able to cross at a ford not passable for artillery, Custer and his comrades reached Centreville without "further molestation" by early evening. In common with other elements of the disorganized, demoralized army, they halted there for a few hours to catch their breath and rest their horses. After dark the march resumed in the direction of Washington. Only when the cavalry reached its camps inside the capital's defenses on the rain-spattered morning of the twenty-second did the body- and mind-numbing retreat come to an end. There Custer looked back in wonder at a baptism of fire he could never have envisioned and which he would never forget.[41]

Chapter IV

Rising Star

Custer recalled that "I little imagined, when making my night ride from Washington on July 20th, that the night following would find me returning with a defeated and demoralized army." It also found him hungry, thirsty, drenched with rain, coated in mud from the waist down, and exhausted after being in the saddle for almost forty hours. His youth, physical fitness, and the pain-dulling prospect of being overtaken by pursuers kept him alert enough to push through to his destination. Joseph Fought, a bugler in Company D of the 2nd Cavalry, described by his commanding officer as "a small boy" and who would later attach himself to Custer's command, marveled at the lieutenant's stamina on the retreat. As Fought remembered, although almost completely "spent, Custer never let up, never slackened control."

His conduct during the night and into the small hours of the twenty-second capped a respectable performance in battle and campaign. In a twenty-four-page letter sent to Tully McCrea the following month he reported that, to prevent his men from catching the panic of the retreating volunteers, he rode in rear of the unit instead of at its head—"the proper place"—all the way to Arlington Heights. Supposedly his exemplary conduct reaped praise. Bugler Fought claimed that even before he returned from the battlefield "his name was being cited for bravery in the Capital." According to Marguerite Merington, Congressman Bingham would recall that in the post-battle reports of "that miserable fiasco he was mentioned for bravery." Yet the official record includes no mention of a personal citation. When penning his account of the fight, Major Palmer claimed that "the conduct of officers and men throughout the day was in the highest degree praiseworthy." The troopers had not, however, been heavily engaged at any point, as indicated by their casualty count: thirteen enlisted men wounded, five missing and presumed captured.[1]

While Palmer's blanket commendation was not inappropriate, it concealed the fact that because the horsemen had been used so sparingly except when covering the retreat they had contributed little to their army's fortunes; worse, they had impeded them. When shifting about during the fighting in search of maneuvering room the cavalry several times became intermingled with infantry units, breaking up their formations. On one occasion late in the day they had virtually driven a Maine regiment from the field, exposing its brigade to a devastating fire. According to one observer, his command's misadventures had driven Major Palmer, at day's end, to tears.[2]

Custer would write that his company and one other, which directly supported Arnold's battery on the retreat, were the last organized bodies of troops to vacate the battlefield. While this claim is impossible to verify, the timing of his arrival at Arlington, if correct, appears to bear him out. Palmer reported that the vanguard of his worn-out battalion reached its camps at 5:30 in the morning; Custer maintained that Company G did not limp in until shortly before noon. As he wrote, "I scarcely waited for my company to be assigned to its camp before I was stretched at full length under a tree, where from fatigue, hunger, and exhaustion I soon fell asleep, despite the rain and mud, and slept for hours before awakening." When he did, according to Cadet McCrea, Custer was "so stiff and sore he could hardly move."

The physical toll did not prevent him from attempting to make sense of the disastrous encounter he had emerged from: "I could find but little to console or flatter me, and still less to encourage a hopeful view of the success of the Union cause in the future. . . ." And yet he saw no reason to despair. He was right to reject despondency, for the magnitude of the defeat, while demoralizing in the short run, would galvanize the North into a much greater effort to defeat the Rebels.[3]

Subsequent events suggested a better outcome the next time the armies clashed. Though defeated as much by the inexperience and ineptitude of their commanders as by the unduly harsh conditions under which they fought, the Union volunteers had given a good account of themselves on many parts of the field—while already a proud Regular, Custer freely acknowledged their grit and tenacity. Some comfort could be taken from the assertion of a prisoner with whom he conversed, Lieutenant Colonel Bartley Boone of the 2nd Mississippi, that the Federals had been overwhelmed by a superior force, though Boone's figure of ninety thousand was hardly credible. Encouraging signs included the lack of a punishing pursuit or any attempt to capture or besiege the federal capital. This suggested that the Confederates had been as disorganized by victory as their opponents by defeat, which hardly described an enemy of superior discipline, mobility, or resolve. Then too, the overwhelming importance of preserving the Union would undoubtedly force the Lincoln administration to redouble its efforts to place a large, well-equipped, well-trained, and competently led force in the field before the year was out.[4]

Above all, that effort must be made by a commander in whom the government and the army had the utmost trust and confidence. This was not Irvin McDowell, who in the wake of the bitter defeat was castigated by officers and men, editors, and politicians as irresolute, incompetent, even disloyal, charges Custer condemned as "harsh and unjust." The problem was that there were few candidates for the job. General Scott, who could not mount a horse without assistance, was too old and infirm to take the field, and most of the officers who would later rise to high rank were too young and inexperienced. This was only to be expected; not since the war in Mexico had any officer commanded more than a few hundred men in combat, and the campaigns against Native Americans on the western frontier would not measure up to the effort expected of the man who replaced McDowell.

Only one United States officer had achieved even a modicum of strategic or tactical success at this early stage of the conflict, and Lincoln called upon him almost immediately. He was George Brinton McClellan, the second-ranking graduate of the fifty-nine-man West Point Class of 1846 that would contribute twenty general officers to the ranks of the contending armies. Only thirty-four, the man who would become known as "The Young Napoleon" had forged a distinguished career in the Engineer Corps, especially in Mexico where he had been one of Scott's favorite staff officers, and later in the cavalry before resigning his commission in 1857 to become chief engineer of one railroad and later, the president of another.

In 1861 McClellan's military record and railroad experience had recommended him to the governors of several states who were looking for an officer steeped in strategy and logistics to lead volunteers. Governor Dennison of Ohio, who had cordially but noncommittally welcomed Custer's application for a commission, had secured McClellan's services only to lose him to the federal government, which in mid-May appointed him a major general in the regular army, senior to every officer then on duty except Scott himself.[5]

McClellan's initial command was the vast Department of the Ohio, consisting of the states of Ohio, Indiana, and Illinois, as well as portions of Pennsylvania and western Virginia. From the first he proved an excellent administrator, and once he took the field at the head of the troops he had organized and trained he achieved visible success, though on a small scale and against less-than-formidable opponents. The victories McClellan's army won in western Virginia, including Philippi (June 3) and Rich Mountain (July 11), safeguarded the vital Baltimore & Ohio Railroad and secured Unionist enclaves that two years later would form the state of West Virginia.

Although McClellan took credit for these and other successes, some of his subordinates, such as Brigadier General William S. Rosecrans, played a material role in the victories but failed to receive the recognition and celebrity lavished on the handsome, charismatic department commander. Not surprisingly, one day after McDowell's beaten troops took refuge inside the Washington defenses, Lincoln called McClellan to Washington and installed him as head of what would become the Army of the Potomac, then numbering less than fifty thousand strong but within eight months to increase almost threefold.[6]

From the start "Little Mac" was a favorite with the great majority of his troops, whose confidence and morale he built up even as he saw to their organization, training, equipping, and provisioning. One of his earliest champions in Virginia was George Custer, who respected McClellan's military acumen, appreciated his West Point and Ohio ties, and was comfortable with his conservative political orientation. McClellan's mind—like Custer's, and supposedly like Lincoln's—was fixed on defeating secession and restoring the Union and unencumbered with concerns about the status of slaves. "It can also be truthfully said," wrote Custer, "that no officer of either side ever developed or gave evidence of the possession of that high order of military ability . . . which General McClellan brought to the discharge of his duties as the reorganizer and commander of a defeated and demoralized force, and to the formation of a new army composed almost entirely of new levies fresh from the counting-house, the farm, and the workshop."

To the end of his wartime service Custer would be closely associated with the gifted young leader, so much so that he would often be referred to as "a McClellan man." The affiliation would give an early boost to his career. Over time, however, it would become a stigma he was forced to shed for purposes of self-preservation.[7]

* * *

Custer would have cherished being assigned to McClellan's personal staff, for the shortest route to advancement and distinction was to serve under a high-ranking officer with a rising reputation. At this point, however, the army leader was not in need of his services; Custer would have to settle for a position on the staff of a subordinate commander. One opened up a few weeks after the cavalry returned from the Bull Run battlefield.

Army organization at this phase of the war was fluid, to say the least. As a result of legislation enacted on August 3, Custer was no longer an officer in the 2nd United States Cavalry. Having decided to rebrand all of the army's mounted units as cavalry, Congress had decreed that the 1st and 2nd Dragoons should become the 1st and 2nd Cavalry, while the Regiment of Mounted Riflemen was renamed the 3rd Cavalry. The former 1st and 2nd Cavalry thus became, respectively, the 4th and 5th Cavalry, while a sixth regiment was authorized and its recruitment began. Another indication of the dynamic nature of the conflict was the temporary attachment of Company G of the 5th Cavalry to a brigade of New Jersey infantry commanded by one of the most famous and flamboyant soldiers in either army, Brigadier General Philip Kearny.[8]

A twenty-four year veteran of dragoon service, Kearny had made a notable record both in Mexico, where he had lost his left arm to canister and amputation following a hell-for-leather charge at Churubusco, and in the American Northwest against hostile Indians. Bored by long stints of inactive service and the glacial pace of the promotion process, he had resigned his major's rank in 1851. Eight years later he accepted a commission in the French army, where outstanding service in the *Chasseurs d'Afrique* brought him the coveted Legion of Honor. Kearny was highly respected by every officer who knew him well including Winfield Scott, on whose staff he had served in Mexico and who considered his former subordinate the "perfect soldier."[9]

Custer was delighted by the opportunity to join the military family of such a renowned soldier. Supposedly it came about when Kearny, who had only recently received his appointment and needed to form a staff on short notice, asked Custer's superior Lieutenant Drummond if he could part with one of the three officers currently assigned to Company G. Drummond, who could not have refused such a request, agreed to let his junior subordinate go, and Kearny thus acquired his first aide-de-camp.

Custer reported finding "the change from a subaltern in a company to a responsible position on the staff of a most active and enterprising officer both agreeable and beneficial." This feeling contrasts with the nonchalant attitude he affected in a letter to Tully McCrea, who quoted Custer as saying that "he would accept [the appointment] for a few days to see how he liked it." The new aide found Kearny to be "a very peculiar, withal a very gallant leader." He never explained the man's peculiarities except to describe him as something of a martinet who blistered errant or underachieving subordinates—usually the upper echelon, not those of Custer's lowly status—with "a torrent of violent invectives, [and] such varied and expressive epithets, that the limit of language seemed for once to have been reached. . . ."[10]

Kearny's temper was most likely to be heard and felt when he was kept out of action for any length of time. He "was never so contented and happy as when moving to the attack," Custer wrote. "And whether it was the attack of a picket post or the storming of the enemy's breastworks, Kearny was always to be found where the danger was greatest." Although he was fated to serve Kearny for only two months, some of the latter's attributes appear to have rubbed off on Custer, whose strong preference for active service and offensive warfare came to mirror that of his superior. Custer also implies, and at least one of his biographers agrees, that Kearny's insistence on strict discipline greatly influenced him. But to claim that one who failed to learn the importance of discipline during four years at West Point came to appreciate its value during two months under Philip Kearny's tutelage strains credulity.[11]

Thanks to Kearny, Custer experienced the excitement of a nighttime raid inside enemy lines. The general, true to his restless nature, gained permission from higher headquarters to attack and seize one of the main picket posts along the so-called Alexandria Line. Three hundred Jerseymen were assigned to the mission under the direction of officers who had yet to see action to any extent. Their leader, Lieutenant Colonel Samuel L. Buck of the 2nd New Jersey, was less than a stalwart soldier. Called to protect the rear of McDowell's army late in the fighting at Bull Run, without orders Buck had hustled his regiment back to Washington well in advance of the rest of the army. Perhaps with this episode in mind, Kearny had assigned Lieutenant Custer to accompany the expedition and serve as the general's eyes and ears while providing a measure of regular army polish to the undertaking.[12]

Despite its serious intent and important objectives, the mission, almost as soon as underway around 9 p.m. on a cloudy night, struck Custer as resembling "upon a large scale some boyhood scheme." Officers and men alike, woefully undereducated in operations of this sort, proceeded toward their target in comic-opera fashion, "no one being allowed to speak above a whisper" to avoid alerting the enemy's pickets—even when five miles from them. When woods were encountered, secrecy became an even greater concern: "We made our way

. . . as cautiously as if masked batteries, then the *bête noire* of the average volunteer, were bristling from behind every bush. The cracking of a twig in the
distance, or the stumbling of one of the leading files over a concealed log, was
sufficient to cause the entire column to halt. . . ."

The fact that the raiding leader had failed to position men in front and on
the flanks of the column appears to have been lost on Custer. By the time the
fearful crew reached the lane leading to the dwelling that housed their quarry,
nerves were strung so tightly that a misstep would almost certainly scuttle the
mission. This occurred minutes later when, in defiance of the advantage of
stealth so carefully preserved, the clouds suddenly cleared, the moon shone
forth, and the Federals were caught in its light. When a picket's voice boomed
out "Who comes there?", three panic-stricken Jersey boys fired wildly into the
night, and chaos reigned. Custer summed up the inevitable result: "All chance
to effect a surprise having been lost . . . we beat a hasty if not precipitate
retreat." So ended Lieutenant Custer's first opportunity to steal a march on the
enemy and engage him at close quarters.[13]

*   *   *

Custer would state that his brief service with Kearny was terminated by a War
Department directive prohibiting regulars from serving on the staffs of volunteer officers. This explanation lacks credibility on two counts. Other general
officers of volunteers including Ambrose E. Burnside, who was outfitting an
expedition to invade coastal North Carolina, were permitted to keep regular officers on their staffs. Then, too, in a letter to Governor Austin Blair of
Michigan early in 1863 Custer claimed that "I could have retained" the position under Kearny but implied that he chose not to. He also maintained that
after leaving the general's staff he was "kept continually on scouting duty, my
regiment . . . [being] ordered to consolidate in Washington where we were
united with two other regular regiments thus forming the *only* brigade of regular cavalry in the service."[14]

This last statement appears to be off the mark, at least as regards timing.
The formation of the regular cavalry brigade of the Army of the Potomac did
not take place until late November when its components were grouped under
Brigadier General Philip St. George Cooke, a distinguished if rather elderly
(fifty-two-year-old), former dragoon officer, the compiler of a treatise on
mounted tactics authorized by the War Department, and the father-in-law of

a more famous cavalryman, Jeb Stuart. Cooke's credentials would not impress Custer, who wrote that the brigadier, even at this early stage of the war, "had passed the period of his usefulness as a cavalry leader, even had he been granted an opportunity to render effective service." Until his coming the regulars had been distributed piecemeal—by companies or two-company squadrons—to the various infantry divisions of the army. In contrast, a majority of those volunteer regiments that had reached the capital in the aftermath of Bull Run had been kept in a semblance of consolidation under McClellan's newly installed cavalry chief, Brigadier General George Stoneman. By the time Cooke assumed command, Custer was gone from the army on a long furlough from which he would not return until the following February.[15]

It would appear that the real reason he left Kearny's service was not War Department forbiddance but sickness. In his letter to Governor Blair he maintained that because his service at Washington provided him and his fellow officers with "superior advantages to perfect [ourselves] in the cavalry drill . . . I was tendered the choice of every position on the staff of Gen Stoneman Chief of Cavalry but owing to ill health at the time I declined."[16]

The nature of Custer's condition has never been determined, but it was serious enough that he was granted an extended stay far from the scenes of his recent service. One can speculate that he fell victim to one of the many lowland illnesses then ravaging the army, or perhaps he had suffered a recurrence of the sexually transmitted disease contracted during his West Point furlough, gonorrhea at that time not being susceptible to cure or effective long-term treatment. All that is known is that on October 3 he left Virginia for the long train trip home. It seems probable that he first visited his family's new farmstead in Wood County, Ohio. In April 1860 Emmanuel Custer had purchased the forty-acre tract, not far from the larger farm David Kirkpatrick had started four and a half years earlier. Then—presumably after receiving some medical attention—the lieutenant headed west to stay with Ann and David Reed in Monroe. Apparently his illness lingered and then worsened, for his leave, which was scheduled to end in early December, was extended another two months and when it ended he had not yet recovered. Tully McCrea, who received a letter from Custer in April, quoted his old roommate, upon returning to the war zone, as "so sick that he was not expected to live." This diagnosis, however, is open to question.[17]

Sickness was not the only problem he contended with during his leave. One night he socialized so avidly with some civilian friends in Monroe that he got roaring drunk, a condition that threatened long-term consequences for both his personal life and professional career. At least one of Custer's biographers claims that this was the only occasion on which he imbibed to the point of serious inebriation. Lawrence A. Frost blames his condition on Custer's unidentified friends: "On their insistence he entered one of the local saloons to have a drink for old time's sake. Being high-strung and unused to alcohol, he overindulged." The result was that as he left the barroom he could hardly walk as he made his way along the sidewalk bordering Monroe's principal street toward the Reed residence.

It is not known how many townspeople witnessed his stumbling passage up Main Street, but residents who played, or would later play, a major role in his life were appalled by the sight. One was eighteen-year-old Libbie Bacon, who lived across the street from the Reeds and who never forgot "that awful day" that formed her first vivid impression of the man she would later marry. Another observer was Daniel Bacon, who never imagined he would entrust his daughter's happiness to such a dissipated wretch.[18]

The most visceral reaction to Custer's condition came from his sister. Ann Reed helped her rubber-legged sibling inside and put him to bed until he sobered up. Then she read him the proverbial riot act, extracting a promise that he would never again be found in such a state. Because Custer adored the woman who had long served as his second mother, he took the pledge, and as far as can be determined he never violated it. His first biographer, Frederick Whittaker, calls that night "the turning point of young Custer's life. . . ." T. J. Stiles provides context for Custer's subsequent sobriety: "His self-awareness was almost always couched in his sense of himself in society; and his standing in Monroe mattered to him. . . . He yearned to be accepted, to be admired, to belong. If alcohol interfered, he would do without it."[19]

He dedicated the rest of his stay in Monroe to rehabilitating his reputation. He kept his distance from the friends who had led him astray, helped Ann with her daily chores, and assisted David with his business dealings. He accompanied the family to its place of worship, the Monroe Methodist Church, during regular services and Sunday school classes. He either did not notice or did not care that Libbie Bacon was not on hand to monitor his reformation. She was spending the holiday season with friends in Toledo.[20]

He may have given up alcohol, but on his way back to Washington he resumed his partying. During an all-night layover at Cleveland, he attended a ball at his hotel, the invitation coming from a West Point acquaintance he ran into. He must have recovered sufficiently from his illness for he danced away the evening and much of the following morning with "several pretty ladies." He burned the midnight oil again a few nights later, after rejoining his regiment in "Camp Cliffburn," just outside the District limits. The encampment adjoined that of the 3rd Cavalry, the outfit of his West Point buddy Deacon Elbert. Lieutenant Elbert had a sweetheart in the city, and he and Custer secured leave to serenade her. They did the job properly, taking the band of Custer's outfit, every musician in the saddle. In a letter to his sister Custer expressed regret that he "was not blessed with such a treasure" as his friend could claim, although the question mark with which he ended the sentence suggests facetiousness.

He submerged whatever disappointment he may have felt by visiting "several of our lady friends, all of whom invited us in." He did not permit twinges of self-consciousness to spoil his evening. He was delaying having his "likeness" taken for Ann because he had shaved off his mustache and was waiting for the beard he was cultivating "to grow a little more."[21]

He was learning that he did not have to drink to have a good time, especially in the right company. He considered Elbert the best friend he ever had, reliable and trustworthy. They kept no secrets from each other: "I could not think more of him if he was my brother." He hoped that Elbert would accompany him the next time he took leave in Monroe, and he planned to visit his buddy's home in Iowa "if *circumstances* are *favorable*." Neither opportunity arose. Eighteen months later Captain Leroy Elbert was dead, not of battle wounds but of an insidious infection contracted during a steamboat voyage. "He had no finery with him," Custer learned, "no one was with him when he died, no one knew him, his body was thrust on shore among strangers and by accident was recognized by some one, and sent to his friends." To die miserably in the midst of a war that offered so many exalted and honorable ways to depart this life was an act of senselessness that Custer, the quintessential romantic, could neither understand nor accept.[22]

*   *   *

Before he tore himself from the Washington social scene, Custer visited the Capitol to observe lawmakers at work and to witness the presentation of Rebel flags captured during recent battles including those in North Carolina fought by Burnside's Coast Division. By early March he was devoting full attention to his company, which was now a component of Brigadier General William

H. Emory's brigade of Cooke's so-called Cavalry Reserve, a division-size force the Francophile McClellan had created in homage to his sometime namesake, the original Napoleon. The Reserves, like the rest of Little Mac's command—which had swollen with the influx of volunteers and the arrival of regular outfits—were about to move against their enemy for the first time since Bull Run. To President Lincoln, Secretary of War Edwin McMasters Stanton, and virtually every member of Congress, it was about time.[23]

McClellan had determined not to return the army to combat until by his standards it was ready to fight—he would not throw half-trained troops under ignorant officers against an army that had humiliated the government last summer. Lincoln had approved the thorough instructional program that his field leader (since November 1861 the general-in-chief of the army, feeble old General Scott having been forced into retirement) put into effect. But he had not counted on it lasting well into the new year. As the winter waned and Little Mac showed no inclination to leave Washington, the president demanded that an advance get underway by February 22. The deadline came and went, but by early March McClellan finally agreed to consult with his subordinates including the commanders of his four army corps, an organization whose formation Lincoln had forced on him.

The plan that emerged from this meeting—though not a consensus decision—called for the army to be transported down the Chesapeake Bay and up the Rappahannock River to Urbanna on the northern shore of Virginia's Middle Peninsula. That nondescript village lay ninety miles behind the line the Confederates continued to hold between Manassas and Centreville. Those troops were now under the command of General Johnston, Beauregard having been transferred to the western theater to oppose a once-obscure brigadier named Ulysses S. Grant, who had recently gained stunning victories on the Tennessee and Cumberland Rivers.[24]

The situation that underlay McClellan's strategy underwent a major overhaul within hours of its acceptance by his lieutenants. On March 7–8 Johnston, who suspected his opponent would eventually summon the nerve to move against him, began shifting troops toward prepared positions below the Rappahannock, some thirty-five miles closer to Richmond. The move, intended to better protect the Confederate capital while preserving the welfare of Johnston's army, caught McClellan off-guard. Not until the ninth did he move toward the vacated sector, his cavalry in advance and the 5th Regulars in advance of everyone else.

The mounted column, including a half-dozen other regular and volunteer regiments, followed the 2nd New York Cavalry, which had reconnoitered the Manassas area immediately after Johnston began pulling out. The enterprising movement had been made at the direction of the regiment's executive officer, Judson Kilpatrick. Custer's West Point comrade had parlayed his newsworthy wounding at Big Bethel, from which he had fully recovered, to field-grade rank in one of the army's premier volunteer regiments, also known as the "Harris Light Cavalry" for its influential patron, Senator Ira Harris.[25]

As the cavalry moved south, Lieutenant Custer was determined to showcase his own talents should an opportunity present itself. On March 11 the slow-moving vanguard, led by General Stoneman, finally ventured south of Manassas to within a few miles of Johnston's rear guard. On the way the horsemen passed the ruins of abandoned camps and burning supply buildings, some of which housed rations and forage that the Confederates lacked the transportation to carry off.

By the fourteenth the wary Stoneman finally consented to speed up the pursuit. He had General Cooke attach the 5th and 6th Regulars to a small brigade consisting of two volunteer cavalry units and an infantry regiment, which was sent down the Orange & Alexandria Railroad to reconnoiter Johnston's latest position near Catlett's Station. When the command drew within sight of a cavalry-heavy force about a mile and a half north of the depot, Stoneman ordered Custer's commanding officer, Captain Charles J. Whiting, to drive the pickets separating the Federals from Johnston's rear guard to and across Cedar Run. Whiting relayed the order to his assembled subordinates including Custer, who by virtue of the absence of two of his superiors was temporarily leading Company G.[26]

Impetuosity remained a hallmark of Custer's character. As soon as Whiting was done speaking, he volunteered to drive the pickets back on their main force. When asked how many men he wanted for the job, he replied that he would take as many as Whiting saw fit to give him. He was told to take his entire company, at least fifty noncoms and privates. As he took his position at the head of the unit, a second company under Lieutenant John Baillie McIntosh, an officer Custer would serve beside many times over the next three years, deployed to cover Company G's rear.[27]

Heart pounding and adrenaline pumping, the junior lieutenant of the 5th U.S. Cavalry led off down the road to the depot. As he remarked in his memoirs, he advanced "without opposition to the base of the hill upon which the pickets were posted, when within convenient distance I gave the command 'Charge' for the first time. My company responded gallantly, and away we went." In a letter to his parents from Fairfax Court House, eleven miles northeast of Manassas, on the seventeenth he recounted that "when I got about half way to the enemy I ordered my men to draw their revolvers I taking my place on the right and to the front of my company in order to be out of the way of their shots. We then took the gallop and charged the rebels but before we reached them they broke and run, we after them as hard as we could go chasing them a mile or two when they came to a deep ravine or creek which they crossed by a bridge [which] they tore up . . . so that we would not follow them."[28]

A standoff followed, the adversaries dismounting and taking position on opposite sides of the water. "They had the advantage of us," Custer noted, "by having some trees to shelter them." Through field-glasses he examined their defenses, which he estimated to be held by three hundred armed Confederates. At first he planned to "descend the bank and ford the creek when the rebels opened fire upon us. The bullets rattled like hail. Several whizzed close to my head." Later some of his men told him that by remaining in the front rank throughout the fight and riding a gray horse, the only such animal on the field, he had been identified as an officer the enemy must cut down. No ball touched him, but "four shots took effect on my company." Considering it senseless to expose his men any longer, he ordered a withdrawal, one conducted "in good order" under a sometimes heavy fire.

He had done well in his first close-up encounter with the foe, and his professionalism and composure received favorable notice throughout the ranks. The praise was a tonic to him. He enjoyed telling his parents how Stoneman had interviewed him after the fight: "He seemed well pleased with the manner in [which] I performed my duty." He was probably chagrinned when the general failed to mention him in his report of the engagement, but he did not lack for publicity from other sources. Four newspaper correspondents had accompanied Stoneman on the march; once the shooting slackened, they clustered about the lieutenant and interviewed him on the spot, taking down his impressions of his first time under such a concentrated fire. He expected his story to appear within days in the *New York Tribune*, *World*, and *Times* as well as the *Philadelphia Inquirer*, and he was not disappointed. As he informed Ann Reed, accounts of his exploit graced the pages of all four papers as well as at least one in Washington. In every one "I am mentioned in a highly flattering manner."

To his surprise, a Southern newspaper, a copy of which his men later procured, also reported the skirmish though it inflated his force to five hundred men. The paper confirmed that he had faced three hundred of Jeb Stuart's troopers, but it claimed they had killed forty Yankees and taken one hundred prisoners, a gross fabrication, while their figure it gave for Stuart's losses—six killed and almost two hundred wounded—"is not true either." The experience must have shown him how easily facts could be twisted to meet an editor's needs and further the cause for which his readers were fighting.

Such attention was a heady experience for a lowly subaltern, one clothed in a uniform rumpled, wet, and muddy following a thirty-mile march in nasty weather. He told his parents that "I have not had my clothes off for over one week. We are now on our way back to Alexandria where we will arrive tomorrow," there to rest, dry his garments, and get something to eat. He reported weighing 176 pounds, certainly not starvation girth but less than he was used to carrying: "I have undergone some awful hardships during the last week. . . . Some days I got nothing to eat had to lie down with my clothes wet on the ground without even a single blanket and the rain pouring down but I slept comfortably notwithstanding."

His durability and willingness to take on any assignment no matter how demanding were coming to the attention of his superiors. After the fight at Cedar Run both General Stoneman and Lieutenant Colonel William Nicholson Grier of the 1st Cavalry—the latter a Pennsylvania-born cousin of Custer's—slept by his campfire. Around three the next morning Stoneman shook Custer awake "to send me out on a scouting party. I had only been asleep about an hour and he knew it. He asked me how I felt. I told him I was as fresh as if I had slept a week." Colonel Grier, who was also awake, told Stoneman that Custer "is a true *Grier. He can eat and sleep* as much as any one when he has a chance but *when necessary he can do without either.*"

He closed his letter by assuring his family that Emmanuel's recently expressed frustration at the army's slowness to move against the Rebels—an implied rebuke of General McClellan—was misplaced. He enclosed a copy of a recent order by McClellan suggesting that a major campaign was imminent and insisted that "he is in earnest. I have more confidence in him than any man living. I am willing to forsake everything and follow him to the ends of the earth and would lay down my life for him if necessary." He was not alone in pledging unreserved fealty to the commanding general: "Every one officer[s]

& privates worship him. I would fight any one who would say anything against him."[29]

*   *   *

Custer stayed up late to finish his home letter. "It is nearly eleven oclock," he wrote. "Every one is in bed except the Lieutenants. We start soon after daylight to Monroe." He was referring not to his sister's city but to Fortress Monroe at Old Point Comfort on the tip of the Virginia Peninsula, one of two United States Army installations in enemy territory still in Union hands. This was the staging area for the Army of the Potomac's long-deferred movement against the Confederate capital, the result of weeks of prodding by McClellan's civilian superiors.[30]

The logistical details had been worked out at a meeting attended by Little Mac and his ranking subordinates at Fairfax Court House on the thirteenth. Thanks to Johnston's fallback to the Rappahannock, the original plan, to begin operating near the mouth of that river, was a dead letter. Instead, the army would be transported directly to the Peninsula preparatory to a northward march on Richmond. Lincoln, who was desperate to see an offensive underway, had agreed to the revamped strategy as long as McClellan could guarantee the security of Washington. That point, however, would become a source of lingering contention between the president and his field leader, one that would sour their relationship and threaten the success of the unfolding campaign.[31]

The transfer to the Peninsula of resources began less than twenty-four hours after Custer wrote his letter describing the bullets flying thick and fast, although not till March 28 was he at sea. Before shoving off, he wrote his parents from the wharves of Alexandria where "the greatest expedition ever fitted out is now going south under the command of the greatest and best of men Gen McClellan."

He suspected that a battle would be fought at Norfolk, across Hampton Roads from Fort Monroe, but "we are certain of victory for with McClellan to lead us we know no such word as fail." He had witnessed the general on the dock as he surveyed the grand expedition and the armada assembled to convey it south. Even as he wrote, Little Mac was assuring Custer's regimental commander that "all the regulars, us included, were to go with him always, he knows who to rely upon."

The ocean voyage—the first Custer had taken since West Point—may have had an uncertain destination but it was sure to produce a heavy dose of combat. The realization excited as much as sobered him, but he felt compelled to inform his family that if "along with thousands of others I must become a sacrifice on the altar in the service for [the Union's] preservation I hope you will be reconciled by the thought that our cause is a just one and that if I die in its defense I do so willingly with the proud consciousness that I am but doing my duty. . . ." Heroic sentiments indeed, reflecting a radical change from his once-strongly held belief that if war came the righteous stance belonged to those oppressed by the government in Washington.[32]

The ship carrying Custer and his regiment reached Old Point Comfort on or about March 29. They debarked and camped outside the fortress, awaiting marching orders that were not received until McClellan arrived on April 2 amid disorganization and confusion. He found, for one thing, that many of the troops who had preceded him were still aboard ship. The only cavalry units to have disembarked in their entirety were the 5th Regulars and a regiment of Pennsylvania volunteers commanded by now-Colonel William W. Averell.

Numerous elements of McClellan's vast command still rode the waves, but already it was short at least ten thousand troops promised to it but with-held by Lincoln for fear that Washington was threatened by Confederates rampaging through the Shenandoah Valley under the Bull Run hero "Stonewall" Jackson. The move, which came on the eve of the army's sailing, concerned and angered the army leader, as had Lincoln's earlier decision to cancel the transfer of an eighteen-thousand-man corps from the Shenandoah to the Peninsula. McClellan was positively livid when, two days after he left Alexandria aboard the steamer *Commodore*, Lincoln decided to retain within supporting range of the capital the First Army Corps of Irvin McDowell. This action stripped another thirty thousand men from the number originally assigned to the Army of the Potomac. In later years the ever-loyal Custer would fully endorse his leader's apprehensions: "What general commanding an army at any later period of the war, confronting the enemy and about to engage in battle upon matured plans, would have been willing to risk a general engagement with his army reduced unexpectedly more than one-third on the very eve of battle?"[33]

McClellan was convinced that Washington was secure from attack whether by Jackson or anyone else and that he needed every available man, horse, gun, and wagon. He believed exaggerated reports that portrayed Johnston's strength as greater than his own—more than twice the actual number. The general also feared that the enemy he would encounter on the Peninsula, holding the line between Big Bethel and Yorktown, numbered far more than the fourteen thousand available to Brigadier General John Bankhead Magruder. When, as he anticipated, Richmond ordered Johnston to augment Magruder, McClellan envisioned having to contend against two full-size armies.[34]

With more than one hundred thousand officers and men at his disposal, Little Mac could afford the loss of additional troops, but he could not shake the suspicion that he was the victim of government meddling and intrusion. He believed that other commanders, in other theaters, were benefiting from a level of support being withheld from him, making him look inferior by comparison. To bolster this perception he need only point to Ulysses S. Grant, who early in April had won—albeit narrowly—a critical, two-day battle in West Tennessee near Shiloh Meeting House, driving a Confederate army from the state and forging a strategy to divide the western Confederacy along the line of the Mississippi River. Grant was a lightweight but was basking in the favor of Abraham Lincoln while the Young Napoleon was being denied the basic requirements of military success. The commander of the greatest army in American history was being treated shabbily, and he would not hesitate to complain of it to his treacherous superiors.

* * *

Undermanned or not, the Army of the Potomac shook itself into marching formation and beginning on May 4 started up the Peninsula toward Magruder's defenses on the north side of the Warwick River. The advancing columns amounted to approximately sixty thousand men, more than McClellan would face even after Johnston linked with Magruder, but he refused to believe it. Two divisions of Brigadier General Erasmus D. Keyes's Fourth Corps took the road to Warwick Court House while, three miles to the south, two Third Corps divisions under the grizzled General Heintzelman trudged up the road to Yorktown (the roads diverged as the army headed north, placing another two miles between the columns). Custer's outfit, temporarily assigned to Keyes's command, led the way on the left via Young's Mill, while Averell's 3rd Pennsylvania moved in advance of Heintzelman's main body. Thanks to McClellan's thorough training program, the army's horsemen had returned to their principal mission of guiding an army on the march, an especially critical function when that army was negotiating unknown territory.[35]

The forward movement did not get far. By midday of the fifth both columns had bogged down on muddy roads, the result of a morning downpour, well in advance of Magruder's works. Elements of Custer's outfit happened upon a chain of earthworks, apparently well stocked with Confederates, near Lee's Mill where the road to Warwick Court House crossed the Warwick River. Enemy riflemen and cannoneers opened fire on the vanguard of Brigadier General William Farrar ("Baldy") Smith's division, and the entire command shuddered to a halt.

The mud made maneuvering difficult, and the waterway behind which Magruder's people were ensconced was a daunting obstacle. Custer would observe that although the Warwick in its original state was an inconsiderable stream, it had been enlarged and deepened by a series of dams "until it had become an almost impassable barrier to the advance of troops, unless the fire from the protecting batteries and rifle-pits could be silenced." When McClellan heard of Keyes's sudden immobility and the concurrently received news that Heintzelman had been halted by the other end of Magruder's works, "he began to perceive," as Custer wrote, "that what he had supposed would be an undertaking of perhaps a day was likely to detain him indefinitely. . . ."[36]

The march up the Peninsula, which had begun on such a confident note, remained at a dead halt, or something close to it, for a full month. When his chief engineer officer made a cursory examination of Magruder's works and declared they could not be assaulted with any certainty of success, McClellan sent back to Washington for siege artillery. When they arrived he painstakingly placed cannons and mortars at strategic points along his lines; he kept up the work until he was certain he could level not only Magruder's defenses but all of Yorktown as well. Strategically it was a classic blunder because it gave Johnston the time he needed to bring his army, some 47,000 strong, to his subordinate's aid. Moreover, the delay could have been avoided had McClellan's scouts perceived the thinness of the gray lines facing him. Every day the enemy remained in his front Magruder, who had a penchant for amateur theatrics, would march the various components of his meager force back and forth to create the impression of a never-ending line of troops. McClellan never caught on to the deception.[37]

The army may have been stopped short of its objectives, but operations did not cease. Custer informed his sister that "there is scarcely an interval of ten minutes during the day that our men and the rebels do not fire at each other, & both parties keep hidden as well as possible but as soon as either party shows themselves they are fired at."

Refusing to remain inactive, he made himself available for scouting missions and larger-scale reconnaissances no matter the degree of danger. On April 9 he was sent at the head of a "large party" of his regiment to locate some hidden batteries so that they might be neutralized. Riding as close to the enemy position as consistent with concealment, he and his men dismounted, tethered their mounts to trees, then crawled on their hands and knees through underbrush to a point where Custer halted them.

From here he and a fellow officer pushed forward by themselves, "our spyglasses" in hand. They managed to penetrate to within five hundred yards of the nearest battery where they took notes, but as they turned back to their men an artillery shell passed just above their heads: "We saw the discharge and fell flat on our faces in order to avoid it. The shell passed over us and exploded over our party beyond. One of the fragments struck one of our men tearing off his arm. We allowed no grass to grow under our feet after that." Scrambling back to the woods, they gathered up their men and with the wounded trooper in tow galloped back to report to General Smith, to whose command the companies of the 5th Cavalry had been attached. It may be supposed that the division commander was well pleased with the intelligence relayed to him.[38]

The successful mission added to Custer's reputation for enterprise, daring, and courage. These qualities recommended him to commanders who wished to make their positions on the siege lines as formidable as possible. Soon after his command was forced to go to earth, General Smith named Custer assistant to the division's chief engineer, First Lieutenant Nicolas Bowen. Custer formed a close alliance with the highly capable young New Yorker, who had graduated near the top of the West Point Class of 1860 and who in recognition of several instances of gallantry under fire would finish the war as a brevet colonel in both the regular and volunteer services. He would describe his time with Bowen, during which he directed "working parties engaged in making fascines and gabions, and in laying out and erecting field works" as "a most invaluable experience."[39]

Keeping gainfully employed in the midst of stationary operations elevated Custer's mood and solidified his faith in eventual success (as he insisted to Ann Reed, with McClellan on the field, "we are certain of victory"). As busy as he was, he still took time for socializing, as when he visited the camp of the 7th Michigan Infantry, a regiment organized in and around Monroe and whose ranks contained several friends and close acquaintances. The visit left him in high spirits, in contrast to many of his already war-weary comrades: "I know that I am happier than those around me, not because I have more cause to be but simply because my disposition enables me to look on the bright side of everything. I allow no little mishap to discourage or dishearten me and when anything occurs contrary to my wishes I act upon the old saying, 'Never cry for spilled milk'."[40]

That philosophy, however, would soon be put to the test as would his faith in the man whom he counted on to win the war, with or without the support of the warlords of Washington.

Chapter V

Serving the Young Napoleon

Armstrong Custer has sometimes been portrayed as complex because of seemingly contradictory impulses including a cold-blooded attitude toward killing and, as Frederic F. Van de Water puts it, the ability to be "the most sentimental of men." Further, there is his marked courage in battle and seeming indifference to danger contrasted with common phobias such as his fear of heights. Those who read these contradictions as anything more than normal human behavior miss the mark. Most people exhibit contradictions in what they think, say, and do; that does not make them abnormally complicated. The Custer who rose to prominence and high rank during the Civil War was essentially a simple person because the goals he strove to attain, both personally and professionally, were simple. The credo he lived by at West Point remained untouched by the fury of war. He wanted to achieve, to advance, to succeed, but he intended to do so while experiencing as much adventure and pleasure as possible.[1]

As for his fear of heights, the importance of contact with the ground was ingrained in him. As he put it in his memoirs, "although I had chosen the mounted service from preference alone, yet I had a choice as to the character of the mount," and the elevation he achieved in the saddle did not shake his sense of physical security. Thus he was taken aback to learn that his duties as assistant engineer to General Smith before Yorktown included periodic ascents in a tethered balloon under the supervision of Thaddeus Sobieski Constantine Lowe and his assistants.

A self-taught authority on upper air currents, "Professor" Lowe had been conducting flights in balloons of his own construction since 1858; his well-publicized activities had gained him recognition both within and outside the scientific community. In August 1861 one of his many admirers, Abraham Lincoln, had named him chief of army aeronautics with the rank and pay of a colonel. Since that time Lowe had been supplying Union officers with both visual and photographic intelligence, on occasion even directing artillery fire from aloft. He had accompanied General McClellan to the Peninsula along with a portable hydrogen gas generator he had devised to support a fleet of balloons of various capacities, eventually numbering seven.[2]

Lincoln's patronage notwithstanding, the army as a whole appeared doubtful of the value of aerial observation, suspecting that Lowe and his assistants habitually exaggerated their reports of enemy defenses and troop concentrations. General Smith was one of the skeptics. To provide some measure of verification he ordered his newest aide to go aloft from Lowe's base of operations in the Warwick Court House vicinity. Custer was told to carry a field-glass, a compass, and a notebook in which to record his own observations, to be compared with those of the aeronaut.

Custer approached his maiden flight, which he made in company with one of Lowe's assistants, with "no little trepidation." He could not hide his jangling nerves; during a later ascent, the first he made with Lowe himself, the latter found him "white and shivering like an aspen leaf." Lowe observed that "I saw at a glance that he had courage, but that his courage was impulsiveness."[3]

Custer's fears began to diminish when the balloon reached the end of its anchor line, giving him "the finest view I ever had in my life," one encompassing Yorktown, the York and James Rivers, even the distant Chesapeake Bay. It revealed the location of enemy camps and defensive works that could be monitored for changes of position. But although Custer went up often enough to assure himself that it was safe to do so, he never completely acclimated to dangling a thousand feet off the ground from a round bag filled with gas.[4]

During his service with Smith, Custer showed his sentimental side on at least one notable occasion. He was probably aloft on April 16 when McClellan made his first aggressive move since pulling up in front of Yorktown. To force the Rebels to cease strengthening their defenses along the Warwick River near Dam Number 1—work that Custer undoubtedly spotted during one of his ascents—the army leader ordered Baldy Smith to dose the laborers with rifle- and cannon-fire. This tactic appeared to have the desired effect, the work parties being driven to the rear under a heavy fusillade, but then a portion of one of Smith's regiments waded the river on its own initiative in hopes of capturing the vacated position. It was a major mistake; counterattacking Confederates savaged the 4th Vermont Infantry, inflicting more than eighty casualties before repulsing a wave of reinforcements at comparable cost.

"A Dam failure," a witty Federal wrote in his diary. Back in Washington General Smith, who received most of the blame, had to weather baseless charges that he had been drunk during the fighting. The unhappy affair soured the spirits of many soldiers and gave General McClellan grounds for proceeding more cautiously than ever in dealing with the defenders of Yorktown. He riveted his attention to building up his siege works, placing in carefully shielded but strategically situated positions the dozens of cannons and mortars being shipped to him from the arsenals of Washington.[5]

The day after the botched attack Custer left Warwick Court House to visit the nearby camp of the 7th Michigan. The journey led him to the site of the recent carnage, where burial teams were still at work. He found himself drawn to one of the fallen, struck by the man's youthful appearance and handsome face, "which even death had not removed." Questioning some bystanders, members of the man's regiment, he found they "spoke highly of him and informed me that he had married a beautiful girl but a few days previous to his leaving home for the war. I at once thought of the severe shock that awaited her when the news of his death should reach her. I thought she would be glad to get any little trinket he might have as a memento." Taking out his knife, he stooped down to cut open the man's pocket, in which he found a knife and a ring, then sheared off a lock of hair. He handed the items to a comrade from the man's hometown "who promised to send them to her. I then turned away, mounted my horse and continued on my road to the camp of the 7th Mich."[6]

* * *

McClellan relished the thought of unleashing the fury of his artillery on the Yorktown defenses. Under the supervision of engineer officers, work crews had erected and fortified fifteen siege batteries south and west of the river village. These mounted a total of seventy heavy guns including two gigantic two hundred-pounder Parrott rifles and a dozen hundred-pounders as well as forty-one iron-plated mortars, some of which fired shells that weighed more than two hundred pounds. As Stephen W. Sears, historian of the Peninsula Campaign, has written, when they opened simultaneously, "as McClellan intended, these siege guns would rain 7,000 pounds of metal on Yorktown's defenders at each blow. Such firepower dwarfed even that of the Sevastopol siege" during the Crimean War.[7]

In a sense, all of McClellan's preparation went for naught. He had planned to unleash his heavy weapons at dawn on May 5, but he never got the chance. On the evening of the third Custer, at General Smith's order, went up in Lowe's balloon and did so again before reveille on the fourth. Through his glass he could see heavy fires burning in the direction of Yorktown, "resembling the burning of ordinary dwelling houses," but at first he attached no significance to the admittedly unusual observation. Then, as daylight approached, he noted the absence of campfires along Johnston's lines: "A second and more careful examination convinced me that the works of the enemy were deserted."

Descending rapidly, he galloped to division headquarters. There he learned that General Smith, via interviews with a couple of contrabands out of Yorktown, had been informed that "the enemy had evacuated his entire line, and was retreating toward Williamsburg." This report, corroborated by Custer's sightings, was immediately telegraphed to McClellan's headquarters. A message came back ordering the three brigades of Smith's command to advance and occupy the vacated defenses. Custer writes that "as soon as it was definitely determined that the Confederates had withdrawn their forces," the army was sent "to harass the movements of the enemy, and if possible, bring him to bay until the army could overtake and attack him." In fact there was nothing "soon" about the pursuit; hours passed before McClellan, at the continual urging of Stoneman and other subordinates, gave the order to chase down the evacuees.[8]

As expected, the cavalry moved first, with bodies of infantry close behind. Stoneman led out with portions of four regiments including those companies of the 1st and 6th Cavalry attached to his command, the former under Custer's cousin, "Old Billy" Grier. Four batteries of "flying artillery"—each of whose men rode a horse in contrast to the units that accompanied the infantry, whose gunners when in motion rode on the ammunition chests atop their caissons— accompanied the troopers.

By hard riding the horsemen caught up with Jeb Stuart's cavaliers, protecting the rear of the retreat column, about eight miles from Williamsburg. An hour-long fight broke out, the antagonists alternately gaining and losing the advantage. The slugging contest ended when Confederate infantry retraced their steps to man a line of defenses south of the old town including a formidable earthwork named for its architect, General Magruder. When Stoneman learned that the nearest infantry, the division of Brigadier General Joseph Hooker, was moving too slowly to provide the support he needed, he called off the fight and withdrew to defensive positions.[9]

The next day, with enough foot soldiers on hand for a general engagement, a vicious battle swirled around Virginia's colonial capital in a steady rain. Detained at Yorktown, Custer missed the initial fighting but on the fifth—eager as ever to see action and publicize his penchant for undertaking dangerous assignments—he offered his services to one of Smith's brigade commanders, Winfield Scott Hancock. The brigadier, one of the most combative officers the Army of the Potomac would ever know, temporarily added the lieutenant to his staff, thereby giving him "a personal association with the battle of Williamsburg . . . which otherwise would not have been probable."[10]

If he intended to be involved in the thick of the fighting, Custer chose wisely, for late in the day—following an attack by Hooker on Fort Magruder that failed for lack of prompt support—Hancock gained a critical foothold on the Rebel left flank along Cub Creek, held by the forces of Major General James Longstreet. He was permitted to do so through the enterprise of Custer. General Smith had learned from a local guide that a road that crossed the creek at a dam led to a redoubt the Confederates had failed to occupy. Offering to confirm the report, Custer made a personal reconnaissance and located a point at which the stream could be crossed out of sight of the enemy.

At Hancock's assent, Custer escorted the brigade's leading regiment, the 5th Wisconsin, through a concealing woods, across the dam, and into position to envelop the open flank. Following closely behind, Hancock led the rest of the brigade to within a mile of Fort Magruder, where he occupied the redoubt and established a line of battle bolstered by eight cannons. When a brigade of Virginia and North Carolina infantry finally noticed them and tried to gouge them out, Hancock's men counterattacked with a wild fury. "Our troops," Custer would write, "stood firm until the rebels were within twenty paces of them when the General told them to . . . charge [with the] bayonet. They did so and put the enemy to a complete rout killing and capturing a large number of rebels." The enemy's casualties exceeded five hundred, one of their regiments losing almost 70 percent of its strength before turning and racing to safety.

His success notwithstanding, Hancock was ordered by Major General Edwin V. Sumner, the on-scene commander in McClellan's absence, to hold his position and, eventually, to abandon it. Of his sharp-tongued superior Custer would write: "Those who have seen Hancock when affairs with which he was connected were not conducted in conformity with his views can imagine the manner in which he received the order to retire."[11]

In his report of the battle Hancock commended his provisional staff officer for his resourcefulness but omitted other heroics that Custer alluded to in a letter to Ann Reed. He had been "in the thickest of the fight from morning till dark" and had some trophies to show for it: "I captured a Captain and five men without any assistance. I also captured the battle flag of the rebels a large white silk flag with a red cross in the center. It was afterwards sent by Gen McClellan to the President at Washington."[12]

Some accounts have Custer personally escorting a captured flag or flags to the War Department in Washington, but this is incorrect. Some historians also claim that the flag Custer secured had been captured from the 5th North Carolina State Troops of Brigadier General Jubal A. Early's brigade, but more recent research identifies it as a company-level standard of the 24th Virginia Infantry. This flag was not turned in; Custer was permitted to keep it.[13]

The lieutenant performed his dashing deeds without sporting a dashing appearance. According to Frederick Whittaker, throughout the battle "he wore an old slouch hat and a cavalry jacket, with no marks of rank, the jacket flying open, while his muddy boots did not look worth more than a dollar. His hair was beginning to grow long, and aided his careless dress to give him a slouchy appearance. . . . It was not for more than a year after, that he came out as a dandy." As Custer informed Tully McCrea, the unruly mane was the result of a solemn vow to let it grow until he entered Richmond in company with General McClellan. That day would be long in coming. The next time McCrea saw his former roommate his hair was "about a foot long and [it] hangs over his shoulders in curls just like a girl."[14]

After Hancock fell back, the battle raged on in the rain for some hours, but the keys to victory had been lost in the mud. McClellan, who reached the field too late to influence the outcome, would pronounce it a "brilliant victory" since an enemy he considered superior in numbers had broken off the fight. In a letter to his sister Lieutenant Custer echoed his commander's assessment although given his admitted distress over Hancock's recall at the most critical point in the fight it may be assumed that he regretted the lost opportunity to halt Johnston's retreat before fairly underway.

In the aftermath of battle Custer was thrown into contact with a Military Academy classmate in gray. When Johnston's army departed it left behind hundreds of dead and wounded, to be tended to by its enemy. First Lieutenant Alex Pennington, a graduate of the Class of 1860, was passing by a barn that had been converted to a hospital for care of the wounded of both armies. Suddenly a voice called out: "Hello, is that you Pennington?" The latter recalled: "It was Gimlet [Lea]; he was lying in a stall wounded in the leg. I asked him if I could do anything for him. He said no, a Mrs. Durfee [Durfey] in the town had offered to take care of him, and he was to be taken to her house that afternoon." Pennington, who had been detached from his regiment, the 2nd U.S. Artillery, and detailed to engineering duty, remained with the Mississippian for as long as possible; after he left him he located Custer and told him of Lea's whereabouts.[15]

Custer looked him up at his first opportunity. "When we first saw each other," he told his sister, "he shed tears and threw his arms around my neck." Captain John Lea had never expected such kind treatment from his enemy, even one he had known intimately in the old days. He insisted in writing a note that Custer should carry in the event he too was captured, attesting to the consideration shown him: "He wanted me to be treated as well as he had been. I left him at the hospital. His last words were 'God bless you old Boy'."[16]

Three months later the friends would meet again under far more pleasant circumstances.

*   *   *

McClellan made a single effort to halt the Rebels before they reached safe haven but it failed at Eltham's Landing on the York River two days after the fight at Williamsburg. By mid-May Johnston's troops were enfolded in their capital's protective embrace, and McClellan's once-mobile campaign, which had lost all momentum at Yorktown, came to a dead halt outside Richmond. On Tuesday, the twentieth, the vanguard of the Army of the Potomac, part of Smith's division, reached the Chickahominy River at Bottom's Bridge, about twelve miles east of Richmond and nine miles or so from the outer line of the Richmond defenses. The bridge had been burned by the retreating Rebels, as had a railroad span a short distance upstream.

Smith's troops forded the stream without difficulty, as did General McClellan when he arrived next day. Adopting the river as a temporary line of operations, Little Mac oversaw its crossing by other elements of the Fourth Corps, some of which advanced another six miles toward Richmond to anchor the army's left flank at a crossroads called Seven Pines. Three days later other forces extended the Union position as far as Mechanicsville, on the upper bank five miles northeast of the capital.[17]

The Chickahominy, which would play a major role in the fighting to come, was something of a mystery to the newcomers. To solve it McClellan dispatched his chief engineer, Brigadier General John G. Barnard, to reconnoiter its extent, measure its depths, and determine its military applications. When Barnard went down to the river near Bottom's Bridge he found it to be "one of the most formidable obstacles that could be opposed to the advance of an army" although consisting of "a stream of no great volume, a swamp, and bottom land."

Two days later, accompanied by Lieutenant Custer, the venerable engineer extended his reconnaissance upstream to a point about four miles south of Mechanicsville. Near New Bridge Barnard prepared to make soundings, but he assigned the dirty (and wet) work to his companion. At his order Custer dismounted and plunged into the stream that, fortunately, was only about four feet deep. Barnard reported that "he waded across without any difficulty."[18]

Various sources attempt to describe Custer's crossing. His West Point classmate James H. Wilson claimed in his published memoirs that Custer jumped into the river without being ordered to do so, yelling "I'll damn soon show how deep it is!" Barnard was pleased with Custer's initiative, praised his performance, and made a note to use his services, if available, again.[19]

On May 24 Custer's penchant for dash and daring came to the attention of the soldier he admired above all others. That day Brigadier General Andrew A. Humphreys, McClellan's chief of topographical engineers, directed Lieutenant Bowen, whom Custer continued to assist with his mapmaking duties, to reconnoiter the Chickahominy from New Bridge to a point two miles upstream. Because the mission was likely to alert a large force of Rebels on the opposite bank, Bowen was to be escorted by four companies of the 4th Michigan Infantry of Heintzelman's Third Corps and a squadron of the 2nd U.S. Cavalry. He would also be accompanied by several attachés to Humphreys's staff as well as three regular officers including Custer who, it may be imagined, had volunteered for the mission. Custer immediately attached himself to the infantrymen, several of whom hailed from Monroe and knew him well.

Reaching a point about two hundred yards from the river, the vanguard of Bowen's force approached a passable ford that Custer had helped locate the previous day. At a given signal thirty Federal skirmishers dashed out of a woods that had obscured them from enemy view and moved as stealthily as possible toward New Bridge. "About 300 yards from the crossing," Bowen reported, "we found the enemy and charged them." The skirmishers quickly put the nearest Rebels on the run; the cavalry detachment tried to cut them off but failed to find a fordable point. The remainder of Bowen's escort then crossed the river "under a severe fire, the water in places being up to their armpits," cartridge boxes held above the men's heads to keep the powder dry.

The Michiganders drove the Rebels beyond rifle-range to a point where they were reinforced and gained artillery support. A heavy shelling brought the Federal pursuit to a sudden halt, after which elements of two Louisiana regiments of Brigadier General Paul J. Semmes's brigade advanced menacingly. Somehow Bowen's escort held them at bay for upwards of four hours before ammunition ran low. At that point Bowen, believing he had all the information he needed, called for a withdrawal, which he claimed was made "in most excellent order" under a storm of musketry and artillery.

The Federals carried off twenty-two prisoners, all of them "Tigers," as the Louisiana troops were habitually known. According to the captives, the Yankees had killed or wounded at least a hundred including several officers. In his report of the mission Bowen named several participants deserving of special consideration including Custer, "who was the first to cross the stream, the first to open fire upon the enemy, and one of the last to leave the field." By Whittaker's account, the lieutenant further distinguished himself by capturing another enemy flag—supposedly the first ever taken by his army—but evidence is lacking.[20]

What was not lacking was official recognition of Custer's performance. When the results of the operation became known to him, General McClellan was highly impressed. Eager to present evidence that his efforts to best the defenders of Richmond were bearing fruit, he quickly cabled news of the affair to President Lincoln, boasting that the "Fourth Michigan about finished Louisiana Tigers; 50 prisoners, 50 killed. Our loss 10 killed and wounded." In a later dispatch to Secretary Stanton, Little Mac claimed that the infantry had covered "a very gallant reconnaissance made by Lieutenants Bowen and Custer, came upon the Louisiana Tigers, and handled them terribly. . . ."[21]

Even before he read Bowen's report, McClellan had heard of Custer's heroics, perhaps from General Humphreys. He sent word that he wanted to see the lieutenant. Apparently in company with Barnard, a nonplussed Custer rode to army headquarters near Gaines's Mill, two miles northeast of New Bridge. He relished the chance to be presented to his personal hero but was embarrassed to meet him in his present condition—as Whittaker describes him: "Dirty and muddy, with unkempt hair, coat not brushed, but all creased from being slept in."[22]

McClellan noted that the young officer was "carelessly dressed," his appearance not enhanced by the sudden onset of rain, but it did not deter him from congratulating Custer on his latest act of gallantry and asking what could be done for him. As McClellan recalled, "he replied very modestly that he had nothing to ask, and evidently did not suppose that he had done anything to deserve extraordinary reward." One was offered him anyway—a position on the general's personal staff.

The invitation floored Custer, but as he had in response to the extraordinary courtesies shown him by General Scott, he stammered out his acceptance of the offer, adding that, as McClellan recalled, "he would regard such service as the most gratifying he could perform." His appointment as assistant aide-de-camp with the rank of captain in the volunteer service was dated May 28. His soiled and ragged days were over; as a representative of his immaculately groomed and handsomely tailored superior Custer would have to look properly attired for the duration of Little Mac's tenure, which his newest aide must have imagined would continue until the last of Joe Johnston's troops had been subdued. In a brief time McClellan would become "much attached" to the aide he called "The Youngster." As he later wrote, "Custer was simply a reckless, gallant boy, undeterred by fatigue, unconscious of fear; but his head was always clear in danger and he always brought me clear and intelligible reports of what he saw under the heaviest fire."[23]

Custer could hardly suppress his delight over his great good fortune. Colonel Edward H. Wright, a senior member of McClellan's staff, recalled sitting alone in his tent during a heavy storm "when a young officer, an entire stranger to me, entered, saying, 'I have just been made an Aid[e] on Genl McClellan's staff with the rank of captain'." Wright shook hands with the newcomer, who had been sent to his abode for temporary shelter, and asked what he had done to merit the appointment. "He replied, 'I will show you,' and stepping to the door of the tent pointed to a group of Confederate prisoners (Louisiana Tigers) standing in the drenching rain, just captured by him and Captain [*sic*] Bowen during a brilliant reconnaissance on the south side of the Chickahominy. . . . From that day we were friends."[24]

* * *

The duties of the position Custer now assumed were many, demanding, and frequently onerous. Military texts of the time defined aides-de-camp as a general's confidential assistants, "employed in representing him, in writing orders, in carrying them in person if necessary, [and] in communicating them verbally upon battle-fields." To carry out these tasks aides "should know well the positions of troops, routes, posts, quarters of generals, composition of columns, and orders of corps; facility in the use of the pen should be joined with *exactness of expression*; upon fields of battle they watch the movements of the enemy; not only grand manoeuvres [*sic*] but special tactics should be familiar to them."[25]

Custer handled these and other duties as assigned throughout the balance of the Peninsula Campaign, although his whereabouts and the exact nature of his service during most of this period have not been recorded. By the end of May McClellan's troops continued to straddle the Chickahominy, all but one of his five corps stationed on the north bank, while General Keyes's Fourth Corps held an exposed position on the south side near Seven Pines and Fair Oaks Station on the Richmond & York River Railroad. The army's divided deployment was an implied criticism of the army commander's logistical skill, supposedly one of his great strengths. It may not have mattered, however, for a brief cessation of activity by Stonewall Jackson in the Shenandoah permitted Lincoln to order the release of McDowell's corps to McClellan. The beefed-up command, 41,000 strong, would join the Army of the Potomac by an overland march from Fredericksburg.

With 140,000 men at his disposal, even the hesitant McClellan was confident of taking Richmond; preparations to that end were almost complete by the last days of the month. But Lincoln would change his mind as a result of Jackson's renewed movements and indecipherable intentions; in the end McClellan received only two divisions from McDowell's corps including the Pennsylvania Reserves of Brigadier General George A. McCall. This was not enough of a reinforcement to soothe Little Mac's mind, uneasy once again.[26]

The army's awkward positioning proved an inviting target for McClellan's opponent, who could not allow his much stronger adversary to attack or besiege Richmond. On May 31 the normally cautious Johnston attacked Keyes's position south of the river with the divisions of James Longstreet and Major General Daniel Harvey Hill; two other divisions advanced farther north in support of the main effort. The promising offensive fell apart almost immediately due to miscommunication, botched assignments, and overcrowding on the roads out of Richmond, but it rocked McClellan's peace of mind and forced him to rush reinforcements to the threatened sector via a rickety bridge over the rain-swollen Chickahominy. By 6 p.m. the wayward assault had run its course, the Confederates having been driven back at critical points.

The fighting, while fierce, had not been decisive. A second day was needed to close out the combat and send the Rebels back to their defenses minus more than six thousand casualties, about a thousand more than their opponents absorbed. Among the wounded and disabled was Johnston, felled late on the thirty-first by a shell fragment in the chest. He was replaced late the next day by General Robert Edward Lee of Virginia, who had served for the previous two and a half months as principal military advisor to Confederate President Jefferson Davis.[27]

Another casualty of the Confederacy's first attack in eastern Virginia was an officer on Johnston's staff, Lieutenant James Barroll Washington, who had been captured on the thirty-first. The young man hailed from an old and distinguished family. Custer had known him at West Point and now he helped him in the same way he had Gimlet Lea. Their association has been graven into history thanks to a photograph of the two posed side-by-side on an ammunition or commissary box with a contraband boy seated on the ground between them.[28]

Despite being stunned into immobility by Johnston's audacity and although he professed to view the wounded man's successor as a lesser opponent, McClellan held his revamped position for almost a month before he dared to reenter combat. By June 25, having moved every element of his army except one south of the Chickahominy, he appeared ready to launch his long-deferred assault. But what ensued was a limited advance toward the southern flank of Lee's Army of Northern Virginia inside a woodland known as Oak Grove. The movement brought on a heated affair that produced some gains but ended inconclusively. The fighting at Oak Grove—the first of a week-long series of engagements known as the Seven Days' Battles—marked the last time Little Mac would assume the offensive while on the Peninsula.[29]

On the twenty-sixth General Lee, animated by the same aggressiveness his predecessor had shown at Seven Pines, lashed out at the Union right wing near Mechanicsville. This position was defended by the only component of the Army of the Potomac that remained north of the river, the Fifth Corps, a provisional organization established under McClellan's most trusted subordinate, Brigadier General Fitz-John Porter. Thanks to a four-day raid by Stuart's cavalry in mid-June that circumvented the entire Army of the Potomac, Lee had determined that McClellan's right was "in the air"—unanchored to a natural defensive position. Lee planned to strike with twice as many troops as Porter could gather to oppose him. One reason for his sudden numerical superiority was the arrival of Jackson's "foot cavalry" via a forced march from the Valley. Again, however, mismanagement produced Confederate defeat, largely the result of Jackson's perplexing failure to attack in furtherance of Lee's plan.[30]

Despite emerging victorious, McClellan was unhinged by the fighting at Mechanicsville and thus began a scrambling, five-day flight to defensible ground not on the York but on the James River, pursued by a smaller but more audacious antagonist. Little Mac finally reached his place of refuge, where his army gained protection from the Union navy, on July 1 following successive retreats from Gaines's Mill, Garnett's and Golding's Farms, Savage's Station, and White Oak Swamp. Each battle had ended in stalemate or tactical success for McClellan, but he was so preoccupied with saving his army from ruin at Lee's hands to notice his run of success.[31]

Custer was actively involved in the fighting on all but one of the Seven Days (the exception being Savage's Station) but most of his activities have been lost to history. Whittaker notes only that "in all of these battles, Custer and Bowen, who seem to have been inseparable, were seen together, carrying orders from one part of the field to another cheerful in spite of the disaster" overtaking their army. On the twenty-sixth Custer relayed an order to General McCall, who held a precarious position behind Beaver Dam Creek, to "maintain the honor of Pennsylvania in that fight." The division commander did so; his men stood firm, repulsing a spirited but unsupported attack by Major General A. P. Hill. At Gaines's Mill the next day Custer guided the brigade of Brigadier General William H. French across the Chickahominy on the so-called Grapevine Bridge in an effort to bolster Porter's hard-pressed division.[32]

The fighting at Gaines's Mill created personal tragedy for Custer. When the reinforcements he sent up failed to prevent a section of Porter's flank from caving in early that evening, the 5th U.S. Cavalry under Captain Whiting was thrown into the breach with disastrous results. Forced to cross three hundred yards of rifle-swept ground, Custer's regiment was shot to pieces well short of its objective. Whiting and his second-in-command were wounded and captured; total casualties ran to fifty-eight officers and men.

Custer grieved for the loss of so many comrades including Lieutenant John J. Sweet, who had been a member of his tactical company at West Point. Sweet was later found to have been the only officer killed in the attack. "They died in the discharge of their duty," Custer wrote. "It is better to die an honored death than to live in dishonor." Dishonor descended on General Cooke who, having ordered the attack without Porter's approval, absorbed much of the blame for the day's outcome. His reputation in shambles, he never again commanded troops in the field.[33]

Throughout the evening of the twenty-seventh, McClellan led his army across the Chickahominy, putting a natural barrier between him and his pursuers. Custer, as he wrote, was tasked with "sending as many of our wounded across [the river] as were able to walk as the bridges were to be destroyed in order to prevent the rebels from following us."[34]

By July 1 the Army of the Potomac was at Malvern Hill, huddling behind hastily erected works shielded by one hundred field guns placed nearly hub-to-hub across the mile-wide crest. His fighting blood up, an overconfident Lee attacked without thoroughly examining the ground or properly coordinating his subordinates' operations. The result was the loss of some 5,600 men killed or wounded during a series of day-long assaults against McClellan's multi-layered defenses.

The Army of the Potomac was safe at last but immediately after the shooting ceased it gave up its formidable perch to make an eight-mile retreat to Harrison's Landing on the James. There, at last, Captain Custer could stand down after being "in the saddle four consecutive nights as well as every day during the march to this place." As he informed his sister, despite eating only one meal a day for the past week "I was never very hungry nor did I become weary or fatigued, the excitement was probably the cause. . . ." His daily fare consisted mainly of hardtack and coffee. He was concerned that Ann Reed might think he liked his preferred beverage "too strong," but "so long as I use nothing stronger than coffee you need have no fears."[35]

Evidently Billy Grier's observation on Custer's capacity for hard and continuous work although underfed and sleep-deprived held true, as did Armstrong's sobriety pledge.

* * *

McClellan's claims that he had saved his army from destruction at the hands of an enemy of superior strength did not fool those in Washington. A week after turning back Lee at Malvern Hill, he hosted several high-ranking visitors including Lincoln himself. In one sense it was a courtesy visit; the president reviewed the defeated but unbowed army and questioned its leader about future operations. Already, however, Lincoln was thinking of using McClellan's troops— with or without McClellan—in another offensive, either on the Peninsula or in Southside Virginia, perhaps in concert with the Army of Virginia, an amalgam of the several commands that had failed to bring Stonewall Jackson to bay in the Shenandoah.

Now operating in central Virginia some eighty miles west of Harrison's Landing, the newly created command had been entrusted to a transferee from the western theater, Major General John Pope. Another two-star general called in from the West soon after the presidential party returned to Washington, Henry Wager Halleck, signified Lincoln's distrust in McClellan's capacity to fill the dual role of field commander and advisor to the president. On July 11 Halleck, a strategist of such supposed brilliance that he was known by the sobriquet "Old Brains," replaced Little Mac as general-in-chief.[36]

On July 25 McClellan's successor, along with other high-ranking soldiers including Quartermaster General Montgomery C. Meigs and Ambrose E. Burnside, followed the president to Harrison's Landing. Through close questioning Halleck learned to his disapproval that Little Mac's plans included renewing the offensive on the Peninsula but only if he received at least fifty thousand additional troops including everyone assigned to Burnside. The next day, after Halleck returned to Washington, Custer mentioned the confab in a letter to his cousin Augusta Ward but knew nothing of the upshot. Otherwise, "nothing interesting or exciting is transpiring here now except the reviewing of the different Corps d'Armee by their commanders and General McClellan. Everything is quiet along the lines and promises to be so for a period. . . ."[37]

For Captain Custer of the volunteer army—who as of July 17 was also a first lieutenant in the regular service—the quiet time ended on August 3, when he accompanied a reconnaissance south of the James supervised by William Averell, now commanding the 1st Brigade of Stoneman's cavalry division. Supposedly the mission was a prelude to McClellan's reoccupation of Malvern Hill, which the Army of Northern Virginia had taken over after the battle there. The three-hundred-man force of mixed arms, half of it drawn from the 5th Cavalry, intended to cross the river under cover of darkness, but stealth proved to be lacking and Confederate pickets fired on the column. The more numerous Federals put their adversaries to flight across rain-soaked roads, but near Sycamore Church they rallied, were reinforced, and a standoff ensued. After capturing and burning the local encampment Averell declared his mission accomplished and turned back to Harrison's Landing. In his report he cited both Custer and Lieutenant Bowen as having taken an "active part" in the operation, without providing details.[38]

Two days later Custer joined Averell on another scouting mission, this part of a large-scale effort to wrest Malvern Hill from the foe. The overall effort had been assigned to General Hooker, whose division of the Third Corps took the advance via Nelson's Farm and Charles City Cross Roads at sunrise on August 5. Averell led four hundred troopers, members of the 5th Regulars and 3rd Pennsylvania, out the Long Bridge Road to St. Mary's Church and as far as the bridge over White Oak Swamp, scene of the battle of June 30. Irish-born Lieutenant Richard Byrnes of the 5th led the advance guard, accompanied by Custer.

Approaching the swampland bridge, Byrnes spotted a force of about forty Rebel horsemen. As per his orders from Averell, he "dash[ed] at once upon the enemy." After crossing the span his detachment split up to run down various groups of antagonists, Byrnes and Custer taking the left-hand road toward Malvern Hill and, as Averell wrote, "chasing, shooting, or capturing all the pickets that came from that direction."[39]

Custer described the wild ride in a letter to Lydia Ann on the eighth: "Away we went, whooping and yelling with all our might. The rebels broke and scattered in all directions, we following as fast as our horses could go. As soon as we came close enough, we began firing at them with our revolvers. Quite a number of them surrendered when they saw that their escape was cut off; others, who had good horses, were not of this way of thinking, but continued the race."

Early on, Custer became separated from the rest of his detachment except for "a bugler boy of my company"—otherwise unidentified. The bugler, who was being pursued by a couple of the more combative Rebels, cried out to Custer, asking for help. The captain spurred his black charger at one of the assailants, who immediately turned and raced off. His mount being faster than the enemy's, Custer rapidly closed the distance between them, firing a shot above his head, and calling on him to surrender. The man, who was armed with a carbine, made a quick inventory of his options before dropping the weapon and raising his hands.

Finding that the bugler had outrun his other pursuer, Custer handed his captive over to a guard detail; then he and Byrnes "started out again. We had not gone far until we saw an officer and fifteen or twenty men riding toward us with the intention of making their way through and joining their main body." Suddenly the Rebels wheeled about and attempted to flee. Byrnes called out: "Custer, you take the right hand and I'll take the left!" Custer agreed; spurring onward, he zeroed in on an officer on a "splendid horse," so fleet-footed that he had to circle around to head him off: "If I had been compelled to follow *behind* him I could never have overtaken him."

The race went on for several minutes, Custer gradually gaining on his opponent, careful to avoid a patch of spongy ground that was slowing the other horse ever so slightly. Finally coming into pistol range, he twice called on the rider to surrender, without effect. "Taking as good aim as was possible on horseback," he fired but missed. After a more careful sighting he fired again and saw his opponent tumble from the saddle. Carried away by momentum, he overran the scene of the encounter but later learned that the Confederate "rose to his feet, turned around, threw up his hands and fell to the ground with a stream of blood gushing from his mouth."

By the time Custer reined in his mount, he had become enmeshed with the troopers of Byrnes's party, "fighting right and left." He rode with the lieutenant for some distance, capturing a Rebel who had tried to escape through a woods, before everyone was recalled to Averell's main body. En route to the rear he recognized and appropriated for his future use his victim's mount, "a perfect beauty, a bright bay, and as fleet as a deer." He also acquired the horse's saddle, covered in black morocco ornamented with silver nails, as well as the dead man's saber and a "splendid double-barreled shotgun." The gun he would send home as a gift for his thirteen-year-old brother, Boston.

So ended Custer's telling of what he called "the most exciting sport I ever engaged in." In contrast to the many emotional letters he sent his sister during his months in the army, this one, while in places dramatically rendered, is basically a matter-of-fact account. Not a drop of sentimentality can be wrung from his description of how he dispatched the first man he could be certain had died at his hands. "It was his own fault," he insisted to Ann Reed. "I told him twice to surrender but was compelled to shoot him."[40]

*   *   *

In the end, Hooker's operation bogged down against enemy resistance and came to naught. Even had McClellan managed to secure Malvern Hill, the feat would have been devoid of strategic value. On July 30, General Halleck had issued his decree to evacuate the army from Harrison's Landing and transport it to Washington to assist Pope in his operations between the Rappahannock and Rapidan Rivers. McClellan's advance had been an insubordinate attempt to protest and block Halleck's action or, as one historian has described it, "one final, convulsive effort to turn back the tide of events." Its failure signaled, once and for all, the end of a promising campaign to take the enemy's capital by attack or siege.[41]

By August 16, with the evacuation of Harrison's Landing complete, an irate McClellan, accompanied by Custer and other members of the staff, left Harrison's Landing for Alexandria "by easy marches." Reaching Williamsburg the next day, Custer looked up his friend Gimlet Lea, who had been released from a POW camp on parole. He found him at Bassett Hall, the home of the Durfey family, whose matriarch and her daughters had ministered to the wounded Mississippian following the battle fought outside their town. Custer visited the house, where he met "a cordial reception although the entire family were strong 'secesh'." They had been informed of the kindnesses Custer had extended to their houseguest, who was now nearly recovered from the effects of his wound.[42]

Custer's reunion with Lea and his caregivers was initially brief, but he secured permission from McClellan to return to Bassett Hall to spend the night. He was treated to a lavish (for wartime) dinner, followed by an evening of music and song. He found himself drawn to the company of "two beautiful young ladies" with whom he spent pleasant hours—the older of whom, Mrs. Durfey's eighteen-year-old daughter Margaret, had become engaged to Captain Lea, the couple having fallen in love during his convalescence. Custer congratulated his classmate "on the wisdom of his choice and wished him every imaginable success." Lea replied that he wanted Custer to be present at the wedding, set for the following week. Lea's guest was willing, but he could not vouch for his whereabouts on that date, whereupon, after a quick consultation with "all the parties concerned, it was decided that the ceremony should be performed the next evening in order that I might be present. No strangers were to be there but myself."

On the eighteenth he returned to McClellan's temporary headquarters just long enough to dress for the wedding, which would take place at nine that evening. At the appointed time Custer was back at Bassett Hall for the unorthodox proceedings. Groom and best man were "both struck by the strange fortune which had thrown us together again, and under such remarkable circumstances."

Custer wrote that when the ceremony was over he was the first to address Margaret as "Mrs. Lea." He noticed that "everyone seemed happy except the young lady who had been my partner on the floor. She kissed the bride and sat down crying." Gimlet began to tease her: "Cousin Maggie, what are you crying for. . . . Oh I know. You are crying because you are not married; well here is the minister and here is Captain Custer, who I know would be glad to carry off such a pretty bride from the Southern Confederacy." The butt of his humor managed to reply that Lea was "just as mean as you can be."

Custer attempted to dry her tears by leading her to the supper table. There, joining in the fun, he asked "how so strong a secessionist as she could consent to take the arm of a Union officer." Maggie replied that her escort ought to be wearing gray instead of blue, whereupon he asked her "what she would give if I would resign in the Northern army and join the Southern." She looked up with a start and inquired: "You are not in earnest, are you?" Custer just smiled at her.[43]

Chapter VI

War Lover

Southern hospitality had waylaid Captain Custer; he found it almost impossible to pry himself from Bassett Hall. As an officer on the army's command staff, he seems to have enjoyed carte blanche, or something close to it, to come and go as he pleased. He used that authority to remain with the Durfey family for two weeks after the wedding of August 18. McClellan himself returned to Fort Monroe on the nineteenth and from there eventually to Washington to consult with Lincoln, Stanton, and Halleck, and to protest their decision to transfer much of his army to John Pope's current area of operations north of the Rapidan.

Custer considered himself very much at home in the abode of avowed secessionists. As he told his sister, his hosts "did all in their power to render my visit pleasant." Every evening was spent in the parlor where Maggie played the piano and regaled the family with songs notably including "Dixie," "Maryland, My Maryland," and "The Bonnie Blue Flag." Custer did not seem to mind the countless Confederate allusions. Nor was he upset when they played a card game with a wartime theme, Lea "representing the South, I the North," and he bowed to his friend every time.[1]

He was not the only loser in a contest to determine the survival of the Southern nation. While Custer shuffled cards in Mrs. Durfey's parlor, John Pope was being beaten in a much more consequential game of chance, the campaign of Second Bull Run. Less than two weeks earlier the commander of the Army of Virginia had begun to descend on the Gordonsville-Charlottesville vicinity, threatening the Virginia Central Railroad, Richmond's lifeline to the provision-rich Shenandoah Valley. McClellan's quiescence on the Peninsula had permitted Lee to shift twelve thousand troops under Jackson to deal with Pope. Following the Army of the Potomac's withdrawal from Harrison's Landing, Lee moved most of the rest of his command, under Longstreet, to join Jackson before McClellan could reinforce Pope.

Even before Longstreet arrived, Jackson dealt a large segment of Pope's army a bitter defeat at Cedar Mountain on August 9. Three weeks later Lee's combined forces enveloped and smashed the Army of Virginia on the fringes of the battlefield of July 1861. Pope's survivors retreated to the Washington defenses. En route they again lost heavily when Lee attacked near Chantilly on September 1, a chaotic, rain-spattered clash in which Custer's first military patron, General Kearney, was mortally wounded.[2]

Pope's downfall came as a relief not only to Robert E. Lee but also to George B. McClellan, who regarded his conceited, boastful colleague with utter contempt and gloried in his humiliating defeat. Little Mac, who had been stripped of his army after his failure on the Peninsula, was suddenly back in power. As soon as Pope's weary, battered troops came within supporting distance of the Washington defenses their commander was summarily relieved of command. Left with few alternatives, Lincoln placed McClellan in command of an expanded Army of the Potomac, Pope's troops having been added to it. McClellan was directed to secure Washington and as soon as he accomplished that to retake the field against Lee. Lincoln's decision to reinstate the man was a desperate gamble especially since he suspected that McClellan had undermined Pope by failing to reinforce him, as ordered, in time to confront Lee, Longstreet, and Jackson.[3]

Even with his old superior back in power, Custer does not seem to have been unduly concerned with reconnecting with him. Apparently he did not leave the Peninsula via ship for Fort Monroe along with his orderly, his two horses—the black charger and the newly acquired bay—and his favorite hunting dog, Rose, until the last days of August. He landed at Baltimore, where he took the train to Washington. He informed his sister that McClellan was then at Alexandria (he had arrived on the twenty-sixth) reorganizing his enlarged command and preparing it for the field but was expected to return to the capital within a matter of days.[4]

Custer lingered in Washington until McClellan arrived on September 1. He told Ann Reed that they spent about two weeks in the capital before his commander was finally prepared to start in search of his enemy. This cannot be true, for by September 3 McClellan knew that the Rebels pursuing Pope had broken off contact; they were nowhere to be found within sight of Washington. Then came reports that the Army of Northern Virginia was advancing toward the Potomac, apparently intent on invading Maryland. On the sixth, having moved elements of the army to the vicinity of Tenallytown in the northern part of the District, McClellan went to the front at Rockville to assume field command. Three days later he was at Frederick, forty miles northwest of Washington, which Stonewall Jackson's occupiers had recently vacated.[5]

It may be assumed that Custer was at or near McClellan's side when on the thirteenth army headquarters came into possession of a copy of the orders Lee had recently issued to guide his troops' future movements. The lost document divided the Army of Northern Virginia into components of approximately equal size under Jackson, who was directed to seize the Union communications hub at Harpers Ferry, and Longstreet, a large portion of whose command was to move toward Boonsboro. McClellan declared that he would take full advantage of this nearly miraculous opportunity to defeat Lee's army in detail. But, as usual, he moved slowly and irresolutely, with predictable results.[6]

Ranging west through the northern extension of the Blue Ridge, the next day McClellan's forces caught up with the division of Major General D. H. Hill inside three passes in the South Mountain chain. The upshot included a couple of all-day slugging matches. Major General William B. Franklin's Sixth Corps broke through at Crampton's Gap but only after critical delays that enabled Jackson to capture Harpers Ferry and its twelve thousand defenders. Eight miles to the south at Turner's and Fox's Gaps, the First and Ninth Corps (the latter an element of Pope's army that had been transferred to McClellan) eventually compelled the Rebels to release their hold on the mountain. When Lee broke contact he led Longstreet's troops westward to the village of Sharpsburg, on Antietam Creek, near where he hoped to reunite with Jackson. McClellan pursued, cautiously as ever, but on the seventeenth felt compelled to offer battle. He struck Lee's line west of the creek in a series of piecemeal, uncoordinated attacks that produced the bloodiest single day in American military history, 12,400 Federals and some 13,300 Confederates being killed, wounded, or gone missing.[7]

*   *   *

As was true of Custer's participation in the Seven Days, his service during the Antietam campaign is limited to fleeting glimpses that obscure as much as they reveal. It may be supposed that throughout the push to Sharpsburg he would have been in the saddle for hours, if not days, at a time, delivering orders to front-line troops and reporting their progress to McClellan's headquarters, well in the army's rear. As Custer had already come to appreciate, his commander preferred to fight his battles at a distance, placing the outcome in the hands of his corps and division leaders.

T. J. Stiles tracks Custer's participation during and after the fighting on South Mountain on the fourteenth and fifteenth, during which he was temporarily attached to the army's First Cavalry Division, commanded now by Brigadier General Alfred Pleasonton. The Union horsemen, pursuing Lee's westward column, overtook its rear guard near Boonsboro and crashed into it. Custer took part in the hell-for-leather charge, which like most mounted attacks probably produced as much confusion in his own ranks as in those of the Confederates, who turned to meet it but were overwhelmed and forced to flee. Custer was clearly delighted, writing McClellan that "we captured between two & three hundred prisoners. . . . The rebels are scattering all over the country." That they would quickly regroup and though heavily outnumbered give McClellan all he could handle two days later, he did not think possible.[8]

Stiles makes three suggestions about Custer's mindset at this stage of the campaign. He raises the prospect that the captain joined in discussions of a cabal against the officials of the government, an effort hatched by members of McClellan's inner circle including some of his senior subordinates. The supposed intent was an army-wide march on Washington to intimidate Lincoln into doing something against his will, the exact nature of which was not revealed. Differences in war policy, stark and deep-seated, had long generated friction and animosity between president and general. But considering that he had restored Little Mac to control of an army larger and more powerful than the one he had led on the Peninsula, it seems unlikely that Lincoln could have done more for his senior field leader.

Stiles also theorizes that Custer, based on the wording of a dispatch he sent to army headquarters late on the fifteenth, had begun to distance himself from his long-time patron. Stiles likewise posits that Custer was no longer content with being a mere staff officer and "passive observer" of war—he had become captivated by, if not addicted to, combat. Yet the surviving letters Custer wrote at this point in the conflict do not reflect a changed attitude toward battle. From the outset—at least once he got over the shock of Bull Run—he had embraced the adrenalin rush that battle generated, especially the thrill of the mounted charge. Boonsboro was not the first time, and certainly not the last, that he would respond to these sensations.[9]

Nor do Custer's writings at this time suggest an effort to disconnect from his commander. He continued to praise McClellan's acumen, to defend him

against any and all detractors, and to declare him the victor in every engagement. After the campaign ended he would write Ann that "we have fought
three battles, one of which was the greatest battle ever fought on this continent,
and in all were victorious." These achievements had placed McClellan "beyond
the power of his lying enemies to injure him."[10]

Custer's link to McClellan remained strong through the balance of the
campaign. By the fifteenth he had left Pleasonton's side to ride with Hooker's
First Army Corps. He did his best to keep McClellan informed of unfolding
events and recent results, but the dispatches he submitted to army headquarters,
some of them based on his interrogation of civilians in and around Boonsboro,
contained mistakes. He reported erroneously that Lee had lost fifteen thousand
men at South Mountain, twice the actual number, and that (as Hooker told
him) "the rebel army is completely demoralized." Custer had the Confederates
heading for the Potomac River at Shepherdstown, which was not far off the
mark as that village was only six miles from Sharpsburg, but he brimmed with
overconfidence when he declared that "everything is as we wish."[11]

On the seventeenth, however, nothing was as the Army of the Potomac
wished, thanks to Lee's ability to anticipate and counter every threat to what
Custer on the fifteenth called his "perfect [line] about a mile and a half
long." The most critical blow, directed at Lee's embattled right late in the
day, was overcome by a decisive counterattack by A. P. Hill's division. From
various observation posts, Custer tried to keep track of the rapidly expanding
battle. But it was beyond his ability to make strategic sense of the ghastly
bloodbath.[12]

The extent of the carnage did provide a strategic benefit: it helped per-
suade Lee to end his invasion. Late on the eighteenth he started his blood-
spattered command toward the Potomac and crossed it into Virginia. Before
the Confederates could fully withdraw, however, Custer was after them, having
again traded staff duties for field service. According to one account, without
orders he led a company of the 8th Illinois Cavalry commanded by Captain
Elon J. Farnsworth on a dash against a weak point in the enemy's line, capturing at least one cannon. In a hastily penciled note to the headquarters staff,
he wrote: "We have just captured one three inch gun and its caisson on the road
from the Hagerst[ow]n Pike to Sharps town [*sic*]. Col. Hunt [Henry Jackson
Hunt, McClellan's chief of artillery] had better send out for it. We cannot take
it with us. . . ." A half-hour later he reported that "we have captured another
gun—a 12 pdr. brass howitzer."[13]

Supposedly, this latest exposure to danger and harm—sure to come to the attention of the high command—further embellished Custer's reputation for bold action. But if he hoped it would gain him even higher standing with Little Mac, he was doomed to disappointment. In the wake of Antietam the world of McClellan was on the verge of exploding, and the career of every member of his staff would suffer collateral damage.

Before the axe fell, Custer wrung as many benefits as possible from his position. By September 26 the Army of the Potomac had gone into camp on the east bank of its namesake river, sprawled across the ravaged countryside between Sharpsburg and Harpers Ferry. Here McClellan remained for five weeks, tending to the physical needs of his command. Although it had turned back Lee's invasion, the Army of the Potomac had suffered more heavily than its less numerous adversary, and its spirit was equally in need of repair.

Custer used the period of relative inactivity to his advantage, passing over the river under a flag of truce while escorting several Confederates who had been captured, then paroled. The assignment enabled him to inquire of West Point classmates who had followed their states into secession and he wrote notes to several of them including John Lea.[14]

The following day he penned a letter to his cousin Augusta, expounding on his attitudes toward fighting a war in which his opponents were not necessarily his enemies. "You ask me if I will not be glad when the last battle is fought. So far as my country is concerned I, of course, must wish for peace, and will be glad when the war is ended, but if I answer for myself alone, I must say that I shall regret to see the war end. I would be willing, yes glad, to see a battle every day during my life."

Many who read these words will condemn the writer as a self-absorbed idiot for whom war was nothing more than entertainment. More charitable readers credit him for his honesty in describing the allure certain aspects of warfare held for him while not ignoring the larger picture: "When I think of the pain & misery produced to individuals as well as the miserable sorrow caused throughout the land I cannot but earnestly hope for peace at an early date."[15]

* * *

As the army slowly recuperated, Little Mac engaged in a heated conflict with his civilian and military superiors. In addition to his evident distaste for reengaging Lee, this war of words proved his undoing. He complained to Halleck that the general-in-chief found fault in everything he said and did. He clamored inces-santly of Stanton for reinforcements and the filling up of regiments skeletonized by battle. He dispensed uninvited advice on a wide range of military matters including the operations of forces not assigned to him.

Initially he avoided direct conflict with Lincoln, but after September 22, when the president issued a preliminary draft of his Emancipation Proclamation, McClellan furiously assailed him in letters to political friends for "at one stroke of the pen changing our free institutions into a despotism." The general was far from alone in condemning Lincoln's writ, which freed slaves in Southern territory as yet unoccupied by Union forces. A majority of his soldiers, at least initially, considered the decree a flagrant case of executive overreach. Custer, given his deep-seated anti-abolitionist views, undoubtedly shared his commander's opinion.[16]

On the first day of October Lincoln unexpectedly visited the army outside Sharpsburg. He spent the next four days inspecting its ranks and camps, being escorted over the recent battlefields by officers who may well have included Custer, and urging McClellan to get moving as soon as possible. The general did not pay heed; when on the twenty-sixth he finally began to cross the army over the Potomac he did so with such lethargy that Lincoln had no choice but to fire him. He acted on November 5, replacing him with Ambrose Burnside, an old friend of Little Mac's who had twice previously resisted the president's urging that he take the reins. Burnside was sufficiently honest with himself, and with Lincoln, to admit that he was not up to the challenge of army com-mand, but he felt compelled to make an effort.[17]

McClellan's downfall set his staff officers adrift. As Frederick Whittaker has written, once the general was returned to his residence in Trenton, New Jersey, to await orders that would never arrive, "and as the status of his aides depended on him, they also went home on 'waiting orders'." As a newly pro-moted first lieutenant, Custer was now the executive officer of Company M of the 5th Cavalry, but until his staff appointment was officially revoked, he had no orders to join his regiment.

Whittaker claims that McClellan advised Custer to go home to Monroe "and see his people." Recently he had been entirely willing to do so; in a September 27 letter to Ann Reed he wrote playfully that "if I am successful in procuring a leave of absence I intend to make myself as troublesome as possible, and I would not be surprised if I still 'have an engagement down town!'" Now, however, he could not be quite as happy to leave Virginia.[18]

Hoping to rejuvenate his spirits, he took McClellan's advice. At the railroad junction adjacent to army's new concentration point at Warrenton, he caught a train to Washington prior to the two-day-plus journey westward. He left the army on the morning Little Mac bade an emotional farewell to his troops, whom one of them described as "wild with excitement. They . . . cheered their old commander as long as his escort was in sight." Others bemoaned the spectacle of a cherished leader brought low. Given the adulation he inspired in his army up to the very end, one wonders if that nascent coup against the government, if carried out, might not have succeeded.[19]

*   *   *

What Custer felt during his long trip west can only be imagined. Whittaker suggests that upon reaching Monroe he was "thoroughly miserable," longing "to be back sharing the dangers of his comrades in the army." No doubt the kind of dangers he had faced at Williamsburg, during the Seven Days and at Antietam held an allure, but upon returning to his sister's home he seems to have done his best to repress his career disappointments and to enjoy himself as much as possible. He would have drawn pleasure as well as emotional strength from his reunion with Ann, David, and their children, especially little Autie.[20]

Then, too, there were male friends in town with whom to recall old times and share new ones, though without indulging in the carousing that had gotten him into so much trouble during his last visit. Others, previously available, were away in the army, having joined local regiments such as the 15th Michigan, recruited in response to the government's July 1 call for thousands of additional troops. As for young women, there were enough of them in Monroe to capture and hold his attention. In the letters he had written her over the past year he had asked his sister to remember him to several including Marie Miller, Mary Arnold, Helen Wing, Nellie Van Wormer, and Fannie Fifield. Some or all of these girls, especially the last two, he had determinedly pursued, if only for a time. Before his return in November, his relationship with Nellie seems to have run its course although Miss Fifield, the daughter of a wealthy merchant, continued to pique his interest. Despite the respectability her family's prominence lent her, Fannie understood the ways of the world and was not hesitant to use that knowledge to advantage. Her reputation among the young set of Monroe ranged from harmless flirt to brazen hussy. She had made conquests of many of the local boys; now she set had her sights on the young army officer.[21]

Custer may have loved Fannie, but her sexual availability seems to have been her greatest attraction. Still, he was open to new relationships. Seeking entertainment, on the evening of November 27 he attended a Thanksgiving party given by the staff of Monroe's leading academy of higher education, the Young Ladies' Seminary and Collegiate Institute, from which Fannie had graduated and that Nellie continued to attend. Custer paid proper attention to both women, engaging in the small talk common to such an occasion.

At one point he was motioned to by an acquaintance who had been speaking with another former student Custer did not at first recognize, a petite, brown-haired, blue-gray-eyed beauty in stylish attire, whom he quickly recalled as the daughter of Judge Bacon of the probate court. The circumstances of his introduction to twenty-year-old Libbie Bacon are obscure. Whittaker claims it came about through the agency of Annette ("Nettie") Humphrey, whose father operated a popular local hotel. Nettie, a close friend and confidant of Libbie's, would serve as an intermediary for the couple once their romance bloomed. Libbie herself, though she could remember little of their first conversation, recalled that one of her many beaux, Conway Noble, had "fearfully vexed" her that evening for some cause, whereupon "to propitiate me he said 'Shall I introduce Captain Custer?' I assented merely to be rid of him."[22]

It would be too tidy to suppose that for either Captain Custer or Miss Bacon it was love at first sight. According to Whittaker, "she was not disposed to like him; his war record went for nothing with her. . . . She only knew that she had heard of him as a dissipated young man, a desperate flirt, and that she had herself seen him, on one occasion, intoxicated," and he a fallen-away Methodist. Then, too, the boundaries of politics and social status served to distance the daughter of a prominent Republican official from the son of a working-class family notable for its Democratic partisanship. Marguerite Merington has Libbie at their first meeting inquiring politely but with an air of disinterest about Custer's military career, observing that his rise through the ranks had been "very rapid," to which he replied, "I have been very fortunate."[23]

Other sources depict a different encounter. Stiles writes, "on meeting, a current sparked between them, and Custer felt it. So began his siege of her doorstep, his patrol of her routine." They met again the day after the party, when she saw him coming toward her as she walked to the home of a seamstress with a coat to be altered. Apparently they did not speak but after Libbie pulled the bell cord on the woman's porch she turned and (as she recalled long afterward in a letter to Custer) "there you were, looking at me." She admitted to having been a little flustered by the chance encounter, "but, oh, how pleased I was."[24]

By early December the captain was still in town, awaiting orders. He looked increasingly downcast, at loose ends with his career and with life in general, his mood in sharp contrast to the effervescent spirit he had displayed at the Thanksgiving party. Thanks to his pursuit of her, Libbie and he had begun to meet and speak with some frequency, eventually to the point that he felt confident enough to let his feelings show. It was not long before his name appeared in the journal she assiduously kept. One day she quoted him as declaring that "nobody could entertain him but me over an hour without his being lonely."[25]

Although Custer had a facility for charming young woman with whom he had no romantic interest, Libbie Bacon intrigued him in a way foreign to his experience. Her social status ought to have made her unapproachable, but he saw her as an unfinished product capable of development by the right man: educated (valedictorian of her class) but not sophisticated, talented but not accomplished, self-composed but not fully self-aware. That kind of incompleteness, added to the spark of vitality and the genteel sexuality she exuded, was quite appealing. [26]

Their union did not come about quickly for it was apparent to Custer that Judge Bacon did not favor him as a potential suitor for his daughter. In addition to his unprepossessing antecedents and affiliations, the captain had demonstrated his social unfitness by drinking himself sick in public. Having lost three children as well as Libbie's mother to deadly illnesses (he had remarried three years ago), the judge was a zealous guardian of his surviving daughter, on whom he had long doted. Her social reputation was his uppermost concern; he would not besmirch it by allowing a professional soldier, especially one known for his scandalous behavior, into her life.

But what exactly did Judge Bacon know and feel about Custer, and how informed was he of the nature of the latter's relationship with his daughter? There is a major disconnection on this issue. Marguerite Merington claims that almost from the start the judge was aware of Custer's intentions and strongly opposed them, to the point that the Bacon home was "heavy with disapproval." First Custer simply was not invited to the house; then Libbie was forbidden to have anything to do with him. Merington stresses Custer's drunken escapade of the previous winter as having prejudiced Bacon against the young man. She notes his outrage at seeing Custer pay close personal attention to his daughter, and how strongly he reacted when she spoke to him of her outings with the young man.

Yet Merington also asserts that near the close of Custer's time in Monroe he "struck up a warm personal friendship with Judge Bacon." Supposedly this occurred when both happened to be in the clubroom of the Humphrey House. Custer was being plied with war-related questions by some of the patrons and Bacon was impressed by his sound, well-crafted replies. Merington claims this to be the first time the two had met, for she has the judge asking Levi Humphrey to introduce them.[27]

Custer historian Lawrence Frost accepts this account of the meeting but implies that it occurred some weeks before Custer left Monroe. Frost claims that at the time Bacon was introduced to Custer he was "not aware of Autie's beginning siege for the attention of Libbie." Supposedly he remained ignorant of the affair for some time afterward since Libbie's name never came up during their first conversation. Both accounts appear at variance with facts and logic. Merington's version of events is not credible; nor is her contention that the two "struck up a warm personal friendship." Equally hard to accept is Frost's claim that the reputation-obsessed Bacon, even after he happened upon Custer at the four-story hotel on Washington Street, remained deaf to rumors linking him with Libbie, rumors well known to other townspeople including Levi Humphrey.[28]

When Captain Custer finally nerved himself to call on Miss Bacon, she, fully aware of the judge's attitude toward unsuitable suitors, turned him away. Later, when he asked her to accompany him in public, she refused. Instead of permitting him to escort her to a seminary concert, she went with her father. At evening's end he appeared unexpectedly at the school, but the judge and his daughter ignored him until a balky gate barred their way. Custer swooped in to open it for them; she acknowledged his gallantry with a simple "Thank you, sir," and continued on her father's arm.

But his persistent attentions were beginning to have an effect. When Libbie learned, a week before Christmas, that Captain Custer was about to return to Virginia, she expressed a measure of regret, confiding to her diary that "I feel sorry for him. I think I had something to do with his going." She was aware of how attracted he was to her, and the knowledge excited her.[29]

* * *

On or about December 17 Custer rode to the local depot and for the second time in ten months boarded an eastbound train. Three days later he was back in Washington, but not to rejoin his regiment. Undoubtedly he inquired at the War Department, but no orders awaited him. Because this was not unexpected, historians have wondered why he returned to the capital at all. The answer probably lies in the battle fought at Fredericksburg, Virginia, four days before he left. It had been a horrific affair, the carnage rivaling that of Antietam, but this time the disparity in casualties was striking: nearly thirteen thousand for the Army of the Potomac, more than twice the losses suffered by Lee's command.

The unmitigated disaster had been the work of Ambrose Burnside, who, thwarted by delays in the delivery of materials to bridge the Rappahannock River in preparation for attacking a suddenly wide-open Richmond, had permitted Lee the time he needed to build impregnable defenses across the river from Falmouth. The criminally stubborn Burnside had attacked those works throughout the thirteenth, refusing to desist till long after dark, by which time the dead and wounded lay in piles. The defeat had created a crisis both in the army and in Washington. Lincoln held emergency meetings with his cabinet members, three of whom offered to resign. Disaffected elements in the army threatened another, more powerful, revolt if Burnside was not relieved, and high-ranking emissaries went directly to Lincoln in a thinly disguised effort to remove the army leader by pleading wholesale demoralization in the ranks.

The preferred solution in many quarters, military and political, was to reinstate McClellan to command; as one general officer wrote in a letter home, "we *must* have McClellan back with unlimited and unfettered powers. His name is a tower of strength to everyone here. . . ." This was an effort that Little Mac was all too willing to promote. It is possible that in preparation for his restoration he called to his side Custer and other members of his disbanded staff. It is also possible that Custer, anticipating McClellan's return to power, made the trip on his own initiative to be close at hand when dramatic events unfolded at the seat of government.[30]

Regardless of his reasons for returning, Custer would have been deeply disappointed by the upshot, for by the time he reached the capital the Army of the Potomac was beginning to recover from its wounds and to maneuver toward another confrontation with its enemy. Lincoln had decided to keep Burnside in command, at least in the short run, while he responded to (and subsequently rejected) a proposal by William B. Franklin and Baldy Smith to abandon the Rappahannock and return the army to the Peninsula, from which Richmond could again be threatened. By the twenty-second, having observed no ground-swell of support for McClellan's return, Custer boarded another train and headed back to Monroe. Arriving on Christmas Day, he almost immediately returned his attention and energy to courting Elizabeth Bacon.

He did so with extreme conspicuousness. According to the object of his affection, he passed her house "forty times a day." His abject surrender to her charms aroused Libbie's vanity but also put her on guard. He was coming on far too strong, "tho' I admire his perseverance." Two days before New Year's she gave in to her feelings enough to present him with a holiday gift, a package of candy. They would meet, with increasing frequency, at parties and social gatherings. Early in January he carried her bodily across a muddy crosswalk, "an act," Frost writes, "that left a deep impression." Having finally gained her heartfelt attention, he mentioned marriage. The proposal came wrapped in romantic avowals, but she was strong enough to resist them. "He tells me he would sacrifice every earthly hope to gain my love," she wrote in her journal, "and I tell him if I could I would give it to him."[31]

But she remained unsure of his level of commitment and conscious of her father's unyielding disapproval. Having welcomed his advances, now she rebuffed them. By February, playing the jilted lover, Custer was seen squiring Fannie Fifield about town. Disturbed by the renewed relationship but affecting indifference, in February Libbie decided to accompany a visiting friend to her home in Toledo. The judge was delighted—for at least the second time in Custer's life, the father of a girl he loved seized the opportunity to distance his daughter from the undesirable youth pursuing her. And therefore Bacon was furious when Custer showed up at the train station to see Libbie off—and, if possible, to accompany her and her friend to Ohio. Not only did he help load the women's luggage, but he also had the effrontery to touch Libbie's elbow when assisting her into the passenger coach.[32]

Libbie spent a few weeks in the mid-size city, attending lectures, concerts, and at least one grand ball. When she sent home for a formal dress, however, her strict Presbyterian father wrote back in anger. He also took the opportunity to censure her relationship with Armstrong Custer. His disapproval, and the way he expressed it, had an unintended effect. Instead of meekly accepting his criticism, she replied that she had consistently resisted Custer's advances, "*all for you. I like him very well*," she explained, "*and it is pleasant always to have an escort to depend on. But I am sorry I have been with him so much. . . . You have never been a girl, Father, and you cannot tell how hard a trial this was for me.*"[33]

Though the judge's displeasure troubled her, the father-daughter blowup served to draw her closer to Custer, who had continued his attentions to Fannie during Libbie's absence from Monroe. Thus far, acutely conscious of her standing as a proper upper-middle-class young lady, Elizabeth Clift Bacon had restrained her impulse to pursue a man in the unfettered way Fannie did, but upon her return from Toledo, through Nettie Humphrey's agency, she studiously courted Armstrong Custer. At various times during the winter Nettie sent him notes from Libbie as well as her ambrotype and a ring with the engraved letters "L" and "A." Subsequently, fearing her father's reaction should he learn of the gifts, especially the photograph, she pledged Custer to show it to no one (he would break his promise, then lie about it). By February Libbie was frequenting the Humphrey House, ostensibly to visit the friend who lived there but in fact hoping to find Custer.

At her instigation, the two were thrown together at various functions including a supper where they broke from a crowd to talk privately upon a loveseat. Charmed by the intimate setting, she spoke some words that Custer mistook for an invitation to enfold her and attempt a kiss. Libbie, believing that things had gone too far, disentangled herself and, cheeks flushing, blurted out that she was not Fannie Fifield or Helen Wing, another rumored rival for Custer's affections. As though slapped in the face, he drew back, composed himself, and declared emphatically that he had never thought of her that way.[34]

February morphed into March, and suddenly the couple was not seen together in public as frequently as before. He continued, however, to escort Fannie, as though the misunderstanding at the supper had permanently damaged his intimacy with the woman whose company he preferred. By early April he had received notice that he was wanted in Washington, apparently to rejoin his regiment in the field. Their separation might consume months; there was no guarantee the relationship would survive it.

Thus it was that on the eighth Custer took the train that would carry him, via connecting routes, to the capital. It is not known if Libbie saw him off although given her father's sentiments she was probably disinclined to chance it. Besides, her feelings toward him had undergone a change. Only days before he left Monroe they had separately attended a gathering at Fannie's home, perhaps a sendoff for him. He had recently seen her sample an alcoholic drink at the Humphrey House and now he criticized her for it in front of the other guests. When she angrily defended herself, he grew petulant—a flare-up of the dark mood that sometimes overtook him when unhappy or depressed. Later in the evening he joined a card game but could not restrain himself from making sarcastic remarks about her within her hearing.

The ugly confrontation prompted a journal entry the following day in which she questioned her attraction to him: "I am glad I saw him last night as I did," for his behavior had revealed his character flaws in a new and troubling light. With Nettie Humphrey's assistance she might still consent to receive letters from him after he returned to the army, but it was best they kept a substantial distance. "I don't have as much fun now C is gone," she wrote, "but I know very well now that it is best he has gone. I am doing my duty and away from temptation."[35]

So she wrote at the time. Months later she would tell a friend that Custer "proposed to me last winter but I refused him more than once, on account of Father's apparently unconquerable prejudice. I never *even thought of marrying him*. Indeed I did not know I loved him so until he left Monroe in the spring."[36]

* * *

Custer reached Washington on the evening of May 10. When he reported to the War Department he was surprised to learn that he was not heading back to Virginia—at least not yet. He was wanted, instead, in New York City, where General McClellan was now residing. Little Mac had asked for Custer's presence at his side; apparently the matter was urgent. Custer had no inkling of what lay in store, but the next day he took the morning train for New York, arriving at seven that night and learning that his literary, not his military, skills were responsible for the assignment.[37]

McClellan remained in War Department-imposed Coventry. Instead of being called on to save the army after the debacle of Fredericksburg, he had become a pariah whose influence would never again be allowed to infect the Army of the Potomac. In late January Lincoln, finally convinced of Burnside's incapacity, had ignored McClellan's availability when appointing to army command Joseph Hooker, a severe but relatively discreet critic of both of his predecessors.[38]

The no-longer-young Napoleon had retreated to a townhouse in a fashionable section of Manhattan, where he resigned himself to the end of his active military career. Now he was strongly considering a life in politics, a realm in which he had much experience. Already he was being touted by Democratic leaders and anti-administration editors as one who could block Lincoln's reelection in 1864. A stepping-stone to a return to public acceptance was the report Little Mac was required to submit to army headquarters, covering his tenure in command—he had been working on it ever since being shelved. It would require careful wording to make it clear, without appearing to be insubordinate or disloyal, that he had been consistently successful in managing his campaigns in Virginia and Maryland and would have prevailed had the government supported him properly.

When assembling the notes and documents he needed to prepare his effort at self-exoneration, McClellan had petitioned the army to assign to him, on temporary duty, thirteen members of his staff. It is not known how many were released to him, but they had not included Custer because the general had not specifically asked for him. Custer later told his sister that he would have been called on sooner but McClellan had been "ignorant of my whereabouts as my letter to him had miscarried"—a statement at variance with the report that the general had told him to go home to his family in the Northwest.[39]

Belatedly or not, McClellan had decided he needed his former aide to jog his memory on names, dates, and events. Then, too, he could use novel suggestions for phrasing his defense of the charges that had been leveled against him by his political and military critics. These included, but did not encompass, his failures on the Peninsula, his post-Antietam lethargy, and his foot-dragging when ordered to reinforce Pope prior to Second Bull Run.

Custer was pleased to be reunited with his superior, but the assignment, and its timing, had its disagreeable aspects. As he informed Ann, had he foreseen the assignment "I should have come better prepared both in money and clothes." Because his trunk, with his clothing and personal effects (including Libbie's likeness), had yet to reach him, "I fear I will be compelled to purchase a new suit of citizens clothes and if I do not get them from Monroe I will have to get some new shirts &c." Moreover, "I am living at great expense." He was staying at the swanky Metropolitan Hotel, a five-floor brownstone on Broadway and Prince Streets known for its steam-heated rooms, three meals a day on the American Plan, and the largest plate-glass mirrors in the country. The socially conscious McClellan had arranged a room for him at almost three dollars per day and Custer had no idea how long he would have to foot the bill.

The workload was, however, tolerable and its unique nature appealed to him. He enjoyed poring over records and trying to mold them into an effective narrative. "I am occupied in Gen McClellan's office," he told Ann, "from

10 in the morning until 3 in the afternoon. The report when complete will make quite a large volume." (One edition, published in a book from two years later, ran to almost five hundred pages.) The schedule left him ample time for socializing; he had met "a vast number of my friends since I came away from Monroe." But the work forced him to skip the midday meal included in his room and board. He breakfasted every morning at 9:30 and dined at 6 p.m., "the fashionable hours here."[40]

The only drawback to the assignment was that it kept his military career on hold, even after a six-month absence from active duty. He had expected upon arriving in Washington to quickly rejoin his regiment at the front, but he had been mistaken. Another career setback occurred three days after he reached New York: he was officially mustered out of the volunteer service, causing him to revert to his former rank of first lieutenant, 5th Cavalry, an action backdated to March 31. Given the glacial pace of promotion in the regular service, there was no guarantee he would rise as high again, at least not for years. By then the fighting would probably be over, returning the military establishment to pre-war stagnation and congressional neglect.[41]

The more he pondered his future, the more convinced he became that the path to advancement lay in the volunteer service. If he could regain a commission in the volunteers his education and experience would ensure a steady rise through the officer corps. And whatever rank he held at war's end—especially if he had distinguished himself—was likely to translate into something more than a lieutenancy when he was returned to the regulars.

He had already taken the first step to revive his career. Shortly after arriving in Monroe the previous fall he had received a request from Isaac P. Christiancy, an associate justice of the Michigan Supreme Court and one of the founders of the state Republican Party. Christiancy, who hailed from Monroe, was also a journalist, owner of the town's Republican organ, the *Commercial*. Despite their family's political differences, Custer was a close friend of the judge's son, Captain Henry Clay Christiancy of the 1st Michigan Infantry (Custer had visited Henry at his regiment's camp at Warrenton the day before he left Virginia). The judge asked his correspondent's help in expediting Henry's pending appointment to the staff of General Humphreys, Custer's superior during the latter's service on the topographical engineering staff. Humphreys was now a division commander in the Fifth Army Corps, although the 1st Michigan was not one of his regiments. The judge believed that a recommendation from Custer would carry weight given his past association with the brigadier.

In his reply Custer, who agreed that a staff appointment would open opportunities for advancement for Henry, agreed to try to move along the vetting process. He would seek the help of an aide to Major General Daniel Butterfield, the army's chief of staff, as well as General Humphreys himself, with whom he claimed to be "intimately acquainted." His intervention may have done some good—before the end of November Captain Christiancy received the coveted appointment—but since it occurred less than a week after Custer's pledge of support, his influence does not appear to have been a decisive factor in the outcome.[42]

Even so, the elder Christiancy was grateful for his willingness to help—ever after he showed himself to be an avid supporter of Custer's career. Since the justice had the ear of high-ranking officials in the state capital at Lansing including Governor Blair, that support should stand Custer in good stead. It gave him hope that he had a future in the Army of the Potomac even now that the leader who claimed his undying loyalty was gone. By itself Custer's gesture would not advance him far on the road to promotion, but it was a start.

Chapter VII

A Resurrected Career

On April 13, only two days after Custer reached New York, the War Department directed him to report to his regiment in Virginia. The order was counter-manded three days later; on the thirteenth eight companies of the 5th Cavalry had accompanied ten thousand other horsemen under General Stoneman on an expedition from Joe Hooker's base at Falmouth toward Richmond with the intention of cutting enemy communications in advance of a general move-ment by the army. In accordance with orders issued on the sixteenth, Custer was to join his own company, newly detached from the 5th and assigned to the defense forces of Washington. When Custer reported he would assume command of Company M, its senior officer, Captain William McLean, having recently succumbed to a fatal illness.[1]

Although pleased that he would soon be returned to the business of fighting Rebels and developing opportunities for advancement, he did not rejoin his company straightaway. He parted with McClellan on the nineteenth and reached the capital the following day. He checked in at the Ebbitt House, the hostelry he had visited the day before Bull Run. That day or the next he left the rooming house to visit a cavalry encampment—not that of the 5th Regulars, but of a regiment of volunteers from his adopted state.[2]

The trip was prompted by a suggestion from Austin Blair that made Custer hopeful of gaining higher rank and responsibility than he could have acquired in the regulars. It appears that when in Michigan he had traveled to Jackson, historic birthplace of the Republican Party and hometown of the governor, to press his chances of gaining the colonelcy of the 5th Michigan Volunteer Cavalry. That a lowly subaltern could jump four grades in a single bound appeared unlikely, but virtually anything seemed possible in the anomalous world of military affairs in mid-1863. A desperate need for educated leaders had enabled more than a few mid-level officers in the regular service to make that leap.

Custer's initial effort to gain a volunteer commission had been made two and a half months earlier, after having learned that "there are vacancies in the command of the regiment of 'Lancers' at Detroit and the regiment stationed at Monroe." As he had when contacting Congressman Bingham about a West Point berth, Custer boldly introduced himself to Governor Blair, who had the authority to appoint field-level officers for Michigan regiments. Custer touted his finished education and experience in the field, which, although of only six months' duration, he considered "more perhaps than most junior officers." He went on to describe his staff service under Phil Kearny, the positions supposedly tendered him by Stoneman, and the opportunities he had gained to perfect his skills as a cavalryman. And yet, he was not absolutely committed to mounted service. He claimed to be "equally qualified to occupy a position in an infantry regiment" based on his knowledge of the tactics and organization of that arm of the service.[3]

The 5th Michigan was currently in a state of turmoil. Colonel Freeman Norvell had submitted his resignation under a professional cloud. Although by most accounts a capable officer who had the respect of his men and some of his superiors, Norvell had several times been accused of drunkenness on and off duty. "If you think the efficiency and usefulness of the 5th Cav'y will be promoted by giving me command of the regiment," Custer inquired of the governor, "I should be proud and most happy to accept it." He stressed that in applying "I am actuated by the desire of serving my country. I am not content to remain idle at a moment of national peril like the present. . . . I am anxious to again enter active service."[4]

Custer's carefully modulated efforts at self-promotion would go for naught. Given the well-known political leanings of his family, he stood no chance of making a favorable impression on a staunch Republican like Blair. The governor, however, was unwilling to make the basis of his refusal clear. To avoid the impression that he was acting purely from political motives, he suggested that Custer, once back in Virginia, should visit the camp of the 5th to meet its officers and gauge their reaction to his candidacy.

At this time the regiment was stationed at Fairfax Court House, fifteen miles southwest of Washington, where it formed the nucleus of an all-Michigan cavalry brigade assigned to the defense forces of Washington. The larger command was headed by Brigadier General Joseph Tarr Copeland of Pontiac, a former state supreme court justice of considerable political influence but no pronounced military aptitude. In addition to Norvell's regiment, recruited largely from the Detroit area, Copeland's brigade consisted of the 6th Michigan, which hailed from Grand Rapids and was commanded by Colonel George Gray, and Colonel William D. Mann's 7th Michigan, also organized at Grand Rapids. The 5th and 6th had been serving on the outskirts of the capital since the previous December, while Mann's outfit had arrived in February, cementing the identity of the "Wolverine Brigade." Due to slow recruiting, the 7th Michigan consisted of ten companies, two shy of the War Department standard for volunteer cavalry regiments. Companies L and M would not leave Michigan, fully staffed, until early in the summer.[5]

Blair probably supposed that his feigned interest in Custer's candidacy would cost him nothing while perhaps producing a small measure of nonpartisan goodwill. Undoubtedly he was certain that Custer's bid would founder on the overwhelming opposition of the officers of the 5th, especially that of Lieutenant Colonel Ebenezer Gould, who coveted the command for himself. Another contender was one of the regiment's three's majors, Luther S. Trowbridge, brother of U.S. Congressman Roland E. Trowbridge. Then there was the equally ambitious Lieutenant Colonel Russell A. Alger of the 6th Michigan, who believed he was a better fit than either Gould or Trowbridge, and demonstrably preferable to an outsider like Custer. Even so, Custer was heartened by Blair's apparent support, which he must have believed stemmed from his affiliation with renowned commanders—never realizing that it was his closeness to McClellan that stood in his way.[6]

Custer's trip to Fairfax Court House produced mixed results, but he remained encouraged. Returning to Washington one day later, he informed Blair that he had been unable to speak to more than a few of the regiment's officers. To those he found in camp "I explained the object of my visit and asked their views." He quoted Major Noah Ferry, the regiment's acting executive officer, to the effect that he was "glad someone who has had experience was coming to take command of the regiment" because as things stood "the regiment is going to ruin."[7]

One reason for Custer's apparent acceptance by the officers of the 5th was the recommendations he had secured from some notable supporters. These included Major General Julius Stahel, the Hungarian-born commander of the cavalry division of which Copeland's brigade was a part, as well as Stahel's departmental superior, Major General Heintzelman. Stahel had written that although Colonel Norvell had "many good qualities," his return to the command of the 5th would be "productive of more injury than good." He also believed that Custer possessed "the requisite qualifications to render him a most valuable and efficient officer. Such an officer is very much needed in the 5th Michigan Cavalry. . . ." Heintzelman stated that "I fully concur in Gen. Stahel's recommendation. So much depends upon a suitable Colonel to have a Regiment to do honor to the State that I hope this recommendation will receive your favorable consideration."[8]

The weightiest endorsement was provided by General Copeland, who as a Michigander not only had Blair's ear but also his support. Copeland had received his original appointment from the governor, and his success was also Blair's success. During his visit to Fairfax Custer called on the brigadier, winning his support contingent on the acceptance of Colonel Norvell's resignation, which the latter was thinking of rescinding. From a sense of loyalty Copeland conditionally supported Norvell's return, observing that the colonel had fallen off the wagon only once during the past few months. Yet he admitted that he would "much prefer to see" Custer at the regiment's head, whereupon who would transfer Norvell to the brigade staff, "a position he is willing to accept."

Custer prevailed on Copeland to write a letter to Blair recommending him for the colonelcy "in the event of your coming to the conclusion that you cannot consistently re-appoint Col. Norvell, but will appoint some other outside officer, a resident of our State." If that were to happen, "judging from the antecedents of Capt. C, and from the high character of the recommendations he presents, I have no doubt he possesses the requisite qualifications in an eminent degree, and that he will prove himself an able commander."[9]

The strength of these high-level endorsements—added to recommendations from Isaac Christiancy, repaying Custer's favor in behalf of his son, and from Edwin Willitts, formerly of the judge's law office and now the editor of his Republican-oriented newspaper—threatened to complicate Blair's unyielding position regarding Custer's candidacy. The governor had already replied to Christiancy's letter of support: "Custer is using you to his own advantage, just as he used Bingham. His people are Rebel Democrats. He himself is a McClellan man, indeed McClellan's fair-haired boy, I should say. Sorry, your Honor, I cannot [appoint him] . . . whatever his qualification."[10]

Blair's appraisal of the Custer clan as a nest of Copperheads was well off the mark. Emmanuel Custer, at least early in the conflict, supported some of Lincoln's military and political policies. As for the family's commitment to the war effort, not only was Emmanuel's eldest son a Union officer but Armstrong's brother Tom was serving in an Ohio infantry regiment; by war's end, he would be a brevet major of volunteers as well as a double recipient of the Congressional Medal of Honor. In any case, Blair would now have to consider the strong statements of support Custer had obtained from two major generals and a brigadier with strong Republican credentials. Unless he could provide a more acceptable reason for blocking Custer than his opinion of the loyalty of the man's family, he might make an embarrassing misstep.[11]

Custer, in the dark as to the governor's motivations, kept pressing his case and submitting high-level testimonials to his fitness to command. On May 30, shortly after Blair returned to Michigan after a brief visit to the government in Washington and the army in Virginia, Custer wrote him again. To his deep regret, "close occupation to my duties" had prevented him from seeing the governor. He hoped to recover from the lost opportunity by sending Blair two of the most impressive statements of recommendation yet acquired. The first was from General Pleasonton, who had recently succeeded to the command of every cavalryman in Joe Hooker's army. The second was a brief but "very favorable" endorsement from Hooker himself. The following day Custer wrote Justice Christiancy—who appears not to have informed the lieutenant of Blair's animus—mentioning these latest testimonials and observing, more accurately than he knew, that "if the Governor refuses to appoint me it will be for some other reason than a lack of recommendations."[12]

Fortunately for Blair, his original supposition, that the officers of the 5th Michigan would not welcome the interposition of an outsider, proved accurate, furnishing him with ammunition to use against Custer's supporters as well as a more publicly acceptable basis for his action. One of the regiment's officers, Captain Samuel Harris, recalled that after meeting Custer the officers considered him too young for the position he sought. But Harris did not accurately characterize his comrades' objections, which appear to have had nothing to do with the youth of the applicant. Two weeks after Custer's visit a petition was sent to Blair bearing the signatures of almost three dozen captains and lieutenants of the 5th. It conveyed their concern that, according to rumor, a regular army officer was going to be appointed as their leader. Such an action "would be against our own, and the wishes of the entire rank and file."[13]

The petitioners cited two reasons for opposing Custer. They considered it "an imputation upon the officers and upon the regiment to go outside it for our commander." They also claimed, supposedly from observed experience, that "very few volunteer regiments had done well, under the command of Regular Army officers and their efficiency is quite often entirely destroyed thereby . . .

We therefore *earnestly* but respectfully protest against such appointment, and beg that the promotion in this case may be regularly made from the officers of the regiment."[14]

In the end, the captains and lieutenants got half of what they asked for. Custer was out—he heard no more from Blair about available positions in the state volunteers. But when the governor filled the vacant berth on June 11 it went not to any of those who had protested Custer but to Lieutenant Colonel Alger of the 6th. Alger was not a professional soldier, but the 5th would find that he was a disciplinarian of the first stripe, always a complaint of volunteers when regular army officers were appointed to command them and probably the underlying basis of the petition.

*   *   *

Weeks before Blair announced his decision, Custer had plotted his course in the event his application failed of success. If he could not gain regimental command in the volunteers, he would gravitate back to staff duty under an influential commander. He had discovered long ago that such a life offered many advantages. It rescued an officer from the dull routine and arduous responsibilities of small-unit command and provided an elevated platform from which to observe war. Further, it granted opportunities for exciting service including crossing dangerous ground with important messages and taking part in attacks and skirmishes.

By April 22, Custer was back in Washington, where he drew an issuance of clothing and other items—coat, trousers, and blanket— from the local quartermaster. According to T. J. Stiles, these were "the tangible signs that the young man was just a first lieutenant once more, with orders to take charge of a company in the 5th U.S. Cavalry." The return to his roots in the regulars, however, would be brief. As of May 5 Custer was with his company but no longer operating under the orders of the local commander, Brigadier General John H. Martindale. His unit had been assigned to the command headed by Alfred Pleasonton, at whose side he had ridden prior to Antietam. At Pleasonton's direction Company M made a seventy-five-mile march from Washington to Hooker's headquarters at Falmouth. Here Custer's association with the 5th Cavalry again came to a close. He would not rejoin the regiment during the war.[15]

The following day, the sixth, Custer was at Pleasonton's field headquarters adjacent to the Lacy House, also known as "Chatham Manor," at Falmouth, one of the most notable landmarks of the Fredericksburg campaign (Burnside's army had appropriated the ground around the dwelling as an observation post during the battle of December 13). Here Custer appears to have begun seeking another staff appointment. Pleasonton, impressed by the aide's combativeness and daring at Boonsboro and elsewhere during the Maryland campaign, was no doubt amenable to the idea, but the assignment did not come about right away, perhaps because Custer had his sights set on an even loftier position: aide to the army leader, "Fighting Joe" Hooker.

As was true of almost everyone who had come under Hooker's command, Custer had developed a favorable opinion of Ambrose Burnside's successor. Almost immediately after taking the reins, Hooker had implemented a series of organizational and administrative reforms aimed at restoring the strength and morale of the army including better rations, more attentive medical care, and a more regular issuance of pay and furloughs. Everyone who gave the improvements fair trial agreed that they had gone a long way to rehabilitate the army physically and psychologically.[16]

Of greatest interest to Custer and his colleagues, Hooker had instituted badly needed improvements in his mounted arm. On February 5 he had grouped the army's cavalry into a single, full-sized corps, nine thousand strong, thereby putting it on an equal footing organizationally with the army's infantry components. The move provided the cavalry, for the first time, with a truly effective structure and by removing it from the clutches of infantry commanders offered it a chance to realize its potential as a combat force as well as an intelligence-gathering service. Hooker had further pleased his horsemen by appointing one of their own to command, though some were surprised and chagrined by his choice: George Stoneman, McClellan's well-meaning but underperforming mounted leader—an officer afflicted by an overly conservative mindset. Stoneman's shortcomings had forced McClellan to relieve him, and he had gravitated to an infantry command during the Fredericksburg campaign. Now Hooker not only restored him to his former branch but procured a second star for him.[17]

Stoneman's assignment deeply disappointed the officer with whom Custer was trying to forge a close relationship. Alfred Pleasonton had proposed a cavalry corps in advance of Hooker's coming; being instrumental in its conception, he felt entitled to lead it. Instead, as the cavalry's senior brigadier, he took charge of the first of Stoneman's three divisions, consisting of seven regiments and one squadron of volunteers and a battery of horse artillery. The other divisions, all composed of volunteers, were led by William Averell and Brigadier General David McMurtrie Gregg. The army's regular regiments—five of them, including the 5th Cavalry—had been grouped into a separate Reserve Brigade under Brigadier General John Buford.[18]

Its morale and stability restored, the Army of the Potomac fully expected to give a stronger account of itself when it was returned to action against Lee's troops, now entrenched west and south of Fredericksburg. Fighting Joe promised to make it happen. In the end, however, he failed miserably—in a sense, more miserably than Burnside—in that Hooker's army, in battle against Lee's, suffered more than seventeen thousand casualties, albeit the losses were spread across several days of fighting.

In the last days of April—a week after Custer visited the 5th Michigan's camp at Fairfax—Hooker led one-third of his 134,000-man command downriver from Falmouth, across the Rappahannock at Kelly's and U. S. Fords, and into the rear of the Army of Northern Virginia. Thanks largely to a diversionary attack below Fredericksburg by a division under Major General John Sedgwick, Hooker's offensive came as a rude surprise to Lee.

Once fully aware of the threat, the Confederate commander acted swiftly and decisively. Leaving enough men at Fredericksburg to deal with Sedgwick, he led the rest, under Stonewall Jackson, toward the point of the Union advance. His response should have come too late to save his army, but Hooker, as soon as challenged, pulled back and went over to the defensive. During the next three days his forfeiture of the initiative turned a promising movement into yet another massive defeat. In the end, following some of the most bitter and confused combat of the war—most of it fought inside the clotted, movement-impeding woodland known as the Virginia Wilderness—Hooker retreated to Falmouth in abject defeat.[19]

Fighting Joe's newly reinvigorated cavalry comported itself just as poorly as its patron. Ordered to strike Lee's links to Richmond two weeks before the main army advanced, Stoneman proved unable to cross the rain-swollen Rappahannock until the day the infantry broke camp. Hooker had expected the horsemen to inflict enough damage in Lee's rear to force him out of his trenches and back upon Richmond. But instead of exploiting his command's newly-achieved cohesion Stoneman, from a central location, dispatched raiding parties that landed feeble, uncoordinated blows on railroads, canals, and supply depots before hastening back to him, pursued by small groups of Stuart's cavalry. Most of the detachments returned to Falmouth by May 8;

one, under Judson Kilpatrick, finding itself cut off from Stoneman, fled down the Peninsula to the Union outpost at Gloucester Point, more than a hundred miles from the expedition's starting-point.[20]

Hooker was infuriated by Stoneman's equally wretched performance. Disappointed by the horsemen on whom he had lavished so much care and in need of a scapegoat for his own failures, he lopped off a couple of heads. First to fall was Averell, whose column had moved the slowest and achieved the least of the forces involved; Hooker relieved him from command on May 3 and handed his division to Pleasonton. The latter was further rewarded soon afterward. When Stoneman and his raiders returned to the Falmouth area, Hooker sent him home on leave. On May 22 Pleasonton replaced him in corps command.[21]

Alfred Pleasonton thrived because he had escaped blame for the raid's outcome. Hoping to deny Pleasonton the glory of accompanying him, Stoneman had left his pushy subordinate behind, attached to the main army and reduced to the command of a single brigade in close support of the infantry. It was obvious to every observer, most certainly including Armstrong Custer, that the brigadier had outlasted, if he had not upstaged, his superior, and was now the man at the top, to be courted and cultivated. Custer, who understood the survivor's mentality, intended to do just that.

* * *

On May 6, the day the larger portion of the army recrossed the Rappahannock and headed for Falmouth, Custer was already there. His company was standing idly at Pleasonton's headquarters, awaiting the return of the body of its regiment from its raid in the enemy's rear. Custer, lounging in the shadows of Chatham Manor, was in one of his foul moods. The army's drubbing was an established fact, and he knew who was to blame. He also knew that George B. McClellan would enjoy hearing the bad news.

"I know you must be anxious," he wrote Little Mac, "to know how *your* army is, and has been doing, particularly if, as is reported here, the papers are prohibited from publishing the news. I cannot give you any of the details nor is it necessary, it is sufficient to know the general result. We are defeated, driven back on the left bank of the Rappahannock, with a loss which I suppose will exceed our entire loss during the seven days battle[s]." In this he was correct, although Lee had suffered severely as well: thirteen thousand casualties, nearly one-quarter of his aggregate force, the most sobering being the mortal wounding of the soldier he called "my right arm," Thomas J. Jackson.[22]

Despite pleading an inability to particularize, Custer proceeded to provide enough details to give his old boss a fair understanding of what had occurred over the past week: "Our left wing with Sedgwick crossed and captured Fredericksburg and the heights in rear advanced five miles were defeated and driven over the river to the left bank. . . . The right wing [Hooker's turning column] crossed up the river at Banks and U.S. fords. The enemy offering little or no resistance until our forces had crossed and advanced about five miles when they attacked Hooker's right, driving him towards the river." Evidently the fighting was all but over for "the firing is growing less rapid and distinct." Fears were entertained that the rear guard, under Major General George Gordon Meade, had been cut off from the river and perhaps captured en masse. In the end, however, Meade would make his way to safety with minimal loss.[23]

McClellan's informant, like everyone else at Falmouth, was in the dark as to the results of the great cavalry raid. News of the outcome should have been received by now but because it had not, "great solicitude is felt here by all concerning Stoneman. . . ." The informant reported Averell's demise and attributed it correctly: "Hooker was displeased because affairs did not succeed as he wished and *somebody had to suffer*. Pleasonton commands *all* the cavalry with the army now. . . ."

The corporate morale that Hooker had restored over the past three months was long gone. "To say that everything is gloomy and discouraging," Custer wrote, "does not express the state of affairs here." A rumor of Hooker's being incapacitated during the battle would soon be verified. On the third he had been stunned by the bursting of an artillery round that struck a pillar on the porch of the house he had appropriated for his headquarters, slamming a large piece against his skull. The blow knocked him unconscious and contributed to the instability he exhibited after appearing to regain his senses.[24]

Custer signed off in a manner calculated to flatter his correspondent: "You will not be surprised when I inform you that the universal cry is 'Give us McClellan.' Every one is speaking of this all are unanimous in saying that you alone can extricate the country from its present difficulties. If I am not mistaken there will be such a howl go up from the conservative press and people of the north which will [leave] but one course open for the administration to pursue, I need not say what that course is."[25]

Eleven days later, still at Pleasonton's headquarters, Custer wrote Judge Christiancy on the same subject—the army's downfall in the Wilderness—but in a slightly different tone. The judge being a high Republican figure and Hooker being a darling of Congressional Republicans, Custer went easier on the man he blamed for the army's latest drubbing. He emphasized that Hooker's less-than-inspired performance below the Rappahannock had not destroyed the command. Much of the army, especially the portion under Sedgwick "on the left, did nobly. Had our right wing kept the enemy's left occupied, as they might well have, all would have been well."[26]

Though it had suffered losses that would have crippled most fighting forces, "what remains of the army, except perhaps for the 11th Corps, it certainly is in excellent condition and spirits. The men and officers are united in their refusal to acknowledge the late contest [as] a defeat on our part, nor is it to be wondered at when it is known that not one half, probably the better half, was engaged at all." Custer 's mention of the Eleventh Army Corps was a reference to that segment of the army that, holding an exposed position on Hooker's right flank, had been attacked and routed by Stonewall Jackson late on May 2, the first link in the chain of events that produced defeat and retreat.[27]

Custer's most severe stricture on his army's leader was his observation that Hooker "allowed Lee to adopt the tactics of Napoleon in permitting him to engage his entire force against fractions of our own"—a claim at variance with facts, as Lee had divided his army no fewer than three times in order to counter an enemy advance or launch one of his own. Even in defeat, "we captured nearly, if not quite as many cannons as we lost. The Rebels probably took more prisoners than we, but in the loss of arms and blankets, provisions etc., theirs bears no comparison to ours." Here again Custer misspoke; he was closer to the mark when asserting that "the loss of Stonewall Jackson was a much greater one than all their entire loss in men and material."[28]

The next time he wrote to Justice Christiancy, at the end of May, Custer was less sparing in his criticism of Hooker, who, having failed to demonstrate an inclination to reengage Lee, was now viewed not only as a commander who had lost the confidence of his troops but, in the minds of many, a lame duck. It appeared a matter of time before Lincoln worked up the nerve to challenge the radicals in his party and send Fighting Joe into the ranks of the unemployed. This assumed, of course, that a capable replacement was available.

On this occasion Custer castigated Hooker for his unwillingness to accept even a dollop of responsibility for Chancellorsville. Above all, he resented

Hooker's claim that he had banished Stoneman because the cavalry leader "had accomplished nothing by his late raid and did not carry out his instructions, but on the contrary he injured us more than he did the rebels." Custer believed that it was in Hooker's interests "to place as low an estimate upon Stoneman's services as possible." He insisted, however, that "Stoneman stands very high in the estimation of the entire Army and his raid is considered to surpass any that Stuart ever made, even the rebel prisoners we have taken since the battle admit that Stoneman has excelled Stuart." But it had become ingrained in the army's mentality that when failure occurred "it is not proposed to find that one who really is responsible but to discern the most *available* man. . . . Stoneman is the man to select as a 'peace offering' as no other leader aside from the General Commanding bore a part in the late struggle of sufficient importance to render them in any way liable. . . ."[29]

*   *   *

Custer accepted the rules of the game of self-preservation. While they were unfair and sometimes cruel, he understood the need for them and was willing to abide by them. His attacks on Hooker's military capacity and lack of integrity did not prevent him from exploiting an opportunity to profit from the relationship he claimed to have forged with Fighting Joe. Sometime between May 6 and 12 he managed to secure an appointment on the army headquarters staff. The transfer back to the volunteer service, apparently with the rank of captain, enabled him to ignore an order, issued on or about the twelfth, to return to his unit. By this point Company M of the 5th Regulars had rejoined the balance of the cavalry corps. Still under Stoneman, the command was resting and resupplying near Potomac Creek, north of Falmouth, following its debilitating expedition.[30]

It seems Custer's attachment to Hooker's staff was a temporary posting, for on the seventeenth he informed Judge Christiancy that he had accepted an appointment with Pleasonton. As a result of the transfer, he was once again a first lieutenant; the rank did not increase upon Pleasonton's promotion to corps command. The whirlwind succession of personnel changes suggests that through the latter half of May and probably well into June Custer was continually transitioning between the staffs of the two generals. Officially he was an aide at Headquarters Cavalry Corps, Army of the Potomac, but when Hooker had an assignment for him, he returned to army headquarters on a provisional basis.[31]

He had remained in touch with the cavalry leader following the Antietam Campaign. As late as November 7 Custer was again serving with Pleasonton when the Federals clashed with Stuart's horsemen at Barbee's Cross Roads, near Chester Gap in the Blue Ridge. On that occasion Custer took up an exposed position behind the guns of his friend Alexander Pennington's Battery M, 2nd United States Artillery. He observed the outcome when, as a *New York Herald* correspondent reported, "columns of rebel cavalry came sweeping down on the roads to the right and left," only to be countercharged, turned back, and harried by pursuers under one of Pleasonton's most combative subordinates, Colonel Benjamin F. ("Grimes") Davis of the 8th New York.[32]

For the most part the workload of Pleasonton's newest aide was not nearly so exciting. One of his first duties, in the role of divisional ordnance officer, was to turn in an array of serviceable weaponry at the army's chief supply base at Aquia Creek on the Potomac, ten miles northeast of Falmouth. Even so, the job had its perks. On May 16 he informed Ann Reed that he was in excellent health and had been ever since his return to the army. One reason for the "much better appetite than I had in Monroe" was the abundance of victuals at Pleasonton's table "when we are not moving. He sends to Baltimore daily for vegetables and other delicacies; we have onions radishes and *ripe tomatoes* asparagus, fresh fish, mackerel beef, mutton, veal, *Bacon*, pound cake oranges ginger snaps candies eggs *peas* warm biscuits (instead of hard bread) fresh milk butter and cheese and everything I could desire."

Pleasonton employed as cooks an African American couple who accompanied the command on the march. Thanks to the wife, "an excellent cook" known to everyone at the headquarters as Aunt Hannah, "we do not suffer much from hunger when we are not marching or fighting." Other amenities at headquarters included a "fine band," one of best in the army.[33]

In this letter Custer alluded to the women he had left behind in Michigan. He told Ann that he had received two letters from Fannie, who had called at his sister's house but had yet to receive a visit in return. Indicating his continuing interest in the young woman, he reminded Ann to tend to that social obligation. Only in closing did he speak of Libbie, sending his regrets at the news, recently received, of her stepmother's illness, which was said to be serious (but that she would survive). Noting that Rhoda Bacon's death would deal a severe blow, he remarked, rather curiously, that Libbie "has a sweet disposition and is the *most sensible* young lady I ever met. There are not more than a dozen girls in Monroe who I like better than Libbie, and that is the truth."[34]

But was it the truth? Given the lengths he had gone to win her hand, one suspects he was downplaying his true feelings. The impression, perhaps deliberately produced, is that he had steeled himself to move on from the judge's daughter in his pursuit of intimacy and love. But since he remained in regular communication with Miss Bacon, one doubts he rated her as low on his list of desirable females as he claimed.

* * *

Four days after his most recent letter to his sister Lieutenant Custer was again on the move, by order of Pleasonton but at the behest of Hooker. On May 20 cavalry corps headquarters sent to Captain George Thompson, commanding Companies E and F of the 3rd Indiana Cavalry at Potomac Creek, a recently acquired issue of the *Richmond Whig*, "showing that passengers are en route to Urbanna on the Rappahannock and will probably reach there tomorrow. Rebel mails may also accompany the party. The CG [Pleasonton] directs that you proceed with your squadron, by water, to Heathsville, which is on the Potomac about fifteen miles from Urbanna, with a view to capture the party expected [there], together with all mails, besides destroying all boats and other conveyances which cannot be brought off." Pleasonton, desiring a report from a source independent of Thompson, ordered Custer to accompany the expedition.[35]

Apparently Union authorities suspected that the "mails" included communications from the Confederate capital to Lee's army in the field. It is also possible that passengers on the Rappahannock were suspected of carrying funds with which to purchase foodstuffs and other goods from Confederate agents on Virginia's Northern Neck and Middle Peninsula. Federal patrols had been combing those areas for months seeking to break up the sources of the illicit trade.

The information brought to Pleasonton's attention undoubtedly came from Hooker's recently organized Bureau of Military Information (BMI). Headed by Colonel George H. Sharpe, the BMI would prove to be most effective intelligence-gathering apparatus of the war. Sharpe's resourceful and meticulous operatives considered Southern newspapers a major source of information on enemy plans and movements, which often came disguised as innocent, everyday news. The 3rd Indiana was a logical choice to handle the present assignment: the regiment had long supported many of Sharpe's operations and Sergeant Milton Cline of the 3rd was one of his most reliable scouts.[36]

Custer rendezvoused with Thompson's squadron at Aquia Creek on the evening of May 20. The local quartermaster provided the seventy-five-man expeditionary force with two transports, which carried the Hoosiers and their mounts down the Potomac. They landed at the mouth of a tidal tributary, the Wicomico River, shortly before noon of the twenty-second. Men and horses debarked on the Northern Neck and moved stealthily inland. Passing through Heathsville and Lancaster Court House, they bivouacked that night at Chowning's Ferry. The trip had taken longer than Captain Thompson had anticipated, and the rowboats the party carried to enable them to cross the Rappahannock were found to be leaky, requiring repairs. The lost time made it appear that if the suspicious travelers reached Urbanna on schedule Thompson's men would fail to intercept them. Presumably Custer, charged with evaluating the performance of all involved, took note of these vexing difficulties.

Thompson managed to place twenty of his men in two boats and shove off early on the twenty-third. During the passage he spied a boat heading his way, piloted by civilians whom Thompson would later identify as members of the party he was seeking to detain. Upon being sighted, the pilot turned about and attempted to flee, but was overtaken. Before Thompson could secure the boat several crewmembers scrambled to land and fled. Thompson was able to detain a man claiming to be a refugee from the Confederacy, his wife, and their four children. The man was found to be carrying more than a hundred dollars in Confederate money. Made captive, he was sent to Pleasonton's headquarters for interrogation.

His seizure was one of the raid's few accomplishments. As he had feared, Thompson reached Urbanna too late to encounter the rest of the passengers from Richmond, who had departed the previous day. Other achievements included the destruction of all boats found on that stretch of the river, the capture of three Rebel deserters, and the taking of fifteen horses. The latter were brought back in the boats and, upon their return to Aquia Creek were turned over to Pleasonton's quartermasters. The transaction was signed for by Custer, who had personally captured two of the horses.[37]

Custer's official report, which he submitted on May 24, provides details that Captain Thompson overlooked in his own report. Possibly because the officers had served apart during much of the operation, Custer's account also contains statements that conflict with Thompson's. He corrects the captain's error regarding chronology, noting that the expedition got underway on the evening of the twenty-first, not the twentieth. Unlike Thompson, Custer definitively identifies the target of the operation as "bearer[s] of rebel dispatches" although, probably based on information obtained during their interrogation, he has them bound not for Lee's army but for Philadelphia. His account of the pursuit and overtaking of the "small sailing vessel" on the Rappahannock is somewhat at variance with Thompson's. He fails to identify the detained passengers as members of the same family. He notes only that much Confederate money was found in their possession, but he agrees that the travelers, "by their own statement proved to be the party we were in quest of."

Custer's report includes an observation missing from the captain's account, based on a discovery that he considered "infinitely more important than all the other results of the expedition combined." He wished Hooker and Pleasonton to know of the existence of a "strong Union sentiment which prevails among a large portion of the inhabitants of Lancaster, Westmoreland, and Northumberland Counties." He based his findings on the many residents who had been found concealed in the woods and marshes of the Northern Neck in hopes of evading Confederate conscription officers then sweeping the region. Other locals had hidden their possessions from Rebel quartermasters, also active on the Northern Neck. Some had even expressed a wish that the Federals would "take possession of their horses rather than that they should become the property of the enemy."[38]

Custer's report may have conflicted at a few points with the raiding leader's, but his private accounts of the expedition, written on successive days to Ann Reed and Nettie Humphrey (and thus also to Libbie Bacon), offer a much more detailed record of the operation while dramatically expanding his role in it. He speaks of embarking from Aquia Creek with "*my* little party of seventy-five men (cavalry)" and reaching, late the following day, the Wicomico River landing. A fatiguing journey brought the squadron to the Rappahannock within sight of Urbanna. He described the trip as "the most rapid march I ever made since being in the army. We marched forty miles in but little over five hours, several of the men and horses gave out from exhaustion."[39]

While Thompson and the main body proceeded to Urbanna, Custer was detached to scout the other side of the river. As he reported, "taking nine men and another officer [Lieutenant Abner L. Shannon] in a small canoe, the only boat we could find, *I* started in pursuit of a small sailing vessel which was coming down from the direction of Urbana." After a ten-mile chase, Custer's boat overtook the other, causing it to ground on the south bank. This enabled him to seize several passengers from Richmond with "quite a large sum of

Confederate money in their possession . . . [whom] I was compelled to make prisoners of. With four of *my* men I made my way on shore."

The river at that point being too shallow to approach the objective by boat, he and the other raiders had to wade ashore. Upon reaching dry ground they proceeded to the nearest house, "a fine country mansion." On its piazza he spied Lieutenant William B. Hardy, engrossed in a volume of Shakespeare. So absorbed in his reading was the officer, who was home after being detached from his Virginia artillery unit, that by the time he looked up from his book he had no hope of escape. From his prisoner Custer learned that no other Confederates were within six miles of the place, easing his fear that his little band was being lured into a trap.[40]

Handing the officer over to Lieutenant Shannon's men, Custer entered the manor house to confront the man's sisters, who remained unaware of the lieutenant's fate. Custer explained their brother's situation and appears to have apologized for being a party to it, reflecting that "I could not but feel sorry that they were to be made unhappy through any act of mine." The other members of the expedition were less considerate in their treatment of the family. After Shannon's party reunited with Thompson's main force, men and women alike were herded back to the waiting transports on the Wicomico. Custer was gallant enough, however, to find suitable transportation for the ladies, pressing into the service a family carriage, horse, and driver.

The raiders and their captives traveled across the Northern Neck until 2 a.m. on the twenty-third. After camping for the night "to avoid pursuit and capture," they reached the transports at noon the next day and headed home. After an uneventful run up the Potomac the vessels offloaded their cargo at Aquia including the two horses seized by Custer. One was a black charger whom he named Harry for his favorite nephew. The other, one "of the finest horses I ever saw," was an iron-grey blooded stallion named "Roanoke," supposedly worth upwards of a thousand dollars. Only two weeks later, he would expose Roanoke to enemy bullets, with unfortunate results.[41]

Neither in his report nor in his private letters did Custer identify the exact nature of the mission. Although it appears that the expeditionary force was indeed in search of dispatch bearers on the Rappahannock, it seems clear that the mission—especially Custer's part in it—also aimed to search for evidence of contraband trade. This operation involved unscrupulous Northern businessmen conspiring with enemy agents to buy tobacco, cotton, and other agricultural products confiscated from local farmers in exchange for cash (preferably

Yankee greenbacks, Confederate currency if necessary), weapons, or medical stores of value to the Rebel armies. Even as Thompson's raiders scoured the two peninsulas, the 8th Illinois Cavalry, supported by three regiments of infantry, was capturing suspects and destroying $30,000 worth of contraband goods at trading stations elsewhere on the Northern Neck. The Illinoisans' expedition, unlike Thompson's, would prove so successful that Pleasonton would describe it to General Hooker as "the greatest raid of the war." Custer's several references to detainees carrying large amounts of money folds into this narrative as does his conspicuous mention of Jewish civilians. Custer must have known that Union officials had long accused Jewish businessmen (without conclusive evidence) of being major players in the contraband trade.[42]

Though the expedition boasted no major accomplishments, Custer emerged from it with a reputation not only intact but growing. The day after he returned he was called to army headquarters where Hooker "complimented me very highly upon the manner in which I carried out his orders. He said it could not have been done better." Equally gratifying was the army leader's promise "that he would have something more for me to do soon." With high-level commendations such as these, Custer dared believe that his career, so recently threatened with stagnation, was again on the rise.[43]

Chapter VIII

Boy General of the Golden Locks

Around the time Custer returned from the Urbanna mission, rumors began circulating of an impending raid into the North by at least a portion of Lee's army. The Rebels had invaded Union territory shortly before Antietam, and their recent victory along the Rappahannock fueled speculation of a repeat performance. Federal observers knew that the Army of Northern Virginia, despite its battlefield successes, was in some ways a hollow force, suffering from inadequate rations and forage and in need of more and better horses, weaponry, and equipment. An invasion of hitherto inviolate territory appeared to offer an opportunity to restock at the Union's expense and to temporarily relieve war-ravaged Virginia of the presence of the destructive Yankee.

As early as May 18, with Joe Hooker showing no signs of leaving his safe haven at Falmouth, General-in-Chief Halleck had advised Secretary of War Stanton of several potential moves by Lee in the wake of his opponent's inactivity. Only one—a demonstration (essentially, a feint) toward Maryland, Harpers Ferry, or Washington, DC—Halleck considered likely, although a more general movement toward any of those objectives was feasible, "as Lee's army can move with much greater rapidity than ours." Halleck's final point was ominous: whatever plan Lee adopted, "we shall probably know his real intentions only after the blow is actually struck."[1]

By the end of the month the accepted belief in some quarters, including the Army of the Potomac's intelligence-gathering community, was that, whether or not Lee launched a general movement, his cavalry was preparing to raid northward. Jeb Stuart might be heading for any of the locations Halleck had suggested, and possibly others as well, perhaps via the Shenandoah Valley. The reports seemed confirmed by the twenty-seventh, when Colonel Sharpe of the army's BMI learned that three of Stuart's brigades, under Brigadier Generals Wade Hampton, Fitzhugh Lee (Lee's nephew), and W. H. F. "Rooney" Lee (the commander's second son) had shifted to Culpeper County, well to the west and north of the Fredericksburg vicinity. In and around the local courthouse men and horses were resting in preparation for a large-scale movement, destination unknown.

Stuart's cavalry was not Sharpe's only cause for concern. His scouts had acquired information that Robert E. Lee had called in infantry detachments from distant points and had issued marching orders. Since it appeared unlikely that Lee intended to attack his much stronger enemy, the consensus at the BMI was that he was planning to outflank the Army of the Potomac, perhaps in prelude to invasion. If so, Stuart, rather than planning an independent operation, might be preparing to support the main army, covering its front and flanks on the march. Hooker had taken pains to develop a top-drawer intelligence service, but he ignored these warnings and also the reports of numerous civilian observers who believed they knew that Lee was up to something big.[2]

For his part, Abraham Lincoln did not know what to make of the rumors but, well aware of Lee's capacity for craft and boldness, suspected that the "Gray Fox" was about to take the offensive. The president had hoped that Hooker himself would make some sort of forward movement, if not to offer battle, then to strike at the enemy's communications. Union forces in other theaters were moving aggressively. One had only to point to the operations on the Mississippi, where Grant's Army of the Tennessee, having fought its way inland, had begun to besiege strategic Vicksburg. It was becoming increasingly clear to Lincoln that his commander in Virginia was no Grant.[3]

Affairs on the Rappahannock began to heat up on the twenty-seventh, by which time Custer was serving Hooker rather than Pleasonton. A message sent that afternoon, moving the cavalry corps a quarter mile southwest of its present location, bore his signature as a member of the army headquarters staff. How long his reattachment to Hooker lasted cannot be determined, but within days Custer was again at Pleasonton's side, monitoring activities at the cavalry's outposts and poring over scouting reports as they came in from the field.[4]

By early June Custer was attached to Pleasonton on a full-time basis; he would remain so for the remainder of his career as a staff officer. In short order he made himself indispensable to his superior, who came to rely on Custer's rapid and precise delivery of orders, his willingness to hazard all battlefield conditions, and his insistence on being in the forefront of the action so as to provide what later generations of military analysts would call real-time strategic intelligence. He was also attentive to the placement of the cavalry's outposts.

Custer's birthplace, New Rumley, Ohio. (Harrison County Historical Society)

Custer holding a photograph of his first sweetheart, Mary Jane "Mollie" Holland. (Harrison County Historical Society)

Congressman John A. Bingham of Ohio, who secured Custer's admission to West Point. (Library of Congress)

Cadet Custer, Class of June 1861. (U.S.M.A. Archives)

Major General George B. McClellan. (Library of Congress)

Brigadier General Philip Kearny, Custer's first military patron. (Library of Congress)

Major General George Stoneman, Chief of Cavalry,
Army of the Potomac, 1861–63. (Library of
Congress)

Custer and Lieutenant Nicolas Bowen of the
Topographical Engineers (right) on the Virginia
Peninsula, spring 1862. Between them is Lieutenant
William G. Jones of the 10th U.S. Infantry, a West
Point acquaintance of Custer. (Library of Congress)

Drawing of Lieutenant Custer on a reconnaissance of the Chickahominy River, May 22, 1862. (Whittaker, *Complete Life of Gen. George A. Custer*)

Captain Custer, staff officer. (Monroe County Historical Museum)

Custer and his captive, Lieutenant James B. Washington, C.S.A., June 1862. (Library of Congress)

Custer and one of his many canine companions. (Library of Congress)

Elizabeth "Libbie" Clift Bacon. (Library of Congress)

Major General James E. B. Stuart, C. S. A. (Library of Congress)

Drawing of Battle of Second Brandy Station, June 9, 1863. (Library of Congress)

Custer and Major General Alfred Pleasonton (right). (Library of Congress)

Major General George Gordon Meade.
(Library of Congress)

Brigadier General Custer. (Library of
Congress)

Brigadier General H. Judson Kilpatrick.
(Library of Congress)

Brigadier General David McMurtrie Gregg.
(Library of Congress)

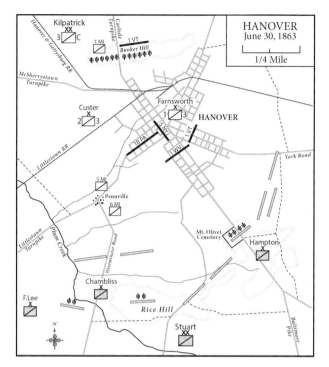

Hanover.

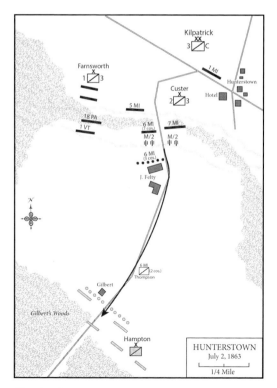

Hunterstown.

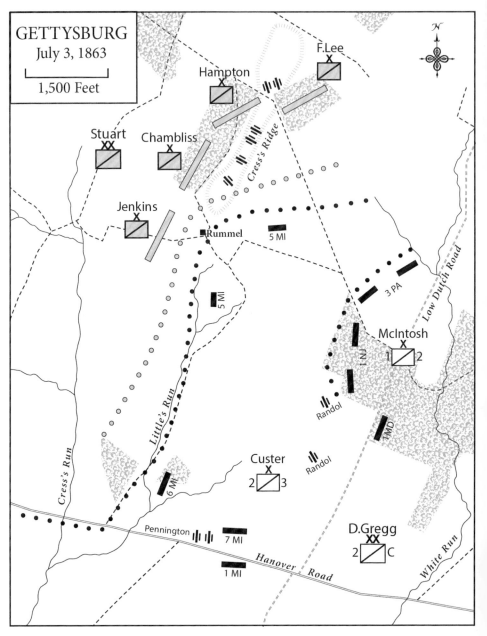

GETTYSBURG
July 3, 1863

1,500 Feet

N

F.Lee

Hampton

Stuart   Chambliss

Cress's Ridge

Jenkins

Rummel   5 MI

3 PA

Low Dutch Road

5 MI

McIntosh
1   2

1 NJ

Randol

Little's Run

1 MD

Cress's Run

6 MI

Custer
2   3

Randol

D.Gregg
2   C

White Run

Pennington   7 MI

Hanover Road

1 MI

Gettysburg.

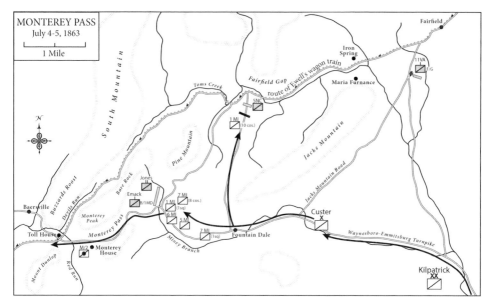

Monterey Pass.

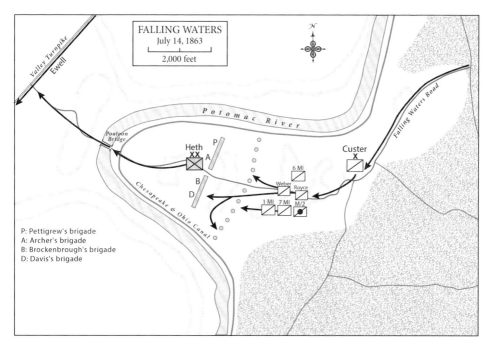

Falling Waters.

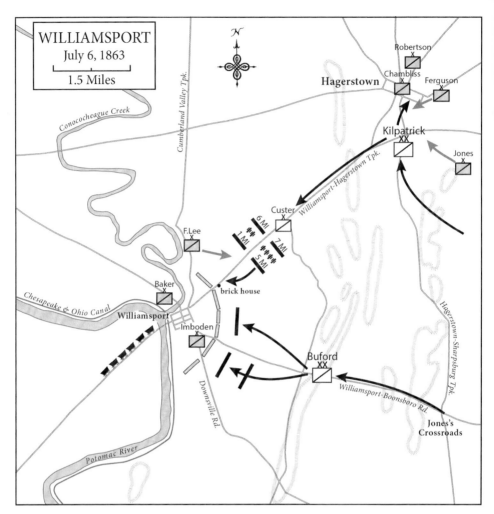

WILLIAMSPORT
July 6, 1863

1.5 Miles

N

Conococheague Creek

Cumberland Valley Tpk.

Hagerstown

Robertson
X

Chambliss
X

Ferguson
X

Kilpatrick
XX

Jones
X

Williamsport-Hagerstown Tpk.

Custer
X

6 MI.

1 MI.

7 MI.

5 MI.

F. Lee
X

Baker
X

brick house

Chesapeake & Ohio Canal

Williamsport

Imboden
X

Downsville Rd.

Buford
XX

Hagerstown-Sharpsburg Tpk.

Williamsport-Boonsboro Rd.

Jones's
Crossroads

Potomac River

Williamsport.

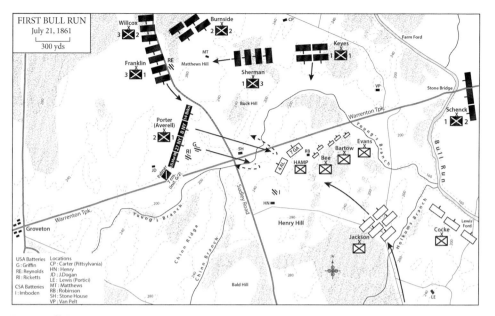

First Bull Run.

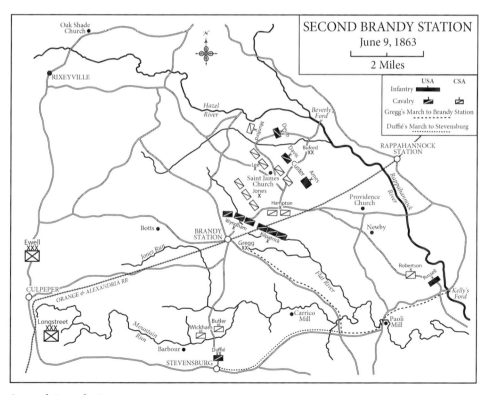

Second Brandy Station.

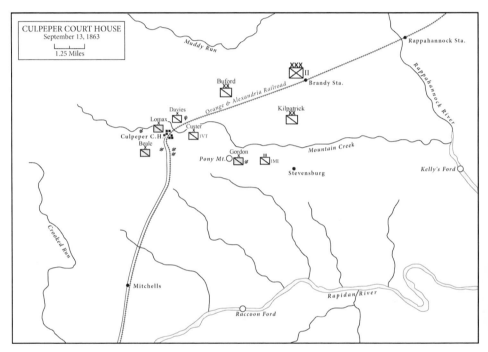

Culpeper Court House.

Joseph Fought, the teenaged bugler now serving as Custer's orderly, noted that Custer was "very careful with our defences [*sic*]. He made it a point not to depend on others in placing pickets, but saw to it himself. In consequence we were often out together at all hours of the night, and ran terrible risks."

Custer may have felt comfortable at the cavalry's forward locations, but the same was not always true of his boss. There were many in the army, including more than a few of his own officers, who viewed Pleasonton as a desk general out of his element and beyond his depth in the field. Much in the manner of McClellan, whenever possible he preferred to let his subordinates do the fighting for him. Even Private Fought, who professed to consider Pleasonton "a very active officer," admitted that he often led from the rear, "and in that respect his Trusties [aides] were more valuable to him than his brigade commanders. If Lt. Custer observed that it was important to make a movement or charge he would tell the [subordinate] commander to do it, because he knew Lt. Custer was working under Genl. Pleasonton, who would confirm every one of his instructions and movements."[5]

Over time the Custer-Pleasonton relationship would become a close one, to the point that Custer would declare that "I do not believe a father could love his son more than Genl. Pleasonton loves me. He is as solicitous about me and my safety as a mother about her only child. . . ." At other times, their relationship was of a more fraternal nature. Perhaps for obvious reasons, Custer shared with Ann Reed but withheld from Nettie Humphrey an anecdote that dramatized the personal side of his connection to his superior: "This morning I showed Fannie's photograph (the full length one) to General Pleasonton. He was much pleased with it and paid her some very high compliments. He told me to ask her for one from him and that he will send her his in return."[6]

At this time Custer forged other relationships. He told his sister that he had added to his ever-constant pack of canine companions: "I have got another dog, a hound pup about two months old." He also acquired a second attendant—a valet named Johnny Cisco. A homeless white lad who had wandered into camp looking for food and warmth, Johnny had attached himself to the lieutenant, offering to cook for him and do his laundry. He slept in Custer's tent, usually next to the puppy, and in quick time became devoted to his protector. "I think he would rather starve," Custer declared, "than see me go hungry. I have dressed him in soldiers' clothes. . . . He rides one of my horses on the march." It wasn't every staff officer who had a staff of his own, and Custer took pride in the unusual arrangement.[7]

* * *

Reports of enemy activity below the river increased in quantity and quality as result of the movement order Custer had composed on May 27, which placed all three of Pleasonton's divisions in a better position to keep tabs on the enemy to the south. As of the first week in June, however, nothing definite had been learned of Lee's intentions. Now Hooker was under pressure to do something that made him look aggressive, or at least proactive. On June 7 Fighting Joe called his cavalry chief away from his field headquarters at Warrenton Junction on the Orange & Alexandria Railroad and ordered him to prove his stated belief that Stuart, and Stuart alone, was about to go raiding. Pleasonton was ordered to locate the main body of the Confederate cavalry and pitch into it, damaging it so severely that it would not be going anywhere anytime soon. Or so Hooker recalled; Pleasonton, however, would insist that he was told to engage Stuart merely to determine the size and location of his force and, if possible, discover his intentions.[8]

The next day Pleasonton, with the help of Custer and other members of his staff, hauled his ten thousand officers and men out of their camps and headed southwest in two columns. A total of twelve pieces of horse artillery accompanied the troopers. A brigade of infantry from Meade's Fifth Corps marched in rear of each column to lend it staying-power in the unlikely event that Rebel foot soldiers were found within supporting distance of Culpeper Court House. In point of fact, Lee's Second Corps, under Lieutenant General Richard S. Ewell, successor to the recently deceased Stonewall Jackson, was in the area as was Longstreet's command, as if waiting for the Yankees to come looking for them.

Longstreet's and Ewell's presence was one facet of a remarkable, and inexcusable, breakdown of intelligence at Hooker's headquarters. Fighting Joe was unaware that fully two-thirds of Lee's infantry had departed the Fredericksburg area beginning on June 3. The few efforts Hooker had made to confirm Lee's continued presence around Fredericksburg proved inadequate. Forces under Sedgwick, sent across the river on the sixth, merely revealed that A. P. Hill's corps, which Lee had left behind to hold Hooker's attention, remained in the position it had taken up six and a half months earlier. The rest of the army had slipped away under Pleasonton's nose.[9]

Although the extent of the infantry's presence at Culpeper remained unknown to Hooker, Stuart's stationing there supposedly was well established.

The Union commander was ignorant, however, of other significant facts. Stuart, rather than planning a raid, was preparing to escort the Army of Northern Virginia to the Shenandoah, screening its advance and guarding its flanks. His troopers were scheduled to cross the river on the morning of the ninth. Hooker also lacked an accurate estimate of Stuart's strength. Having been reinforced for the coming campaign, the Confederate cavalry now numbered more than nine thousand—the odds for the coming encounter with Pleasonton had been evened. Finally, and perhaps most significantly, Stuart's men were no longer in and around Culpeper Court House; on the eighth they had moved six miles east to the fields surrounding the O & A depot of Brandy Station.[10]

Pleasonton's battle plan, such as it was, hinged on crossing the Rappahannock at two divergent points. The troops of John Buford, who had inherited Pleasonton's First Division, would cross at Beverly Ford. The Second Division of Colonel Alfred Duffié (successor to the departed Averell) and the Third Division of David M. Gregg, both under Gregg's overall command, would hit the river at Kelly's Ford, almost six miles to the southeast. The wings would meet at the depot before proceeding to Culpeper. Pleasonton had taken pains to mask the movement of his troops from Warrenton—Stuart was ignorant of his adversary's proximity, and his camps were lightly guarded. But the element of surprise is considerably diminished when an attacking force proposes to concentrate in the midst of the enemy.

In blissful ignorance of what was to come, Lieutenant Custer bedded down late on June 8 a few miles from Beverly Ford. At Pleasonton's direction he had attached himself to the column of General Buford, consisting of two brigades of volunteers led by Grimes Davis—whose grit Custer had witnessed at Barbee's Cross Roads—and Thomas C. Devin. Buford's division also included his former command, the Reserve Brigade, mostly composed of regular outfits including the 5th Cavalry; it was led by now-Major Whiting, who had been paroled and exchanged following his wounding and capture at Gaines's Mill. Attached to Buford was Captain James M. Robertson's battery of the 2nd U.S. Artillery and the infantry brigade of Brigadier General Adelbert Ames.[11]

By 10 p.m. most of the officers and men under Buford had fallen asleep on their blankets, Pleasonton among them. He had left word to be awakened at two in the morning, about two hours before the crossing at Beverly Ford was to begin. Custer, who as officer of the day was required to remain awake for another hour or two, sat on his spread-out bedroll writing what might become his last letter to his sister in Michigan.[12]

Custer knew the fighting would be sharp and long-lasting, but he was confident that the enemy would be roughly handled. If so, it would mark the first time in the war that Union forces in the Virginia theater had demonstrated superiority over their foe. They had shown promise in at least one nearby engagement. In mid-March, 2,100 troopers under William Averell, then in his heyday as a mounted leader, had attacked a smaller yet substantial number of cavalry and horse artillery under Fitz Lee, an action in which Custer's West Point comrade John Pelham fell mortally wounded. But the scale of the coming fight would dwarf Averell's limited victory at Kelly's Ford. Only then would a statement about the power and skill of the cavalry of the Army of the Potomac be made.[13]

Near the close of his letter to Ann Reed, Custer touched on a more personal note. He had left word with Pleasonton's adjutant general that should anything happen to him in the morning his trunk was to be sent to Monroe. In that event Ann should burn the letters he had sent her since entering the service to keep from public view the terms of endearment he had bestowed on certain young women and the criticisms he had leveled at various military leaders and political officials. Then, perhaps to dispel the gloom his instructions had generated, he assured his sister that "I never was in better spirits than I am at this moment." Had another soldier made this claim it might have smacked of desperate bravado, but there is no reason to doubt that Custer meant exactly what he said.[14]

*   *   *

Given the general misunderstanding of the enemy's positions, it must have come as a shock to Custer, as to thousands of his comrades, when Buford's column splashed across Beverly Ford at about 4:30 on the foggy morning of June 9 and, after snatching up the nearest pickets, found itself confronting hundreds of Rebels within two miles of the river. An equally unpleasant surprise was the crossing of Duffié and Gregg downriver at Kelly's Ford. The operation fell hours behind schedule, the result of the incompetence or treachery of a guide who shunted Duffié's division onto the wrong road. Forced to countermarch, Duffié crossed too late to lend maximum support to Buford. While he wandered astray, Gregg's men in the rear sat idle in their saddles.[15]

Unaware of the breakdown in operations, Buford's vanguard headed inland toward the camps of Brigadier General William E. Jones's "Laurel Brigade." Near the head of the blue column rode Grimes Davis and, somewhere farther back, the action-hungry Lieutenant Custer, accompanied by his faithful orderly. In violation of his stated pledge to keep his most valuable horse out of combat, he was riding a captured stallion. He supposed that the former mount of a Confederate officer was accustomed to dodging bullets, but the truth would come as a rude shock to its rider.

Davis's brigade was heading for a clearing beside an Episcopal chapel, St. James Church, where Stuart's horse artillery was parked, apparently ripe for the talking. Just before he struck the nearest Confederates the feisty colonel was heard to shout to those following him: "Stand ready, men, and begin firing as soon as you see anything!" Taken by surprise, cut off from their horses, dozens of Jones's Virginians were forced to surrender. As they were herded toward the river in the dissipating fog, comrades farther from the scene of action vaulted into the saddle and charged the invaders, arms at the ready.[16]

The opposing bodies collided with a bone-shattering crunch. As the combatants sorted themselves out, pistol and saber duels broke out in the fields around St. James Church. Not every combatant fought in the saddle; members of Davis's 8th New York, who were sent in as dismounted skirmishers, fell prey to counterattacking Confederates who rode over them, scrambling their ranks and promoting a wild rush to the rear. Hoping to stem the tide, Davis, a master swordsman, singled out a Confederate officer whose head he nearly took off with a powerful swipe. Barely duckling the blow, the Rebel bobbed up and fired a pistol ball into the colonel's skull.[17]

Supposedly, Custer was close enough to the scene to see Davis topple, mortally wounded, from his saddle. Carried to the rear on a blanket, the old regular would succumb to his wound some eight hours later. According to Fought's account of the battle, Custer brought word of Davis's fall to the nearest body of Federals, the gunners of Robertson's battery; presumably, many were shocked by the news. Fought's claim, however, appears to lack credibility. At this point Robertson's unit had yet to go into battery, and word of Davis's wounding had already spread along the firing lines, leaving few ignorant of his fate. The brigade leader's fall caused a charge by the mounted members of the 8th New York to stall and then die out, whereupon the regiment, as if entirely leaderless, began to fall back in confusion. Its withdrawal, which saved Stuart's guns from capture en masse, had a pernicious, long-range effect on Buford's command. Suddenly the entire offensive was in danger of falling apart.[18]

Thanks to the combat inexperience of his horse, Custer's role in the fighting on Buford's front appears to have been both brief and harrowing. With an unknown degree of verisimilitude, Joseph Fought would claim that on the road from Beverly Ford, he and Custer encountered enemy pickets on the edge of a woods: "We clipped along towards them, and they fired at us, and we fired back. One kept on the road, and the Lt. said I shot him, and I said he did." The other pickets disappeared, but minutes later more combative members of Jones's brigade charged out of the trees: "All at once we saw the Rebels coming in a body, full speed, and we met them in the narrow road. . . . Lt. Custer's horse and mine had never been in a fight before, and they rammed themselves into a fence and would not budge, but just stood together and neighed."

The new arrivals unleashed a hail of rifle and carbine fire at the immobile pair. Cursing, tugging at the reins, and kicking with all their might, Custer and his orderly finally got their animals turned about. They had no recourse but to head for the nearest shelter, a low stone wall across which Yankees and Rebels were firing promiscuously. Fought wrote that the two of them "put spurs to our horses at the same moment, expecting to go down at any minute. My horse took the wall, but the Lieutenant was long-legged and his horse not large, and he fell in going over, but was up again immediately."[19]

Nothing more is known of Custer's part in the battle that would become known as Second Brandy Station. As he had predicted, the fighting was uniformly fierce, the antagonists trading pistol shots and saber blows for nearly twelve hours with brief lulls in between. The battle was also disjointed and on many parts of the field chaotic and as a result indecisive. Once a flabbergasted Stuart rose to the challenge and committed Hampton's and Rooney Lee's brigades, the Federal advance was largely contained and sometimes placed in jeopardy. More than once Buford's column appeared on the brink of defeat, but it rallied each time and held on until when, around noon, Gregg's division moved into striking distance of the enemy's all-but-unguarded rear. Barely in time, Stuart wheeled about and met the attack, parrying every blow including one delivered by the brigade of Colonel (soon to be Brigadier General) Judson Kilpatrick. Meanwhile, two regiments detached from Stuart's main body neutralized the threat posed to the Confederate right flank by Duffié's timid, halting advance on Stevensburg, three miles south of Brandy Station.[20]

Critical delays, squandered opportunities, and a general lack of coordination cost Pleasonton victory and compelled him to settle for a bloody, exhausting draw. But when he finally disengaged at afternoon's end and led his horsemen and artillerists to the north side of the river, he could claim credit not only for (literally) catching Stuart sleeping but for fighting Jeb's cavaliers to a standstill on a grand scale. Lieutenant Custer could take little credit for the outcome. Even so, having emerged from the maelstrom shaken but exhilarated, he would have been content to bask in the afterglow of an imperfect triumph.

* * *

Because Pleasonton never reached his initial objective—Culpeper Court House—he came away from the battle ignorant of the full extent of Lee's presence in that vicinity. The fighting on the ninth left Stuart's cavalry in no condition to escort Ewell's and Longstreet's foot soldiers; the Rebel troopers would require almost a week to refit, reorganize, and patch the holes in their ranks before starting for the Mason-Dixon Line. But the main army would not wait for them; accompanied by some two thousand horsemen from western Virginia, Ewell's corps left Culpeper on the tenth heading for Sperryville and, beyond, the Shenandoah. Longstreet would remain behind for five days before joining the march.[21]

For three days after Ewell departed Culpeper, Pleasonton, unaware that anyone had left his front, held to his pre-battle positions on the upper bank of the Rappahannock. Not till June 13 did he receive credible reports that he had been outflanked. Even then, he was inclined to dismiss them, aware that Stuart was tied to the Brandy Station area. All doubt was swept away, however, on the fifteenth, when Hooker's headquarters received word that Ewell had attacked and overrun the major Valley outpost of Winchester. One day later came reports that Rebel forces were rampaging through southern Pennsylvania. In a belated response, an angry and embarrassed Hooker ordered the advance of his army—three corps under Major General John F. Reynolds, who had set in motion Custer's court-martial at West Point—to head north in pursuit. As soon as the rest of the army hit the roads, Hooker would transfer his headquarters to Fairfax Station, almost twenty miles from the federal capital he had been enjoined to protect at all costs.[22]

After refitting his troopers for the march—he had as many battle wounds to salve as Stuart—Pleasonton, presumably determined to make amends for his lapses at reconnaissance, prepared to locate and overtake his enemy. On the sixteenth Hooker ordered him to send his entire corps toward the village of Aldie, just north of the Bull Run Mountain chain (the command now consisted of two divisions under Buford and Gregg, Duffié's underperforming command having been broken up, its regiments assimilated into the others). Beyond Aldie lay the entrance to the Loudoun Valley, a corridor through which portions of Lee's army—now including Hill's corps as well as Stuart's refurbished division—were believed to be marching.[23]

Custer, as usual, was at the forefront of the westward movement. In the immediate aftermath of Second Brandy Station the lieutenant, while still on Pleasonton's staff, had been temporarily attached to army headquarters. The assignment put him in motion almost immediately. On the eleventh he had traveled by boat from Aquia Creek to deliver "important dispatches" from Hooker to Washington and upon his return carried orders from the War Department to the army leader. A few days later he was riding with the vanguard of Gregg's division, the brigade of his old Academy cohort Kilpatrick, as it prepared to enter the Loudoun Valley in search of Stuart's horsemen.[24]

Part of Stuart's force was found on June 17; the result was a four-hour battle that raged along two thoroughfares branching west from Aldie toward the Blue Ridge. The encounter began as a back-and-forth struggle on the lower road, the Little River Turnpike, between a squadron of Kilpatrick's 2nd New York and elements of Fitz Lee's brigade led by Colonel Thomas T. Munford. As the fighting heated up, Kilpatrick brought up and deployed the remainder of his command, unlimbered his horse artillery, and conferred with General Gregg, who had just reached the field of action.

That day Custer, as he had on many past occasions, was serving as Pleasonton's representative at the front. Prudently he had clothed himself in a way designed to disguise his rank and prevent his becoming a target for enemy sharpshooters. An observer described him as "dressed like an ordinary enlisted man, his trousers tucked in a pair of short-legged government boots, his horse equipments being those of an ordinary wagonmaster." His ensemble included a wide-brimmed straw hat in place of the usual officer's slouch hat. A Fifth Corps staff officer described him as "a singular looking fellow . . . presenting a crazy appearance, but it is only so in looks as he is a good officer, & everyone likes him."[25]

Custer's appearance suffered further when, before the shooting started, he watered his horse in the Little River, which flowed south, east, and west of Aldie. He was riding his black charger, whom he considered a stouter warrior than the battle-skittish grey. His choice of steeds came into question when Harry, after drinking, stumbled on the river bank and horse and rider pitched into the stream in full view of Gregg's staff. One officer, who joined in the guffaws of his colleagues, called the soaking-wet aide "an object that one can better imagine than I can describe."[26]

The remainder of Custer's day went much better. In mid-afternoon, Munford advanced both mounted and dismounted portions of the 5th Virginia Cavalry led by Tom Rosser, Custer's close friend at the Military Academy. The 2nd New York charged and drove in Rosser's pickets but was stopped dead when struck by a saber charge. A wild melee broke out up and down the road, claiming numerous casualties on both sides. A lull finally ended this phase of the fighting, allowing the antagonists to pull back and reorganize. Action would flare up again, continuing through the remainder of the afternoon, but most of it shifted north to the turnpike that connected Aldie with Snickersville.[27]

The struggle for control of the upper road spawned a frenetic series of charges and countercharges. Kilpatrick sent in his units piecemeal; the inevitable result was that each was halted and turned back either by enemy resistance or by the exhaustion of horses forced into one extended gallop after another. The primary victims of this uninspired strategy were several squadrons of the 1st Massachusetts, which went forward unsupported, to be cut apart by larger numbers of pistol- and saber-wielding Rebels. The latter included the larger part of Rosser's outfit, which Munford had ordered up from the lower turnpike along with another regiment and two guns of Major James Breathed's battery. Still other opponents included a phalanx of dismounted sharpshooters crouching behind stone walls on the north side of the pike.[28]

Despite the prevailing conditions, the officer who would win the unenviable sobriquet "Kill-Cavalry" continued to commit his forces one at a time, with predictable results. With sundown approaching and time for further maneuvering fleeting, his brigade had been beaten to a standstill, held short of the valley through which Gregg had ordered him to pass en route to the Potomac River at Noland's Ferry. Acutely aware that his superior was watching him closely and critically, the newly minted brigadier may have feared that his career was in jeopardy. Thus he grasped at the opportunity to commit a regiment on loan to him from the brigade of Colonel John Irvin Gregg, the division commander's cousin. Riding to the head of the just-arrived 1st Maine, Kilpatrick placed himself beside Colonel Calvin S. Douty and ordered him to charge the Rebels who continued to block the Snickersville Pike: members of Colonel Thomas Owen's 3rd Virginia, supported on either flank by portions of two other regiments including Rosser's.[29]

Another West Pointer was poised to enter the fight. For the past three hours, Custer had been a rapt observer of the succession of attack and counterattack that had swept both turnpikes. No longer able to curb his urge to be involved, he had broken from the rearward gaggle of staff officers to accompany Kilpatrick to the head of Douty's column. When the Mainers started forward the lieutenant dug his spurs into Harry's flanks and flew along with them. Minutes before, Munford, in response to an order from Stuart's headquarters inside Loudoun Valley, had begun to withdraw his brigade. Now, seeing the Federals rushing toward him, he halted the movement and prepared to meet the threat.[30]

Swept up in the fury of the charge, Custer was heard to shout to those around him, "Come on boys!" He punctuated his entreaty by holding aloft a straight blade of Toledo steel that he had seized the previous summer after claiming his first victim in close-up combat. Supposedly the weapon was so heavy that, according to Frederick Whittaker, "hardly an arm in the service could be found strong enough to wield that blade, save Custer's alone." The blade carried an inscription in Spanish that warned its bearer never to draw it without provocation or to sheathe it without honor, a sentiment Custer embraced.[31]

Mere seconds after the charge began the opposing forces slammed together in the narrow road. Horses and riders congealed into a giant tangle, many tumbling to the ground in heaps large and small. Most of those who maintained their seat halted to shoot and swipe at one another, while others plowed ahead in an effort to penetrate the enemy's ranks and gain his rear. Custer unexpectedly found himself among the latter group. Unnerved, Custer's mount suddenly bolted, carrying his powerless owner at breakneck speed through the ranks of Munford's Virginians.

Custer must have expected that at any second and without warning he would be unhorsed by pistol ball or saber thrust. He could not believe his good fortune when no gray-jacketed horseman paid attention to him. In a letter written eight days after the battle he informed Ann Reed that "I was surrounded by rebels, and cut off from my own men, but I made my way out safely but I made my way out safely. . . . The rebels at first thought I was one of their own men, and did not attack me, except one, who rushed at me with his saber, but I struck him across the face with my saber, knocking him off his horse. I then put spurs to 'Harry' and made my escape." As he did so, Confederates turned around by Douty's attack streamed past him. On the way back to his own lines the fortunate horseman made a prisoner of a second antagonist, who, having been sent sprawling by Custer's hefty sword, "was glad to surrender and be taken in."[32]

Custer's gyrations and miraculous escape were witnessed by members of the 1st Maine, and word of it got back to Kilpatrick, Gregg, and their staffs. If he had been looking to make an impression on those who could promote a soldier's career, he seems to have achieved his purpose. Correspondent E. A. Paul of the *New York Times* mentioned Custer's participation in the charge on the Snickersville Pike although without providing the overly dramatic and highly implausible details contained in Whittaker's biography and other contemporary sources. Michigan newspapers, including the *Monroe Commercial*, picked up the story and gave it fuller coverage. The Northern press also lauded the Federal cavalry as a body for again demonstrating its ability to give Stuart all he could handle, though at a heavy cost: more than three hundred casualties including Colonel Douty, who had fallen to sharpshooter fire, as against 119 Confederate losses.[33]

Over time, Custer's wild ride would be deemed so improbable that historians would consider it the stuff of fiction. However, a member of Meade's staff, an officer not closely acquainted with Custer and therefore not disposed to inflate his reputation, corroborated his colleague's account in a letter to his wife two weeks after Aldie. Custer, the captain told his wife, "got into the rebel lines during the last fight. They mistook him for one of their own men, and to get out he charged with the rebels upon our troops, & when he got close to our lines turned round & whacked two rebels over the head. At least that is the story I heard." And that story, thanks to its wide and timely circulation, would reshape the military career of George Armstrong Custer.[34]

* * *

In his post-Aldie letter to his sister Custer had remarked that "General Pleasonton has been promoted to be a major-general. This will make me a captain again." It was true that as his superior rose, so too would he, but he could not have imagined how high.[35]

Alfred Pleasonton had his share of deficiencies and he was not well-regarded by many of his officers. A cavalry surgeon, commenting on Pleasonton's succession to Stoneman's position, pronounced him "about as fit for it as any 2nd Leutenant [*sic*] in the command." Another critic was Captain Charles F. Adams, Jr., of the 1st Massachusetts. Pleasonton had battled Stuart's to a standstill at Brandy Station, an outcome that stoked the pride and confidence of almost every trooper involved while bringing down Southern ire on Stuart. Still, "a good cavalry officer would have whipped Stuart out of his boots, but Pleasonton is not and never will be that." One of the general's most notable faults was his never-ending quest for publicity. Adams called him "pure and simple a newspaper humbug."[36]

But Pleasonton had his supporters too—many in high places—and he cultivated them assiduously. One was John Franklin Farnsworth, who for fourteen months prior to his recent election to the U.S. House of Representatives had been a brigade leader under Stoneman and Pleasonton. As a friend and supporter of fellow Illinois Republican Abraham Lincoln, Farnsworth was in a position to grant important favors. To further this connection Pleasonton had recently added to his staff the congressman's nephew, Captain Elon J. Farnsworth. Now he induced the young officer to press his relative for help in securing Pleasonton's promotion. Unaware of the governor's feelings toward Custer, Pleasonton may have placed Custer on his staff in hopes of currying favor with Austin Blair. Perhaps for this same reason he had granted Custer's wish that a friend from Monroe, Lieutenant George W. Yates of the 4th Michigan Infantry, likewise join the cavalry corps staff (later another Monroe native, Henry Christiancy's nineteen-year-old brother Jim, would gain a staff position under Custer).[37]

Pleasonton had his eyes on two prizes. One was a second star, the other command of the cavalry attached to the Washington defenses. The addition of Major General Julius Stahel's division, some 3,600 horsemen, would enlarge his command—now the smallest corps in the army—to a size that might support his quest to obtain the major generalship that had not accompanied his promotion. Pleasonton, who believed that "in every instance" foreign-born officers "have injured our cause," detested the German-speaking Hungarian who outranked him, insisting that "I will not *fight* under the order of a *Dutchman*."[38]

In some respects Pleasonton appeared deserving of promotion and not only because corps command usually came with two stars. Not only had his troopers fought well at Aldie, holding the field at day's end, but over the next four days they had given a generally strong account of themselves in two engagements inside the Loudoun Valley at Middleburg and Upperville (no details of Custer's participation in either battle are available). However, not until late on June 21 did Pleasonton, via a reconnaissance of Ashby's Gap in the Blue Ridge, discover that at least two of Lee's infantry corps were in the Shenandoah Valley within reach of Pennsylvania. He relayed this intelligence—which he should have acquired days earlier—to Hooker, but not until the twenty-fifth did the army begin crossing the Potomac River into Maryland.[39]

Hooker's lethargy and seeming lack of interest in protecting Pennsylvania and Washington, added to his unstable performance at Chancellorsville, had put him in a bad light at the White House and the War Department. On June 27, after Halleck refused Hooker's petulant demand for additional troops, the army commander tendered his resignation. Lincoln accepted it, replacing him with the army's most available corps commander, George Meade. Pleasonton may have feared that given his lackluster record as an intelligence officer he too was headed into retirement. Instead, the shakeup at army headquarters left him standing, even rising. On the twenty-eighth he received word of his promotion to major general. That same day Stahel's cavalry was absorbed into the Army of the Potomac and its commander was banished to Pennsylvania to lead a small mounted force in defending the state.[40]

The ousted division leader appears to have been more resourceful and proactive than the man who replaced him. Shortly before he was decapitated Stahel had dispatched most of his horsemen into areas recently occupied by Lee's army. On the twenty-eighth the 5th and 6th Michigan, led by General Copeland, crossed the Mason-Dixon Line and entered the Adams County seat of Gettysburg. Two days earlier the village had played unwilling host to a brigade of Ewell's infantry and a battalion of hard-bitten cavalrymen. The locals had been terrorized by the invaders, who the following day departed for points east, carrying off much booty. Copeland commiserated with the residents, but after gathering as much information as he could he pulled out of town and headed southwest to rejoin Stahel.

En route to Emmitsburg, Maryland, Copeland was overtaken by a courier from Meade's headquarters. The man brought word that Stahel had been removed from command and his troopers assigned to Pleasonton. Copeland was informed that he, too, was out of a job. Shocked and infuriated, the brigadier immediately sought out the man behind the action. Pleasonton told him that he regretted having to relieve Copeland but insisted that as ranking officer of cavalry operating in Virginia he had the right to name his subordinates. He had decided to replace Copeland with a talented and energetic officer well known to him: Brigadier General George Armstrong Custer.[41]

* * *

It appears that shortly before Pleasonton received his second star Custer had an inkling that he would be the beneficiary of his superior's good fortune, though whether he expected a star of his own is doubtful. His hopes rose dramatically on the twenty-eighth, when Pleasonton, returning from his first conference with the new army leader, informed Custer that Meade had approved several of his recommendations for reorganizing the cavalry corps including the promoting of deserving subordinates.

Trained as a topographical engineer and in command of infantry since August 1861, Meade had a limited knowledge of cavalry's organizational needs and even less of an appreciation of its value except as a reconnaissance arm. Having been handed command of an army with which he was largely unfamiliar and perhaps only days from battling the invaders of his home state, he was entirely willing to allow the commander of one of his corps to make staff assignments. As Pleasonton recalled the meeting, Meade "acknowledged his ignorance with regard to the army in general, and said he would be obliged to depend a great deal upon me to assist him."

Taking the cue, Pleasonton called his superior's attention to Stahel's cavalry, "which he might place under my command, and [if so] I would like to have officers I would name specially assigned to it, as I expected to have some desperate work to do. The general assented to my request, and upon my naming the officers, he immediately telegraphed to have them appointed brigadier generals." This action, Meade informed an undoubtedly surprised General Halleck, was deemed necessary "to organize with efficiency the cav'lry force now with this army." Along with Custer, Elon Farnsworth and Captain Wesley Merritt of the 2nd U.S. Cavalry suddenly became general officers, their appointments dating from June 29.[42]

Whether or not he had received advance word of his promotion, Custer claimed to be shocked by it, as he undoubtedly was once the enormity of it finally sank in. With a single stroke of a War Department functionary's pen, Custer had become, at twenty-three, the youngest general officer in the army. One imagines that he could barely contain his excitement—perhaps to the point of being tempted to violate his sobriety pledge. On the day his promotion came through an officer at Pleasonton's headquarters telegraphed a quartermaster making a supply run up north: "The Gen'l Comd'g directs that you hurry back as we most probably move tomorrow. Custer & Farnsworth are Brigadiers & wish you to christen the star in four (4) five (5) gallon kegs of best whiskey."[43]

Custer would later describe his reaction to his good fortune in a letter to Isaac Christiancy. A month had passed since the promotion was announced and he could report objectively on the emotions he had experienced and the aspirations that underlay his quest for higher rank. "I was never more surprised," he declared, "than when I was informed of my appointment. . . . It was a position I had never in the faintest measure asked for. I will be candid enough to admit that my ambition long since caused me to hope in course of time to render me worthy of a 'star.' "

He recounted how the news was broached to him upon Pleasonton's return from Meade's side around 3 p.m. on the twenty-eighth. Custer, suspecting nothing, had been called to the room the cavalry commander was occupying in the City Hotel in Frederick, Maryland. There he was informed that "the Cavalry was to set out next day in search of the rebel army and leaders were needed," and that his appointment had been recommended to the War Department. He remembered almost wishing that the news had been withheld from him because his age, rank, and lack of a "friend at court" militated against its acceptance, thus dashing his hopes.[44]

But six hours later a telegram from Washington confirmed the appointment and ordered Custer, along with Farnsworth and Merritt, to report for duty at their new rank. That night the other recipients of Pleasonton's patronage paid their respects. The cavalry chief would recall how Merritt, tears in his eyes, thanked him effusively for assigning him to lead the Reserve Brigade under John Buford, his long-time superior and mentor in the 2nd Dragoons.[45]

Even before the appointments were confirmed, Pleasonton, accompanied by Custer, rode out to meet and inspect Stahel's troopers at Richfield, a vast tract of land three and a half miles north of Frederick. The force on hand included only two of the four regiments Custer would command, the 1st and 7th Michigan. A trooper of the 1st would note in his diary that "Gen Custer is from Monroe Michigan. He is [of] light complexion has blue eyes & yellow hair which rests in ringlets on his shoulders. He is about five feet eight inches high & by profession a soldier. We call him the boy General of the Golden Lock[s]." Other Wolverines had a more imperfect knowledge of their leader. A member of the 7th Michigan referred to him in a letter home as "General Custerd."[46]

According to Custer, Pleasonton spent that night and the next morning planning the reorganization of the corps. He transferred each of Stahel's regiments into his new Third Division and appointed Kilpatrick, the senior brigade leader, to lead it. The division, to consist of two brigades, would be the smallest in the corps; Buford's and Gregg's each comprised three brigades. Farnsworth and Custer, respectively, were assigned to head the new commands. Farnsworth took charge of four regiments from New York, Pennsylvania, Vermont, and West Virginia, while Custer received command of the regiments that had served under Copeland, plus one other. As he informed Judge Christiancy, during his meeting with Pleasonton on the twenty-eighth Custer stated "that I had but one request to make which was to assign me to the command of the Michigan brigade adding to it the 1st Mich Cav. which had previously been attached to another brigade."[47]

Historians appear skeptical of some of the claims Custer made in his letter to the judge, but if this is how the Wolverine Brigade was enlarged, the inclusion of Colonel Charles H. Town's 1st Michigan, a veteran of one battle and many skirmishes since reaching Virginia in December 1861, was a smart move. It marked a propitious start to the career of a young general who probably slept no longer that night than the officer who had enabled him to realize his loftiest ambitions.[48]

*   *   *

One day after his promotion was confirmed, Custer was sized up by Captain James H. Kidd of the 6th Michigan as his regiment prepared to enter battle on the outskirts of Hanover, Pennsylvania. It was a meeting the details of which Kidd would never forget. "Looking at him closely, this is what I saw: An officer superbly mounted who sat his charger as if to the manor born. Tall, lithe, active, muscular, straight as an Indian and as quick in his movements, he had the fair complexion of a school girl. He was clad in a suit of black velvet, elaborately trimmed with gold lace, which ran down the outer seams of his trousers, and almost covered the sleeves of his cavalry jacket. The wide collar of a blue navy shirt was turned down over the collar of his velvet jacket, and a necktie of brilliant crimson was tied in a graceful knot at the throat. . . ." The garish ensemble was completed with "a soft, black hat with wide brim adorned with gilt cord, and rosette encircling a silver star . . . worn turned down on one side giving him a rakish air."[49]

Where Custer came up with the idea for this costume, which made him look, as other observers wrote, like a "popinjay" or "a circus rider gone mad," is unknown. Elements of it may have been procured by Private Fought, the shirt supposedly acquired through the generosity of a crewman on a warship. It has been suggested that Custer's choice of apparel was inspired by his nattily attired superior, but Pleasonton's tastes never went to such extremes.[50]

Custer had reached Hanover from Frederick, which he departed late on the rainy morning of the twenty-ninth when seeking the balance of his far-flung command. In response to orders, he led Town's 1st and William Mann's 7th Michigan to Emmitsburg, twenty-one miles north of Frederick and just below the Pennsylvania line. By 11 p.m. both regiments had crossed the border, bivouacking outside the village of Littlestown, where they found Kilpatrick and Farnsworth. Here Custer introduced himself to his newly acquired subordinates and began to assemble a staff, one mainly composed of friends from Monroe. Here too he renewed acquaintances not only with Kilpatrick but also with Alexander Pennington, whose battery of six three-inch rifled cannons had been assigned to Custer, much to the latter's delight.[51]

The 5th and 6th Michigan, having been detached from the brigade to scout farther south, were still in Maryland; they would not join Custer to complete the composition of the 2nd Brigade, Third Cavalry Division—some 2,300 officers and men—until after Kilpatrick's command reached its next objective, Hanover, shortly after noon on the thirtieth. The men of Town and Mann were riding at the head of the elongated column, followed by Pennington's battery and the division's trains with Farnsworth's brigade bringing up the rear, when a full-fledged battle broke out south of town, the 1st Brigade being suddenly attacked by Confederate cavalry. By now Custer's regiments had left Hanover heading north, having spent several hours in the town while their leader and his superior conferred with local citizens as to reported enemy movements. As soon as the shooting reached his ears, Kilpatrick, at the head of the column, ordered Custer to countermarch. Then he rode back to Hanover at a pace so furious it killed his horse.[52]

Farnsworth's command had been struck by the vanguard of a three-brigade raiding force under Jeb Stuart. One week earlier, as Robert E. Lee prepared to enter lower Pennsylvania in full force, he had approved Stuart's request to cut loose from the army and raid behind enemy lines, destroying Union communications and confiscating foodstuffs and supplies from the provision-rich Yankee countryside. Stuart had intended to reunite with Lee somewhere in the vicinity of York, Pennsylvania, but a series of unexpected encounters with Federal forces had caused him to detour so far to the east that his rendezvous with the army was long overdue. To worsen matters, Stuart, when near Rockville, Maryland, had delayed long enough to capture and assimilate a 125-wagon supply train bound for the Army of the Potomac. The drag caused by this prize of war further impeded his progress. At Hanover he would be delayed again, with further damage to his timetable.[53]

Farnsworth's attackers were members of a Virginia and North Carolina brigade assigned to Rooney Lee, who had been disabled by a wound at Brandy Station. Now led by Colonel James R. Chambliss, the brigade had marched up the road from Westminster, Maryland. Some distance behind Chambliss, both on and to the west of that road, the all-Virginia brigade of Fitz Lee was also approaching Hanover. A six-gun battery of horse artillery supported the newcomers. The brigade of Wade Hampton, Stuart's senior lieutenant, was stationed well to the rear of the column, separated from the main force by the raiders' supply train and the wagons captured at Rockville.[54]

The first phase of the fighting at Hanover did not directly involve Custer, whose 1st and 7th Michigan did not return to Hanover until Farnsworth and Chambliss had engaged in a heated battle for control of the town, neither side gaining a decisive advantage. Meanwhile, the estranged 5th and 6th Michigan spent the early afternoon in a fight for survival independent of the combat inside the town. At perhaps 1 p.m., Colonel Gray's regiment, approaching Hanover via the Littlestown Road, also encountered elements of Chambliss's brigade. Opposed by a force four times his size, Gray rapidly shifted westward, only to run into Fitz Lee's 1st Virginia Cavalry, the most storied mounted regiment in Confederate service. Again badly outnumbered, the 6th was forced into a fighting retreat by the left flank. Thanks largely to a staunch rear-guard action by two companies under Major Peter A. Weber, the regiment avoided encirclement.[55]

Numerous troopers were cut off during the withdrawal and captured; others fled back down the road to Littlestown. Many were rescued by comrades in the 5th Michigan, just then arriving from the lower village. The 5th had delayed its move from Littlestown until Meade's Twelfth Corps drew within marching distance of the town, thus establishing a communications link between the main army and its forward echelon. Colonel Alger's regiment was the largest in the brigade—more than seven hundred strong—and its men were armed with state-of-the-art weaponry, seven-shot Spencer repeating rifles. Fighting afoot, they were more than a match for Fitz Lee's men, who eventually withdrew closer to Hanover. Then Alger's people remounted and joined the 6th Michigan in shifting west. By noon both outfits had reached the outskirts of Hanover.[56]

When Custer returned to the town in the wake of Stuart's attack, he established his headquarters in a house on Frederick Street. Later he conferred with Kilpatrick at the latter's headquarters in the Central Hotel; later still he joined Kilpatrick in observing the fighting from the steeple of a church on Chestnut

Street. Initially, Custer had only the 1st and the two-battalion 7th Michigan at his disposal. With little maneuvering room available in the heart of town, he held both regiments north of it. He made his first dispositions as a brigade commander by advancing four companies of the 7th under Lieutenant Colonel Allyne C. Litchfield to the northwest boundary of Hanover, while deploying the rest of the regiment and the entire 1st Michigan to guard Pennington's guns, which unlimbered atop an elevation, Bunker Hill, about a quarter-mile northwest of Hanover's Centre Square.

Upon the arrival of the 5th and 6th Regiments, Custer rode to meet them and direct their operations. His hurried introduction to Colonel Gray would have been a perfunctory affair, but one wonders how cordially he was greeted by the commander of the 5th Michigan. Russell Alger must have believed that Custer's promotion should have been his own. Then there were those thirty-three subalterns who had strenuously objected to his affiliation with the regiment. They were not alone in their objections. Joseph Fought claimed that every officer in the brigade, at least initially, was "exceedingly jealous of him. Not one of them but would have thrown a stone in his way to make him lose his prestige." According to Frederick Whittaker, Custer was acutely conscious that "his subordinates disliked, suspected, and distrusted him." To counter this attitude he affected an "abrupt and distant manner" by which he "made himself felt as master from the first hour."[57]

While Fought and Whittaker probably exaggerated the prevailing attitude, it was true that not everyone in the corps approved of Custer's elevation. J. Irvin Gregg, for one, claimed that the promotions of Custer, Farnsworth, and Merritt were not welcomed "by th[os]e most favorably disposed" to the three officers. He singled out "Lieut Custer [who] had never commanded even a squadron in the field."[58]

Jealous or not, Custer's subordinates listened when he spoke. At his order, relayed from Kilpatrick, James Kidd accompanied some 350 dismounted men of the 6th Michigan in advancing beyond the tracks of the Littlestown-Gettysburg Railroad. The detachment then crossed the Littlestown Road, topped a low ridge, and thrashed through farm fields toward Chambliss's Virginians and Carolinians. Thanks to the close support they received from the gunners of Pennington and Lieutenant Samuel S. Elder's Battery E, 4th U.S. Artillery, attached to Farnsworth's brigade, as well as to the power of their own arms—four companies carried Spencers, other men easily reloadable single-shot carbines—the Wolverines pressed back the Confederates and held them in check. Stuart's men had never encountered so much firepower; the effect must have been unnerving.[59]

After an hour or more of skirmishing, Custer withdrew Gray's men to the line of the railroad just west of town. The operation, which was conducted in good order, concluded the major portion of the day's fighting; for the next few hours, the opposing artilleries dominated the fighting. Pennington's and Elder's gunners gave better than they received from the ammunition-poor Confederates. Eventually, the latter ceased firing, limbered up, and passed to the rear, enabling the Federal cannoneers to occupy Centre Square.

Custer's decision to send a single regiment against a full brigade with a second enemy brigade within supporting range may have courted disaster, but neither Chambliss nor Lee launched a major counterattack. By now Stuart had decided he could not fight his way through Hanover to gain a northward-running road on which to hunt for Lee. Early in the evening, he directed Fitz Lee to assume control of the captured wagons while Hampton's brigade deployed to guard the rear. Soon every Confederate was pulling up stakes and heading east toward the town of Jefferson, from there to turn north in the direction of Dover and Carlisle.[60]

Both Kilpatrick and Stuart claimed success at Hanover; each was probably entitled to do so for the fighting had been, in the end, a stalemate. On the Union's front, however, the Michigan Brigade had done a better job of holding off its enemy, maintaining cohesion, and escaping from tight corners than the troopers under Farnsworth, some of whom had fled in panic when first attacked although comrades stabilized and maintained the brigade's position through the balance of the fighting.

Custer himself could take only so much credit for his tactical decision-making in this, his first battle in command. Most of the fighting had occurred before the 5th and 6th Michigan came under his direction. Even so, he had comported himself well, working in close cooperation with officers with whom he was unfamiliar, many of them, perhaps, hostile to him. Throughout the fight he had maintained a businesslike manner and a cool head, issuing orders, as James Kidd wrote, "in clear, resonant tones, and in a calm and confident manner, at once resolute and reassuring." Such qualities boded well for General Custer's future and that of the soon-to-be-reckoned-with Michigan Cavalry Brigade.[61]

Chapter IX

Charge, and Charge Again

After the Confederates pulled out of Hanover, their route should have been easy enough to follow. Instead, Judson Kilpatrick, channeling Alfred Pleasonton's abilities at intelligence collecting, lost track of his enemy. He spent the morning of July 1 dispatching patrols in various directions seeking Stuart but without success. During this time Custer, Farnsworth, and their subordinates tended to their battle-worn commands. Custer's regimental commanders would report relatively few casualties as result of the fighting, but they included a number of wounded men who would die over the next few days or weeks. The evening of July 1 these men were tended to along with some wounded and captured Confederates. Recently dismounted troopers scoured the region for remounts, confiscating animals from almost every citizen including the pastor of a local church.

Not until 2 p.m. did Kilpatrick assemble his regiments and lead them north to Abbottstown, all the way seizing supplies. Custer's troopers, many of whom briefly bivouacked on farmland along the road to York, were particularly active in confiscating fodder. The 6th Michigan carried off four tons of newly cut hay piled in one farmer's field; other Wolverines seized a dozen bushels of corn from his barn. Custer ensured that the brigade's quartermasters distributed receipts for the appropriated goods, though whether the vouchers were honored is uncertain.[1]

These efforts helped restore the strength of men and horses weakened by hard marching and hard fighting, but they did not appear to serve the needs of Union strategy. Custer had never forged a close relationship with Kilpatrick despite the several occasions on which they had been thrown together. He may have questioned his division commander's performance at Hanover, where Kilpatrick had exercised minimal influence on Custer's part of the field. He would have faulted Kilpatrick's inability to keep tabs on Stuart following the battle. And when he learned that Kilpatrick, late on the thirtieth, reported to

Pleasonton that Robert E. Lee's army was in East Berlin, almost forty miles from his actual headquarters at Chambersburg, he would have felt utterly disgusted.[2]

In the broader scheme of things, it was fortunate that Kill-Cavalry failed to locate Stuart's whereabouts after Hanover, for if he had he undoubtedly would have followed, intent on renewing combat. Such a reaction would have led him astray, for his primary mission was to screen the Union forces in upper Maryland and lower Pennsylvania and gather intelligence on the movements of Lee's infantry. Chasing down Stuart, who was obviously raiding far afield of his army, would have helped George Meade little or not at all.

Because he did not pursue Stuart, early on the morning of July 2, when Kilpatrick learned that a major battle was in progress at Gettysburg, the Third Division was in position to contribute to the fighting relatively quickly. Turning in that direction, Kilpatrick's column, with Farnsworth's brigade in the van, moved toward the steadily growing thump of cannon fire. By 2 p.m. the division was near Gulden's Station on the Hanover-Gettysburg Railroad, about four miles from the battlefield and the far right flank of Meade's army. There Kilpatrick was met by a courier from Pleasonton who escorted him to the field headquarters of David Gregg. The latter's Second Cavalry Division had reached the fringes of the battlefield about three hours earlier after a debilitating march from Westminster and Hanover and had taken up a position astride the intersection of the Hanover and Low Dutch (or Salem Church) Roads.[3]

Kilpatrick reported to Gregg, his superior on the basis of seniority, and through him received orders to turn his column about, move over to the road from Abbottstown to Gettysburg, "and see that the enemy did not turn our flank." The instructions came from Pleasonton, whose headquarters adjoined Meade's. The latter, who viewed Pleasonton as a glorified staff officer, was intent on keeping him pinned to the main army. Instead of taking an active role in managing the operations of his far-flung brigades and divisions (a role that did not seem to match his talents), Pleasonton was forced to keep abreast of their movements through aides and couriers whom he sent galloping all over the combat zone. On the thirtieth one of these, Lieutenant Colonel Andrew J. Alexander, had been in Littlestown, close enough to the fighting at Hanover to receive reports from Kilpatrick and gather reinforcements for him.[4]

When Kilpatrick's column countermarched up the York Pike, Custer's brigade took the lead. Close to 4 p.m., the Wolverines turned left onto a narrow lane that led, two miles farther on, to the village of Hunterstown. Around 4:30

Custer's lead regiment, the 6th Michigan, entered the place, which it found occupied by a small force of gray-clad riders, a fragment of the rear guard of Wade Hampton's brigade. Strictly by happenstance, Kilpatrick had found the enemy that had slipped away from him forty-eight hours earlier.

Hampton had been in the area, guarding the five roads that emanated from Hunterstown, since early morning. The South Carolinian was now bringing up the rear of Stuart's column, keeping close watch over the divisional supply train and the long line of vehicles stolen from Joe Hooker's quartermasters. Stuart, who after leaving Hanover wandered to Carlisle, fifteen miles north of Gettysburg, had received word from a scout just after midnight that he was needed immediately on the field of battle. Stuart marched there forthwith with Lee's and Chambliss's men. He was about to send back for Hampton and the wagons when Custer's men appeared on the scene.[5]

With Kilpatrick and Farnsworth some distance to the rear, it was Custer's job to deal with the Rebels south of Hunterstown. He had Gray's men drive the nearest pickets from the village square, past the local hostelry, the Grass Hotel, down the fence-lined road to Gettysburg, and toward Hampton's main body. It is not known whether Custer identified the displaced troopers as members of Cobb's Georgia Legion, a regimental-sized unit commanded by his West Point classmate and friendly debate opponent, Pierce M. B. Young.[6]

Custer accompanied the 6th Michigan to a point a few hundred yards below the village. He halted the outfit atop a ridge that offered a good view of Hampton's position. Through his field glasses he spied a line of mounted Confederates blocking his path and dismounted sharpshooters deployed on either side of the road, huddling behind the fences. Not far below the road-block the bulk of Hampton's brigade, seventeen hundred strong, was waiting to provide a warm reception to any Yankees who ventured its way.[6]

A more experienced leader would have viewed the situation as a trap waiting to spring. Though he justified his next move as a means of clearing ground for the placement of Pennington's battery, which was trundling along in the middle of the brigade column and thus several minutes from Hunterstown, Custer saw an opportunity to display his brigade's strength and resolve. He turned to Captain Henry E. Thompson, commander of Company A of the 6th, and told him to charge the mounted Rebels, sharpshooters be damned. Custer's credo, which he would spell out in a letter to Nettie Humphrey, guided him now: having decided on a course, however perilous and uncertain, "I allow nothing to swerve me from my purpose."

He was quickly learning, but as yet he lacked the ability, so necessary in a commander, to send other men into danger while he remained behind. According to Frederick Whittaker, just before it started forward, the black-clad Custer "dashed out in front of Co. A with the careless laughing remark, 'I'll lead you this time, boys. Come on!'" And off he went at a gallop, Thompson's fifty-some men close behind. To some extent their way was paved by the dismounted carbineers of the 6th—three companies' worth—deployed on the west side of the road, and on the opposite flank a larger detachment of the 7th Michigan, also fighting afoot.[7]

Captain Thompson was a fighter—two days before he and his company had provided strong support to Alger's regiment when the latter fought to escape envelopment south of Hanover. Even he, however, could not hope to penetrate deeply into a force the size of the one he was attacking. A few yards from the farmhouse of John Gilbert, Thompson's front rank slammed into the stationary riders in the road. The collision sent men and horses sprawling; others went down when caught in the flanking fire of dismounted riflemen. "It was a great wonder that we was not all killed," wrote a semi-literate member of Company A.[8]

Those who remained in the saddle blasted away at one another, but most of the Federals continued south at an only slightly reduced speed, evicted Confederates fleeing before then. Pierce Young, the rear guard commander, galloped south with his men but only until reaching the main body of his outfit—four companies' strong—just south of the Gilbert farm. At his shouted command, the Cobb Legion launched a countercharge that rocked Thompson's men and slowly drove them back up the road in a whirlpool of shooting and hacking.

Heavy casualties on both sides were inevitable, especially due to the enfilading fire. Among the most notable, Thompson suffered a pistol wound in the arm that would render him unfit for active duty for almost three months. Three major combatants had their horses shot from under them, including Young, who escaped serious injury, and Lieutenant S. H. Ballard of Thompson's company, who was lifted from the ground by his enemy and made prisoner. Another who flew from the saddle of a downed horse was George Custer. Slammed to the ground, he lay dazed by the fall while a Confederate trooper advanced on him, intending to kill or capture an easily identifiable general officer.[9]

Custer was saved from either of these undesirable fates when Private Norvill F. Churchill of Company L of the 1st Michigan came to his aid. Churchill's regiment, which had traveled to Hunterstown in the approximate middle of the brigade column, had just reached the field, and the twenty-three-year-old trooper was in the right place at the right time to play the role of hero. Without thinking twice, he galloped to Custer's side, helped him mount behind him, and raced back up the road to safety amid a rain of rifle bullets.[10]

Custer probably never saw the battle's denouement. The victorious Georgians chased Thompson's survivors back to the starting point of their charge, only to be cut up in turn by members of the 6th Michigan, firing through the door and windows of John Felty's barn. One of Pennington's sections was now in position farther north, the 1st and 7th Michigan were bracing Custer's eastern flank, and Farnsworth's brigade was deploying on the other side of the road to lend additional assistance. The combined might of cannon- and carbine-fire forced the attackers to halt and then withdraw minus numerous men and horses felled by a crossfire every bit as deadly as the one that had ambushed Custer and Thompson.[11]

By now, evening was fast approaching. Visibility fading, the artillery forces, as they had at Hanover, were called on to complete a hard-fought engagement that ended as a tactical standoff. In salvaging the draw, Custer's brigade had suffered thirty-two officers and men killed, wounded, or missing, most of the casualties coming, not surprisingly, from Company A. One more name might have been—perhaps should have been—added to the list of killed or captured, but thanks to the courage and quick thinking of an otherwise unremarkable young cavalryman, Custer's luck continued to hold.[12]

* * *

Although smarting from his dive over the head of his wounded horse—the consequences of impacting hard ground would have been felt for hours, if not days—Custer was heartened by the day's results, believing he had displayed the dash, savvy, and grit his men expected of their leader, even one as young and untried as he. Under his direction, the Wolverines had proved a match for the vaunted cavaliers of Stuart. They had stymied a substantial portion of Hampton's brigade, and the casualties they had absorbed indicated that the fighting had been extensive and consequential.[13]

Officially, Custer had not been in command at Hunterstown. Judson Kilpatrick had been there, too, although leading from the rear. While the results of the encounter with Hampton had been mixed, Custer was confident that he had won his superior's approval of what had transpired. To be sure, his tactics had not been especially inspired. But Kilpatrick, who had a reputation for favoring an offensive in almost every situation, had been impressed. In his report of the campaign he would declare that the Second Cavalry Brigade had "fought most handsomely," while bestowing particular praise on those units that had supported Custer the most, Gray's Michiganders and Pennington's regulars.[14]

Kilpatrick's approval would have been sweet news to Custer; he wished their relationship to be a cordial one, regardless of his opinion of the man's ability as a tactician and intelligence gatherer. Custer was very much aware that he had something to prove. Kilpatrick may have had reasons for questioning his fitness to command a brigade, or even win a commission. The suspicion may have dated from their West Point association. Then, too, the fact that Custer, despite his lowly status at war's start, had gone on to a remarkable career—one virtually unique in the annals of the American military—could not have pleased his division leader, who believed he had risen to the top on merits that his subordinate lacked. Whatever its source and despite Custer's best efforts, over time their collaboration would be fraught with competitiveness, distrust, and even suspicion.

Not long after leading his brigade out of Hunterstown, Custer for the first time found himself in his superior's bad graces. This was not his fault; he was following orders from higher headquarters—but the move displeased Kilpatrick because it did not originate with him. Moreover, it would deprive him of half of his command at a critical time, when hastening to join in the major fighting at to the west.

A dispatch from Pleasonton, received late on July 2, called on Kilpatrick to reach the field of battle via Two Taverns, a hamlet athwart the Baltimore Pike midway between Gettysburg and Littlestown. The Third Cavalry Division made the journey in good order, trotting seven miles south from Hunterstown in the early evening. The route of march would place Kilpatrick in position to guard the left flank and rear of the main army against multiple threats including attempts by Stuart to strike from that direction.[15]

Custer's command, which led the march, experienced little opposition as it wound down the narrow country roads in stop-start fashion. To its rear, however, Farnsworth's brigade fended off intermittent strikes from some of Hampton's troopers who had been assigned to monitor the Yankee withdrawal. The column crossed the York Pike, then the road from Hanover, before grinding to a halt in the Two Taverns vicinity shortly before 4 a.m. on July 3. Custer's men pulled up at the twin shops, while Farnsworth's troopers filed off into the fields to the west, bivouacking on either side of the turnpike. In both areas, dead-tired cavalrymen were permitted to dismount but in expectation of impending action were forbidden to unsaddle. After seeing to their mounts' needs, the division was granted a few precious hours of slumber.

By 8 p.m. the rest period was over, Kilpatrick having received orders to proceed to Gettysburg and the lower end of Meade's battle line. Kill-Cavalry, anticipating another opportunity to showcase the talents of his command, started off promptly, ignoring the groans and curses of sleep-deprived troopers who felt they had every right to call their commander by his infamous nickname. This morning Farnsworth led the march, accompanied by Kilpatrick and his staff. The First Brigade pressed on until reaching the road from Taneytown, Maryland, within supporting range of Union infantry and artillery almost three miles below Gettysburg.[16]

As Farnsworth's men began to deploy in positions selected for them by Pleasonton's aides, Kilpatrick searched for Custer—and could not find him. With the exception of an advance guard that had closed up in Farnsworth's rear, the bulk of the Second Brigade had effectively disappeared. It is not known how long it took Kilpatrick to learn what had lured away almost 2,500 horsemen and a battery of light artillery, but until he did he probably blamed his subordinate for an error capable of visiting disaster on the Third Division and perhaps on the entire army. Instead, Custer's failure to follow Farnsworth would prove decisive to Meade's ability to remain at Gettysburg long enough to fight Lee to conclusion, assured that his army's right flank and rear were protected from attack and overthrow.[17]

Sometime after daybreak on July 3, Kilpatrick and Farnsworth having departed Two Taverns, a dispatch had reached Custer's bivouac delivered by an aide to General Gregg. Throughout the previous afternoon Gregg, at the head of two of his brigades (the third was guarding the far rear of the army), had sparred with roving Confederates west of the Hanover-Low Dutch Roads intersection. By pinning down a substantial force of Rebel infantry—the famed Stonewall Brigade—Gregg's men had diluted the strength of a late-afternoon attack on Culp's Hill, along Meade's upper flank, which had failed through a lack of manpower.[18]

Even before their debilitating, hours-long fight under a blistering sun, Gregg's brigades had been worn down by days of hard marching relieved by few rest halts. About midnight July 2–3, hours after the Rebels ceased opposing him and drew closer to Gettysburg, Gregg led his main body south of the crossroads and into bivouac at a point where the Baltimore Turnpike crossed White Run. There his exhausted riders enjoyed the rest that had eluded them for so long.

The move to the rear was not Gregg's idea. Suspecting that the Confederates would return to the crossroads on the third, he feared relinquishing the ground on which his dismounted troopers had established a defensive position. The breastworks they had crouched behind, though hastily erected, had sheltered them from enemy missiles on the second and presumably would serve the same purpose on the third.

The transfer to the Baltimore Pike had been Pleasonton's doing. So too was the decision, conveyed to Gregg's field headquarters around 6 a.m. on July 3, to move up the turnpike and occupy a commanding ridge along Rock Creek. Gregg agreed that the move would provide benefits—it would enable him to support his own army's infantry, then clinging to positions on Culp's Hill. Even so, he requested that it be delayed until certain the previous day's position was secure. His mild protest was no avail; sometime after daylight, a communiqué from corps headquarters insisted that he move as directed. Gregg was somewhat mollified by securing a pledge that the vacated crossroads would be occupied by enough cavalry to hold it.[19]

True to his word, Pleasonton sent a galloper to Two Taverns to inform Kilpatrick of the need to detach a force to spell Gregg. Upon arriving the courier found that a small portion of the Michigan Brigade had left the area but that Custer's main body was still there, most of it drawn up in column. At this point, Custer was faced with his first command relations dilemma. No time should be lost in hastening to Gettysburg. But a higher ranking superior—his corps commander—wanted him elsewhere. Without hesitating, Custer ordered the column turned about, heading northeast.

Perhaps a half-hour later the head of the Wolverine Brigade reached the position Gregg had withdrawn from the previous evening. It found there a band of mounted men whom the division commander had left behind to picket the crossroads. At once Custer threw out skirmishers, mounted and afoot, in several directions. Although the sounds of combat from the battlefield were rising with the morning sun, no Rebels were in sight. Yet the flat, open ground around the intersection was fringed by enough woods to conceal large numbers of potential opponents.

Initial dispositions complete, Custer, accompanied by Pleasonton's emissary, galloped off to General Gregg's headquarters near White Run where he reported to his superior. From intermittent contact with Gregg over the past months, especially at Aldie, he had formed a highly favorable opinion of the man, as had virtually everyone who knew him. Tall and imposing with his patriarchal beard, prominent nose, and hooded eyes, the thirty-year-old Gregg was the antithesis of the Kilpatricks and Pleasontons of the army: dignified, soft-spoken, unaffected, and unflappable. Gaining prominence in the eastern theater, he had performed with distinction and becoming modesty on every field from the early phases of the Peninsula Campaign to the recent clashes in Loudoun Valley. His men regarded him with a degree of respect and trust bestowed on no other cavalryman in the army with the possible exception of John Buford, whose First Division had held Gettysburg on July 1 against daunting odds until the vanguard of Meade's army arrived. Describing Gregg, a high-ranking colleague would invoke Napoleon's legendary cavalry chief: "As steady as a clock, and as gallant as Murat."[20]

Having gained a situation report from the division leader and some of his subordinates, Custer saluted and rode back to join his men, who were spreading out north and west. As yet they had not made contact with the enemy; for this reason, Custer's initial dispositions were somewhat improvised. He had Pennington unlimber in the southwestern angle of the road junction, facing west. He would soon learn, however, that the threat to his new position would come from the north via a long, tree-lined rise known as Cress's Ridge. At that point, around noon, the Wolverines would encounter Stuart's cavalry in its entirety.[21]

Late on July 2 Stuart had reestablished contact with the army he had cut loose from a week earlier. Upon reporting at Lee's headquarters northwest of Gettysburg, the cavalry chief had suffered through a tension-filled reunion with his superior. In the end Lee, laboring to keep his temper in check, ordered his long-absent subordinate to take his four brigades (including the western Virginia cavalry of Brigadier General Albert G. Jenkins, which had accompanied Ewell's corps throughout the invasion) and two-and-a-half batteries of horse artillery out the York Turnpike eastward from Gettysburg and gain a position well in rear of the Federal battle line.

Lee expected that at some point in the fighting on the third Stuart would have an opportunity to deal Meade an unexpected blow. That afternoon Lee would launch a larger attack, with massed ranks of infantry, against the Union front and center, although one not known to be closely coordinated with Stuart's operations. The Confederate commander had high hopes for a breakthrough in front but, unlike a strike from the rear, this assault would surprise no one. Every Union soldier crouching behind breastworks on Cemetery Ridge would see it coming and be prepared to meet it. Lee, who had begun to believe his underequipped but robust and fearless troops could achieve anything he asked of them, would find he had made a major miscalculation. Blown apart almost before it began, Pickett's Charge would doom Lee's hopes for a decisive victory on enemy soil.[22]

* * *

In his first battle report as a general officer, Custer would observe that upon reaching Gregg's former position he looked far and wide for the Rebels who had given the Second Cavalry Division a hard fight the previous day. "I immediately placed my brigade in position," he wrote, "facing toward Gettysburg. At the same time I caused reconnaissances to be made on my front, right, and rear, but failed to discover any considerable force of the enemy." Given Gregg's vocal belief that the cavalry would see fighting on the same ground today, this was both curious and troubling.[23]

However, shortly before noon (in his official report Custer erroneously estimated the time as 10 a.m.) the situation changed dramatically. Perhaps because Cress's Ridge was so heavily wooded, or because the patrols sent in that direction were not sufficiently vigilant, Custer did not realize that Stuart was so near his position until cannon blasts sounded from the high ground to the north. In more or less rapid succession, a Parrott rifle from the Maryland horse artillery battery of Captain William H. Griffin unleashed salvos in each compass direction. Stuart's intention remains unclear, though the firing may have been a signal to Lee that he had gained a foothold behind the Yankee army.[24]

The shelling may have come as a shock to the blue-coated troopers and their inexperienced general, but because it had not been directed at a specific target, it told Custer that Stuart, too, was ignorant of his enemy's proximity. Minutes later, however, Rebel artillery began to seek out Custer's position, suggesting that Stuart was no longer deceived. Before chaos could erupt on his line, the leader of the Wolverines took action. Repositioning Pennington's rifles and placing most of the 6th Michigan to guard them as well as to cover a long stretch of the Hanover Road, he "shifted the remaining portion of my command, forming a new line of battle at right angles to my former line."

The swerve to the north caught Stuart's attention, and within minutes, as Custer noted, "the enemy had obtained correct range of my new position, and was pouring solid shot and shell into my command with great accuracy." He expressed some relief when Pennington's cannons began to throw so many shells, so accurately, that the guns on the wooded crest temporarily fell silent. Having performed admirably at Hanover and Hunterstown, Battery M would win even brighter laurels on this field. Custer could not have asked for more powerful support than Pennington's gunners would lend his cavalrymen throughout the day.

In his report Custer described his new, elongated position: "My line, as it then existed, was shaped like the letter L. The shorter branch formed one section [i.e., two guns] of Battery M, supported by four squadrons of the 6th Michigan Cavalry, faced toward Gettysburg . . . the long branch, composed of the remaining two sections of Battery M, 2d Artillery, [was] supported by a portion of the 6th Michigan Cavalry on the left and the 1st Michigan Cavalry on the right. . . ." He held Colonel Mann's 7th Michigan still further to the right, ready to repel any attack Stuart might make from the east.[25]

With most of the command guarding Pennington's battery or committed to the defensive until the extent of Stuart's dispositions could be determined, only Russell Alger's 5th Michigan was available for mobile operations. With their Spencer rifles, the men of the 5th were a source of trouble for almost any opponent. Their colonel, however, was a potential source of trouble for Custer. Alger would not have been human had he not resented Custer's almost inexplicable rise to the position he held. In the months to come he would sometimes show himself to be a difficult subordinate, willing to substitute his own judgment for his superior's, but on the present occasion he saluted and moved out smartly.

Custer had ordered him to dismount and advance toward Stuart's assumed position in skirmisher formation. Taking the same route as Gregg's men the previous day, the 5th moved steadily north through fields of wheat and clover. They did so in the face of a new round of cannon-fire and volleys served up by the Rebels. En route the regiment skirted the banks of a sluggish stream, Little's Run, before angling west toward the farm of John Rummel, whose property had hosted some of the fighting on the second.[26]

After ordering up Alger, Custer deployed the balance of the brigade in such a way as to safeguard other segments of his line. To shore up his right flank, he

ordered fifty members of the 6th Michigan to advance about a mile and a half up
the Low Dutch Road. To guard the far left a detachment of similar size trotted
west and then a mile or more along the turnpike between Gettysburg and York.
Both units were under the command of Major Weber, who had performed with
distinction at Hanover. Custer held Town's 1st Michigan near the crossroads in
column of squadrons to observe Stuart's movements and stand ready for action.
These were standard dispositions, but they admirably covered the extent of the
brigade's position, suggesting that the young general knew his business or at least
was open to advice from subordinates familiar with such operations.[27]

Alger's men, given the salient-like position they assumed when moving forward of the main line, absorbed the brunt of the day's early fighting. When the
first Confederates arrived to oppose them—dismounted members of Jenkins's
brigade, led by Colonel Milton Ferguson—Alger's men held them at bay with
their seven-shot repeaters. But then the Virginians shifted toward the left flank
of the 5th Michigan, blazing away with their English-made Enfield rifles that,
while more cumbersome to reload than the cavalry's standard arm, the carbine,
could inflict damage at longer range.

Under this fusillade Alger's line began to waver and his ability to hold his
position, shielding the brigade, suddenly seemed in doubt. Custer, who was
keeping a close eye on the proceedings, frequently riding to and from the front,
sized up the threat with growing concern. Aware that Stuart would soon add
much greater weight to the fighting, he began to wonder if he could remain on
the field until relieved by another force—if any could be found.[28]

In fact, help was on the way. Even before the day's fighting began, Gregg
had decided to disobey his orders to vacate the Baltimore Pike and move to
Rock Creek. Corps headquarters was three miles away from Custer's position;
at such a distance Alfred Pleasonton could not have appreciated the magnitude
of the looming threat to the army's right and rear. Therefore Gregg ordered the
commander of his First Brigade, Colonel John Baillie McIntosh, a hard-bitten
veteran of numerous battles and skirmishes—including Cedar Run, where he
had supported Custer's first charge—to take his regiments back the way they
had come the previous evening. In response, McIntosh moved into a position
roughly midway between the Baltimore Pike and the Hanover Road, where he
halted to await the go-ahead to augment or spell Custer's men.

By rejecting Pleasonton's desires, Gregg realized that was placing himself
in an unenviable position—an insubordination charge could scuttle a career
even as sterling as his. Sometime after noon, however, vindication arrived in

the form of another dispatch from cavalry headquarters. This one conveyed an hours-old warning from Major General Oliver O. Howard, whose Eleventh Corps pickets south of Gettysburg had observed a long column of gray horsemen, artillery, and wagons marching out the York Pike toward the army's rear. Here was a threat that even a distant superior could not ignore. At long last Pleasonton approved Gregg's request to return to the field on July 2. Yet, as if he had yet to fully appreciate the unfolding situation, Pleasonton believed the crossroads could be held by a single brigade. Upon arriving there, McIntosh was to relieve Custer and send him on to Kilpatrick.[29]

Gregg intended to comply, but with misgivings. A misguided directive from army headquarters had detached his Third Brigade, commanded by his cousin, Irvin Gregg, which had been sent to study enemy dispositions inside Gettysburg. The order had been countermanded but not before Colonel Gregg reported to Meade's headquarters. Until he returned to the far right, his relative's division was reduced to about fourteen hundred troopers available for duty. It seemed clear to the commander of the Second Cavalry Division that if he was to stop Stuart in his tracks, he was going to need help.[30]

* * *

About 1 p.m., McIntosh got the word to move forward and began heading for Custer's position. Earlier, before the fighting there had heated up, the colonel had ridden ahead to inform the leader of the Wolverines of Gregg's intentions. It appears that McIntosh had not expected to find such a large force on the ground because he asked Custer where his "fine body of men" had come from. As he recalled, Custer made no reply but remarked that he was glad McIntosh had come on the scene before his own command had fully deployed. When McIntosh inquired about the enemy's whereabouts, Custer, "laughing said, I think you will find the woods out there (pointing towards Rummells) full of them."[31]

Even before McIntosh arrived, Custer had gotten word that he was going to be relieved. Around noon, he had received a peremptory order from Kilpatrick—finally apprised as to why his Second Brigade had gone astray—to hasten to his side. The division commander had big plans for dealing with the Rebels threatening Meade's lower flank, and he had no intention of doing so at half-strength. Custer, who appreciated his superior's situation, returned most of his dismounted men to the saddle and pointed them toward Gettysburg.[32]

Alger's troopers, unable to disengage so quickly from their exposed position, continued to hold on as newly arriving Confederates pressed their front and flank. McIntosh's brigade began to move up to the firing lines, but the process was cumbersome and took time. Custer must have believed that his own brigade would not be fully in motion for at least half an hour, meaning that it would be mid-afternoon or later before he could reconnect with Kilpatrick.[33]

His withdrawal was barely underway when General Gregg arrived on the field at the head of the rest of his command—Irvin Gregg's brigade was just then closing on McIntosh's rear although at least one of its regiments remained detached. Furthermore, McIntosh's horse artillery, under Captain Alanson M. Randol, would take time to get into position to replace Pennington's battery. At once Gregg called Custer to his side. From what he could see of the fighting, and from what Custer told him of Stuart's efforts to outflank him—Weber's patrols on the Low Dutch Road had been driven in—Gregg doubted that his two brigades could adequately oppose the major attack likely to come. Now he told Custer to remain in position, to be augmented, not replaced, by McIntosh's three regiments and a single attached company of Maryland cavalry, while Irvin Gregg's four regiments took position in the rear, below the Hanover Road.

Appreciating Gregg's logic, Custer readily complied. While some of McIntosh's units moved into position along the wooded fringe of the Low Dutch Road and others started heading west in the direction of the Rummel farm, Custer urged Colonel Alger to hold his position "at all hazards." Soon Alger, while opposed by Rebels coming at him from Cress's Ridge including Chambliss's brigade, was devoting increasing attention to supporting those of McIntosh's troopers who had begun to square off with Ferguson's mounted riflemen along Little's Run. The dual mission took a toll, especially when elements of Fitzhugh Lee's brigade—the cream of Stuart's command—descended the high ground to add their weight to the fight against McIntosh. However, the effective shelling of Pennington's battery, eventually complemented by the four guns of Randol's combined Batteries E and G of the 1st U.S. Artillery, enabled the embattled Federals to hold the line, at least for now.[34]

So far the 5th Michigan had fought admirably under pressure. Assisted by able subordinates such as Majors Noah Ferry and Luther Trowbridge, Colonel Alger shifted elements of his regiment from one position to another to contain the pressure being applied by Ferguson, Chambliss, and Lee. Custer attributed the 5th's tenacity to the firepower generated by repeating rifles "in the hands of brave, determined men." But Alger could not be expected to hold his ground forever in the face of quickly renewed opposition. By 2 p.m., Stuart was close to launching the full-scale attack David Gregg had been expecting, and Alger's ammunition had begun to run low (all too often repeating arms encouraged profligate firing). Then Major Ferry, one of the most respected field-grade officers in the brigade, was cut down by a rifle bullet while encouraging his men in the advance.[35]

Alger's men were not the only Federals with a dwindling supply of cartridges. Two dismounted battalions of McIntosh's 1st New Jersey Cavalry, which had taken position between Little's Run and the Rummel farm, were also running low. In mid-afternoon, upon the brief withdrawal of some of their opponents, the Jerseymen attempted to disengage and reload, only to be pounded so heavily by Stuart's artillery they dared neither advance nor retreat. Then the vanguard of Lee's brigade—some units mounted, others afoot—arrived on the scene in such numbers as to make McIntosh's withdrawal a necessity regardless of the risk involved.

Through his field glasses, Custer saw his comrade's predicament and attempted to help. He ordered four squadrons of the 6th Michigan, heretofore supporting Pennington's guns, to bolster McIntosh's right flank, but the reinforcements were stymied by cannon- and rifle-fire. The only other potential supports near the point of danger were Alger's men. Although he appreciated the vulnerability of the regiment's position, Custer felt compelled to order the 5th to extend its line toward Rummel's to relieve the pressure on its comrades. An understandably harassed Alger moved his left-flank companies to a post-and-rail fence running at a ninety-degree angle to the line along Little's Run, where they opened a brisk fire on the nearest Confederates. Pressure temporarily relieved, many of McIntosh's men scurried to safety.[36]

Custer realized that the revamped line would hold only so long—too many Confederates were already battering it, and others, still arriving on the scene, could break it to bits. The end seemed even nearer when around 2:30 Stuart ordered Lee's brigade, led by the storied 1st Virginia, to attack. Superbly mounted and armed to the teeth with rifles, pistols, and sabers, the veteran troopers prepared to surge forward, sweeping all before them. Now, if not earlier, Custer must have wondered if this, his first full-scale engagement in brigade command, would also be his last.

*   *   *

Before the fighting became general, the 7th Michigan had quit its initial position astride the crossroads in response to Pleasonton's order, delivered by Gregg, that the Wolverine Brigade should depart the field and rejoin Kilpatrick. Custer had countermanded the order, but only now was the 7th returning to the battlefield in column of fours. They arrived just in time to counter the approach of the 1st Virginia with an advance of their own. But, although unfamiliar with the capabilities of many of his units, Custer understood that by committing this regiment to an attack he would be throwing the dice of war.

The 7th Michigan was the least experienced outfit in the brigade, having broken training camp less than five months ago. It was also the youngest of Custer's regiments, the average age of its enlisted force being eighteen. Like the brigade's most seasoned outfit, the 1st Michigan, the 7th had been armed not with repeating rifles but with swords, pistols, and single-shot carbines. Along with the 1st, it was considered a saber regiment, expected to fight primarily in the saddle, relying on cold steel in close-quarters fighting. Trusting in the saber, however, did not come easily to pea-green troopers, most of whom preferred to kill at a distance rather than in the faces of shooting, screaming Rebels. Another notable deficiency was the regiment's strength: ten companies, approximately 420 officers and men available for duty, a little more than half the size of the brigade's largest component, the 5th Michigan. Only recently had enlistments picked up: Companies L and M were aboard a train bound for Virginia, but they would not arrive for another week.[37]

These were daunting handicaps, to be sure, but perhaps the 7th's most critical shortcoming was its lack of reliable leadership. Its twenty-four-year-old colonel, a former line officer in the 1st Michigan who had helped recruit both the 6th and 7th, was an erratic commander whose "rather perplexing" behavior and seeming disregard for his outfit's welfare had alienated many including Lieutenant Colonel Litchfield. There were also whispers in the ranks that Colonel Mann was not the "follow me" type. More so than in the other combat branches, cavalry officers were expected to fight alongside their men, inspiring them with their cool-headedness and disdain of fear. But Litchfield, in letters home and in correspondence with Governor Blair, accused his superior of always looking out for himself.[38]

Even so, the 7th was available for action and Custer was desperate to counter a thrust that might scatter not only the dismounted men on the front line but their supports to the rear, imperiling Pennington's and Randol's batteries. Thus he rode to the head of Mann's column, pointed it north, and ordered everyone to draw sabers. The collective rasp of steel was followed by a bugler blowing the call to charge. A moment later Custer, aboard Roanoke, still his favorite charger, led off at full tilt. After some hesitation and perhaps an understandable amount of confusion, Mann and his troopers followed.

Looking back, Custer gestured the men to greater speed, crying for all to hear, "Come on, you Wolverines!" Heeding his injunction, carried away by the thrill of their first charge, the youngsters began to shout and cheer, the sound quickly spreading down the length of the column. Soon everyone was moving at an extended gallop, sixteen hundred hooves thundering across alternately open and plowed ground, stalks of wheat and clots of dirt and grass flying.

By now the 1st Virginia had begun its attack, heading directly for Mann's vanguard. To avoid being caught between the converging forces, dismounted Federals scattered for cover, giving the 7th what appeared to be an unobstructed path. But the way was not clear; carried away by their momentum and enthusiasm, the rookies failed to notice that at least two dismounted regiments of Chambliss's brigade remained ahead of them, many of their men crouching behind farm fences, ready to pour fire into the Wolverines' flanks as they passed.

The 7th Michigan sliced through the first rank of the enemy without difficulty, but the second, Chambliss's 13th Virginia, unleashed a volley that drove a wedge through the mass of men and horses. The main body, Custer at its head, continued along a northwest track toward the Rummel farmstead, where Stuart's horse batteries had gone into position, but at some point short of his objective Custer realized that Mann and the rest of the 7th were no longer with him. The colonel, initially at Custer's side, had dropped down the column; when the 13th Virginia opened up, Mann and those riding with him had curved to the left to avoid the blizzard of bullets. The change of direction sent the detachment hurtling toward the fence line from which Alger's men and their supports had fled. Unable to halt their furiously pounding steeds, the Wolverines struck the barrier head-on, horses and riders tumbling into a gigantic pile-up.[39]

Chaos ruled. In his report Custer claimed that Mann's men "discharged their revolvers in the very face of the foe." According to numerous participants, however, the fence prevented anyone in that tangle of downed riders from getting off an effective fire at close range. Instead, Mann's detachment fell prey to the 1st Virginia, whose men, likewise stymied by the fence, were savvy enough to halt their charge short of it. Dismounting, they fired away from the other side, inflicting numerous casualties.

One whose horse hit the fence, Sergeant Edwin Havens, observed that it was no wonder the charge failed, it having been made "against a large force of dismounted skirmishers armed with long range guns and protected by a fence and line of bushes, and made with drawn sabres. . . . We could not touch them [the enemy] with our sabres, and were led through a narrow gap where our men were huddled together and the rebs pouring a destructive fire among us." According to Havens, some of his comrades made an effort to pass around or through a gap in the fences, only to be forced back with heavy loss. The sergeant's comments amount to criticism of the brigade's inexperienced leader. It would not be the last time Custer's impulsiveness—and, as in this case, his ignorance of the nature of the terrain in his front—would be faulted by those he led into the cauldron of battle.[40]

Mann's detachment had gone astray, strung out and scattered by the length of its charge. Around two hundred yards short of the Rummel farm Custer turned his men about and led them and their winded horses to the starting-point of the attack. They managed to break free although some Rebels staged a close pursuit that inflicted further casualties, one finally halted by rounds from Pennington's and Randol's guns.

When the survivors of Mann's wayward charge straggled in over the next half-hour or so, the colonel was nowhere to be found. Mann had seen some action, but as though unwilling to press his luck, he seems to have passed out of the fighting at some point. Allyne Litchfield, who had been shot off his horse at the height of the attack and when on foot picked up a discarded carbine to fight alongside the men, made no comment on his superior's conduct this day. However, following another encounter less than a week later, he reported that Mann had "evinced great fear all day . . . his pluck has all played out in my opinion."[41]

The 7th Michigan's introduction to the perils of the mounted charge had taken a grievous toll. According to Litchfield, fourteen men had been killed, five officers and forty-five men had been wounded, and no fewer than two officers and sixty-seven men were missing in action. An uncounted number of horses had been lost, the majority killed during the fighting, others, disabled after crashing into the fence, being deliberately shot. As one historian has noted, "these losses, the highest in the brigade that day, were staggering, but the regiment had sustained an even more damaging loss to their morale."

Litchfield spoke for many survivors when he wrote that following the regiment's repulse he had gone to the rear "very much exhausted, but . . . ashamed even in that state to leave the field."[42]

* * *

But that field had not yet been won, and Custer was determined that it would be. When he returned, unharmed, to the main body of the brigade, he saw that yet another phase—the most critical phase—of the fighting was about to begin. By now it was sometime after 3 p.m. The combat on the battlefield at Gettysburg was reaching its apogee as Pickett's men hurled themselves at the center of Meade's line. But time remained for Stuart to add his weight to that effort by smashing his way through from the rear. If he were to do so, the instrument of success would be the last arrow in his quiver, the hitherto lightly engaged brigade of Wade Hampton, just now coming on the field at full strength.

Hampton's advance began prematurely, the result of miscommunication. When the South Carolinian rode south to reconnoiter the ground in front of him, his adjutant supposed he was signaling the entire command to charge. The officer gave orders to that effect to each of Hampton's subordinates. One unit, the Cobb Legion, still recovering from the beating it had absorbed at Hunterstown, was left behind on the high ground, but the remainder of the brigade—the 1st North Carolina, the 1st and 2nd South Carolina, and two regimental-sized legions from Alabama, Georgia, and Mississippi—moved to the attack.[43]

The sight was most inspiring. From his perch along the Low Dutch Road one of McIntosh's officers, Captain William E. Miller of the 3rd Pennsylvania, would recall that "a grander spectacle than their advance has rarely been beheld. They marched with well-aligned fronts and steady reins. Their polished saber-blades dazzled in the sun." When Hampton, who had decided to make the most of the premature movement, gestured his men forward with upraised saber, the crisis of the day appeared to have come. Whether or not the effort could carry the Confederates all the way to Gettysburg, it appeared capable of throwing Custer and Gregg into chaos.

McIntosh's men were too scattered to mount an effective counterattack although able to support one by attacking from their several positions—Irvin Gregg's people were too far in the rear to provide immediate help. The main effort, therefore, devolved on Custer, who had at least one intact, fully mounted force available for immediate use: the veteran 1st Michigan. A more prudent commander might have considered striking the flanks of the enemy to minimize casualties and perhaps gain his rear, but Custer appreciated the impact a head-on attack was capable of. Although Company A's charge at Hunterstown had not carried the day, it had gouged Hampton's line, creating confusion in the ranks. Custer was confident that this time, if applied forcefully, it would prevail.

Riding to the head of the 1st Michigan, he reportedly remarked, "Colonel Town, I shall have to ask you to charge, and I want to go in with you." His subordinate, though in no shape to lead any attack, told him to give the order. Charles Town was slowly dying of consumption, now so feeble that he required help to mount his charger. He might not survive the war, but he intended to go down fighting.[44]

Once Custer's order to draw sabers and charge was passed down the line, another column of several hundred horsemen rumbled into motion. It crossed a field not only cut up by fences but littered with fallen men and horses. As before, dismounted Federals hastened to the flanks to let it pass. Other troopers held their positions so they might lace the approaching Rebels with carbine- and pistol-fire. At first it seemed unlikely that these efforts would have an effect. James Kidd, watching from the rear, would write his parents that "on swept the rebel cavalry, yelling like demons, right toward the battery we were supporting apparently sweeping everything before them."[45]

Intent on avoiding the fences that had ambushed the 7th Michigan, Custer hurled Town's troopers at the head of Hampton's column. The opposing lines met with a crash supposedly heard for miles around. Captain Miller likened the sound to "the falling of timber" and described the collision as "so sudden and violent . . . that many of the horses were turned end over end and crushed their riders beneath them. The clashing of sabers, the firing of pistols, the demands for surrender and cries of the combatants now filled the air."[46]

Dozens of small battles broke out across the contested ground as men in blue and gray or butternut-brown grappled with one another from the saddle. Relying on his Toledo blade, Custer cut down one opponent after another, while dodging pistol fire from many directions. Eventually, perhaps inevitably, he fell prey to the most effective way to disable a cavalryman: a rifle ball tore into Roanoke's foreleg, causing him to stumble and then collapse. Unlike at Hunterstown, Custer was able to dismount before striking the ground. His prized steed would recover from the wound to see further service, but for now Custer had to leave him behind and seek a remount. His luck very much intact, he caught a riderless horse from whose saddle he resumed swiping at any Rebel who drew near. Around him, Town's veterans fought furiously to carve a path through the enemy's ranks.[47]

Opposed as they were by a much larger force than their own, the Wolverines might not have prevailed but for the timely assistance of McIntosh's men, many of whom mounted and crashed into Hampton's flanks. Detachments of the 5th Michigan also attacked both mounted and afoot including one under Major Trowbridge, who like Custer had his horse shot from under him. For thirty minutes or more the fighting raged at white heat, saber- and pistol-wielding antagonists striving desperately for the advantage. Eventually, the inroads made in front by the 1st Michigan and on either side by their supports caused the enemy to give way, slowly at first but more precipitately when their route of withdrawal came under threat, and Wade Hampton was wounded and forced to the rear. At last Stuart, sensing that his chances of reaching Meade's lines had come and gone, broke off the fight and grudgingly withdrew to Cress's Ridge.[48]

Once he confirmed Hampton's withdrawal, Custer rallied and re-formed Town's scattered ranks before leading the 1st Michigan, with defiant deliberation, to the rear. For some hours both cavalries made sporadic, small-scale advances but none reignited the fighting. The cavalry battle on the right flank at Gettysburg was over. Neither antagonist had achieved an unambiguous victory, but Stuart's menacing advance toward the Union rear had been repulsed and the Michigan Brigade had made a major contribution to that outcome.

In doing so the Wolverines had won the admiration of every onlooker. Years later Lieutenant Pennington would recall that "I saw the charge and in all [the others] I was ever in I never saw a more picturesque sight." William Miller's comrade Lieutenant William Rawle Brooke felt the same way: "The charge of the 1st Mich. led by Custer himself . . . was the finest thing I witnessed during nearly three years of the war." Praise also came from an unexpected quarter. According to one of Stuart's regimental commanders, at day's end the cavalry leader expressed himself as "full of admiration for the Federal troops who so gallantly charged our lines."[49]

If he had not already done so at Hanover or Hunterstown, the Wolverines' leader had proved his mettle, and most of his tactics, while unpolished and perhaps unorthodox, had been effective. Heretofore officers and men had wondered if their commander possessed the skill, the poise, and the personality to bond with them and lead them to success. One of the doubters, Sam Harris of the 5th Michigan, had openly questioned Custer's youth and inexperience. Late on July 3 he spoke with Lieutenant Pennington, whose battery had been saved from certain capture by Custer's and Town's heroics. "Well, Harris," the artilleryman asked, "what do you think of the boy General Custer now?" Harris had to admit that, like virtually everyone who had witnessed the fresh-faced brigadier in action on July 3, 1863, he had come away highly impressed.[50]

Chapter X

Driving out the Rebels

Official casualty figures for the Michigan Cavalry Brigade in the fighting on July 3 are largely incorrect. In his report, submitted seven weeks after the battle, Custer enumerated the command's losses as nine officers and sixty-nine men killed, twenty-five officers and 207 men wounded, and 225 men missing. The grand total—542 casualties—actually represents the brigade's losses for the Gettysburg campaign in its entirety. James H. Kidd, in his memoir of service under Custer published almost fifty years after Gettysburg, provides more reliable figures for the day: one officer (Major Ferry) and twenty-eight men killed, eleven officers and 112 men wounded, and sixty-seven men missing, for a total of 219, or more than six times as many casualties as Gregg's division suffered on the third. Even discounting Custer's exaggerated numbers, the Wolverines' losses testify to the severity of the contest and the scope of the brigade's commitment to a critical phase of a pivotal battle.[1]

Custer's troopers deserved rest and recuperation commensurate with their exertion and sacrifice. This was largely denied to them. What passed for repose was a few hours of relative inactivity that ended at twilight. By then Custer had taken his leave of General Gregg, who must have expressed his great appreciation of the assistance the young brigadier had provided to the truncated and hard-pressed Second Cavalry Division. In gathering darkness, the Wolverines moved wearily south until reaching the Baltimore Pike not far from the Two Taverns vicinity where they had spent the previous night.

At daybreak, after a few more hours of much-interrupted rest, the brigade was winding down southwestward-leading trails toward Emmitsburg. In that Maryland village it reestablished contact with General Kilpatrick and the First Brigade. Possibly Custer had some explaining to do although by this point his division leader would certainly have learned of the basis for his prolonged absence. In turn, Kilpatrick had to explain what had happened to the other half of the division while Custer was tangling with Stuart.[2]

Reduced to half his assigned command, Kill-Cavalry had spent most of July 3 skirmishing at long range with infantry and artillery anchoring Lee's far-right flank three miles from Gettysburg. Late that afternoon, when he learned of the failure of Pickett's Charge, Kilpatrick anticipated a counter-stroke all along the line. Determined to play a role in the proceedings and reap some of the glory that his rather anomalous position had denied him, he considered striking the forces in his front, between the Taneytown and Emmitsburg Roads.

The nearest Rebels, west of the heavily-forested eminence known as Round Top, enjoyed secure positions on ground hemmed in by farm fences and studded with trees, rocks, and ditches. The terrain was by no means suitable for mounted operations, but Kilpatrick was of the opinion that cavalry, properly led, could operate successfully anywhere on land. Moreover, Pleasonton had directed him to "press the enemy, to threaten him at every point, and to strike at the first opportunity."

Kilpatrick found such an opportunity after 5 p.m. when he proposed to attack the division of Brigadier General Evander M. Law. With limited success, he had probed the positions of Law's Alabama and Georgia infantry with his own troops as well as with the regulars of Wesley Merritt, operating farther to the north. Now he ordered Elon Farnsworth, at the head a battalion of the 1st Vermont Cavalry, to charge across the wooded and hilly ground against Law's flanks. Farnsworth protested the maneuver as suicidal—a view shared by the majority of the Vermonters—but Kilpatrick appears to have goaded him into leading it by impugning his courage. The young brigadier, determined to prove his mettle, made the attack as ordered. In the process he was killed; sixty-four other participants were killed, wounded, or captured; and no discernable advantage was achieved. Many of those who witnessed what one Confederate officer called a "wholesale slaughter" believed that Kilpatrick had deliberately sent Congressman Farnsworth's favorite nephew to his death.[3]

Custer's opinion of the attack remains unknown, but he would have heard the rumors and, given his knowledge of Kilpatrick's military persona, may well have believed them. In essence Kilpatrick's approach to offensive warfare—his penchant for risk-taking—tallied closely with Custer's, with two exceptions. Custer was apt to act boldly when conditions appeared to warrant it. Kilpatrick dared unnecessarily—often, it seemed, merely to make himself look aggressive and proactive. And when Custer committed his troops to a chancy maneuver, he usually rode with them and in front of them. Kilpatrick, like Pleasonton, was fond of shouting "attack" but not necessarily "follow me." Custer was ever impulsive, but he was not reckless. Kilpatrick was both.

*   *   *

As if to make amends for his misadventures on this field, Kilpatrick moved rapidly south, as directed, on the morning of the fourth, Custer's brigade in the vanguard. In leaving Gettysburg he parted ways with Merritt, who eventually returned to Buford's side. When Kilpatrick reached Emmitsburg in mid-afternoon, he bulked up his command by temporarily adding Colonel Pennock Huey's brigade of New York, Ohio, and Pennsylvania troopers and the attached artillery battery of Lieutenant William D. Fuller. For the past five days Huey had been guarding the army's supply base at Manchester, Maryland, a duty that had deprived David Gregg, his division commander, of his services on July 2–3.[4]

At Emmitsburg Kilpatrick received orders from corps headquarters to turn his column around and return to Pennsylvania. The northwestward movement was intended to interrupt if not halt Lee's retreat, which had begun early that morning. Kilpatrick had been informed that "a heavy train of wagons was moving on the road to Hagerstown; that I was expected to take with me my entire division . . . destroy this train, and operate on the enemy's rear and flanks." The assignment had much appeal for him. To waylay a supply train carrying not only an army's baggage, rations, and forage but an immense amount of spoils would be a glorious coup. The mission appeared entirely viable, for reports had the train moving toward South Mountain without infantry support.[5]

The line of vehicles that had come to Kilpatrick's attention hauled the impedimenta of the Second Corps, Army of Northern Virginia: subsistence and quartermaster's wagons, interspersed with herds of captured horses, mules, cattle, and hogs, as well as a long line of ambulances conveying wounded and ill officers and men. The train had left Gettysburg on the Hagerstown Road, the most direct route to the Potomac, via the village of Fairfield and Monterey Pass in South Mountain. Other Confederate supply trains were taking a more northerly course via the Cashtown Gap; still others were trundling south via Cavetown and Hagerstown to the river at Williamsport.

Of major interest to Kilpatrick were the two roads that forked around Jack's Mountain peak in the Alleghany chain southwest of Fairfield. The upper fork, known locally as the Maria Furnace Road, was the route that Ewell's train would take. This steeply climbing road swerved its way through the several mountain ranges in the vicinity. While the local terrain would make life difficult for wagons, horses, and mules, it posed even greater obstacles to any military force that attempted to fight there.[6]

These considerations did not prevent Kilpatrick from going after the beckoning prize. Assembling his regiments, he made a little speech in which he heaped high praise on their conduct on July 3. James Kidd quoted him as announcing that they would now cut loose from their army and "go to the enemy's right and rear," a mission that would keep them apart from their comrades for an indefinite period. After allowing the men time to prepare three days' rations, Kilpatrick led them out the turnpike toward Waynesboro and the South Mountain range. Despite a continual rain and intermittent downpours, his enlarged command moved at an impressive pace, Custer's Wolverines still in the advance. While Farnsworth's men had served ably at Gettysburg, Kilpatrick was aware how exceptionally the Michigan Brigade had performed in the right rear of the army. It had earned the post of honor on the march.[7]

About two hours before midnight, the head of the column reached the intersection with the Jack's Mountain Road en route to Fountain Dale. Through reports from local residents Kilpatrick learned that he was not too late to overtake Ewell's train short of South Mountain. Moving on, the wagons and ambulances had already cleared Fairfield Gap and were approaching the nearby Monterey Pass. It was Custer who relayed the information to his superior; Kilpatrick immediately ordered him to gallop on to Monterey.

Ewell's wagons were being escorted by members of the mounted brigades of William E. Jones and Brigadier General Beverly H. Robertson. Both units had been added to Stuart's command strictly for the invasion. He had a favorable opinion of neither leader as a fighting man—hence their relegation to a seemingly mundane but important mission apart from Stuart's main body, which was protecting the rear and flanks of Lee's army against pursuing cavalry and infantry. Robertson had positioned a small force within striking distance of the turnpike, but it was chased away by one of Huey's regiments. Other escort units had established positions between Fairfield and its namesake gap, guarding the far rear of the train.[8]

While the bulk of his command—the 5th, 6th, and 7th Michigan, Pennington's Battery M, and a squadron of the 1st Michigan—surged ahead on the macadamized road, Custer detached the balance of his lead regiment.

At or just beyond Fountain Dale he sent Colonel Town, with his remaining ten companies, up a winding mountain trail toward Fairfield Gap. By this route the 1st could gain the Maria Furnace Road, securing the right flank and rear of the division during the fighting to come.

Town started out briskly, but short of the gap he encountered Robertson's 5th North Carolina, dug in behind works and backed by a battery of horse artillery. Town lacked cannons of his own, a consideration that made the imminent confrontation difficult under any circumstances. When his men drew within striking range, Town proposed to disperse the enemy with a mounted attack. He called up a single squadron, placed it under Lieutenant Colonel Peter Stagg, and sent it into action. Despite battling what he described inaccurately as "superior numbers," Stagg eventually surmounted the defenses and propelled their occupants into retreat. The cost, however, was steep: two officers and men killed; Stagg himself was seriously injured when shot off his horse. His superior would report that "the enemy were driven out and the Gap [was] held until the entire [Union] column and train had passed."[9]

Custer was not on the scene to oversee Town's operations; he rode with the balance of the brigade as it pounded up the turnpike in a raging thunderstorm. Perhaps two miles from the east slope of Monterey Pass his outriders encountered a teenage girl whose family lived nearby. She informed the new arrivals that the Rebels had emplaced several cannons at the mouth of the pass and warned them to proceed with extreme caution. Her advice went back to Custer, then to Kilpatrick, who ordered the advance to resume at full speed. When it did, the girl rode behind a trooper of the 1st Michigan, guiding the column up a muddy road through darkness.[10]

The Wolverines' ordeal worsened when, within a few hundred yards of the pass, a cannon began to shell the lead companies. The shot, which had come from thirty feet above the Federals, had been fired by a tiny detachment of mounted horsemen armed with a single, ammunition-poor gun. The unit, commanded by Captain George M. Emack of Company B, 1st Maryland, a component of Fitz Lee's brigade, had been left by some mistake at the entrance to the pass miles apart from Jones and Robertson.

Unable to see who had fired the round and how many opponents they were facing, the startled Wolverines stopped dead, then reeled backward when Emack's men dosed them with carbines and rifles, all the while screaming the Rebel Yell. One Federal described the unseen opposition as "a confused mass of . . . demons whose shouts and carbine shots, mingled with the lightning's red glare and the thunder's crash, made it appear as if we were in the infernal regions."[11]

When Custer's vanguard pulled back, Captain Emack ordered every man at his immediate disposal—all eight of them—to dismount and take position on both sides of the road. For the next hour or more they frustrated efforts by Custer and Kilpatrick to outflank them by clambering up the frighteningly steep sides of the pass. When members of the brigade formerly commanded by Farnsworth and now led by Colonel Nathaniel Richmond of the 1st West Virginia dismounted on the south side of the road, Emack merely pulled his men and gun two hundred yards to the rear and fought on.

While Kilpatrick plotted other efforts to gain the pass, Custer led his reorganized troopers against Emack's new position, which had been augmented by a few other Marylanders with additional reinforcements supposedly on the way. Again the Wolverines, led by the squadron of the 1st Michigan that had not accompanied Town toward Fairfield, fell back, cowed more by the conditions than by their opponents. Finally enough troopers were on hand to bull their way ahead, reaching the Monterey House hotel at the eastern summit of the defile. Custer emplaced two of Pennington's rifled guns in a clearing just west of the hostelry. Covered by their accurate fire, the Michiganders forced Emack's men to withdraw up the mountain. Behind them Ewell's trains continued moving through the pass. The Federals still had a chance to capture and disable enough wagons to seriously disrupt the retreat of the Army of Northern Virginia.

At Kilpatrick's order, Custer replaced the squadron of the 1st Michigan with the main body of the 6th and led its dismounted men, backed by elements of the 5th Michigan, along the north side of the pike toward the enemy's new position. By now Emack had made contact with General Jones and detachments of two regiments totaling a little over two hundred men had reached the pass to lend their support. Other potential reinforcements, blocked by the mass of wagons and led animals on the Maria Furnace Road, were struggling to reach the scene.[12]

Emack had enough men on hand to cause Custer's brigade additional trouble. The advance of the 6th Michigan, which initially made satisfactory progress, began to wane thanks to the horrid conditions. Kidd, whose company had deployed as skirmishers inside a woodlot that skirted the turnpike, recalled that it was "so dark that we could locate them [the Rebels] only by the flashes of their guns. . . . One had to be guided by sound and not sight."[13]

With the 6th stymied, Custer sent in the entire 5th Michigan, which fared little better, being halted by a deep gorge spanned by a wooden bridge over rain-swollen Red Run. The condition of the bridge was unknown, but according to skirmishers sent forward to reconnoiter, it appeared stout enough to support the weight of an attacking force. According to Colonel Alger, without seeking approval from either Kilpatrick or Custer, whom he claimed to be too far off for a quick consultation, around midnight he led the larger portion of his regiment across the span. Their coming muffled by the driving rain, the dismounted troopers reached the opposite bank without difficulty. They spread out on both sides of the pike, forming a line of battle that stretched to within sixty yards of the Rebel wagons. Once informed of Alger's success, Custer prepared to lead a climactic charge through the pass.[14]

Eyewitness accounts differ markedly as to what happened next. Alger would claim that his regiment gained access to Ewell's train, ensuring its wholesale destruction. For his part, the historian of Company A, 1st Ohio Cavalry, Kilpatrick's headquarters escort, claimed that when it advanced the lead squadron of Alger's regiment made some captures "but as soon as the rebels opened on them with their artillery they turned and came scampering down the road like a drove of frightened cattle." Alger would forever insist that "the 5th Michigan Cavalry was never driven back one inch." But he called into question the accuracy of his testimony when he claimed in his official report that his regiment had been opposed by "two howitzers, charged with grape shot" and that the bridge over Red Run "was guarded by over one thousand of the enemy's infantry."[15]

Captain Noah Jones of Company A agreed that Emack's cannon "caused no little wavering and excitement" in Alger's ranks. As a result, when Kilpatrick reached the scene of the 5th Michigan's repulse he "became very angry and censured General Custer for the conduct of his men." Jones may have been prejudiced against Custer since the 5th's retreat had broken the ranks of his company, which had been supporting Battery M, carrying several Ohioans to the rear along with Alger's men. Lacking knowledge of the facts, Kilpatrick not only berated Company A but questioned its courage, a charge the escort greatly resented.

Determined to refute the imputation of cowardice, Captain Jones and several of his men volunteered to make the charge that Alger's squadron had botched. Supposedly Kilpatrick hesitated to throw his escort into the fray, preferring that Custer made a second attempt to break through the pass. According to Jones, who did not identify the regiment assigned to make the movement, "Custer ordered his men to charge, but they refused, when he reported to General Kilpatrick that he did not think we could capture the train."

Kilpatrick hastily consulted with his staff as to committing the escort. The aides counseled against it but in the end, around 3 a.m. on July 5, Kilpatrick ordered the company to advance. According to Jones, Custer approached him, shook his hand, and said: "Do your duty, and God bless you." By this account, which present-day historians have accepted, Jones's unit, accompanied by one hundred members of Major Charles E. Capehart's 1st West Virginia and aided by volleys from Pennington's guns, made a saber charge, "whooping and yelling," that carried it into Emack's paper-thin ranks. The Marylander, whose gun had run out of ammunition, attempted to meet the thrust with a charge of his own. The result, as Capehart put it, was a "wild and desolating" collision.[16]

Whether or not he had informed Jones of his intention, Custer, perhaps stung by Kilpatrick's reflection on his brigade's fortitude, determined to join the attack. Placing himself at the head of a mixed force of the 5th and 6th Michigan, he led it in on the heels of Jones and Capehart. He did not, however, get far. For the third time in as many days he was unhorsed, this time when his mount stumbled and collapsed. Slightly dazed but otherwise functional, the brigadier struggled to his feet, a target for oncoming Confederates. As at Hunterstown, he managed to evade capture; the details of this latest escape, however, went unrecorded.

The attack of Jones's, Capehart's, and Custer's troopers destroyed the opposing force. Emack's men were shot down or ridden over. Their leader was hit several times by bullets and struck by shrapnel; his horse, too, went down, ending his improbable defensive effort. General Jones, who had reached the scene with additional reinforcements, also emulated Custer by narrowly escaping capture. The oncoming Federals at last penetrated the pass and fell upon the train, whose drivers they called on to surrender and whose guards they shot or sabered. The wagons that came into their possession they overturned, ran off the road and down the mountainside, or rendered immobile by shooting down their teams. When Lieutenant Pennington moved forward one of his guns, shells tore apart other wagons and ambulances (the latter presumably after their occupants had been removed), creating roadblocks that would take hours to clear.[17]

Beyond the entrance to Monterey Pass, sections of Ewell's train well forward of the rest also fell victim to the rampaging cavalrymen. In a matter of hours every quartermaster's vehicle for miles around had been seized and were in the throes of destruction. An ecstatic Kilpatrick would report that by daylight on the fifth "Ewell's large train had been entirely destroyed, save [for] eight forges, thirty wagons, and a few ambulances loaded with wounded rebel officers. . . ." In a postwar addendum to his official report of the campaign, Custer would estimate the number of wagons overtaken as four hundred while boasting that the Michigan Brigade "made most if not all the captures."[18]

Custer may have claimed too much for his command, but many of his men gave him an immoderate share of the credit for the outcome. One praised his conduct throughout the fight and described him as "full of resources and always cheerful in the darkest hour." A trooper of the 7th Michigan called him "a glorious fellow, full of energy, quick to plan and bold to execute, and with us has never failed in any attempt he has yet made." Another enlisted man declared that under Custer's leadership "it is an honor to belong to [the] Mich cavalry."[19]

It is doubtful that any trooper who survived that demonic night ever forgot the experience. Kidd spoke for many when calling it "one of the most exciting engagements we ever had, for while the actual number engaged was small, and the casualties were not great [forty-three in Kilpatrick's ranks], the time, the place, the circumstances, the darkness, the uncertainty, all combined to make 'the midnight fight at Monterey' one of unique interest."[20]

*　　*　　*

Overcome by the physical and mental stress of their efforts, once the fight was over Custer's men gave way to fatigue. Their leader undoubtedly stayed awake for many hours, seeing to the maximum destruction of the train and taking inventory of the damage, but most of his men collapsed in their saddles. Kidd fell into a sound sleep that lasted till dawn, and when he awoke, he saw no one he recognized. He beheld, instead, "a moving mass of horses with motionless riders all wrapped in slumber. The horses were moving along with drooping heads and eyes half-closed." Unattended mounts moved ahead of their companions, while others dropped back in the column. As a result "few men found themselves in the same society in the morning with which they started at midnight."[21]

As the riders regained their senses they found themselves moving down the mountain past piles of overturned wagons and dead horses. The line of march wound south across the Maryland border in the direction of Smithsburg. Accompanying the Federals were almost fourteen hundred prisoners, principally teamsters and train guards, as well as large numbers of horses and mules that the invaders had attached to their own wagons. Kilpatrick's division moved toward the Potomac with great caution. It had become known that Lee intended to cross his troops, and the hundreds of supply vehicles that had not fallen to his pursuers, into Virginia at or near the river at Williamsport, and that is where Kilpatrick was heading.

Relatively little fighting took place during the balance of July 5 although, according to Kilpatrick, Stuart attempted to intercept and waylay his division well short of the river. Late that afternoon Confederate horsemen emerged from South Mountain passes near Smithsburg as if to offer battle. They were forced to fall back by the well-directed shelling of Kilpatrick's artillery, his left flank being guarded by Battery M, closely supported by dismounted troopers under Custer's supervision.

Unable to nail down a position in the face of such resistance, Stuart, although outnumbering his adversary, withdrew. His advance had been so threatening, however, that Kilpatrick refused to pursue him and instead headed south "to save my prisoners, animals, and wagons." The perhaps-unintentional note of anxiety in his report was echoed by at least one of Custer's men, who wrote home that as "their number was so much more than ours we fell back fast."[22]

From Smithsburg the Third Cavalry Division trotted toward Boonsboro, Maryland. Near that town, late in the day, it made contact with an outpost manned by former members of the Harpers Ferry garrison under Major General William H. French. Here Kilpatrick unloaded his prisoners and captured property. From French's troops he learned that Stuart had withdrawn to Hagerstown, where he was barricading roads to protect the main body of Lee's supply train at Williamsport as well as to secure a path to the Potomac for the main army.[23]

Freed of his human and animal baggage, Kilpatrick made plans to attack the enemy in strength. He found he could do so in tandem with Buford's division, which had reached Boonsboro in pursuit of Stuart's cavalry. The two brigadiers met, compared notes, and devised a cooperative effort. Kilpatrick would operate against Rebel infantry and cavalry at Hagerstown while Buford moved against Williamsport, where teamsters and wagon guards were waiting for the rain-swollen Potomac to recede.

Early on July 6 Kilpatrick proceeded to Hagerstown, Richmond's brigade in advance, followed by Huey's, then Custer's. The division leader reported that Stuart, "expecting me from the direction of Gettysburg," was found, surprised, and routed at Hagerstown, but the reports of his subordinates do not bear him out. Huey, on the left of the town, and Richmond, on the right, fought what the latter described as a "vastly superior force" of cavalry and foot soldiers for at least three hours, hurling back several attacks, until forced to withdraw. Kilpatrick claimed that he left Hagerstown because he learned from prisoners taken there that a mass of Confederate infantry was bearing down on Buford at Williamsport.[24]

Custer, having been held in the rear throughout morning and most of the afternoon without being heavily engaged, led the way down the turnpike to Williamsport, displacing groups of enemy pickets at every point. At about 4 p.m. his vanguard topped a rise less than a mile north of Williamsport. There it burst upon the scene of a battle raging between Buford and Brigadier General John D. Imboden, whose brigade of cavalry and mounted infantry had escorted Lee's principal wagon train to the river.

Imboden's force, though small, was augmented by several batteries of artillery and dozens of wounded men capable of wielding firearms. The escort force had been formidable enough to give Buford all he could handle, and the fight was hanging in the balance when Custer arrived and placed his command astride the turnpike off the right flank of the First Cavalry Division. Calls for help from Imboden had persuaded Stuart to send him the better part of two brigades under Fitz Lee and Colonel Laurence S. Baker (formerly Hampton's). Stuart's men opposed Custer both in front and on the right, threatening Pennington's guns west of the pike. Meanwhile, reports from Hagerstown had the remainder of the Confederate cavalry and at least one brigade of infantry battling Richmond's brigade, which Kilpatrick had left outside the town to guard the rear.[25]

To ease pressure on Buford's division along the Boonsboro Road, Custer advanced his lead regiment, the 5th Michigan, toward the center of Williamsport. The 5th moved south, the 1st Michigan close behind; Pennington followed the 1st, while the rest of the brigade strove to connect with Colonel Richmond. A squadron of Russell Alger's regiment suddenly galloped down the pike, driving in the enemy's pickets. Then Alger prepared to lead a saber charge, uprooting the Rebels and seizing an even larger cache of supply wagons than the one that had fallen into the brigade's hands two nights earlier.

It is not known whether Custer intended to accompany the attackers as he had on at least three previous occasions, but if he did he never got the chance. Alger had barely given the command "Trot, march!" when the order was countermanded by a courier from Kilpatrick. At that moment one of Imboden's guns sent a shell into the leading ranks of the 5th. Alger reacted by dismounting most of his men and placing them "in a sheltered place behind some rocks on the left of the road." The 1st Michigan, though relatively inexperienced at fighting afoot, formed a skirmish line on the 5th's right flank that extended to the other side of the road. Pennington unlimbered his guns to support both regiments, placing two sections behind Alger and the third in rear of Colonel Town.[26]

With his men pinioned between two sizable forces, unable to go forward or backward without incurring great risk, Custer held them in place for the balance of the afternoon, hoping at some point to slip away to a more defensible position. For two hours or more Alger and Town exchanged fire with dismounted skirmishers while ducking round after round of shrapnel, shell, and canister. Town's outfit had an especially rough time of it; his men repeatedly charged a sharpshooter's nest in a brick house on the outskirts of the village. Just as frequently they were turned away by rifle-, carbine- and shotgun-fire.[27]

Near nightfall, the time to move—somewhere—had come. Buford's troopers had fought themselves out against Imboden's main body, and the slowly approaching Confederate infantry was threatening to get in their rear and cut off their line of withdrawal. Then Kilpatrick informed Custer that the First Brigade, following hours of fighting against heavier numbers, was about to be evicted from Hagerstown. The break came only minutes later. As the retreating Federals pounded down the turnpike, Custer gave the word to clear out before they could arrive, plow into his brigade, and cause untold consternation.

Though Custer voiced the order, it came down from on high. Edward Paul, the *New York Times* reporter who rode at the division leader's side, wrote that "never was a command in a more critical situation; never before was a man cooler, or did one display more real generalship than General Kilpatrick on this occasion . . . by a dashing movement, [he] saved the cavalry corps from disaster." The dashing movement consisted of countermarching the regiments that had led Colonel Richmond's retreat from Hagerstown. At just the right moment Kilpatrick "fell into the breach with a yell, and, sword in hand, drove back the enemy, relieving the exhausted rear-guard, and holding the enemy in check until the whole command was disposed of as to fall back, which they did in good order, fighting as they went."[28]

What Custer thought as he read this dispatch when it appeared in the *Times* two weeks after the battle can only be surmised. Whether he considered it representative of the highest standards of military journalism is doubtful, but he knew from experience the value of favorable reporting. For that reason he probably made a mental note to acquire an E. A. Paul of his own at the earliest opportunity.

Custer's withdrawal from Williamsport was no mean feat. By now the Rebel infantry, having shoved their antagonists out of Hagerstown, were advancing on and east of the pike, interposing between Richmond's evacuees and the Wolverine Brigade. Suddenly, however, the gray column ground to a halt as if intimidated by the gathering darkness. Because it held the most advanced position, the 5th Michigan was the last of Custer's regiments to disengage—not realizing that the rest of the brigade was already gone. Colonel Alger reported that his men, their movements cloaked by the night sky, began to retire, "passing along within two hundred yards of the enemy's infantry for more than a quarter of a mile." His outfit was saved from a vicious beating and possible destruction only because the Rebels "had stacked arms in the road where we had passed down [and] saw us march by unmolested, evidently supposing we belonged to their army."

Understandably, Alger complained that "this movement was only participated in by my regiment, the balance of the command having moved away much earlier, but being on our extreme right the orders had not reached me until it was found that my command was missing. I was holding a position to guard the front only, supposing that others were attending to the rear." The foul-up may have been a matter of sloppy staff work but Alger, feeling neglected and mistreated, no doubt entered a black mark against the name of his brigade leader.[29]

* * *

Falling in behind Buford's column, Custer withdrew toward Boonsboro, heading three miles southeast. For much of that distance, he was harassed by some of the less timid Confederates—he got no help from Colonel Richmond's command, which, Kilpatrick at its head, retreated by another road. Custer's ordeal did not cease until shortly before the exhausted troopers were allowed to bivouac for the balance of the night. At that point, Colonel Thomas Devin's brigade of Buford's division assumed the rear-guard duties.[30]

The following morning, July 7, Custer's men completed the march to Boonsboro. For the rest of the day, they remained in temporary camp, enjoying the relative peace long denied to them although forced to endure a reprise of what Captain Kidd called "the Fourth of July rain storm." It can be imagined, however, that Custer was not overjoyed by the spate of inactivity. Lee's army, despite its relative mobility, had been trapped inside Maryland by an engorged river. That stream would be passable as soon as the rains ceased, but Lee's enemy had yet to strike a blow.

The infantry of the Army of the Potomac was days away from reaching the Potomac—by the seventh it was only beginning to depart Gettysburg in force, Meade transferring his headquarters from the battlefield to Frederick— and until it arrived only the cavalry was in a position to mount an effective pursuit. On the seventh, Kidd saw some heavy cannons come down the road to Boonsboro. He and his men expected "a big battle . . . to begin at any moment," but it did not happen, and "we wondered why there was so much deliberation."[31]

Lee expected to be attacked, forcing him to fight his way across the river. He had set his men to construct a line of works from Williamsport to Downsville, ten miles to the southeast; they enclosed several potential crossing points including one at a bend in the river called Falling Waters. At that site the army's engineers were slowly reassembling a pontoon bridge on which Lee had intended to cross his army—four days ago Union raiders had seized it and broken it up.[32]

A fight of some substance took place on July 8, when Buford was attacked near Boonsboro and Kilpatrick was called on to secure the rear of his division. Thanks to his help, Buford reported that following an all-day fight he displaced Stuart's cavaliers and drove them four miles. As Kidd recalled, "most of the fighting was done dismounted, the commands being deployed as skirmishers." Custer's brigade occupied the extreme left of Kilpatrick's line where it kept at bay a force of Rebels who tried several times to leave their cover and attack the 6th Michigan. Custer nodded approvingly at the resistance offered by those members of the 6th armed with Spencer rifles, especially when, at his order, they advanced near day's end and ejected the enemy from a woods, an operation that, according to Kidd, "was done in gallant style, the whole line joining." During this advance, which ended the day's fighting, Colonel Alger was disabled by a wound in the left leg, forcing him to pass command of the regiment to Lieutenant Colonel Gould. Alger would spend the next six weeks recuperating at his home in Grand Rapids. Colonel Gray of the 6th was also wounded during the action; the wounds refused to heal, eventually forcing him to resign his commission.[33]

The day's fighting, while sharp and spirited, settled nothing. Stuart was now in position to cover the extent of Lee's front, and without infantry assistance, Buford and Kilpatrick had little chance of breaking through that protective screen. Even so, the cavalry was buoyed by the knowledge that it was doing damage to Lee's stalwarts—on the verge of sweeping them out of the North even if unable to bag the lot of them. Sergeant Andrew Buck of the 7th Michigan exulted in a letter to his family: "At last we have fell on highly important times. [We] are now practicing war not theory[iz]ing it." Hope continued to burn in many a heart. Lieutenant George Barse, 5th Michigan, declared in a letter to a hometown editor, "Although much worn down by fatigue and need of rest, the cry is, 'No rest until the rebels are driven from the State. We can whip them, and must do so, cost what it will'."[34]

Over the next two days little action occurred on Custer's front, no doubt increasing the anxiety the boy general shared with Kidd and many others that Lee would be permitted to reach Virginia without further molestation. Late on the ninth the head of Meade's columns finally poked through the South Mountain gaps north of Boonsboro. The infantry did not seem disposed to pitch into Lee, but it brought word of a great victory won in Mississippi. The day after Meade turned back Pickett's charge, Ulysses S. Grant had forced the surrender of Vicksburg following a seven-week siege of that strategic fortress. Grant's triumph, which placed the full extent of the Mississippi River in Union hands, had effectively split the Confederacy in two.

On the morning of July 11, after two days of fighting that had devolved almost entirely on Buford's command, Kilpatrick led his now-rested division up the road to Funkstown and the tag end of Lee's army. Taking Funkstown would give the cavalry a foothold from which to strike the Confederate rear, an operation it could now perform in cooperation with Meade's slowly advancing foot soldiers. The day was a success: Custer's men chased the few remaining troops out of the village and planted themselves a mile and a half south of Hagerstown, connecting there with the right flank of John Sedgwick's Sixth Corps. This placed the Third Cavalry Division on the far right of Meade's army, which at last had settled into positions opposite Lee's extended bridgehead.[35]

But the cavalry-infantry link-up had come late in the game. With his defenses at the river now complete and fully manned, the Confederate commander was on the verge of abandoning Hagerstown and concentrating his forces near Williamsport and Falling Waters. Meade appeared uncertain as to whether those defenses were capable of being carried without suffering unacceptable losses. He ordered a reconnaissance-in-force, to be converted into an all-out attack if the prospects were favorable, but not for some days would it be put in motion. Custer must have wondered if the general commanding would be just as happy to see his antagonist escape. The fighting would then return to Virginia, and the contending forces could start all over again. Perhaps it was from this hour that he began to see Meade as too cautious, too concerned with what Lee might do him should he miscalculate, to essay anything daring or decisive. This attitude would grow stronger in the months ahead as Custer witnessed time and again what he considered a severe, if not fatal, lack of resolve in the army leader.[36]

While Meade dithered, his horsemen marked time. By late on the twelfth Lee had evacuated Hagerstown; his entire army was now inside its breastworks, poised to cross to Virginia thanks to the cessation of days of rain and rising waters. That morning Custer led the way as the Third Division galloped through the streets that had hosted so much recent fighting and that remained strewn with barricades left behind by the enemy. According to Trooper John Morey, the 5th Michigan "charge[d] through the town and of all the screaming and yelling you ever saw or heard[,] we done." Custer's men rampaged through the place, snatching up stragglers, taking custody of severely wounded Confederates who had been left to the clemency of the enemy, and skirmishing with Lee's rearguard on the roads to the Potomac.[37]

On July 13, as Meade personally reconnoitered Lee's defenses, an operation that persuaded him to approve an advance by the entire army the following morning, Custer and his Wolverines enjoyed another respite. Gearing up for a climactic confrontation on the fourteenth, Kilpatrick spent the day probing the enemy's far left on the Hagerstown road with a portion of the First Brigade. Curiously, he bolstered his force with a few hundred Pennsylvania militia who had joined Meade's columns after departing their home state under the command of Custer's Peninsula Campaign superior, Baldy Smith. Repeating his mishandling of the regiment at Gettysburg, Kilpatrick without authority from army headquarters ordered the 1st Vermont Cavalry to charge some heavily occupied works outside the town. As a result Kilpatrick received a message from Meade rebuking him for having "disarranged" the commanding general's plans.[38]

The mistimed attack was a prelude to Kill-Cavalry's performance on the fourteenth, the day Lee began to cross his army over the river—some four hours before Meade's offensive was scheduled to begin. The water had receded sufficiently to enable most of the Army of Northern Virginia to ford at Williamsport. Three miles downriver at Falling Waters, a pontoon bridge capable of accommodating vehicles as well as troops had been laid after days of strenuous labor by fatigue teams working under the guidance of engineer officers.

Before dawn on that foggy morning, Kilpatrick's scouts informed him that the nearest enemy pickets had suddenly disappeared. By daylight Federal troopers seized a crest the enemy had occupied only hours earlier. Sent in pursuit of the departed ones, Custer overtook some stragglers from whom he learned that Lee's men were crossing at Williamsport. Upon hearing the news, Kilpatrick ordered Custer there posthaste, but when the 5th Michigan reached the river it was too late. As Captain Kidd reported, lines of carefully erected breastworks remained in and around the town but "there was no enemy there. Lee had given Meade the slip."[39]

Kidd exaggerated, but only slightly. When his comrades in the 5th, under Lieutenant Colonel Gould, charged into Williamsport they "encountered no considerable force." Even so, under Custer's direction they located and attacked elements of Lee's rearguard, which they drove across the Potomac, in the process taking several prisoners. Enough fighting took place to produce a few casualties including the severe wounding of Gould, who was succeeded by Major Trowbridge. According to Private Victor Comte of the 5th, Custer personally dispatched at least one Rebel who resisted being forced into retreat. The French-born Comte, who was uncertain of his commander's name but well aware of his affinity for combat, saw "General Koster . . . plunge his saber into the belly of a rebel who was trying to kill him. You can guess how bravely soldiers fight for such a general."[40]

As it happened, the day was not entirely lost. As Kidd recalled, "word came that they [the Confederates] were not all across after all"—the passage at Falling Waters was still underway. At Kilpatrick's frantic order, Custer turned his column about and led the 6th Michigan toward the bend in the river where breastworks and entrenchments still manned by thousands of infantrymen and artillerists protected Lee's precious pontoon bridge.

Custer, Kilpatrick at his side, covered the five miles to Falling Waters "in hot haste." In advance of the main body of the 6th rode Peter Weber with two companies of the regiment. Despite the slowly dissipating fog and the excessively muddy roads, under the major's vocal prodding the squadron far outdistanced the body of its outfit. Kidd, riding well back in the column, observed that upon nearing the river the column angled off the main road through a woods that skirted farm fields. Coming up suddenly on the right of the road was a line of field works on elevated ground overlooking the bridge: "Behind the earthwork a considerable force of Confederate infantry was seen in bivouac, evidently taking a rest, with arms stacked." The captain believed the position was held by two brigades. In fact, the works were extensive enough to accommodate almost the entire division of Major General Henry Heth, comprising the brigades of Brigadier Generals James Johnston Pettigrew, James J. Archer, and Joseph R. Davis, and Colonel J. M. Brockenbrough.

Kilpatrick and Custer, catching up with Weber's detachment at around 11:30 a.m., had differing ideas on how to engage the Southerners. Custer prudently ordered the major to dismount his men, throw out a line of skirmishers, and size up the opposition. He was emphatically overruled by Kilpatrick, who directed Weber to remount and charge the high ground. In disbelief Custer stood helplessly by as Weber obeyed the order. Kidd reported the result: Weber "placed himself at their head and giving the order 'Forward,' emerged from the woods into the open field, took the trot until near the top of the slope, close to the earthworks, and then with a shout the little band of less than a hundred men charged right into the midst of ten times their number of veteran troops. . . . Weber, cutting right and left with his saber, and cheering on his men, pierced the first line, but there could be but one result."[41]

At first stunned by the attack—Heth and his subordinates had mistaken the Yankees for a body of Stuart's cavalry—the languid Confederates quickly recovered their composure, seized their rifles, and shot their assailants out of the saddle. The attackers lost thirty men including six officers. Weber and Lieutenant Charles E. Bolza were killed; four others were wounded, including Kidd, who took a minié ball through his right foot.[42]

The enemy saw Weber's charge ("the most gallant ever made," according to Kilpatrick) as a prelude to a larger attack; it expedited the flight of many of Heth's men across the pontoons. His main body, however, stood firm when the balance of Custer's brigade reached the scene and dismounted to lash the bridgehead with their Spencers. The Confederates again took a toll on the

6th Michigan, driving it back and cutting down several of its men including Captain David G. Royce, who fell dead at the head of his company.

At about this time the 1st Michigan, followed by the 7th and Pennington's battery, came up on the left and rear of the 6th, halting the latter's rush to the rear. The 1st, too, was held at arm's length until Heth ordered everyone to head for the bridge. At that point—more than two hours after the fighting had begun—Town's regiment closed in, capturing five officers and sixty-five men of a Virginia regiment in Brockenbrough's brigade along with two battle flags. Meanwhile, the 7th, under Lieutenant Colonel Litchfield, attacked dismounted against the enemy's far left, seizing a cannon and turning it against its former owners. The Confederates' most prominent casualty was General Pettigrew, mortally wounded by a carbine round fired by a trooper of the 6th.[43]

Supposedly, Kilpatrick had coordinated operations with John Buford, who was closing in on Falling Waters from the east. Buford's advance reached the bridgehead on schedule, but Kilpatrick's decision to have Weber attack immediately upon arrival ensured that the First Division got there too late. Buford's men trapped a few hundred Rebels, a fraction of the total they might have bagged had Kilpatrick attacked as planned. Soon after Buford appeared, the rearmost Confederates crossed the river and the pontoon bridge was cut loose from the Virginia side, dashing any hopes of further pursuit. Kidd was saddened and disgusted by the outcome. So were a great many of his comrades in and outside the Michigan Cavalry Brigade. So was George Armstrong Custer.[44]

* * *

Exhausted and covered with battle scars, Custer's command rested by the river through the remainder of the day before taking up the march at sunup on the fifteenth. Along with the remainder of the Third Cavalry Division, the Wolverines trotted back to Hagerstown and Funkstown and then took the turnpike to Boonsboro. Though worn and weary, many were in high spirits. They had failed to land a decisive blow against Lee, but they had helped send him back to Virginia with the exultant cheers of Yankee cavalrymen ringing in his ears. In a letter to his father, William Ball of the 5th Michigan boasted that "we have sent old lee out of PA, and crost Maryland into old verginne. We lict him [every] time we atacked him." The men felt they could take a substantial amount of the credit for the enemy's enforced departure. Writing to the editor of a Battle Creek newspaper, Adjutant George G. Briggs of the 6th Michigan declared that "the world has never seen such Cavalry fighting as we have done, which is the testimony of the best Cavalry officers in the service." The 1st Michigan's Benjamin Clark believed that the Army of Northern Virginia "will remember Gen Killpatrick's [sic] Cavalry for some time."[45]

If Judson Kilpatrick had his way, that memory would be even sharper, reflecting more brightly on his leadership. In his report of the fight at Falling Waters, completed late in July, he bragged that he "routed the enemy at all points, and drove him toward the river," killing dozens of defenders and capturing two pieces of artillery, two caissons, a large number of small arms, three battle flags, and "upward of 1,500 prisoners." His claims were outlandish and indefensible, but he did not care, and neither did most of his men, for his boasts elevated their reputations as well as his.[46]

This time, however, Kilpatrick's exaggerations provoked an angry response—not from any of his colleagues or superiors, but from the enemy. On August 7 Robert E. Lee, who had read Kill-Cavalry's report in a Richmond newspaper that had copied its publication in the *New York Times*, took the unusual step of filing a formal protest with Meade. Lee contended that the report was grossly incorrect: "The enemy did not capture any organized body of men on that occasion, but only stragglers and such as were left asleep on the road. . . . The number of stragglers thus lost I am unable to state with accuracy, but it is greatly exaggerated in the dispatch referred to." The battery horses had likewise been exhausted, forcing General Heth to leave behind the two cannons Kilpatrick claimed to have captured in the fight.[47]

After receiving Lee's communication, Meade called on Kilpatrick to provide evidence to support his claims. The division leader played for time, procuring a twenty-days' leave on account of "a severe pain in my side" (Kilpatrick suffered from a chronic kidney condition that would eventually take his life) and also to visit his home in New York where his wife had just given birth to the couple's first child. He left Maryland on the fifteenth, leaving Custer to succeed him. Barely two weeks after achieving brigade command, Custer was now temporarily commanding a full division of horsemen, some 3,500 strong.[48]

It was enough to make one's head spin. By all accounts, however, the young general's would remain firmly in place.

Chapter XI

Apprenticeship Complete

On July 15 Custer received his first orders as commander of the Third Cavalry Division. Pleasonton told him to cross one of his brigades over the river opposite Harpers Ferry, where a pontoon span had been laid. Proceeding south, "marching as safely as practicable," he was to locate and kill, capture, or disperse enemy troops who had fired on the army's supply trains near Point of Rocks on the Potomac. With the rest of his command Custer was to continue south in advance of the main army, reconnoitering the various gaps in the Blue Ridge, on the other side of which Lee's army was in motion.[1]

Custer assigned the search-and-destroy mission to the First Brigade, now under the command of Colonel Othneil De Forrest. He then he led the Wolverines over the river on another floating bridge at Berlin, Maryland, six miles east of Harpers Ferry. The brigade was initially commanded by Charles Town, but when the colonel's failing health interfered George Gray replaced him. The following day, the seventeenth, Gray's advance echelon, the 5th Michigan under Major Trowbridge, encountered a segment of Stuart's cavalry—members of Jones's brigade—in a driving rainstorm at Snicker's Gap. Although Custer did not gain definitive information on Lee's heading or intentions, his men roughly handled the Rebels, "routing them with no loss" to the brigade, according to John Morey of the 5th Michigan, and driving them from the pass.[2]

The Michiganders continued on toward a series of defiles, any one of which Lee might take to transfer his army from the Shenandoah Valley to the line of the Rappahannock, his assumed destination. On the twentieth, after passing through the Loudoun Valley on ground fought over during the run-up to Gettysburg, Gray's brigade again attacked and dispersed Rebel pickets a short distance in front of Ashby's Gap. Through information from prisoners taken there Custer believed that Longstreet's corps, leading Lee's column, had been prevented from driving through Ashby's and forced to continue south. To make sure the Rebels did not change their mind and seek to access the Loudoun Valley, Custer left Gray's men within reach of the gap until the twenty-second.[3]

Although much scouting and a certain amount of fighting were asked of Custer's men, their leader managed to carve out time to communicate with his family through correspondence, something he had been unable to do since the commencement of the campaign in Maryland and Pennsylvania. One of his first letters, written from Amissville, Virginia, went to Ann Reed, for whom he summarized his activities over the past month and to whom he expressed his delight at being "the youngest General in the U.S. Army by over two years." He observed that "I have been through many dangers since I last wrote to you. . . . I had three horses shot under me." Since returning to Virginia "I have had the post of honor . . . that is I have had the advance with my division." He described in some detail the composition of his command and stressed that "I would not exchange it [the Wolverine Brigade] for any other brigade in the Army." He made sure that Ann understood that "the regiment in which I endeavored to obtain the colonelcy (5th) belongs to my brigade so that I rather outwitted the Governor who did not see fit to give it to me." If he had his way, Austin Blair would never cease to regret his politically inspired error in judgment.

Over the past six weeks or so Custer had lacked the opportunity to consider the course of his pursuit of the women in his life. Although his romantic interests appeared to be wide-ranging and almost indiscriminate (he asked Ann to remember him "to all the girls in town"), his focus had narrowed to two, and perhaps to one. His infatuation with Fannie Fifield appeared to dominate his interests. He had asked Pleasonton if upon Kilpatrick's return to the army he might take leave in Monroe. The corps commander had promised that "I can have a leave but only on this condition"—that he go home and marry Fannie. He asked Ann (playfully, one supposes), "Shall I come?"[4]

Even before he wrote his sister Custer had sent at least one letter to Nettie Humphrey, signifying his intention to keep in close touch, through her intercession, with Libbie Bacon. He wrote to give Nettie, as he had his sister, a glimpse into his daily life and an appreciation of the demands made on his time as commander of two brigades of cavalry and two batteries of artillery: "I have but a few minutes, as I intend to march several miles before night and to attack the enemy cavalry early in the morning."[5]

His real reason for writing, however, was to explain away an incident that had upset Libbie and for which she blamed him. He had learned that Fannie had described to other people the ambrotype Libbie had given him, something the judge's daughter had feared might happen. Though Libbie claimed that Fannie's access to the photograph did not bother her, in her journal she fumed that Custer "had no business to write the passionate messages he has about me & to me [via Nettie] when he has been writing so constantly & lovelike to Fan." The mixed signals left her with conflicting feelings toward the man who had proposed to her six months ago: "He is nothing to me. He never will be. . . . [yet] I like him much."[6]

Custer was insistent that Nettie should present his side of the story to the woman he had come to care for deeply: "I never showed it, or even described it, to Fannie. How Fannie was able to describe it I cannot tell, unless she got the information from the picture gallery." Whether or not he was being truthful, he added an unambiguous statement of his feelings toward Miss Bacon: "Fannie *has nothing in her power to bestow that w*[oul]*d. induce me to show her that ambrotype.* I know nothing of what representations of our intimacy she has made to Libbie. It is no different from what I told her. . . ."[7]

If this declaration was not enough to convince Libbie of his true feelings toward her, an event that took place in Monroe on July 5 should have. That day David Reed paid an unexpected visit to the Bacon home carrying what Libbie called a "huge envelope like the affairs of state!" It contained an equally large drawing of Custer's charge at Aldie, detailing the unorthodox uniform he had worn including the "rebel hat" that allowed him to escape detection by the enemy whose ranks he invaded on his runaway horse. It had been sketched by Alfred Waud, a noted artist-correspondent for *Harper's Weekly*. The drawing, which indicated the celebrity Custer had gained even before winning his brigadier's star, must have impressed Libbie, although perhaps less so when David explained that it was a gift not to her but to the Reed family, one its subject wished to be shown to his many friends including Fannie. Still, Custer had stipulated that Libbie, above all others, should see it.

Before he left, David handed Libbie a letter that he and Ann had received shortly after Aldie, in which Custer detailed the dangers he had faced and his near-miraculous escape. Libbie read it without apparent interest and expressed a wish that David would relay to his brother-in-law her gratitude for the "great many pleasant times last winter," during which "he was so gallant & polite." As David turned to go, she casually mentioned a piece of news that her romantic rival had made certain she heard: Custer planned to take leave from the army sometime in the fall, return to Monroe, and marry Fannie. Her incredulous visitor spun around and asked why she believed this to be true, the clear implication being that she was very wrong. Alert to David's words and body language, Libbie suddenly realized that Custer loved her, and her alone.[8]

*   *   *

Custer enjoyed division command and not just because of the additional power and authority it conferred. He could make himself known to a wider audience while renewing acquaintances with officers he had served with intermittently during the recent campaigning. The heavier workload and additional responsibilities were burdens to be endured, but the routine of high command was still fresh to him, his physical stamina was not in question, and he embraced the challenges as they cropped up. In his letter to his sister he spoke matter-of-factly of the new order of things: "I am at work night and day usually get up before daylight [and] go to bed late and [am] called up several times during the night so that you can readily see I have little time for matters outside of my official duties."[9]

An example of those duties and the urgency with which he must attend to them came in the form of a telegram he received from Pleasonton's adjutant only five days after returning his command to Virginia: "The Maj Gen Comdg directs me to seek from you again a field return of your command. Both of the other divisions have complied with the request and given me the best one they could. Please send one in early tomorrow as Gen Williams [Brigadier General Seth Williams, Meade's adjutant general] is most urgent for the most accurate report he can obtain tomorrow. . . ." The order must have jarred Custer at least a little. It told him that it mattered not that he had just emerged from a campaign in which he had distinguished himself on numerous occasions, making a major contribution to his army's successes despite a complete lack of experience in his newly assigned position. As far as the army's front office was concerned, he was just another delinquent subordinate who needed to be prodded into action via a peremptory demand.[10]

Two days after Custer was admonished for his tardiness, Meade directed General French, now commanding the Third Corps, to drive through Manassas Gap and attack Lee's army on the other side, thus cutting off his retreat. On July 23 French relieved Buford's cavalry inside the gap, but upon nearing the Confederate flank he found himself held at bay by a single brigade of infantry. Thanks to his timidity and ineptitude, Longstreet's corps, followed by that of A. P. Hill, continued its withdrawal.[11]

To gain a position from which to monitor the enemy's progress, Custer on the twenty-third led his division, this day reduced to six regiments and two batteries, from Upperville, across the tracks of the Manassas Gap Railroad, and over Hedgeman's River, a Rappahannock tributary. At 5 p.m. Colonel Gray's brigade reached Amissville, about four miles from the foot of the Blue Ridge and fourteen miles north of Culpeper Court House. On the way, Custer learned of French's failure to intercept Longstreet, whose column had passed through Chester Gap, seven miles below the point at which it had been accosted. Hill's troops were only a few hours' march to the rear, while most of Ewell's corps had crossed the mountains at Thornton's Gap, fifteen miles below Longstreet's avenue of passage.[12]

Custer was determined to keep tabs on the Rebel columns before they could settle in at one of their old haunts in Culpeper County. On the way to Amissville, he sent a regiment westward via the Sperryville-Alexandria Turnpike to Gaines's Cross Roads, where enemy activity had been reported. Not far beyond Amissville, the regiment encountered skirmishers, whom it drove to within a mile of the crossroads. At that point, as Custer later reported, his main body found the "enemy in force and in such position as prevented our farther advance. We sustained a loss of 6 or 7 wounded." He had the regiment hold its advanced position about one mile from Gaines's. By now Custer should have realized that he was in a precarious spot. An entire Confederate corps was within a few miles of him, a second lurked not far behind, and he was too far from his own army to receive quick support.[13]

Still, all was serene at Amissville. En route Custer had encountered only a few intoxicated stragglers from Stuart's command and a dozen sober comrades who had been herding sheep and cattle for Lee's army. Reliable information on Lee's whereabouts was hard to come by, but one of the prisoners warned Custer that "about one day's march from here" he would meet enough people in gray to "give you all you would want." Custer paid no heed, informing Pleasonton by courier that he would "endeavor to annoy the enemy to-morrow morning as much as it is in my power to do." In other words, he intended not merely to reconnoiter Lee's troops but to pitch into them, speeding them on their way to their designated destination.[14]

This was not a sound plan, because early on the twenty-fourth the straggler's prediction came true. Around daylight Custer, with his five regiments and twelve guns, headed southwest to Newby's Cross Roads, a point from which he might track the movements of the nearest Rebels. Instead, Lee's southward-marching column—infantry, cavalry, and artillery—tracked him to Newby's and also to Gaines's Cross Roads. On the way Custer was informed by a messenger that the outfit at Gaines's was opposed by large numbers of Confederates—members of Longstreet's rear guard, the brigade of Brigadier General Henry L. Benning, supported by detachments of cavalry and artillery. In response, Custer sent two regiments and Elder's Battery E to the threatened point while pushing ahead with the 1st, 5th, and 6th Michigan and Pennington's battery.

He met no resistance until less than two miles from Newby's, at which point he captured stragglers who reported that Longstreet's entire corps was heading straight for him. The prisoners were either misinformed or lying, for Longstreet's column, except for Benning, had cleared the area on the last leg to Culpeper Court House. However, the head of Hill's corps was just now arriving; its approach threatened to catch Custer's truncated division between two weighty forces. Seemingly unconcerned, he marched on.[15]

About a mile from the crossroads, along a lateral extension of an eminence known locally as Battle (or "Bataille") Mountain, the cavalry's vanguard made contact with Hill's skirmishers. Not yet fully aware of the unfolding situation, Custer advanced on the enemy with eight dismounted companies, four each of the 5th and 6th Michigan. The combined force drove the skirmishers back on their main body, which was found posted on a commanding ridge.

Custer, believing he had the advantage, formed a line of battle while ordering Pennington to open with shell and canister. The enemy responded by sending a heavy force to threaten his left flank. Suddenly an equally powerful column appeared about a half mile behind the 5th and 6th, cutting off both regiments from the rear guard, the 1st Michigan, and then spreading out to menace Custer's other flank. Soon the Wolverines were hemmed in on three sides by foot soldiers, with Battle Mountain on the fourth side, leaving "no road . . . to escape by." In his report Custer attributed the enemy's interposition to what he cryptically described as "an un-looked for delay occurring in relieving my skirmishers."[16]

Custer later claimed to have learned that a local resident had warned the Confederates about a force of twenty thousand Federals marching from Amissville to attack them ("this story I know to have been credited by Longstreet, and he made his dispositions accordingly"). In other words, he had been opposed by a force too powerful to contend with due to the untimely receipt of a fictitious report of his strength. This did not serve as an excuse for his predicament, which he had created by failing to reconnoiter the Amissville-Newby's Cross Roads corridor.

Custer was forced to deal quickly with "the most critical [position] I was ever in." By the sheerest of margins he wriggled out of it. Resolving to return to Amissville posthaste, he retrieved one regiment and four of Pennington's rifled guns from their original positions on the left side of the Sperryville-Alexandria Pike. One of the battery's sections, under Lieutenant Carle Woodruff, was almost immediately attacked by Hill's foot soldiers, forcing it still farther to the rear. With minutes to spare, Woodruff limbered up and hauled his guns to safety via what Lieutenant Pennington called "a circuitous route through the woods." Custer would take credit for "cutting a road" through the trees, "to enable the artillery to retire." Then, "taking advantage of a temporary check on our immediate front, I succeeded in uniting my command and withdrew deliberately and in excellent order to Amissville, with a loss not exceeding 15."[17]

A lost opportunity by his opponents appears to have saved Custer. In his memoirs, Sergeant James H. Avery of the 5th Michigan attributed the Wolverines' escape to "an opening between their [the Confederates'] lines and the foot of the mountain. . . . They had bagged their game, but had left a hole in the bag" by failing to extend their flanking movement far enough to the right.[18]

In a follow-up report filed a month after the fight, Custer gave most of the credit for eluding the trap to Colonel Gray and Lieutenant Woodruff and a "display of great courage by both officers and men." Gray had suffered for his effective leadership, having been thrown from his horse and run over by the mounts of the men following him. Custer also updated his casualty count to thirty while insisting that the enemy had suffered "much greater" losses. How he arrived at this conclusion is unknown, but this time Lee chose not to question his enemy's veracity through official channels. He might have taken issue with another of Custer's post-battle statements had it been brought to his attention: "My attack at Newby's Cross-Roads spread great consternation through the entire Rebel column extending beyond Gaines' in the direction of Chester Gap."[19]

*   *   *

Once Custer escaped, Hill and Longstreet resumed their retreat as if the attack at Newby's had been a mere irritant. Hill would dismiss the affair in a single sentence: "The enemy was soon put to flight in confusion, and no more annoyance occurred on the march." Because the Confederates were intent on reaching defensive lines farther south, Custer was permitted to remain unmolested at Amissville, where, as he informed Pleasonton, "I met no enemy; found the roads all clear."[20]

He remained there for the next week, resting and resupplying. The refit was sorely needed for scores of troopers had been unhorsed during the recent campaigning and those mounts still serviceable had gone for days without forage. The division's supply trains were being restocked, however, and the command's mobility was not a problem. The men were another matter; realizing they were short of rations, Custer permitted them to pillage the countryside. The 7th Michigan's Edwin Havens wrote his brother that "our orders now are to take every thing that we want and it is carried out to the letter." John Morey reported that he and his comrades in the 5th Michigan "have plenty of chicken and all kinds of fresh meat that we confiscate" from local secessionists.[21]

For all the troubles he experienced, Custer would not have regretted attacking A. P. Hill. In a letter to Nettie Humphrey two months earlier he had mentioned "a rule which I have always laid down—never to regret anything after it is done." He did, however, grieve over his division's post-battle condition. In addition to the men who had been lost to active duty through wounds or sickness during the Gettysburg Campaign, Newby's Cross Roads had taken a substantial toll. The 1st Michigan, for example, had been reduced to fewer than 280 men fit for active duty; the other regiments had suffered accordingly though perhaps not as severely. Additional losses occurred when, four days after the battle, Custer sent the "played out horses" of the division under Colonel Gray to the remount depot at Giesboro Point on the Anacostia River outside Washington. Upon Custer's application, Lieutenant Pennington, who lacked ammunition and equipage, was also permitted to travel north to obtain the required materiel.[22]

Custer's superiors were equally concerned about the state of his command. On July 28, by which time Meade's infantry had drawn within supporting range of Custer, the army's inspectors were warned they would find his force "small—not more than twelve hundred—until his dismounted men return from Washington." And yet even after his recent travail Custer had not lost the urge to advance and attack. On the day his deficiencies were reported to army headquarters he informed Pleasonton that a large helping of Stuart's cavalry—at least three thousand of them, he believed—had been observed at Little Washington, a Blue Ridge village nestled between Chester and Thornton's Gaps, its pickets extending to within two miles of Gaines's Cross Roads. "If that portion of my command now absent with unserviceable horses were here," he wrote, "I would like to make a demonstration" against the enemy force.

Pleasonton relayed Custer's wishes to Meade's headquarters, which believed that the division's station, due to its proximity to Stuart's forces, should be held. Custer's worn-down command, however, could be allowed to resupply at the railroad if a sufficient force was sent to take its place. Accordingly, on the thirty-first, Gregg's division relieved Custer, whose men marched north to Warrenton Junction.[23]

Before he departed Amissville Custer, along with several of his officers, did a little entertaining. The Union army's movements always acted as a magnet for Virginia slaves who, offered at least a temporary shelter by the presence of blue-coated soldiers, fled in hopes of being escorted out of bondage. The chattels of Rappahannock County were no exception; with the coming of the Third Division scores of slaves had flocked to Amissville.

On the evening of the thirtieth Custer massed the local would-be freedmen. They were informed that they could accompany his column to Warrenton if they could procure transportation or were willing to make the twelve-mile journey afoot; or, if they preferred, they could remain in the area under the protection of General Gregg. The fugitives appear to have appreciated the army's solicitude. That night the more talented among them, or the less inhibited, took part in a "hoe-down" that Custer and his staff attended.[24]

Custer had long been served by a few faithful attendants, notably Joseph Fought and Johnny Cisco. To this little family, he now added eighteen-year-old Eliza Brown, formerly the property of a local farmer, Robert H. Pierce. Despite her severely circumscribed environment, the teenager was bright, plucky, and self-reliant. She would recall that "I didn't set down to wait to have 'em all free *me*. I helped to free myself."[25]

She was also, as she informed Custer, a good cook, and he took her at her word. In Eliza Brown, he had much more than a short-order cook. In quick time the runaway slave, knowledgeable in a variety of domestic arts, would become an integral part of Custer's wartime household. She would also serve as a companion, confidant, and comforter to her employer's future wife. In the end, not only by her culinary skills but also by her nimble mind and generous heart, she would become indispensable to both of them.

* * *

By the first week of August, the contending forces were back in their all-too-familiar positions along opposite sides of the Rappahannock. The Third Cavalry Division covered the far left flank of Meade's army. Its picket lines stretched east from Ellis's Ford, via U.S. Ford, Hartwood Church, and Stafford Court House, to Aquia Creek. While the Wolverines continued their refit at Warrenton Junction, most of the terrain was picketed by the First Brigade, now led by Colonel Edward B. Sawyer of the 1st Vermont Cavalry.

It was along this extended line that Kilpatrick found his command upon his return from leave on August 6. He must have been shocked by the depleted force at his disposal. Five days earlier Custer had found so few troopers equipped for duty that he had been forced to defer taking up the full extent of his assigned position until the Michigan Brigade's refit was complete. Some of its men had been returned to full duty; others had not. That same day, at the direction of corps headquarters, he had sent a "party of 300 picked men" from the 5th and 7th Michigan to hunt down the partisan rangers of Major John Singleton Mosby, who had been sniping at Meade's communication lines around Alexandria and Fairfax Court House with unusual frequency and to great advantage. Mosby had been a major irritant to the Federal armies in Virginia for many months, having outwitted and eluded every party sent to curtail his depredations. Though not a devotee of wishful thinking, Custer indulged in it on this occasion, relaying his "strong hopes" that his men would "capture or drive Mosby out of the country."[26]

The mission, aimed at capturing the Rebels who had waylaid an eighty-mule supply train near Alexandria, failed miserably. Nor were the Michiganders able to overtake another partisan leader, Lieutenant Colonel Elijah V. White, whose 35th Virginia Battalion, according to reports, was about to raid other supply depots in the same vicinity. Perhaps Custer's assignment of Colonel Mann to lead the expedition was the root cause of its failure. The leader of the 7th Michigan had shown himself to be erratic and unreliable on numerous occasions predating Gettysburg, and his subordinates were in the process of drafting a petition seeking his removal.[27]

The Mosby hunt drained the strength of the Third Division, but corps headquarters was not through with making manpower levies on it. Two days before Kilpatrick replaced him in command, Custer was directed to send an additional five hundred troopers on the trail of the "Gray Ghost" and his marauders. Within a matter of hours, Pleasonton upped the required number to between eight hundred and one thousand. Custer was willing to comply, but he warned his superior that due to the detachments sent to Washington and Warrenton Junction he now had fewer than nine hundred men other than those committed to picket duty. Apparently Pleasonton's demand was withdrawn, for a few days later Custer, again in charge of the Second Brigade, was ordered to relieve Sawyer's men on the picket line between U.S. Ford and Stafford Court House with "your entire command."[28]

At his new field headquarters at Hartwood Church, twenty-five miles south of Warrenton Junction, life appeared to improve for Custer—except in his pursuit of the woman he had decided he loved. Most of his men were back on duty and suddenly the war news, or at least the supposed state of the enemy's morale, was encouraging. On the thirteenth he sent Pleasonton a copy of a Richmond newspaper whose editor admitted "the hopelessness with which they regard their prospects. This feeling pervades their entire army." That day he wrote to Nettie of the culinary pleasures he enjoyed with Eliza Brown at the cook stove: "We are living in magnificent style."

He had additional, more personal, reasons for writing Nettie. He wished her to know that her sweetheart, Jacob Lyman Greene, whom he had recently added to his staff as adjutant general of the brigade, "is doing admirably . . . I tried him the other day, took him where bullets flew thick and fast. . . . He never faltered, was as calm and collected as if sitting at his dinner." Already he was attempting to gain a captaincy for his friend from Monroe. Custer also had another back-home personage very much in mind, asking Nettie: "Did Judge Bacon think my promotion deserved or not? Or did he maintain a dignified silence?"[29]

Custer suspected that the only way to gain the good graces of Libbie's father was through professional success and the celebrity it might generate. For this reason he petitioned his aide, James Christiancy, to write Bacon in his behalf, singing his praises as a man and a soldier—under the guise of satisfying the judge's interest in Jim's welfare. Christiancy spoke of riding with Custer during a recent reconnaissance. He cited the courage of several officers but gave the lion's share of the coverage to the brigade leader: "To say that General Custer is a brave man is unnecessary. He has proven himself to be not only that but a very cool and self possessed man. It is indeed very difficult to disturb his mental Equilibrium." The staff officer could not, however, testify to Custer being a qualified suitor—a man of intellect as well as action, a faithful lover, a professed Christian.[30]

On the twenty-fourth Nettie responded to Custer's latest letter by throwing a blanket on his hopes for a sanctioned relationship with Libbie Bacon. In her conversations with Daniel, "your name is seldom if ever mentioned," although he had acknowledged the breathless coverage devoted to Custer's military operations by the *Commercial* and other news outlets. Nettie described Bacon as "a man of strong prejudices," but for all that he was a good man and a devoted father. Because Libbie would never resist his efforts to safeguard her happiness and reputation, Nettie thought Custer's persistence in wooing her "not for the best." At some point he must resolve to "give her up utterly and forever."[31]

He appeared to take Nettie's advice philosophically: "That time may come, perhaps soon. When it does come, I hope it will find me the same soldier I now try to be, as capable of meeting the reverses of life as I am those of war. . . . Rest assured, that whatever fortune may have in store for me will be borne cheerfully." He spoke bravely, but the words were not indicative of what he felt and believed. Because he had not abandoned hope, he searched for an opportunity to return to Monroe for a decisive confrontation with Libbie and her too-controlling father.[32]

* * *

Operational demands remained a concern, specifically the recent substantial increase in guerrilla-style attacks on his picket lines, not all of which could be attributed to Mosby's men. Custer's subordinates had apprehended a number of local civilians accused of either spying on his units or firing on them from concealment. A number of them had been sent to cavalry corps headquarters only to be released, paroled, and returned to their homes. Custer thought this a bad business, telling Pleasonton that the suspected guerrillas "regard their paroles no more than they do so much blank paper, and are as able to injure us by bushwhacking. . . . Complaints have been made to me, and in some cases arrests have been made, but I am powerless to act in consequence of their paroles from the headquarters of the Army of the Potomac. I can suppress bushwhacking, and render every man within the limits of my command practically loyal, if allowed to deal with them as I choose."[33]

Pleasonton replied to Custer's letter by explaining that the civilians had been released because "there was nothing against them except they would not take the Oath of Allegiance. Any citizen that you will arrest under any other charges and send in will be retained and forwarded to Washington."

He then relayed the missive to army headquarters. He appears to have done so because he believed Meade would appreciate reading the Richmond paper Custer included with the letter. But Meade and his staff paid more attention to the brigadier's complaint and especially the words in which he phrased it. Five days earlier Custer's former superior Andrew Humphreys, now Meade's chief of staff, had written to Pleasonton in regard to cavalry officers who arrested Virginia citizens without sufficient evidence of any crimes. Humphreys had directed that "for the present such arrests will not be made, but will be limited to those engaged in . . . [depredations] and such others against whom there is suspicion of having been engaged in them, or of having been guilty of any disloyal act."[34]

Political considerations had compelled the army's hierarchy to step carefully through the world of civil-military relations—too carefully, in the view of officers such as Custer whose commands were suffering daily the effects of guerrilla warfare. Not illogically, Custer believed he had the right to vent his frustration and bring it to the attention of the high command. Thus he must have been shocked to receive Humphreys's reply, through Pleasonton, on the seventeenth. The cavalry chief was directed to remind his disgruntled subordinate that "it is the manifest duty of every officer engaged in the duty General Custer is intrusted with to arrest every one who disregards a parole or pledge. . . . the instructions from these headquarters do not render him, or any other officer, powerless to act whenever any good reason exists for arrest. . . . But . . . the loose statements upon this subject contained in the letter of General Custer do not impress the major-general commanding with the suitableness of intrusting to that officer the discretion he suggests. . . ."[35]

The reprimand was a slap in the face to a complainant whose strictures on the army's handling of disloyal and dangerous civilians were well-taken but also impolitic and perhaps even insubordinate. As one historian has pointed out, because Custer's picket lines had become a favorite target of Rebel raiders and guerrillas, "for the first time the young general may have truly felt the weight of the responsibility resting upon his shoulders." He was learning the lessons of wartime politics as they applied to military commanders. Like Meade, Humphreys, and many another general officer in the Army of the Potomac, Custer was a conservative Democrat, to the point that staunch Republicans such as Austin Blair considered him a Copperhead. From 1861 on he had been a disciple of McClellan, having embraced Little Mac's conservative approach to the conflict, based on persuading the enemy to see the error of his ways rather than crushing his armies, his economy, and his society. Now Custer was viewing events from a different perspective, as the victim of an uncivilized form of warfare.[36]

He had a right to his opinion that Meade was tying his hands, preventing him from returning the blows of an opponent who refused to fight fair. The trouble lay in the words he used to express his chagrin and anger. Like many another young man, he had permitted emotion to trump patience and civility, a dangerous course under any circumstances but especially so when vocally criticizing official policy.

Custer's contretemps with Meade and Humphreys appear to have further damaged his already shaky relationship with Kilpatrick, while also embarrassing Pleasonton. A series of confrontations with both superiors over the next three weeks threatened to divert his attention from his operational duties. Some of the difficulties involved minor administrative issues, but the tone of the communications that passed between Custer and his correspondents, especially Kilpatrick, was sometimes quite severe. Matters appeared to come to a head on August 21 when the division leader upbraided Custer for failing to investigate a subordinate who had unlawfully seized the property of a local citizen, complaining that "instead of doing as you were directed you saw fit to give your opinion and that in a manner most disrespectful to your commanding officer. I have noticed lately in your communications to these headquarters some [hostile] feeling to me. . . . I hope no erroneous ideas will induce you to forget that it is impossible for me to command the division without the willing support of my brigade commanders."[37]

Command relations probably suffered further in early September when Pleasonton admonished Kilpatrick for "a very great want of discipline" in the Third Division. As an example the corps commander cited the disrespect with which some enlisted men treated their officers. Kilpatrick, who never appreciated the concept of accountability, undoubtedly shifted a large helping of the blame onto Custer, whose attitude toward him seemed to typify the general situation.[38]

Yet another incident that suggested a certain amount of ill will between Custer and his superiors derived from a statement he had made in his recent letter of complaint. His men had captured the civilian bearer of some personal letters. They included one written by an aide on the staff of a Confederate general to a young lady on the Falmouth side of the river suggesting, among other things, that a climactic battle was imminent, one sure to "produce peace." When

Pleasonton's headquarters learned of the letters, they ordered Custer to produce them. He could not comply, for he had returned the correspondence, which he considered "of a private character," to their owners. For this act Custer received a stern rebuke and a reminder "that all captured correspondence, private or not, if containing [military-related] information must be retained and forwarded."

Custer was now directed to reacquire the missives. Again, he could not obey. He had not viewed them himself; they had been returned by the officer who had captured them to their bearer, "whose whereabouts I have no knowledge." He added, rather glibly, that "the letters contained nothing whatever of importance except what has been reported." Pleasonton would have preferred to judge for himself, and he made this clear to his subordinate.[39]

These unfortunate incidents made Custer see that he must exercise greater judgment and discretion when handling matters that affected the functioning of his division and corps. Above all, he must keep his superiors informed of his actions even on such a seemingly trivial matter as the seizure of another person's mail. His difficulties with Kilpatrick, at least, would eventually cease. Over the next six months, their relationship would continue to deteriorate. It would not survive the coming winter and when the dust settled only Custer would remain standing.

* * *

The rebel staff officer's suggestion that a major event was coming made Custer keep his eyes peeled for an opportunity to put himself in a better light with his higher-ups. On August 13 Colonel Mann relayed the report of a scout from his regiment who, posing as a Rebel soldier, had infiltrated the camps of General Longstreet opposite U.S. Ford. The scout had learned that Longstreet's entire corps, augmented by five thousand cavalrymen, was preparing to cross the Rappahannock in log rafts, "getting in the rear of General Meade's army, and on to Washington." That same day Pleasonton informed Kilpatrick of a report that a cavalry-only force was about to raid around Meade's left. He directed the division commander to ensure that Custer's pickets "were strong and vigilant in that direction and if his brigade is not strong enough[,] to reinforce him. . . ."[40]

Custer reacted swiftly to the threat, promising not only to bolster vigilance but to extend his picket lines from Falmouth to Belle Plain, six miles to the east, in order to make an end run less feasible. On the seventeenth Kilpatrick assured Pleasonton that the lines on the river as far as Falmouth had been augmented, "each ford being strongly picketed." By then, however, the report of an attack by Longstreet had been discredited, and Kilpatrick had begun to suspect that the scout who made it had been a Rebel spy. Even so, Custer's pickets continued to be assailed from across the river by organized Confederates and in the rear by irregulars who also targeted the trains that made regular supply runs from the railroad at Warrenton Junction.[41]

The attackers sometimes struck directly at Falmouth including the grounds of Chatham, the manor house at the end of Custer's picket line. At other times the Lacy home served as a meeting place for opposing pickets under an informal truce. The gatherings were not always friendly: on August 14 a group of Confederates, supposedly after displaying a truce flag, opened fire on members of the 1st and 6th Michigan as they moved to relieve comrades on picket. The Wolverines replied with rifles and carbines, and for a short time a war ensued on normally neutral ground.

On the nineteenth Custer inspected the scene of the fracas and found some of his pickets conversing freely with their adversaries across the river. Striding down to the left bank of the river, he observed a truce party approaching from the Fredericksburg side. He was hailed by one of its members who requested him to come over in a boat for an "interview." Custer, probably expecting a meeting of some substance, agreed, crossing to the right bank in company with several aides and orderlies. Alighting, he learned that Colonel Robert C. Hill of North Carolina merely wished to inquire about old-army friends in the Union cavalry including Pleasonton and Gregg.

Custer attempted to profit from the parlay by eliciting information about the operations of the nearest enemy forces, but he found Hill "very guarded" and, as he later learned, deceptive about many subjects including his unit affiliation. From talking with him and other Confederates, however, Custer received the impression that a large force of infantry and cavalry occupied several points across from him including an entire division at Fredericksburg. His conversationalists were, as he later told division headquarters, "expecting a general engagement at an early day." This information appeared to tally with a report submitted two days earlier by one of Custer's outpost commanders, that two thousand Rebel horsemen had been observed moving downstream below Fredericksburg. Custer returned to the north bank carrying several Richmond newspapers, some of which appeared to disclose enemy military movements.[42]

While Custer had shown commendable initiative in personally attempting to gain intelligence on the forces confronting him, it has been pointed out that his warning of an imminent attack—which did not materialize—only increased the stress placed on his overworked troopers, who were forced to maintain a state of high alert for several days afterward. It also brought a new round of censure from above. The parlay with Hill, which Kilpatrick considered "undignified and improper," prompted him to issue an order to his command "forbidding all intercourse with the enemy whatever." The disgruntled division leader believed the gesture should have been unnecessary since army headquarters had issued a similar order "last winter," but Custer professed ignorance of the prohibition. Kilpatrick dropped the issue, though he clearly was not pleased with his subordinate's latest transgression.[43]

As when faulted for his involvement with the Rebel mail, Custer sought an opportunity to redeem himself in the eyes of his superiors. On August 25 he led six hundred troopers on a reconnaissance of the lower Rappahannock toward King George Court House. This was the mission that Jim Christiancy had dramatized in hopes of boosting his commander's image in the eyes of Judge Bacon. The operation, which returned Custer to the Northern Neck for the first time since the Urbanna raid, involved not only the 1st and 5th Michigan but also Colonel Sawyer's 1st Vermont, which had recently been added to the no longer all-Michigan Brigade.[44]

Aimed at curtailing the efforts of Rebel infantry and cavalry to sweep the Neck for supplies and to impress local men into their armies, the enterprise was a conditional success. Two miles from King George Court House, Custer encountered the 48th Alabama Infantry, which he found ensconced in a thick woods fronted by a marsh that made maneuvering difficult. He tried to reach the foe by dismounting the Wolverine outfits and placing them on both sides of the river road, he himself between them. "This was of course," Christiancy told Libbie's father, "the most exposed position," in which Custer became a target for bullets that "passed in very uncomfortable proximity" to him but from which he never flinched. The resolve that Custer and his men demonstrated eventually forced the entire brigade of which the 48th was a part to withdraw toward Port Conway on the Rappahannock. Satisfied that he had accomplished as much as possible under the prevailing conditions, Custer retired in turn.[45]

But if he had his way, he was not through with the defenders of the Northern Neck. In his report of the expedition he drew Kilpatrick's attention to an additional force of infantry, cavalry, and artillery (seven guns) near Port Conway, which regularly crossed the river to confiscate "everything they [local civilians] have raised for the subsistence of their families. . . . I would respectfully suggest the propriety of organizing an expedition to capture the force of the enemy on this side of the river which can easily be done. . . ." His suggestion did not produce the response he had in mind, but it led indirectly to Kilpatrick's efforts to damage or sink two Union gunboats that had been captured the week before near the mouth of the Rappahannock by Confederate naval raiders. When the Union navy proved unable to recover the gunboats, on September 2 Kilpatrick blasted the vessels with shoreline artillery, rendering both, as he reported, "about worthless."[46]

* * *

Although Longstreet's corps was not preparing to outflank Custer, as had been reported in mid-August, it was soon moving in an entirely different direction. On September 9 two-thirds of the command departed Virginia by train for Georgia to aid General Braxton Bragg's Army of Tennessee. That same day Bragg had been forced to abandon the communications hub of Chattanooga. The city was immediately occupied by a much larger army under William S. Rosecrans, former subordinate to both McClellan and Grant and now the ranking Union commander in his area of the western theater. The fourteen thousand troops Longstreet transferred via this extended and cumbersome operation, which Lee had reluctantly approved, would enable Bragg to defeat Rosecrans along Chickamauga Creek on September 20 and send him fleeing back to his soon-to-be-besieged stronghold in Tennessee.[47]

With one-third of his army gone, Lee's weakened condition should have been apparent to his enemy, but not until Longstreet started off did Meade get wind of what had taken place. One reason for his ignorance was the distance between the armies. Meade remained north of the Rappahannock while most of the Army of Northern Virginia was now behind defensive works on the Rapidan, some fifteen miles to the south. The ground between the rivers was patrolled by Stuart, whose horsemen did an effective job of keeping developments within their army's ranks from Yankee eyes.[48]

On the eleventh Kilpatrick's scouts reported to army headquarters that several outposts formerly occupied by Lee's infantry had been taken over by cavalry. This news, coupled with rumors of Longstreet's departure that had spilled into Northern newspapers, finally sent Meade into action. On the twelfth he ordered Pleasonton to cross the Rappahannock with his entire command and gain a better idea of Lee's strength and position.[49]

The next morning the cavalry corps was on the move across sixteen miles of alternately rolling and wooded countryside. The ground was familiar to most of the Union troopers, who had fought over it the previous summer. On Pleasonton's right, Gregg's Second Division moved to cross the river at Sulphur Springs before passing down the road to Cedar Mountain. The First Division of John Buford prepared to cross via the railroad bridge at Rappahannock Station. The left flank would be covered by the Third Division—the First Brigade, now under Colonel Henry E. Davies, Jr., in advance—as it poised to cross at Kelly's Ford. In Buford's rear came infantry support from the Second Corps, commanded by Major General G. K. Warren. Not required to add his weight to the coming fight, Warren would venture only as far south as Brandy Station.[50]

Because Stuart's scouts were observant and thanks to a civilian informant, Buford and Kilpatrick had to fight their way across the water. At the railroad bridge and downstream at Kelly's the Federals were contested by the brigade of Brigadier General Lunsford L. Lomax, eventually reinforced by Rooney Lee's brigade (temporarily commanded by Colonel R. L. T. Beale), elements of Laurence's Baker's brigade under Colonel James B. Gordon, and several batteries of horse artillery. Even with the Confederates' advantage in artillery, it was not a fair fight; Buford and Kilpatrick bulled their way across, shoving Lomax and his supports toward Culpeper Court House. There the Confederates made a stand, forming lines of battle across open terrain and placing their guns on high ground along the town's outskirts. Before advancing on them, Buford and Kilpatrick linked forces; they proceeded south in a massive array, several thousand strong.[51]

Custer, as always, was avid for action. Before his brigade reached Culpeper Kilpatrick sent the 1st Michigan under Lieutenant Colonel Stagg toward Stevensburg to guard the far left. About a mile from the town the 1st encountered Gordon's command, which it charged and forced as far west as the foot of Pony Mountain. Later in the day Custer recalled Stagg to his main body, now led by the 1st Vermont.[52]

On Custer's right, across the tracks of the Orange and Alexandria Railroad, came Davies's brigade, the 2nd New York Cavalry in the lead, supported by Lieutenant J. H. Counselman's battery. At Kilpatrick's order, Davies moved by his left flank through the woods and fields north and east of Culpeper. After clearing the trees the colonel led his old regiment, with two others in support, in a saber charge through the village streets, forcing Lomax and Beale to withdraw precipitately and capturing two guns from the batteries of Robert Preston Chew and Marcellus N. Moorman. To follow up Davies's success, Kilpatrick ordered Custer to advance and "gain the hills" south of Culpeper, blocking the enemy's path of retreat.[53]

Custer moved to comply—as well as to halt and capture a Rebel supply train that had chugged into Culpeper minutes before the Yankees arrived. At the head of the 1st Vermont he charged down a country road until stymied by the marshy banks of a creek along the border of the town. Determined to force his way through in order to cut off Lomax, capture more guns, and overtake the train, which had begun to reverse course, Custer struggled through the morass, leaving behind all but a few members of his staff. The old impulsiveness had his way with him, and he launched what some would describe as a one-man attack on his several objectives, one that a member of the 6th Michigan, observing from the rear, called "one of the prettiest charges ever made."[54]

He never got close enough to personally accomplish anything of consequence—even the train managed to outrace him. He did manage another near-miraculous escape from harm, speeding past a line of fencing behind which dismounted Rebels fired round after round at him to no effect. Then, however, he found himself facing a brace of cannons perched on a hill southwest of Culpeper. Seeing him coming straight for his battery, a Confederate gunner got off a hasty shot that nearly found its mark. The round burst under Custer's gray charger, blowing the animal to bits, unhorsing its rider, and gashing his left leg. As the brigadier lay sprawled on the muddy earth, the rest of the 1st Vermont, finally free of the marsh, charged past and around him. With wild cheers they swarmed over the enemy guns, capturing one of them along with seven of its crew.

Before Kilpatrick and Buford could overwhelm them, Stuart's batteries limbered up and followed Lomax and Beale as the cavalry fled toward Raccoon Ford on the Rapidan. Kilpatrick pursued only as far as Pony Mountain before going into bivouac for the night, allowing Buford and Gregg, whose men had initially been checked on their way to Culpeper, to chase the Confederates to within two and a half miles of the Rapidan. The combined divisions had suffered fifty-seven casualties against an untold number of Confederate losses.[55]

With some assistance Custer struggled upright, then hobbled over to Pleasonton to report his wounding, the loss of his transportation, and the ruination of his footwear. He put in an immediate request for a two-weeks' leave of absence. Pleasonton, who in his report of the fight gushed that Custer's "gallantry was distinguished," granted his request just as quickly, and extended it by six days.[56]

Custer must have been ecstatic about the opportunity to return to the place he considered home. Eight days earlier he had requested leave to visit his sick mother. The application was based on a lie; Maria Custer's health, although never robust, remained stable. Pleasonton, suspecting as much, had disapproved it. Thanks to a disabling injury Custer now had a legitimate basis for visiting Monroe, there to pursue to conclusion his campaign to win the hand of Elizabeth Clift Bacon.[57]

* * *

He nearly missed his chance. When he arrived on the sixteenth he found Libbie gone—she had accompanied her father and stepmother on a trip to the Lake Michigan resort of Traverse City. For one miserable day, until her return, he fretted that she might not appear before his leave ended. He spent the day outwardly cheerful, mobbed and coddled by townspeople who had devoured stories of his exploits at Gettysburg and after. Nettie had warned him that all of Monroe would turn out to greet him, fretting that "so much 'brass' will dazzle the eyes of us poor Monroe girls." But he was focused on only one, and his anxiety did not abate until he met her at the train station the following morning.[58]

At first, she did not seem pleased to see him. She wrote in her journal that "I could not avoid him. I tried to, but I did not succeed." Once the two were finally alone, he pressed his case, unequivocally declaring his love and proposing marriage although prevented from doing so on bended knee. Beset by one final pang of indecision, Libbie played for time, but after several meetings over the next two weeks, she vowed to become "his little wife." Perhaps the decision was made when they attended a costume ball held in "honor of Gen. George A. Custer" at the Humphrey House on the evening of the twenty-eighth, she dressed as a gypsy girl, he in the brocade coat and powdered wig of a French monarch. Marguerite Merington claims that "under a tree in the Bacon garden Elizabeth and George Armstrong Custer plighted their troth." Or it may have come during an intimate moment over the midnight dinner that followed the unmasking.[59]

Libbie would later claim that "the general's proposal was as much a cavalry charge as any he ever took in the field." He had proposed before, under different circumstances; she had rejected his offer because she believed it the product of youthful exuberance under wartime pressures. The Custer who had returned from Virginia this time was of a more serious and mature mien, more aware of his mortality following his inexplicable escape from the fate that had befallen his horse. She believed his professions of love to be sincere, and she could not deny his many gifts, physical and otherwise. As she had recently confided to her journal, "every other man seems so ordinary beside my own particular *star*."

She still had her father's feelings to contend with, but they were softening in the face of Custer's newly polished image as a man of promise and prominence. Days after Custer returned to Virginia Libbie would write that "Father is to my surprise on my side," he having realized "how much harm has often been done by parents utterly refusing" their children's preferences in matters of the heart. Daniel Bacon's resistance to Custer as a son-in-law would fade. His reconciliation to his daughter's wishes meant that Libbie's soldier had emerged victorious from a critical struggle, one more difficult and more stressful than any he had waged on the battlefield.[60]

That other conflict he seemed to have mastered. By the autumn of 1863 Custer was well into the accelerated program informally known as professional military development in wartime. The learning curve had been steep, but he had negotiated it deftly. He had become proficient in the duties of a brigade leader while showing an aptitude for higher command. The impulsiveness that had defined him since youth and the willingness to flout the established order, so evident since West Point, continued to color his leadership, but he would learn from the mistakes he had committed at Hunterstown and Newby's Cross Roads. He had made a reputation as one of the most dashing and aggressive leaders in an arm of the service that prized both commodities. Subordinates once uncertain of his fitness to lead had come to depend on him. And he had won the devotion of his men as symbolized by the scarlet neckties almost every member of the Wolverine Brigade was now sporting. George Armstrong Custer's career was flourishing, his prospects were as bright as any man's, and now his personal happiness had been secured. Already, at twenty-three, his life appeared complete.

Endnotes

Abbreviations:

AGO	Adjutant General's Office
BHL	Bentley Historical Library, University of Michigan
EBC	Elizabeth Bacon Custer
EBCC	Elizabeth Bacon Custer Collection
ELRC	Ellis Library and Reference Center
GAC	George Armstrong Custer
HQ	Headquarters
HSP	Historical Society of Pennsylvania
LAFC	Lawrence A. Frost Collection of Custeriana
LAR	Lydia Ann Reed
MMP	Marguerite Merington Papers
MSS	Manuscripts, Papers
NA	National Archives
OR	*War of the Rebellion: A Compilation of the Official Records of the Union and Confederate Armies* (all references are to volumes in Series I)
RG-, E-, M-	Record Group, Entry, Microcopy
USAHEC	U. S. Army Heritage and Education Center
USMA	United States Military Academy

Chapter I

1. Wallace, *Custer's Ohio Boyhood*, 9; Carroll, *General Custer and New Rumley, Ohio*, 4–5, 9–10, 23, 31; Hurless, "Where Was General Custer Really Born?", ELRC.
2. Carroll, *General Custer and New Rumley, Ohio*, 4.
3. Howe, *Historical Collections of Ohio*, 1: 899; Wert, *Custer*, 15; Ronsheim, *Life of General Custer,* [5].

4. Ronsheim, *Life of General Custer*, [5]; Wallace, *Custer's Ohio Boyhood*, 5–6, 31–33; Van de Water, *Glory-Hunter*, 20–21.

5. Howe, *Historical Collections of Ohio*, 1: 900; Wert, *Custer*, 16; Merington, *Custer Story*, 4.

6. Wallace, *Custer's Ohio Boyhood*, 6–7, 9, 31–35; *Tour of Custer's New Rumley*, [2], [12]-[13]; Merington, *Custer Story*, 3.

7. Wallace, *Custer's Ohio Boyhood*, 5–6.

8. Ibid., 9; Monaghan, *Custer*, 4–5. At some point in his life, perhaps as early as his childhood, Nevin Custer was described by his father as "crippled in [the] back": E. H. Custer to GAC, Apr. 18, 1862, LAFC.

9. Wallace, *Custer's Ohio Boyhood*, 11; Wert, *Custer*, 19; Ambrose, *Crazy Horse and Custer*, 88; Ronsheim, *Life of General Custer*, [5]; Van de Water, *Glory-Hunter*, 22. Boston Custer, although never a soldier, served as a civilian foragemaster with his brother's 7th Cavalry on the Plains and was killed along with Armstrong and Tom at the Little Bighorn.

10. Ronsheim, *Life of General Custer*, [5]; *Department of Defense: Selected Manpower Statistics—Fiscal Year 1997*, Table 2–11: "U.S. Military Manpower—1789 to 1997." For the drop-off in the cadet classes at USMA between 1843 and 1847, see *Official Register of the Officers and Cadets of the U. S. Military Academy* for those years.

11. Merington, *Custer Story*, 6.

12. Wing, *History of Monroe County, Michigan*, 318; Nevin Custer to EBC, n.d., MMP. Thanks to Fr. Vince Heier for providing transcriptions and summaries of letters in the Merington Papers.

13. Merington, *Custer Story*, 6.

14. Ibid., 109; Ronsheim, *Life of General Custer*, [7].

15. Nevin Custer to EBC, n.d., MMP.

16. Ibid.; Carroll, *General Custer and New Rumley, Ohio*, 17; Frost, *Custer Legends*, 100.

17. Ronsheim, *Life of General Custer*, [6].

18. Wallace, *Custer's Ohio Boyhood*, 11.

19. Ibid., 11, 37; Merington, *Custer Story*, 78.

20. Wing, *History of Monroe County, Michigan*, 318. Wallace, *Custer's Ohio Boyhood*, 40–41, questions this account of the Custers' move to Michigan in 1842.

21. Wallace, *Custer's Ohio Boyhood*, 13; Wert, *Custer*, 20.

22. Wallace, *Custer's Ohio Boyhood*, 13–14; Ronsheim, *Life of General Custer*, [6].

23. Merington, *Custer Story*, 5; Wallace, *Custer's Ohio Boyhood*, 14; Howe, *Historical Collections of Ohio*, 1: 900.

24. Robbins, *Last in Their Class*, 185.

25. Wallace, *Custer's Ohio Boyhood*, 12.

26. Carroll, *General Custer and New Rumley, Ohio*, 17. Wallace, *Custer's Ohio Boyhood*, 38, questions the generally accepted account of Custer's apprenticeship.

27. Wallace, *Custer's Ohio Boyhood*, 14–15; Ronsheim, *Life of General Custer*, [7]; Merington, *Custer Story*, 6; Wert, *Custer*, 20–21; Whittaker, *Complete Life of Custer*, 9.

28. Ronsheim, *Life of General Custer*, [7]; Frost, *Custer Legends*, 8.

29. Whittaker, *Complete Life of Custer*, 11; Frost, *Custer Legends*, 103.

30. Wallace, *Custer's Ohio Boyhood*, 15.

31. Ibid., 15–16; Whittaker, *Complete Life of Custer*, 11–12.

32. Ronsheim, *Life of General Custer*, [8].

33. Ibid., [7]-[8]; Wallace, *Custer's Ohio Boyhood*, 17–18, 21.

34. Ronsheim, *Life of General Custer*, [8]; Monaghan, *Custer*, 10–11; Wallace, *Custer's Ohio Boyhood*, 22–23; Wert, *Custer*, 22–23.

35. GAC to LAR, Dec. 12, 1856, EBCC; Merington, *Custer Story*, 8.

Chapter II

1. Merington, *Custer Story*, 4; Wallace, *Custer's Ohio Boyhood*, 7, 24; Ambrose, *Crazy Horse and Custer*, 87–88; *Cadiz* (Ohio) *Democratic Sentinel*, Sept. 5, 1855, Aug. 27, 1856.

2. Ronsheim, *Life of General Custer*, [9]; Wallace, *Custer's Ohio Boyhood*, 22.

3. Monaghan, *Custer*, 11; Wert, *Custer*, 22–23.

4. Wallace, *Custer's Ohio Boyhood*, 24.

5. Monaghan, *Custer*, 10–11. See Stiles, *Custer's Trials*, 470, note 58, for commentary on this source. See also GAC to Mary Holland, Nov. 13, 1858, Jan. 1, 1859, Western Americana Collection, Beinecke Rare Book and Manuscript Library, Yale University.

6. Prominent sources that address the issue of Custer's West Point admission, several of which purport to explain Congressman Bingham's role in it include Ronsheim, *Life of General Custer*, [11]; Monaghan, *Custer*, 10–11; Wert, *Custer*, 22–25; Wallace, *Custer's Ohio Boyhood*, 23–24; O'Neill, "Two Men of Ohio: Custer & Bingham," 11; Utley, *Cavalier in Buckskin*, 15; Leckie, *Elizabeth Bacon Custer*, 23; and Stiles, *Custer's Trials*, 18. Not one of these works cites any source that details a plot to separate Custer from his sweetheart; the authors reference one other in a perfect circle of non-information. Occasionally there is a mysterious reference to a source never described beyond a few words: "Boyhood documents called to my attention by Milton Ronsheim" (Monaghan, 411); and "Letter: H. F. Webster to Milton Ronsheim, October 21, 1960" (Wallace, 39). Such citations do not pass for historical documentation.

7.   GAC to John A. Bingham, May 27, 1856, quoted in Whittaker, *Complete Life of Custer*, 13–14. The letters of Custer's included in Whittaker's biography appear to be authentic and transcribed verbatim with the exception of added punctuation.

8.   GAC to John A. Bingham, June 11, 1856, quoted in Whittaker, *Complete Life of Custer*, 14–15; GAC to John A. Bingham, Nov. 18, 1856, M-210, Cadet Application Papers, USMA Archives.

9.   Wallace, *Custer's Ohio Boyhood*, 21–22.

10. Merington, *Custer Story*, 7–8.

11. Wallace, *Custer's Ohio Boyhood*, 24; Wert, *Custer*, 25.

12. Copied in *Cadiz* (Ohio) *Republican*, June 18, 1862.

13. Wallace, *Custer's Ohio Boyhood*, 24; GAC to John Chamberlain, May 5, 1860, Tom Perry Special Collections, Harold B. Lee Library, Brigham Young University.

14. Morrison, *"Best School in the World,"* 114–25, 166–67; Farley, *West Point in the Early Sixties*, 26; Robbins, *Last in Their Class*, 187–88; Carroll, *Custer in the Civil War*, 80.

15. Morrison, *"Best School in the World,"* 68–69.

16. Nevin Custer to EBC, n.d., MMP. Schaff, *Spirit of Old West Point*, 29–30, mentions this messy prank.

17. *Cadiz* (Ohio) *Republican*, July 20, 1876.

18. McCrea, *Dear Belle*, 215; Schaff, *Spirit of Old West Point*, 86.

19. Wert, *Custer*, 29; Stiles, *Custer's Trials*, 19–22; Carroll, *Custer in the Civil War*, 80.

20. Morrison, *"Best School in the World,"* 130; Schaff, *Spirit of Old West Point*, 159.

21. Wert, *Custer*, 28–29; Bushong and Bushong, *Fightin' Tom Rosser, C.S.A.*, 5, 7; Gallagher, *Stephen Dodson Ramseur*, 26–27.

22. Crackel, *Illustrated History of West Point*, 96–97, 132–35; Morrison, *"Best School in the World,"* 77–78; Schaff, *Spirit of Old West Point*, 104.

23. Morrison, *"Best School in the World,"* 91–92, 146–47; Robbins, *Last in Their Class*, xi; Michie, "Reminiscences of Cadet and Army Service," 194.

24. Michie, "Reminiscences of Cadet and Army Service," 194.

25. *Official Register of the Officers and Cadets of the U.S. Military Academy* for the years Custer attended—1858: 14; 1859: 13; 1860: 12; 1861: 11; Morrison, *"Best School in the World,"* 92–94; author's interview of Elaine McConnell, USMA Archives, Aug. 14, 2017.

26. *Official Register of the Officers and Cadets of the U.S. Military Academy*, 1861: 11; Frost, *Custer Legends*, 136; Robbins, *Last in Their Class*, 60.

27. GAC, "The Red Man," May 5, 1858, EBCC

28. Morrison, *"Best School in the World,"* 76–77, 89–91; Ambrose, *Crazy Horse and Custer*, 109–11; Wert, *Custer*, 32; Monaghan, *Custer*, 29; Kirshner, *Class of 1861*, 8.

29. Morrison, *"Best School in the World,"* 51–52, 56, 91–92, 116; Merington, *Custer Story*, 8.
30. Morrison, *"Best School in the World,"* 94–96.
31. Custer, "Aunt Elizabeth as I Knew Her," 3–4.
32. Wright, "West Point Before the War," 18.
33. Farley, *West Point in the Early Sixties*, 78; Robbins, *Last in Their Class*, 186; Frost, *Custer Legends*, 136–37.
34. McCrea, *Dear Belle*, 239.
35. Schaff, *Spirit of Old West Point*, 28, 66–67.
36. Elias V. Andruss to EBC, Sept. 27, 1905, EBCC.
37. "Unsigned, undated fragmentary reminiscence, c. 1917, of West Point experiences," ibid. The "Great Highan-Ki-dank" prank may be the source of the anecdote about Custer and Cadet Henry E. Noyes related in Wert, *Custer*, 30.
38. Elias V. Andruss to EBC, Sept. 27, 1905, EBCC.
39. GAC to LAR, ca. 1860, EBCC; Merington, *Custer Story*, 9; Robbins, *Last in Their Class*, 192; Morrison, *"Best School in the World,"* 79.
40. Frost, *Custer Legends*, 68; Carroll, *Custer in the Civil War*, 86; Averell, *Ten Years in the Saddle*, 38.
41. Kinsley, *Favor the Bold*, 11.
42. McCrea, *Dear Belle*, 215; Tully McCrea to GAC, Aug. 13, 1861, EBCC; Wert, *Custer*, 33.
43. GAC to Mary Holland, Nov. 13, 1858, Western Americana Collection, Beinecke Rare Book and Manuscript Library, Yale University; Stiles, *Custer's Trials*, 18–19.
44. Wert, *Custer*, 34–35; Stiles, *Custer's Trials*, 19.
45. Schaff, *Spirit of Old West Point*, 193–94.
46. Harris, *Major General George A. Custer*, 8; Merington, *Custer Story*, 8; Reynolds, *Civil War Memories of Elizabeth Bacon Custer*, 37–38. Harris's claim that Custer beat up two noncommissioned officers appears to strain credulity. So does EBC's memory of Custer's swimming the Hudson to sneak into a banquet thrown by the parents of his classmate Fred James—the family regularly invited cadets to their home for dinner: Tully McCrea to GAC, Aug. 13, 1861, EBCC.
47. McCrea, *Dear Belle*, 43.
48. Ibid., 43–44; Morrison, *"Best School in the World,"* 84–85; Robbins, *Last in Their Class*, 194.
49. McCrea, *Dear Belle*, 42.
50. Cadet Delinquency Logs, 1857–61, USMA Archives; Robbins, *Last in Their Class*, 188–89; Wert, *Custer*, 31–32; Horn, *"Skinned,"* is the handiest source on this subject, mainly because the original logs feature handwriting so small as to be almost indecipherable under any conditions.

51. Carroll, *Custer in the Civil War*, 84, 87; Robbins, *Last in Their Class*, 190; Reynolds, *Civil War Memories of Elizabeth Bacon Custer*, 38.

52. Robbins, *Last in Their Class*, 190; GAC to "My Dear Brother & Sister," June 30, 1858, EBCC; Merington, *Custer Story*, 8–9.

53. A. C. M. Pennington to EBC, May 8, 1887, MMP; Elias V. Andruss to EBC, Sept. 27, 1905, EBCC.

54. Robbins, *Last in Their Class*, 189; Frost, *Custer Legends*, 134.

Chapter III

1. Carroll, *Custer in the Civil War*, 79.

2. Bingham's biography is Beauregard, *Bingham of the Hills*. On Emmanuel Custer, see Stiles, *Custer's Trials*, 19.

3. GAC to John Chamberlain, Apr. 7, 1860, Tom Perry Special Collections, Harold B. Lee Library, Brigham Young University.

4. GAC to John Chamberlain, May 5, 1860, ibid.

5. GAC to LAR, Nov. 10, 1860, EBCC.

6. Carroll, *Custer in the Civil War*, 80.

7. Schaff, *Spirit of Old West Point*, 144–47; Robbins, *Last in Their Class*, 197–98.

8. Schaff, *Spirit of Old West Point*, 84.

9. Carroll, *Custer in the Civil War*, 81–82. After the war Young wrote that "there had existed between Custer and myself, a warm friendship, which I am happy to say the war never interrupted in either of us. We had been roommates for a time at school, and always friends." Kirshner, *Class of 1861*, 62.

10. McCrea, *Dear Belle*, 77–78.

11. Carroll, *Custer in the Civil War*, 82–83; Ronsheim, *Life of General Custer*, [12]; Frost, *Custer Legends*, 135.

12. Elias V. Andruss to EBC, Sept. 27, 1905, EBCC; "Notes and Queries: Are the West Point Graduates Loyal?", 31–33.

13. Carroll, *Custer in the Civil War*, 85.

14. GAC to LAR, Apr. 10, 1861, EBCC.

15. GAC to LAR, Apr. 10, 26, 1861, ibid.

16. GAC to LAR, May 31, 1861, ibid.

17. Carroll, *Custer in the Civil War*, 87–88; Cadet Delinquency Logs, 1861, USMA Archives; Merington, *Custer Story*, 10–11.

18. Ibid., 88; Stiles, *Custer's Trials*, 4–6, 6–28. Stiles contends that Custer's defense was an effort to win the court's pity, but the words of the accused mainly express the "chagrin and anxiety"—and the genuine grief—he felt at being held back and perhaps dismissed from the army after having graduated and been

commissioned. This is an understandable reaction especially given that, as he observed, the "ordinary circumstances" surrounding his transgression no longer applied in that time of national crisis.

19. Carroll, *Custer in the Civil War*, 88–89. Little is known of the post-Academy career of Cadet Ryerson, who failed to graduate with his class. William Ludlow went on to a distinguished career, winning three brevets for gallantry during the Civil War and thirty-five years later rising to brigadier general: Heitman, *Historical Register and Dictionary*, 1: 646.

20. Frost, *Custer Legends*, 76–77.

21. Carroll, *Custer in the Civil War*, 88–89; Wert, *Custer*, 39–40.

22. Frost, *Custer Legends*, 77; Carroll, *Custer in the Civil War*, 89.

23. Carroll, *Custer in the Civil War*, 89; Wert, *Custer*, 40.

24. Longacre, *Early Morning of War*, 2–18. Stiles, *Custer's Trials*, 472, n3, claims that Custer reached the capital on the nineteenth, not the twentieth, because he spent that night fully awake before seeing Gen. Scott. But Custer writes in his memoirs that he went to the AGO at two o'clock on the twentieth (mistakenly noted as "morning"—in fact, afternoon) and that he returned at 7 p.m. to run the errand for Gen. Scott. The "sleepless night" was his all-night ride to Manassas.

25. Carroll, *Custer in the Civil War*, 89; Heitman, *Historical Register and Dictionary*, 1: 770.

26. Carroll, *Custer in the Civil War*, 90.

27. Averell, *Ten Years in the Saddle*, 35.

28. Carroll, *Custer in the Civil War*, 90–93; McCrea, *Dear Belle*, 104.

29. Longacre, *Early Morning of War*, 231–66, 285–86.

30. Ibid., 298–301; Carroll, *Custer in the Civil War*, 93.

31. Carroll, *Custer in the Civil War*, 93–94.

32. Ibid., 94, 102; *OR*, 2: 393, 403.

33. Carroll, *Custer in the Civil War*, 96, 103; Heitman, *Historical Register and Dictionary*, 1: 996.

34. Carroll, *Custer in the Civil War*, 102; Longacre, *Early Morning of War*, 296, 320–22, 351.

35. Averell, *Ten Years in the Saddle*, 295–97; Carroll, *Custer in the Civil War*, 102.

36. Carroll, *Custer in the Civil War*, 103.

37. Ibid., 103–04. Frank Crawford. Armstrong served as captain, 2nd U.S. Dragoons, at First Bull Run; resigned his commission on Aug. 13; and rose to brigadier general of cavalry in the Confederate army: Heitman, *Historical Register and Dictionary*, 1: 169; Warner, *Generals in Gray*, 12–13, 364–65, n44.

38. *OR*, 2: 319–20, 394, 346–47, 474–77, 481, 488–94.

39. Carroll, *Custer in the Civil War*, 100; *OR*, 2: 403, 482–84; Longacre, *Early Morning of War*, 392–93.
40. Carroll, *Custer in the Civil War*, 104–05, 110; *OR*, 2: 393, 403, 416–17, 483.
41. Carroll, *Custer in the Civil War*, 105, 114.

Chapter IV

1. Carroll, *Custer in the Civil War*, 105; Merington, *Custer Story*, 12–13; *OR*, 2: 393. There are errors in McCrea's letter recounting Custer's role in the battle (*Dear Belle*, 103–04): Custer was not a member of McDowell's bodyguard; he was not in the "thickest of the fight"; and he did not command his company that day. Bugler Fought is described in L. P. Graham to anon., May 13, 1861, RG-94, M-619, NA.
2. Longacre, *Early Morning of War*, 392–93, 427.
3. Carroll, *Custer in the Civil War*, 110; *OR*, 2: 393; McCrea, *Dear Belle*, 105.
4. Carroll, *Custer in the Civil War*, 105; Longacre, *Early Morning of War*, 391, 501–02.
5. Carroll, *Custer in the Civil War*, 111; Warner, *Generals in Blue*, 290–92; Rafuse, *McClellan's War*, 30–49, 92–94.
6. Rafuse, *McClellan's War*, 95–117; Longacre, *Early Morning of War*, 493; Thian, *Notes Illustrating Military Geography*, 83.
7. Carroll, *Custer in the Civil War*, 111–12.
8. Longacre, *Lincoln's Cavalrymen*, 16.
9. Warner, *Generals in Blue*, 258–59; Sears, *Lincoln's Lieutenants*, 89–90.
10. Carroll, *Custer in the Civil War*, 114–15; McCrea, *Dear Belle*, 106.
11. Carroll, *Custer in the Civil War*, 115; Ronsheim, *Life of General Custer*, [13].
12. Longacre, *Early Morning of War*, 445; Bilby and Goble, *"Remember You Are Jerseymen!"*, 64–65.
13. Carroll, *Custer in the Civil War*, 116–17.
14. GAC to Austin Blair, Jan. 31, 1863, Blair MSS, Burton Historical Collection, Detroit Public Library.
15. Carroll, *Custer in the Civil War*, 118; Warner, *Generals in Blue*, 89–90; Whiney and Jamieson, *Attack and Die*, 63–67; Longacre, *Lincoln's Cavalrymen*, 9–11, 66; *OR*, 5: 668.
16. GAC to Austin Blair, Jan. 31, 1863, Blair MSS.
17. Wallace, *Custer's Ohio Boyhood*, 25, 27, 41; Wert, *Custer*, 34–35, 45–46; Whittaker, *Complete Life of Custer*, 88; McCrea, *Dear Belle*, 107.
18. Whittaker, *Complete Life of Custer*, 90; Frost, *Custer Legends*, 13, 15, 68; Ronsheim, *Life of General Custer*, [13]; Ambrose, *Crazy Horse and Custer*, 183.

Frost debunks the oft-told story that a drunken Custer was seen "shooting insula-
tors off the light poles with his service revolver." Merington, *Custer Story*, 48–49,
claims Libbie Bacon did not see Custer drunk that night.

19. Whittaker, *Complete Life of Custer*, 90–91; Stiles, *Custer's Trials*, 36.
20. Frost, *Custer Legends*, 15; Leckie, *Elizabeth Bacon Custer*, 20. Apparently Custer
     was not in a happy frame of mind when he left Monroe; according to a girlfriend,
     he "made a rash vow he would get shot . . . the first chance he had. . . .": Marie
     Miller to GAC, Apr. 23, 1862, LAFC.
21. Stiles, *Custer's Trials*, 36–37; GAC to LAR, Feb. 21, 1862, EBCC.
22. GAC to LAR, Feb. 21, 1862, Oct. 25, 1863, EBCC.
23. GAC to LAR, Feb. 21, 1862; *OR*, 5: 13, 15, 19; Longacre, *Lincoln's Cavalrymen*,
     66.
24. *OR*, 5: 18, 41, 49; Sears, *To the Gates of Richmond*, 3–9.
25. *OR*, 5: 526–32, 548–49; Moore, *Kilpatrick and Our Cavalry*, 39.
26. *OR*, 5: 550; Longacre, *Lincoln's Cavalrymen*, 61–62.
27. Moore, *Rebellion Record*, 4: 296.
28. Carroll, *Custer in the Civil War*, 129–30; Hatch, *Glorious War*, 49–50.
29. Carroll, *Custer in the Civil War*, 130; GAC to "My dear Parents," Mar. 17, 1862,
     EBCC; McCrea, *Dear Belle*, 106–07.
30. GAC to "My dear Parents," Mar. 17, 1862, EBCC.
31. *OR*, 5: 50, 55–56; Sears, *To the Gates of Richmond*, 18–20.
32. GAC to LAR, Mar. 26, 1862; GAC to "Dear Parents," Mar. 28, 1862; both,
     EBCC.
33. *OR*, 11, pt. 3: 66; Sears, *To the Gates of Richmond*, 234–39; Carroll, *Custer in the
     Civil War*, 132–38.
34. Sears, *To the Gates of Richmond*, 29–30, 42–43, 61, 98–99.
35. Ibid., 35–36; *OR*, 11, pt. 1: 9.
36. Carroll, *Custer in the Civil War*, 136–37.
37. Sears, *To the Gates of Richmond*, 37–38. Johnston's manpower figure is from *OR*,
     11, pt. 1: 1086.
38. Carroll, *Custer in the Civil War*, 143; Wert, *Custer*, 50.
39. Carroll, *Custer in the Civil War*, 143; Heitman, *Historical Register and Dictionary*,
     1: 233. Fascines were "long cylindrical fagots of brushwood" for supporting
     defensive works (Scott, *Military Dictionary*, 283, 504–07). Gabions were "cylin-
     drical baskets of various dimensions, open at both ends," usually three feet high
     and two feet in diameter, used to strengthen the embankments of batteries or
     trenches (ibid., 320, 507–08).
40. GAC to LAR, Apr. 19, 1862, EBCC.

Chapter V

1. Van de Water, *Glory-Hunter*, 43.
2. Carroll, *Custer in the Civil War*, 143–46; Evans, *War of the Aeronauts*, 36–39, 112–14, 179–80, 210.
3. Carroll, *Custer in the Civil War*, 146; GAC to LAR, May 15, 1862, EBCC; Kelly, *Generals in Bronze*, 163.
4. Carroll, *Custer in the Civil War*, 147–48; GAC to LAR, May 15, 1862; Evans, *War of the Aeronauts*, 184–88.
5. OR, 11, pt. 1: 364–80; pt. 3: 101–03; Sears, *To the Gates of Richmond*, 55–56.
6. GAC to LAR, Apr. 19, 1862, EBCC.
7. Sears, *To the Gates of Richmond*, 58.
8. GAC to LAR, May 15, 1862, EBCC; Carroll, *Custer in the Civil War*, 149–50; Hatch, *Glorious War*, 56; Evans, *War of the Aeronauts*, 212–13.
9. Longacre, *Lincoln's Cavalrymen*, 75–79; OR, 11, pt. 1: 424–30.
10. Carroll, *Custer in the Civil War*, 151.
11. Ibid., 151–58; Wert, *Custer*, 51–52; Urwin, *Custer Victorious*, 47; Sears, *To the Gates of Richmond*, 70–82; OR, 11, pt. 1: 535–36, 543, 608–13.
12. GAC to LAR, May 15, 1862, EBCC.
13. Whittaker, *Complete Life of Custer*, 104–06; Wert, *Custer*, 52. There has long been controversy over the flags captured in the battle. The flag of the 5th North Carolina was seized by J. R. Ensign of the 5th Wisconsin Infantry; Custer helped carry it to General Hancock although other officers escorted it to Washington. While some accounts have this the first enemy flag to be captured by the Army of the Potomac, Sgt. John N. Coyne of the 70th New York was awarded the Congressional Medal of Honor for taking another flag earlier in the battle. Still other colors are believed to have been seized on earlier occasions by infantry and cavalry units of the army, one of them on the day before the fighting at Williamsburg. The flag Custer snatched up had been carried by a unit—probably a company—of the 24th Virginia. He kept the trophy for the rest of his life. Libbie Custer donated it to the Smithsonian Institution in 1912; thirty-nine years later her nephew, Col. Brice Custer, donated it to Appomattox Court House National Historical Park: Greg Biggs to the author, Sept. 15, 21, Dec. 28, 29, 31, 2017. See also McMahon, "The Flag of the 5th North Carolina . . .," and Custer, "The Hidden Flags . . . (Revisited)."
14. Whittaker, *Complete Life of Custer*, 106; McCrea, *Dear Belle*, 214.
15. Sears, *To the Gates of Richmond*, 82; GAC to LAR, May 15, 1862, EBCC; Schaff, *Spirit of Old West Point*, 180.
16. GAC to LAR, May 15, 1862, EBCC.
17. Sears, *To the Gates of Richmond*, 109–10.

18. *OR*, 11, pt. 1: 110–11.

19. Wilson, *Under the Old Flag*, 1: 101–02; Merington, *Custer Story*, 31; Whittaker, *Complete Life of Custer*, 110–11.

20. *OR*, 11, pt. 1: 111, 652–53, 654 and note; Hatch, *Glorious War*, 61–63. Whittaker, *Complete Life of Custer*, 116–18, presents a fanciful account of this mission. Hatch and Urwin, *Custer Victorious*, 47, repeat Whittaker's claim of Custer having captured the first enemy flag taken by the Army of the Potomac. Whereas Whittaker writes that Custer seized the banner at New Bridge, Urwin and Hatch attribute its capture to the battle of Williamsburg.

21. *OR*, 11, pt. 1: 651.

22. Whittaker, *Complete Life of Custer*, 113.

23. McClellan, *McClellan's Own Story*, 123, 364–65; Merington, *Custer Story*, 31; Reynolds, *Civil War Memories of Elizabeth Bacon Custer*, 5; General Orders #131, HQ Army of the Potomac, May 28, 1862, copy in EBCC.

24. Edward H. Wright to EBC, Apr. 30, 1888, EBCC.

25. Scott, *Military Dictionary*, 21.

26. Sears, *To the Gates of Richmond*, 97–112, 156–57.

27. Ibid., 121–45; Freeman, *R. E. Lee*, 2: 68–74; Freeman, *Lee's Lieutenants*, 1: 225–43.

28. The photo was taken by James Gibson, assistant to Matthew Brady, soon to be celebrated as America's first wartime photo-journalist: Merington, *Custer Story*, 129–30; Monaghan, *Custer*, 33, 35, 203. Reynolds, *Civil War Memories of Elizabeth Bacon Custer*, 25–26, claims that Custer procured Lt. Washington's parole and that the latter induced the boy to sit for the photo in order to illustrate slaves' attachment to their masters. On this subject see Stiles, *Custer's Trials*, 54–55, 477 n16. Less than a month after Custer was reunited with Washington he beheld other familiar faces when Lydia and David Reed visited him at army headquarters. No details of their journey from Monroe to Virginia or the length of their stay are available: Henry C. Christiancy diary, June 23, 1862, Christiancy-Pickett Collection, USAHEC.

29. Sears, *To the Gates of Richmond*, 183–89.

30. Ibid., 197-209; Freeman, *R. E. Lee*, 2: 122–35.

31. Sears, *Lincoln's Lieutenants*, 246–66 passim.

32. Whittaker, *Complete Life of Custer*, 120–21; GAC to "Dear Brother and Sister," July 13, 1862, EBCC; Wert, *Custer*, 56.

33. GAC to "Dear Brother and Sister," July 13, 1862, EBCC; Swift, "Fifth Regiment of Cavalry," 225; Longacre, *Lincoln's Cavalrymen*, 90–92.

34. GAC to "Dear Brother and Sister," July 13, 1862, EBCC.

35. Ibid.; Freeman, *R. E. Lee*, 2: 220–24.

36. Sears, *Lincoln's Lieutenants*, 236, 275–80; Hennessy, *Return to Bull Run*, 5–10.

37. GAC to Augusta Ward, July 26, 1862, Augusta Ward Frary MSS, Rochester Public Library.
38. Heitman, *Historical Register and Dictionary*, 1: 348; *OR*, 11, pt. 2: 946–48; Averell, *Ten Years in the Saddle*, 367.
39. *OR*, 11, pt. 2: 954–56.
40. GAC to "Dear Brother and Sister," Aug. 8, 1862, quoted in Whittaker, *Complete Life of Custer*, 122–24. The reaction of Custer's sister to his letter: "It made me feel sad to hear that you had to kill that man and I think you was in a very dangerous position yourself. I am afraid the next thing I hear you will get shot. . . .", LAR to GAC, Aug. 13, 1862, LAFC.
41. Sears, *To the Gates of Richmond*, 351–54.
42. McClellan, *McClellan's Own Story*, 505–06; GAC to LAR, Sept. 21, 1862, quoted in Whittaker, *Complete Life of Custer*, 125–26.
43. Davis, "Brothers at Bassett Hall"; Merington, *Custer Story*, 34–35; Reynolds, *Civil War Memories of Elizabeth Bacon Custer*, 31; Schaff, *Spirit of Old West Point*, 180–82; GAC to LAR, Sept. 21, 1862, quoted in Whittaker, *Complete Life of Custer*, 126–29.

Chapter VI

1. GAC to LAR, Sept. 21, 1862, quoted in Whittaker, *Complete Life of Custer*, 128.
2. Sears, *Lincoln's Lieutenants*, 299–338; Freeman, *R. E. Lee*, 2: 265–349 passim.
3. McClellan, *McClellan's Own Story*, 535–48; Sears, *Landscape Turned Red*, 11–18.
4. GAC to LAR, Sept. 21, 1862, quoted in Whittaker, *Complete Life of Custer*, 128–29.
5. McClellan, *McClellan's Own Story*, 535, 549; GAC to LAR, Sept. 21, 1862, quoted in Whittaker, *Complete Life of Custer*, 129.
6. Sears, *Landscape Turned Red*, 102–07.
7. Casualty figures are from ibid., 295–96.
8. Stiles, *Custer's Trials*, 69–71; *OR*, 19, pt. 1: 210–11; *Woodstock* (Ill.) *Sentinel*, Sept. 24, 1862.
9. Stiles, *Custer's Trials*, 69–72; Urwin, *Custer Victorious*, 54. For the rumored cabal against Lincoln, see Sears, *Controversies and Commanders*, 133–66.
10. GAC to LAR, Sept. 21, 1862, quoted in Whittaker, *Complete Life of Custer*, 129.
11. GAC to George B. McClellan, Sept. 15, 1862, McClellan MSS, LC.
12. Sears, *Landscape Turned Red*, 158–59; GAC to George B. McClellan, Sept. 17, 1862, McClellan, MSS. This telegram was dated—and evidently misdated—by an archivist; see Stiles, *Custer's Trials*, 71, 480 n69.

13. GAC to A.V. Colburn, Sept. 18, 1862, Gilder Lehrman Collection of American History. This document, dated 10: 30 a.m., is a fragment of a letter contained in the Henry Jackson Hunt MSS, LC, where the second dispatch cited also reposes. My thanks to Sandra Trenholm for background information on both items. Kinsley, *Favor the Bold*, 91–92, provides a dramatic but undocumented account of Custer raiding enemy lines, a mission supposedly on his mind as he slept the previous night. Pleasonton in his official report (*OR*, 19, pt. 1: 212) mentions only that "on the 18th instant my cavalry were engaged in collecting stragglers and feeling the enemy on the different roads." One imagines that if such a dramatic event had occurred the cavalry chief would have publicized it.

14. GAC to LAR, Sept. 27, 1862, EBCC.

15. GAC to Augusta Ward, Oct. 3, 1862, Augusta Ward Frary MSS.

16. Sears, *Landscape Turned Red*, 321–22.

17. Ibid., 323–25, 338–45; *OR*, 19, pt. 2: 545, 557.

18. Whittaker, *Complete Life of Custer*, 134; GAC to LAR, Sept. 27, 1862, EBCC.

19. Long, *Civil War Day by Day*, 286.

20. Whittaker, *Complete Life of Custer*, 134–35; Henry C. Christiancy diary, Nov. 10, 1862, Christiancy-Pickett Collection.

21. Among Custer's many girlfriends in Monroe, his favorites were Fannie, who hoped to marry him; Marie, who offered to make him "my *second* husband if I am fortunate enough to have a *first*"; and Nellie, whom Lydia Ann Reed referred to in a letter to her brother as "your beloved, Nell": Marie Miller to GAC, n.d. [ca. June 1863], LAFC; LAR to GAC, Aug. 13, 1862, ibid. Although Miss Fifield supposedly was a friend of Libbie Bacon, the latter's opinion of Fannie's virtue was not flattering: Leckie, *Elizabeth Bacon Custer*, 25–27.

22. Stiles, *Custer's Trials*, 80–81; Leckie, *Elizabeth Bacon Custer*, 22–23; Merington, *Custer Story*, 46–47; Utley, *Cavalier in Buckskin*, 19–20.

23. Whittaker, *Complete Life of Custer*, 136; Merington, *Custer Story*, 47.

24. Stiles, *Custer's Trials*, 113; Merington, *Custer Story*, 47.

25. Leckie, *Elizabeth Bacon Custer*, 25.

26. Ibid., 24; Stiles, *Custer's Trials*, 113.

27. Merington, *Custer Story*, 52, purports to quote from a letter—GAC to Daniel S. Bacon, May 20, 1863—in which Custer chats about army affairs and McClellan's removal, apparently to strengthen her claim that the correspondents were now close friends. Yet it seems unlikely that a staunch Republican such as the judge would have been "still in favor of our beloved General McClellan." The letter supposedly was written from the "2nd Brigade, 1st Division, 5th Army Corps," at a time when Custer was not attached to any such command but was serving on the army headquarters staff. It is also unlikely that Custer had the time to

write such a letter on the day he started on an expedition to the south bank of the Rappahannock River.

28. Frost, *Custer Legends*, 16–18; Frost, *General Custer's Libbie*, 56–59.

29. Leckie, *Elizabeth Bacon Custer*, 24.

30. Sears, *Controversies & Commanders*, 139–52.

31. Henry C. Christiancy diary, Dec. 21, 1862, Pickett-Christiancy Collection; Leckie, *Elizabeth Bacon Custer*, 24–25; Frost, *General Custer's Libbie*, 58.

32. Leckie, *Elizabeth Bacon Custer*, 25; Frost, *Custer Legends*, 18; Frost, *General Custer's Libbie*, 59; Ambrose, *Crazy Horse and Custer*, 185.

33. Merington, *Custer Story*, 50–51; Leckie, *Elizabeth Bacon Custer*, 25.

34. Leckie, *Elizabeth Bacon Custer*, 25–26; Frost, *General Custer's Libbie*, 58.

35. Leckie, *Elizabeth Bacon Custer*, 26–27; Frost, *Custer Legends*, 18, 233 n9, claims that Custer and Libbie had a two-hour conversation "at Nettie's" (presumably the Humphrey House, where she lived) during which they decided "never to go together again but that they would recognize each other as acquaintances." Frost cites Libbie's journal, which was not in his possession, as his source but he appends no entry date. Leckie, who viewed the journal and cites frequently from it, does not mention this meeting. Stiles, *Custer's Trials*, 83, contends that after the nasty scene at the Fifield residence Custer broke off his courtship of Libbie, but Leckie writes that he began sending her letters through Nettie soon after he left Monroe.

36. Merington, *Custer Story*, 64.

37. Whittaker, *Complete Life of Custer*, 139–40; GAC to LAR, Apr. 13, 1863, EBCC.

38. *OR*, 21: 1005.

39. GAC to LAR, Apr. 13, 1863, EBCC; George B. McClellan to AGO, Dec. 9, 1862, McClellan MSS.

40. GAC to LAR, Apr. 13, 1863, EBCC; Stiles, *Custer's Trials*, 84–85; McClellan, *Report on the Organization and Campaigns of the Army of the Potomac*, was published in several editions, at least one of which was 480 pages long.

41. Special Orders #169, AGO, Apr. 13, 1863, copy in EBCC.

42. GAC to I. P. Christiancy, Nov. 29, 1862, USMA Library; Stiles, *Custer's Trials*, 80; Henry C. Christiancy diary, Nov. 25, 1862, Christiancy-Pickett Collection. Heitman, *Historical Register and Dictionary*, 1: 300, makes it appear that Henry did not receive his staff appointment or promotion to captain until April 5, 1865. This is probably an error; the date should be April 5, 1863, the backdated date of the appointment.

Chapter VII

1. Special Orders #169, AGO, Apr. 13, 1863; Special Orders #174, AGO, Apr. 16, 1863; copies of both in EBCC. Information on Custer's succession to company command: C. W. Canfield to HQ Army of the Potomac, Apr. 13, 1863, RG-94, M-619, NA.
2. GAC to Austin Blair, Feb. 28, Apr. 21, 1863, Blair MSS.
3. GAC to Blair, Jan. 31, 1863, ibid.
4. GAC to Blair, Feb. 28, 1863, ibid. At one point Custer was also interested in a berth in the 8th Michigan Cavalry, which had been organized at Mount Clements in December 1862 and which left the state for service in Kentucky the following May: Dyer, *Compendium of the War of the Rebellion,* 1274.
5. GAC to Blair, Apr. 21, 1863, Blair MSS; Longacre, *Custer and His Wolverines,* 81–98.
6. O'Neill, "George Custer's Ascension to Command the Wolverines," 26–28; Roland E. Trowbridge to Austin Blair, Apr, 17, 1863, Blair MSS; Klement, "Edwin B. Bigelow," 213 n65.
7. GAC to Blair, Apr. 21, 1863, Blair MSS.
8. Julius Stahel to Austin Blair, Apr. 20, 1863, with endorsement by Samuel P. Heintzelman, Apr. 21, 1863, ibid.
9. Joseph T. Copeland to Austin Blair, Apr. 20, 1863, ibid.
10. Edwin Willitts to Austin Blair, Jan. 5, 1863, ibid.; O'Neill, "Two Men of Ohio: Custer and Bingham," 10–13; Beauregard, "The General and the Politician," 6; Stiles, *Custer's Trials,* 84–85; Whittaker, *Complete Life of Custer,* 164–65. Whittaker erroneously claims that Custer was interested in joining the 7th Michigan rather than the 5th.
11. Heitman, *Historical Register and Dictionary,* 1: 348; Hatch, *Glorious War,* 40. In a letter to his eldest son, Feb. 2, 1862, LAFC, Emmanuel does not appear to be hostile to Lincoln: "Old Abe is knocking the abolitioners . . . like a thousand bricks. I am in hopes that they will get a death bloe in this struggle." The elder Custer repeated his distaste of both abolitionists and secessionists in a later letter (to GAC, Apr. 18, 1862, ibid.). On the other hand Custer, midway through the war, would refer to his father, somewhat lightheartedly, as "the same old darned Copper head yet": Howe, *Historical Collections of Ohio,* 1: 900. Thomas Ward Custer would be awarded his Medals of Honor for capturing enemy flags at Namozine Church, Apr. 3, 1865, and, three days later, at Sayler's Creek: Heitman, *Historical Register and Dictionary,* 1:348. Libbie Custer provides some details of Tom's feats in an undated memorandum in EBCC.

12. GAC to Austin Blair, May 30, 1863, Blair MSS; Alfred Pleasonton to Blair, with endorsement by Joseph Hooker, May 30, 1863, USMA Library; GAC to I. P. Christiancy, May 31, 1863, ibid.
13. Harris, *Major General George A. Custer*, 1; Harris, *Michigan Cavalry Brigade at the Battle of Gettysburg*, 3–4.
14. O'Neill, "George Custer's Ascension to Command the Wolverines," 27.
15. Stiles, *Custer's Trials*, 85; *OR*, 25, pt. 2: 183; A. J. Cohen to GAC, May 5, 1863, RG-393, pt. 2, E-1502, NA.
16. Sears, *Chancellorsville*, 63–75, 80–82.
17. *OR*, 25, pt. 2: 51.
18. Ibid., 383; Longacre, *Lincoln's Cavalrymen*, 127–29.
19. The most thorough sources on Hooker's failed campaign are Bigelow, *Campaign of Chancellorsville*, and Sears, *Chancellorsville*.
20. *OR*, 25, pt. 1: 1057–65; Longacre, *Lincoln's Cavalrymen*, 19–45. See also Fordney, *Stoneman at Chancellorsville*.
21. *OR*, 25, pt. 2: 513; Longacre, *Lincoln's Cavalrymen*, 142–47.
22. GAC to George B. McClellan, May 6, 1863, McClellan MSS; Stiles, *Custer's Trials*, 86–87. On Jackson's mortal wounding, see Sears, *Chancellorsville*, 282–307.
23. GAC to George B. McClellan, May 6, 1863, McClellan MSS.
24. Sears, *Chancellorsville*, 336–41. For a defense of Hooker's generalship, see Sears, *Controversies & Commanders*, 169–94.
25. GAC to George B. McClellan, May 6, 1863, McClellan MSS.
26. GAC to I. P. Christiancy, May 17, 1863, Christiancy-Pickett Collection. On Hooker's relations with the Radical Republicans, see Catton, *Glory Road*, 3–4, and Tap, *Over Lincoln's Shoulder*, 192, 235, 257–58.
27. Sears, *Chancellorsville*, 257–87.
28. GAC to I. P. Christiancy, May 17, 1863, Christiancy-Pickett Collection.
29. GAC to George B. McClellan, May 6, 1863, McClellan MSS; GAC to I. P. Christiancy, May 31, 1863, USMA Library. For Hooker's scapegoating tactics, see Fordney, *Stoneman at Chancellorsville*, 47–54.
30. *OR*, 25, pt. 1: 1092–94. An original copy of General Orders #56, HQ Army of the Potomac, May 12, 1863, in the ELRC bears Custer's name and rank as captain and aide-de-camp to Hooker. *OR*, 25, pt. 2: 469, includes the order minus his name. On the same date John Buford's headquarters relayed an order for Custer to rejoin his regiment: HQ Cavalry Reserve to anon,, May 12, 1863, RG-393, pt. 2, E-1449, NA.
31. GAC to I. P. Christiancy, May 17, 1863, Christiancy-Pickett Collection. On Custer's gravitating back and forth from volunteer to regular service while on staff duty, see Price, *Across the Continent with the Fifth Cavalry*, 394–95.

32. *New York Herald*, Nov. 10, 1863.

33. List of quartermaster stores received from Custer, May 16, 1863 (two documents), ELRC; GAC to LAR, May 16, 1863, EBCC.

34. GAC to LAR, May 16, 1863, EBCC.

35. A. J. Cohen to G. H. Thompson, May 20, 1863, E-393, pt. 2, "3rd Indiana Cavalry Miscellaneous Papers," NA.

36. Sears, *Chancellorsville*, 69–70; Knight, *Scouting for Grant and Meade*, xxi–xxvi.

37. Capt. Thompson's report is in *OR*, I, 25, pt. 1: 1116. An account of the raid by an enlisted participant is in *Indianapolis Journal*, May 30, 1863. See also *Richmond Whig*, June 5, 1863. Thompson hardly mentions Custer in his report, perhaps because they served apart during the majority of the operation.

38. Custer's report of the expedition, May 24, 1862 [1863], M-14, ELRC, is not included in *OR*; it was transcribed after the war by a member of his departmental staff in Texas (the staff officer misdated the original report). Thanks to Charmaine Wawrzyniec for bringing unpublished copies of this report and others to my attention.

39. GAC to Annette Humphrey, May 26, 1863, quoted in Whittaker, *Complete Life of Custer*, 149–51; Merington, *Custer Story*, 53–54; *Monroe* (Mich.) *Commercial*, July 2, 1863; GAC to LAR, May 27, 1863, EBCC. Emphasis has been added to the personal pronouns in Custer's report.

40. Lt. Hardy, formerly of the 55th Virginia Infantry and Walker's artillery battalion, had been relieved from duty pending court-martial proceedings following a celebrated run-in with his superior, Brig. Gen. William N. Pendleton: O'Sullivan, *55th Virginia Infantry*, 129. Thanks to Horace Mewborn for help in identifying the doubly unfortunate officer.

41. GAC to Annette Humphrey, May 26, 1863, quoted in Whittaker, *Complete Life of Custer*, 149–51; Merington, *Custer Story*, 53–54; GAC to LAR, May 27, 1863, EBCC.

42. *Indianapolis Journal*, May 30, 1863; *OR*, 25, pt. 1: 1111–15; pt. 2: 494–95, 507–08, 520; Patrick, *Inside Lincoln's Army*, 251.

43. Seth Williams to Alfred Pleasonton, May 27, 1863, RG-393, pt. 2, M-504, NA; GAC to LAR, May 27, 1863, EBCC.

Chapter VIII

1. *OR*, 25, pt. 2: 504–06.

2. Ibid., 509–11, 514–16, 528, 566, 595; Coddington, *Gettysburg Campaign*, 49–50.

3. *OR*, 25, pt. 2: 438, 479.

4. GAC to A. J. Cohen, May 27, 1863, Henry E. Huntington Library.
5. GAC to I. P. Christiancy, May 17, 1863, Christiancy-Pickett Collection; Merington, *Custer Story*, 58.
6. Merington, *Custer Story*, 69; GAC to LAR, May 27, 1863, EBCC. Apparently Fannie sent her photograph to Pleasonton for she spoke of receiving his in return, which she considered "a very fine picture": LAR to GAC, June 23 [1863], LAFC.
7. Stiles, *Custer's Trials*, 89; Whittaker, *Complete Life of Custer*, 148.
8. *OR*, 27, pt. 3: 25–30; Sears, *Gettysburg*, 64, 73; Pleasonton, "Campaign of Gettysburg," 448.
9. *OR*, 27, pt. 3: 12–15; Coddington, *Gettysburg Campaign*, 52; Sears, *Gettysburg*, 60, 64.
10. McClellan, *Life and Campaigns of Stuart*, 262.
11. *OR*, 27, pt. 3: 24; 51, pt. 1: 1047; Newhall, "Battle of Beverly Ford," 137; Coddington, *Gettysburg Campaign*, 55–56; Longacre, *Cavalry at Gettysburg*, 62.
12. GAC to LAR, June 8, 1861 [1863], EBCC.
13. Longacre, *Lincoln's Cavalrymen*, 134–38; Trout, *Galloping Thunder*, 180–81.
14. GAC to LAR, June 8, 1861 [1863], EBCC.
15. *OR*, 27, pt. 1: 1044–45; Newhall, "Battle of Beverly Ford," 138; Longacre, *Cavalry at Gettysburg*, 65–66. For the most detailed accounts of this battle, see Downey, *Clash of Cavalry*, and McKinney, *Brandy Station*. A good brief account is in Sears, *Gettysburg*, 64–74.
16. *OR*, 27, pt. 2: 748–49, 754, 757, 762–63, 765–66, 768–70; Longacre, *Cavalry at Gettysburg*, 65–69.
17. *OR*, 27, pt. 1: 902, 1044–45; Hard, *History of Eighth Cavalry Regiment, Illinois Volunteers*, 65; *New York Times*, June 11, 1863; Newhall, "Battle of Beverly Ford," 139.
18. *OR*, 27, pt. 1: 902; Merington, *Custer Story*, 58–59; Robert F. O'Neill to the author, June 28, 2017; Clark B. Hall to the author, Sept. 4, 2017. Monaghan, *Custer*, 126–28, has Custer assuming command of Davis's brigade after the colonel's fall. In fact, Davis was immediately succeeded by his senior subordinate, Maj. William S. McClure of the 3rd Indiana: *OR*, 27, pt. 1: 1047.
19. Merington, *Custer Story*, 58–59.
20. *OR*, 27, pt. 1: 903, 949–50, 961, 1045.
21. Coddington, *Gettysburg Campaign*, 61–63; *OR*, 27, pt. 2: 293, 295, 357, 439–40.
22. *OR*, 27, pt. 3: 80–85; Longacre, *Cavalry at Gettysburg*, 90, 99–100; Coddington, *Gettysburg Campaign*, 80–82.
23. *OR*, 27, pt. 1: 50, 142; pt. 3: 64, 171–73, 178.
24. A. S. Austin to L. H. Peirce "at Falmouth," June 11, 1863, RG-393, pt. 2, M-504, NA.

25. Meyer, *Civil War Experiences*, 33–34; James C. Biddle to his wife, July 1, 1863, George Gordon Meade MSS, HSP.
26. Meyer, *Civil War Experiences*, 34.
27. Pleasonton's report of Aldie, Middleburg, and Upperville, Sept. 22, 1863, Hooker Papers, Henry E. Huntington Library, does not mention Custer, Merritt, or Farnsworth. Other good accounts of Aldie are: Nye, *Here Come the Rebels!*, 173–81, and O'Neill, *Cavalry Battles of Aldie, Middleburg and Upperville*, the latter being the most detailed and trustworthy account of the battle.
28. Nye, *Here Come the Rebels!*, 174–77, 179–80; O'Neill, *Cavalry Battles of Aldie, Middleburg and Upperville*, 47–56.
29. Nye, *Here Come the Rebels!*, 180; O'Neill, *Cavalry Battles of Aldie, Middleburg and Upperville*, 57–59.
30. Nye, *Here Come the Rebels!*, 180–81; O'Neill, *Cavalry Battles of Aldie, Middleburg and Upperville*, 60–63; Merington, *Custer Story*, 54–56.
31. Whittaker, *Complete Life of Custer*, 156–57; Hatch, *Glorious War*, 73–74. Merington, *Custer Story*, 36, claims the sword was captured not by Custer but by one of his subordinates, who gave it to him as a gift but which Custer wore "only on dress occasions."
32. Custer's letter to his sister, written on June 25, is cited by Ambrose, *Crazy Horse and Custer*, 187, 497 n36, as dated June 19 and as found in EBCC. After extensive searching at the author's request, the archivists at the Little Bighorn Battlefield National Monument could not locate this letter in their collections. Almost certainly the document Ambrose cites is the one quoted in Whittaker, *Complete Life of Custer*, 159. The latter is also the source of the account cited by Merington, *Custer Story*, 55–56, as coming from "a Michigan paper." The reference to Custer's willing prisoner is also from Whittaker, 160.
33. *New York Times*, June 20, 1863; Harris, *Major General George A. Custer*, contains a highly improbable account of Custer leading an attack to capture four guns at Aldie. The casualty count is from Nye, *Here Come the Rebels!*, 181.
34. Wert, *Custer*, 80, describes contemporary accounts of Custer's wild ride at Aldie as "dubious," but they are supported by Capt. Biddle's letter.
35. Excerpt from GAC to LAR, June 25, 1863, quoted in Whittaker, *Complete Life of Custer*, 160.
36. Adams, *Cycle of Adams Letters*, 2: 8, 32; Watson, *Letters of a Civil War Surgeon*, 152; Charles B. Coxe to John Cadwalader, Jr., June 12, 1863, Coxe MSS, HSP; Longacre, *Cavalry at Gettysburg*, 48–49, 89.
37. *OR*, I, 27, pt. 3: 97–98; Elon J. Farnsworth to John F. Farnsworth, June 23, 1863, Alfred Pleasonton MSS, LC. One who believed Pleasonton deserving of promotion was Hooker, who on June 18 wrote General Halleck of the cavalry

leader's "gallant conduct at Chancellorsville, his services there, and his attack and surprise of Stuart's force" on the ninth: *OR*, 27, pt. 3: 51.

38. Alfred Pleasonton to John F. Farnsworth, June 18, 23, 1863, Pleasonton MSS; Longacre, "Alfred Pleasonton, 'The Knight of Romance'," 17–18.

39. *OR*, 27, p. 1: 913; pt. 3: 255; Coddington, *Gettysburg Campaign*, 121–22; Pleasonton, "Campaign of Gettysburg, " 451; Kidd, *Personal Recollections of a Cavalryman*, 113–15; Dexter M. Macomber diary, June 25–26, 1863, Macomber MSS, Central Michigan University Library.

40. *OR*, 27, pt. 1: 61; pt. 3: 373, 496, 730. Apparently there was some confusion about Pleasonton's status. On July 10, 1863, Meade asked Halleck to have Lincoln officially assign Pleasonton to command the cavalry corps, the position Meade "found him in when I assumed command." Halleck replied that while Pleasonton was the senior commander of cavalry there was "an objection to any formal order at present": ibid., pt. 1: 90.

41. Robertson, *Michigan in the War*, 573–74; Longacre, *Cavalry at Gettysburg*, 163–64. According to a member of Copeland's staff, Pleasonton told Copeland that he believed Custer "to be 'the best cavalry officer on the continent' and that his expectations of him had been more than realized": I. P. Christiancy to Austin Blair, Aug. 31, 1863, Blair MSS.

42. Pleasonton, "Campaign of Gettysburg," 452; Wert, *Custer*, 81 (which identifies Custer as a "brevet captain"); Coddington, *Gettysburg Campaign*, 220–21; *OR*, 27, pt. 3: 376.

43. A. J. Cohen to J. W. Spangler, June 28, 1863, RG-393, pt. 2, M-504, NA. Pleasonton's recommendations were received favorably by Meade's staff, one of whom wrote that "Custer & Merritt of the Cavalry are both dashing men . . . and just fitted for that service": James C. Biddle to his wife, July 1, 1863, Meade MSS. Harris, *Major General George A. Custer*, 3–4, tells another fantastical story about Custer, this time how his appointment to brigadier general came about through the extraordinary intervention of Secretary of War Stanton, and how other members of Pleasonton's staff teased him when they knew of his promotion and he did not. The oft-told story of Custer being joshed appears to have originated with Whittaker, *Complete Life of Custer*, 162–63, and has been repeated by such chroniclers as Van de Water, *Glory-Hunter*, 50–51; Monaghan, *Custer*, 133; and Kinsley, *Favor the Bold*, 132–33. The incident forms a prominent scene in Hollywood's heavily fictionalized Custer biopic, *They Died with Their Boots On* (1941). Custer's letter to Judge Christiancy shows that he was fully aware of the pending promotion.

44. GAC to I. P. Christiancy, July 26, 1863, USAHEC. Stiles, *Custer's Trials*, 93, describes Custer as "disingenuously modest" when writing this letter, especially in claiming that he had "not a single 'friend at Court'." In the political realm

he had only one patron, Congressman Bingham, the strength of whose influence in military affairs was unknown. Custer had no supporters among the more radical Republicans who held sway in the Senate including members of its military affairs committee. He had a prominent opponent in the statehouse in Lansing; another adversary on the state level was Ira Grosvenor, staunch Republican and former colonel of the 7th Michigan Volunteers. Custer of course had Christiancy's and Pleasonton's support but it was obvious that the former had no influence in state military matters and the latter, until he received his second star and corps command, lacked the leverage to materially help his subordinate. As for the false modesty of which Stiles accuses him, Custer was forthright in telling Christiancy of his strong ambition, which fueled his hopes of one day securing high rank.

45. Kelly, *Generals in Bronze*, 120. Pleasonton recalled telling Merritt that "I promoted you to fight and if you don't fight, I will break you as quick as I made you." Presumably he gave the same warning to Custer.

46. Servacek, *Custer: His Promotion in Frederick, Maryland*, 18–20, 24; *History of the Eighteenth Regiment of Cavalry, Pennsylvania*, 39; Boudrye, *Historic Records of the Fifth New York Cavalry*, 63; Dexter M. Macomber diary, June 28, 1863, Macomber MSS; John A. Clark to "My dear friend," July 30, 1863, Russell A. Alger MSS, BHL. The reference to "Gen. Custerd" is from Edwin R. Havens to "Father, Mother & Nell," July 9, 1863, Havens MSS, Michigan State University Library.

47. GAC to I. P. Christiancy, July 26, 1863, USAHEC.

48. Wert, *Custer*, 81: "Some of the details he related in the letter [to Judge Christiancy] cannot be documented. . . . Like so many aspects of his life and career, accounts of his promotion to brigadier general have been a mixture of fact and legend." Information on the 1st Michigan prior to Custer's association with the regiment can be found in Longacre, *Custer and His Wolverines*, 23–79.

49. Kidd, *Personal Recollections of a Cavalryman*, 129; Urwin, *Custer Victorious*, 57–58. Wert, *Custer*, 83, speculates that the ensemble was put together "weeks earlier" than the date of Custer's promotion. According to Private Fought, one piece of attire, the sailor shirt, came from a "gunboat on the James" (Merington, *Custer Story*, 60), although how and when this would have occurred is uncertain.

50. Kelly, *Generals in Bronze*, 256; Lyman, *Meade's Headquarters*, 17; Longacre, "Alfred Pleasonton, 'The Knight of Romance,'" 11, 13.

51. For a copy of Custer's Gettysburg report (not in *OR*) see M-14, ELRC. Another, more accessible source is in Robertson, *Michigan in the War*, 582–84. For the formation of Custer's initial staff see Whittaker, *Complete Life of Custer*, 171. A memoir of Custer's relations with his staff officers is provided in "Reminiscences of Chaplain Theodore J. Holmes," n.d., EBCC.

52. *OR*, 27, pt. 1: 986–87, 992; Krepps, *Strong and Sudden Onslaught*, 66–67; Rummel, *Cavalry on the Roads to Gettysburg*, 128–30. Another, earlier book-length source on the battle is *Encounter at Hanover*.
53. Longacre, *Cavalry at Gettysburg*, 148–60, 193–202. For a fuller treatment of Stuart's misadventures on the road to Gettysburg, see Wittenberg and Petruzzi, *Plenty of Blame to Go Around*.
54. *OR*, 27, pt. 2: 695–96; Krepps, *Strong and Sudden Onslaught*, 31–36.
55. *OR*, 27, pt. 1: 999; Robertson, *Michigan in the War*, 580; Kidd, *Personal Recollections of a Cavalryman*, 126–28; Rummel, *Cavalry on the Roads to Gettysburg*, 277–85; George W. Barbour diary, June 30, 1863, BHL; Daniel Stewart to "Dear Margaret," July 24, 1863, Western Michigan University Library.
56. Robertson, *Michigan in the War*, 578; Avery, *Under Custer's Command*, 31–32; Krepps, *Strong and Sudden Onslaught*, 72–75; Rummel, *Cavalry on the Roads to Gettysburg*, 191–92, 244.
57. Robertson, *Michigan in the War*, 581; Merington, *Custer Story*, 60; Whittaker, *Complete Life of Custer*, 170; Hanson, "Civil War Custer," 26.
58. John Irvin Gregg, "Private & Confidential" memo, n.d., Gratz Collection, HSP.
59. *OR*, 27, pt. 1: 999; George W. Barbour diary, June 30, 1863; Kidd, *Personal Recollections of a Cavalryman*, 128; Krepps, *Strong and Sudden Onslaught*, 81–82; Rummel, *Cavalry on the Roads to Gettysburg*, 286–88.
60. Krepps, *Strong and Sudden Onslaught*, 82–83; *OR*, 27, pt. 2: 695–96.
61. Kidd, *Recollections of a Cavalryman*, 128; Krepps, *Strong and Sudden Onslaught*, 82–83.

Chapter IX

1. Krepps, *Strong and Sudden Onslaught*, 94–96.
2. Rummel, *Cavalry on the Roads to Gettysburg*, 296–98, 321–22; Shevchuk, "Battle of Hunterstown," 94, 98; Longacre, *Cavalry at Gettysburg*, 178–79.
3. *OR*, 27, pt. 1: 992; Rummel, *Cavalry on the Roads to Gettysburg*, 325–33.
4. *OR*, 27, pt. 1: 992; Longacre, *Cavalry at Gettysburg*, 203–04; Rummel, *Cavalry on the Roads to Gettysburg*, 295–96.
5. Robertson, *Michigan in the War*, 576; Kidd, *Personal Recollections of a Cavalryman*, 134; Nye, "Affair at Hunterstown," 30.
6. *New York Times*, July 21, 1863; Rummel, *Cavalry on the Roads to Gettysburg*, 339–43; Shevchuk, "Battle of Hunterstown," 98.
7. Robertson, *Michigan in the War*, 581; Rummel, *Cavalry on the Roads to Gettysburg*, 346–49; Whittaker, *Complete Life of Custer*, 173, 212; Merington, *Custer Story*, 65.

8. Robertson, *Michigan in the War*, 580; Rummel, *Cavalry on the Roads to Gettysburg*, 283–87; Ronemus, "Letter from a Young Michigan Cavalryman," 79; Nye, "Affair at Hunterstown," 33.

9. Henry E. Thompson to James H. Kidd, Sept. 30, 1863, Kidd MSS, BHL; *Kidd, Personal Recollections of a Cavalryman, 134–35;* William G. Deloney to "My Dear Rosa," July 7, 1863, Hargrett Library, University of Georgia; *New York Times*, July 21, 1863; *Grand Rapids Daily Eagle*, July 21, 1863; Rummel, *Cavalry on the Roads to Gettysburg*, 357–59; Shevchuk, "Battle of Hunterstown," 99, 102.

10. Rummel, *Cavalry on the Roads to Gettysburg*, 358; Shevchuk, "Battle of Hunterstown," 100, 102.

11. *OR*, 27, pt. 1: 998–1000; John A. Clark to "My Dear Friend," July 30, 1863, Alger MSS; Edwin R. Havens to anon., July 6, 1863, Havens MSS; Rummel, *Cavalry on the Roads to Gettysburg*, 348–50; Shevchuk, "Battle of Hunterstown," 99. The 5th Michigan was the only member of Custer's brigade to see no action during the fight: Avery, Under *Custer's Command, 33–34.*

12. Casualty figures for Company A range from twenty-seven (Shevchuk, "Battle of Hunterstown," 100) to thirty-two (Kilpatrick's report, *OR*, 27, pt. 1:. 992) to forty-four (Wert, *Custer*, 89). Nye, "Affair at Hunterstown," 34, estimates Hampton's loss as 100.

13. *OR*, 27, pt. 1: 992; Shevchuk, "Battle of Hunterstown," 104.

14. *OR*, 27, pt. 1: 992.

15. Ibid.; Rummel, *Cavalry on the Roads to Gettysburg*, 373.

16. *OR*, 27, pt. 1: 992–93; Longacre, *Cavalry at Gettysburg*, 223.

17. *OR*, 27, pt. 1: 992–93. Martin, *Kill-Cavalry*, 112, makes the absurd claim that although in obedience to an order from a superior officer, Custer's move to Gettysburg constituted an "act of gross insubordination."

18. Robertson, *Michigan in the War*, 582; *OR*, 27, pt. 1: 956.

19. *OR*, 27, pt. 3: 502; Gregg, *Second Cavalry Division of the Army of the Potomac*, 10; Rawle, *With Gregg in the Gettysburg Campaign*, 17.

20. Robertson, *Michigan in the War*, 582; Weigley, "David McMurtrie Gregg," 11–13, 28–30; Wilson, *Under the Old Flag*, 1: 364.

21. Robertson, *Michigan in the War*, 582.

22. *OR*, 27, pt. 2: 697; McClellan, *Life and Campaigns of Stuart*, 332–37.

23. Robertson, *Michigan in the War*, 582.

24. McClellan, *Life and Campaigns of Stuart*, 338.

25. Robertson, *Michigan in the War*, 581–83; Isham, *Historical Sketch of the Seventh Michigan Volunteer Cavalry*, 22.

26. Robertson, *Michigan in the War*, 578, 582–83; Avery, *Under Custer's Command*, 35; Russell A. Alger to John B. Bachelder, Jan. 1, 1886, Alger MSS; Luther S. Trowbridge to "My dear precious Julia," July 7, 1863, Trowbridge MSS, BHL.

27. Robertson, *Michigan in the War*, 583.
28. Ibid., 582–83; James H. Kidd to "Dear Father & Mother," July 9, 1863, Kidd MSS; Longacre, *Cavalry at Gettysburg*, 222–24.
29. Miller, "Cavalry Battle Near Gettysburg," 401; Kempster, "Cavalry at Gettysburg," 426. McIntosh (*OR*, 27, pt. 1: 1051) claims that he was instrumental in persuading Gregg to retain Custer's services.
30. *Pennsylvania at Gettysburg*, 2: 847, 855; Longacre, *Cavalry at Gettysburg*, 224.
31. William Brooke Rawle, "Notes as to the Cavalry Fight on the Right Flank at Gettysburg," n.d., Brooke Rawle MSS, HSP.
32. J. B. McIntosh to William Brooke Rawle, June 21, 1878, ibid.
33. *OR*, 27, pt. 1: 1050–51; Miller, "Cavalry Battle Near Gettysburg," 400–02; Longacre, *Cavalry at Gettysburg*, 225, 228–29.
34. Robertson, *Michigan in the War*, 583; Kidd, *Personal Recollections of a Cavalryman*, 146; Harris, *Major General George A. Custer*, 5; Miller, "Cavalry Battle Near Gettysburg," 402–03; *OR*, 27, pt. 2: 698.
35. Robertson, *Michigan in the War*, 578, 583, 585; *Detroit Advertiser & Tribune*, July 18, 1863; Cooper, *Obituary Discourse on Noah Henry Ferry*, 20–22; William Brooke Rawle, "Notes as to the Cavalry Fight," Brooke Rawle MSS; Luther S. Trowbridge to "My dear precious Julia," July 7, 1863, Trowbridge MSS; Avery, *Under Custer's Command*, 37.
36. Kidd, *Personal Recollections of a Cavalryman*, 145–47; Miller, "Cavalry Battle Near Gettysburg," 403; Russell A. Alger to William Brooke Rawle, Nov. 10, 1884, Brooke Rawle MSS; Alger to John B. Bachelder, Jan. 1, Feb. 8, 1886, Alger MSS; Hampton S. Thomas to John B. Bachelder, July 1, 1886, Bachelder MSS.
37. Longacre, *Custer and His Wolverines*, 94–98; Isham, *Historical Sketch of the Seventh Michigan Volunteer Cavalry*, 7–21.
38. Edwin R. Havens to "Dear Brother Nell," Dec. 14, 1862, Havens MSS.
39. Robertson, *Michigan in the War*, 578, 582–83; Isham, *Historical Sketch of the Seventh Michigan Volunteer Cavalry*, 27–28; Lee, *Personal and Historical Sketches . . . Seventh Regiment Michigan Volunteer Cavalry*, 56; Kidd, *Personal Recollections of Cavalryman*, 148–151; *Battle Creek Journal*, July 24, 1863; Edwin R. Havens to anon., July 6, 1863, Havens MSS; Andrew N. Buck to "Brother & Sister," July 9, 1863, Buck MSS, BHL; John A. Clark to "My dear friend," July 30, 1863, Alger MSS. Carhart, *Lost Triumph*, 269, advances the dubious thesis that on July 3 Custer singlehandedly won the battle and thereby saved the Union, while General Gregg added little or nothing to the day's success. Carhart's book is filled with hyperbolic assertions of this sort, wholly unsupported by evidence.
40. Robertson, *Michigan in the War*, 583; Kidd, "Address . . . at the Dedication of Michigan Monuments," 58.

41. Miller, "Cavalry Battle Near Gettysburg," 404; Allyne Litchfield to "My Dear Wife," July 9, 1863, Litchfield-French MSS, William L. Clements Library, University of Michigan.

42. Allyne Litchfield to "My Dear Wife," July 7, 1863, Litchfield-French MSS.

43. *OR*, 27, pt. 2: 697–98, 724–25.

44. Miller, "Cavalry Battle Near Gettysburg," 404; Harris, *Major General George A. Custer*, 5–6; Hampton S. Thomas to John B. Bachelder, July 1, 1886, Bachelder MSS.

45. James H. Kidd to "Dear Father & Mother," July 9, 1863, Kidd MSS.

46. Miller, "Cavalry Battle Near Gettysburg," 404; Robertson, *Michigan in the War*, 576, 583–84; Kidd, *Personal Recollections of a Cavalryman*, 154–55; Dexter M. Macomber diary, July 3, 1863, Macomber MSS; Hewett, *Supplement to the Official Records*, 5: 257–58. Kidd claims that both Gregg and Custer gave the 1st Michigan the order to charge.

47. GAC to LAR, July 26, 1863, EBCC.

48. Robertson, *Michigan in the War*, 578, 587; Luther S. Trowbridge to "My dear precious Julia," July 7, 1863, Trowbridge MSS; *OR*, 27, pt. 2: 698; McClellan, *Life and Campaigns of Stuart*, 340–41; Miller, "Cavalry Battle Near Gettysburg," 404–05; Kelly, *Generals in Bronze*, 259.

49. William Brooke Rawle to John B. Bachelder, May 22, 1878, Brooke Rawle MSS [the writer changed the order of his surname after the war]; Kelly, *Generals in Bronze*, 256; V. A. Witcher to the U.S. War Department, Aug. 2, 1898, Alger MSS.

50. Kelly, *Generals in Bronze*, 256; Harris, *Major General George A. Custer*, 6. Custer's heroics on July 3 would gain him the brevet rank of major in the regular army, the first of five such honors awarded him during his war service including that of major general, to rank from Mar. 13, 1865: Heitman, *Historical Register and Dictionary*, 1: 348.

Chapter X

1. Robertson, *Michigan in the War*, 584; Kidd, *Personal Recollections of a Cavalryman*, 155–56; William Brooke Rawle to John B. Bachelder, Mar. 20, 1886, Brooke Rawle MSS; William Brooke Rawle to William E. Miller, Apr. 1, 1886, ibid. In discounting Custer's casualty figures, Brooke Rawle told Bachelder that the brigadier "was as you may know an abominable l—r."

2. *OR*, 27, pt. 1: 993; Robertson, *Michigan in the War*, 576, 585, 587.

3. *OR*, 27, pt. 1: 992–93, 1005; Parsons, "Farnsworth's Charge and Death," 393–96; Longacre, *Cavalry at Gettysburg*, 232–33, 242–44.

4. *OR*, 27, pt. 1: 970, 993; Hoke, *Great Invasion*, 452; Moore, *Kilpatrick and Our Cavalry*, 99.
5. *OR*, 27, pt. 1: 993; 124, Brown, *Retreat from Gettysburg*, 128–29.
6. Wittenberg, Petruzzi, and Nugent, *One Continuous Fight*, 49–50; Brown, *Retreat from Gettysburg*, 69–70.
7. Kidd, *Personal Recollections of a Cavalryman*, 165–66.
8. *OR*, 27, pt. 1: 993–94; pt. 2: 752–53, 764; Brown, *Retreat from Gettysburg*, 128–30; Wittenberg, Petruzzi, and Nugent, *One Continuous Fight*, 61–62.
9. *OR*, 27, pt. 1: 998; Robertson, *Michigan in the War*, 576–77, 585; *Detroit Advertiser & Tribune*, July 15, 1863. There is a discrepancy between Brown, *Retreat from Gettysburg*, and Wittenberg, Petruzzi, and Nugent, *One Continuous Fight*, regarding the action seen by the 1st Michigan on July 4. The latter's explanation that Col. Town was confused when reporting that his men fought near Fairfield Gap rather than Monterey Pass (421, note 35) is not convincing. Had he made such a mistake in his official report, Custer, who did not file his own report of the campaign until late August, would have had plenty of time to correct his subordinate. In his report Town clearly shows that he was fighting near the gap, which he reached via a road from Fountain Dale, not at the pass farther west. His statements are verified by one of his men, Pvt. Dexter M. Macomber, who noted in his diary that the 1st fought at "Fairfax" (Fairfield) Gap; he clearly separated this action, as Town did, from the struggle at Monterey Pass. Further confirmation comes from Kidd, *Personal Recollections of a Cavalryman*, 168. Although not shown on most maps, a road connected the Emmitsburg-Waynesboro Turnpike and the road to Fairfield Gap—this is the road Town took (Hartley, *Lee's Tarheels*, 241).
10. Brown, *Retreat from Gettysburg*, 130–31.
11. Driver, *First & Second Maryland Cavalry*, 55–59; Hoke, *Great Invasion*, 453.
12. *OR*, 27, pt. 1: 994, 1019; pt. 2: 753; McClellan, *Life and Campaigns of Stuart*, 353–55; Gillespie, *History of Company A, First Ohio Cavalry*, 155–56; Brown, *Retreat from Gettysburg*, 131–34.
13. Kidd, *Personal Recollections of a Cavalryman*, 169; Ronemus, "Letter from a Young Michigan Cavalryman," 79.
14. In his official report Alger implies that his regiment alone crossed the bridge. In a postwar letter (to L. G. Estes, Feb. 12, 1897, Alger MSS) he wrote that "we charged also" as another force crossed the bridge; he identified it as Kilpatrick's escort unit. In a letter to Secretary of War D. S. Lamont, Feb. 11, 1897 (in Alger's Appointment, Commission, and Personal Branch Files, RG-94, M-1395, NA) Estes claimed that Alger made the attack "voluntarily" rather than ordered to do so.

15. Gillespie, *History of Company A, First Ohio Cavalry*, 155; Russell A. Alger to L. G. Estes, Feb. 12, 1897, Alger MSS; R. A. Alger to S. L. Gillespie, Apr. 17, 1899, ibid.; Robertson, *Michigan in the War*, 579.

16. Gillespie, *History of Company A, First Ohio Cavalry*, 155–59; *OR*, 27, pt. 1: 994, 1019; Brown, *Retreat from Gettysburg*, 136–37; Whittaker, *Complete Life of Custer*, 182–83.

17. Kidd, *Personal Recollections of a Cavalryman*, 171; Brown, *Retreat from Gettysburg*, 136–37; Hewett, *Supplement to the Official Records*, 5: 285–86; Urwin, *Custer Victorious*, 88.

18. *OR*, 27, pt. 1: 994; Note to GAC, "Report of the Battle of Gettysburg," Nov. 13, 1865, ELRC.

19. Gillespie, *History of Company A, First Ohio Cavalry*, 155; Edwin R. Havens to "Dear Father, Mother & Nell," July 9, 1863, Havens MSS; Edward Corselius to "Dear Mother," July 4, 1863, Corselius MSS, BHL.

20. Kidd, *Personal Recollections of a Cavalryman*, 170–71.

21. Ibid., 171–72; *OR*, 27, pt. 1: 994; James H. Kidd to "Dear Father and Mother," July 9, 1863, Kidd MSS July 5, 1863, Morey MSS, BHL.

22. *OR*, 27, pt. 1: 994–95; pt. 2: 700; William Ball to "dear father and mother brothers and sister," July 8, 1863, Ball MSS, Western Michigan University Library.

23. *OR*, 27, pt. 1: 488–89, 995.

24. Ibid., 971, 995, 1006, 1020; John R. Morey diary, July 6, 1863, Morey MSS.

25. *OR*, 27, pt. 1: 995, 1006–07, 1020; pt. 2: 701–02, 754, 764; McClellan, *Life and Campaigns of Stuart*, 359–60; Victor E. Comte to "Dear Elise," July 7, 1863, Comte MSS, BHL; William V. Stuart to "Dearest friend," July 8, 1863, Stuart MSS, Burton Historical Collection; Luther S. Trowbridge to "my dear precious Julia," July 7, 1863, Trowbridge MSS; Dexter M. Macomber diary, July 6, 1863, Macomber MSS; Avery, *Under Custer's Command*, 39–40; Hewett, *Supplement to the Official Records*, 5: 286–87; Wittenberg, Petruzzi, and Nugent, *One Continuous Fight*, 134–40.

26. Robertson, *Michigan in the War*, 579; Kidd, *Personal Recollections of a Cavalryman*, 172–74.

27. Robertson, *Michigan in the War*, 587.

28. *New York Times*, July 21, 1863. Kidd, *Personal Recollections of a Cavalryman*, 174, paints a much different portrait of Kilpatrick on this occasion: "His face was pale. His eyes were gazing fixedly to the front and he looked neither to the right nor to the left. The look of anxiety on his countenance was apparent."

29. Robertson, *Michigan in the War*, 579. Kidd, *Personal Recollections of a Cavalryman*, 176–77, claims that Maj. Weber's battalion of the 6th Michigan was the last unit to leave Williamsport.

30. Whittaker, *Complete Life of Custer*, 187.

31. Kidd, *Personal Recollections of a Cavalryman*, 178.
32. Longacre, *Cavalry at Gettysburg*, 258, 266; *OR*, 27, pt. 1: 489.
33. Robertson, *Michigan in the War*, 579, 585; *New York Times*, July 12, 1863; *Detroit Advertiser & Tribune*, July 8, 1863; William H. Rockwell to "My dear wife," July 9, 1863, Rockwell MSS, Western Michigan University Library; William Ball to "dear father and mother brothers and sister," July 9, 1863, Ball MSS; Avery, *Under Custer's Command*, 40; Hewett, *Supplement to the Official Records*, 5: 274; Kidd, *Personal Recollections of a Cavalryman*, 178–79; George Gray to anon., May 14, 1864, Gray's Military Pension File, RG-94, M-1064, NA.
34. Andrew N. Buck to "Brother & Sister," July 9, 1863, Buck MSS; *Detroit Advertiser & Tribune*, July 17, 1863.
35. *OR*, 27, pt. 1: 83, 146, 996, 999–1000; pt. 3: 621; Andrew N. Buck to "Brother & Sister," July 9, 1863, Buck MSS; Robertson, *Michigan in the War*, 581; Kidd, *Personal Recollections of a Cavalryman*, 181–82.
36. *OR*, 27, pt. 1: 118; pt. 3: 675; Coddington, *Gettysburg Campaign*, 567–68. By autumn Custer had lost patience with Meade's cautious tendencies: GAC to anon., Oct. 29, 1863, USMA Library.
37. Robertson, *Michigan in the War*, 579; Dexter M. Macomber diary, July 12, 1863, Macomber MSS; Avery, *Under Custer's Command*, 41, 43; John R. Morey diary, July 12, 1863, Morey MSS. Gillespie, *History of Company A, First Ohio Cavalry*, 164, claims that Custer refused an order from Kilpatrick to send a regiment to disperse a unit of Stuart's troopers who were firing on the occupiers of Hagerstown from behind a stone fence. Supposedly Custer protested that the Rebels were shielded by a battery and other supporting forces, whereupon Company A of the 1st Ohio advanced and captured the harassers. The author of the history, referencing an earlier incident of similar nature during the fighting at Monterey Pass, writes that "this was the second time we had charged where Custer and his Michigan men refused to go." Neither of these claims rings true or is corroborated by other sources.
38. *OR*, 27, pt. 1: 996, 1016–17; pt. 2: 226, 246, 309–10; James H. Kidd to "Dear Parents," July 16, 1863, Kidd MSS; Gillespie, *History of Company A, First Ohio Cavalry*, 165–66; Longacre, *Cavalry at Gettysburg*, 266–67.
39. *OR*, 27, pt. 1: 990; 2: 310; Kidd, *Personal Recollections of a Cavalryman*, 183.
40. *OR*, 27, pt. 1: 999; Victor E. Comte to "Dear Elise," July 16, 1863, Comte MSS.
41. Kidd, *Personal Recollections of a Cavalryman*, 184–86.
42. Ibid., 186–89; *OR*, I, 27, pt. 2, pp. 310, 323, 640–41.
43. *OR*, 27, pt. 1: 990, 998, 1000; Robertson, *Michigan in the War*, 577, 581–82; Charles H. Town to L. G. Estes, Sept. 9, 1863, Town's Compiled Military Service File, RG-94, E-519, NA; Allyne Litchfield to "My Dear Wife," July 14, 1863, Litchfield-French MSS; Dexter M. Macomber diary, July 14, 1863, Macomber

MSS; Kidd, *Personal Recollections of a Cavalryman*, 189; Bush, "Sixth Michigan Cavalry at Falling Waters," 113–15; Brown, *Retreat from Gettysburg*, 343–50; Urwin, *Custer Victorious*, 92.

44. *OR*, 27, pt. 1: 929, 936, 942, 990; Coddington, *Gettysburg Campaign*, 57–72.

45. William Ball to "Dear father," July 25, 1863, Ball MSS; *Battle Creek Journal*, July 24, 1863; Benjamin J. Clark to "Dear Brothers & Sisters," July 17, 1863, Clark MSS, Clarke Historical Library, Central Michigan University.

46. *OR*, 27, pt. 1: 990. The commander of Buford's First Brigade, writing to the adjutant general of Illinois one day before the fight at Falling Waters, remarked that "we do the *fighting*, and Kilpatrick does the *blowing* in the newspapers (a la Barnum)": William Gamble to A. C. Fuller, July 13, 1863, Gratz Collection, HSP.

47. *OR*, 27, pt. 1: 991.

48. Ibid., 1004; GAC to I. P. Christiancy, July 26, 1863, USAHEC; Martin, *Kill-Cavalry*, 126–27.

Chapter XI

1. *OR*, 27, pt. 1: 1004; pt. 3: 702–03; A. J. Alexander to GAC and D. M. Gregg, July 15, 1863; both, C. R. Smith MSS, USAHEC. Alexander's message to Gregg informed him that enemy forces had fired on the army's trains between Berlin and Point of Rocks on the Potomac; he was to send one brigade to picket the river.

2. *OR*, 27, pt. 1: 1004; Dexter M. Macomber diary, July 16, 1863, Macomber MSS; John R. Morey diary, July 17, 1863, Morey MSS.

3. *OR*, 27, pt. 1: 1001, 1004; John R. Morey diary, July 20–22, 1863, Morey MSS.

4. GAC to LAR, July 26, 1863, EBCC.

5. GAC to Annette Humphrey, July 19, 1863, quoted in Merington, *Custer Story*, 62.

6. Leckie, *Elizabeth Bacon Custer*, 30–31. Leckie mistakes the outfit Custer wore at Aldie, featured in Waud's sketch, for the more garish attire he wore at Gettysburg.

7. GAC to Annette Humphrey, July 19, 1863, quoted in Merington, *Custer Story*, 62.

8. Leckie, *Elizabeth Bacon Custer*, 31. As Ann Reed informed her brother, when David took the sketch to Libbie he "had quite a talk with her. I told him to write to you about [it] but he said you had not written to him": LAR to GAC, July 25, 1863, LAFC. Stiles, *Custer's Trials*, 108–09, believes David's "bitter rebuke" indicates "a growing irritation with Armstrong's assumption that David and Ann should be his agents" in communicating with Libbie. In fact that role was filled,

and apparently cheerfully, by Annette Humphrey; no evidence suggests that David was called on to run additional errands of this sort for his brother-in-law.

9. GAC to LAR, July 26, 1863, EBCC.

10. HQ Cavalry Corps, Army of the Potomac to GAC, July 20, 1863, C. R. Smith MSS.

11. *OR*, 27, pt. 1: 97–99, 489–90, 945.

12. Ibid., 1001–02, 1004; pt. 3: 740–41, 753–54; *Grand Rapids Daily Eagle*, Aug. 8, 1863; John R. Morey diary, July 23, 1863, Morey MSS; *OR*, 27, pt. 3: 740–41.

13. *OR*, 27, pt. 1: 1001–02.

14. Ibid., pt. 3: 753–54.

15. Ibid., pt. 1: 1002, 1004; pt. 2: 362, 418–19, 609; pt. 3: 765–66; John R. Morey diary, July 24, 1863, Morey MSS.

16. *OR*, 27, pt. 1: 1002–04; John R. Morey diary, July 24, 1863, Morey MSS; Dexter M. Macomber diary, July 24, 1863, Macomber MSS; *Detroit Free Press*, Aug. 2, 1863; *History of the Eighteenth Regiment of Cavalry, Pennsylvania*, 42. Battle Mountain derived its name from a local family named Bataille who had settled in the area during the eighteenth century.

17. *OR*, 27, pt. 1: 1002–03; Hewett, *Supplement to the Official Records*, 5: 287–88.

18. Avery, *Under Custer's Command*, 46–47.

19. *OR*, 27, pt. 1: 1003; pt. 3: 766; Hewett, *Supplement to the Official Records*, 5: 287–89.

20. Robertson, *A. P. Hill*, 229; *OR*, 27, pt. 3: 765.

21. *OR*, 27, pt. 3: 775; Edwin R. Havens to "Dear Nell," July 28, 1863, Havens MSS; John R. Morey to "Dear Cousin Willie," July 29, 1863, Morey MSS.

22. *OR*, 27, pt. 3: 775–76, 792; GAC to "Dear Friend," May 26, 1863, quoted in Whittaker, *Complete Life of Custer*, 151; Dexter M. Macomber diary, July 27–28, 1863, Macomber MSS; Benjamin J. Clark to "Dear Brother & Sister," July 17, 1863, Clark MSS.

23. *OR*, 27, pt. 3: 775–76, 792.

24. *Detroit Free Press*, Aug. 8, 1863.

25. Stiles, *Custer's Trials*, 118–21, 126–28, provides an excellent sketch of Eliza Brown. Stiles repeats, although he doubts, the charge lodged by Custer's enemies that he slept with the runaway slave, an act that would have made him no better a person than the master from whom she escaped.

26. GAC to Pleasonton, Aug. 2, 1863, RG-393, pt. 2, E-1449, NA. For reports of Mosby's activities at this time, see: Rufus King (commanding division, Defenses of Washington) to H. H. Wells, Aug. 3, 1863; King to J. H. Taylor, Aug. 3, 1863; Wells to King, Aug. 3, 7, 1863; C. H. Potter to King, Aug. 4, 1863; and C. R. Lowell to anon., Aug. 8, 1863; all, RG-107, M-504, NA.

27. *OR*, 27, pt. 2: 992–94; *Grand Rapids Daily Eagle*, Aug. 20, 1863. Blair sympathized with the complainants; he urged Lt. Col. Litchfield, who described Mann as "regarded with hatred and utter contempt" by the regiment, to press charges against him: Litchfield to Blair, July 9, 1863, Blair MSS. Mann would seek what amounted to terminal leave in November and had his resignation accepted the following March.

28. GAC to Pleasonton, Aug. 4, 1863, Gilder Lehrman Institute of American History; L. G. Estes to GAC, Aug. 10, 11, 1863, RG-393, pt. 2, E-1593, NA.

29. *OR*, 29, pt. 2: 38; GAC to Annette Humphrey, Aug. 13, 1863, quoted in Merington, *Custer Story*, 63; GAC to Austin Blair, Sept. 5, 1863, Blair MSS; Hatch, *Glorious War*, 184; Heitman, *Historical Register and Dictionary*, 1: 475.

30. GAC to Annette Humphrey, Aug. 13, 1863, quoted in Merington, *Custer Story*, 63; James I. Christiancy to Daniel S. Bacon, Aug. 27, 1863, EBCC.

31. Annette Humphrey to GAC, Aug. 24, 1863, LAFC; Frost, *General Custer's Libbie*, 69.

32. GAC to Annette Humphrey, ca. Sept. 7, 1863, quoted in Whittaker, *Complete Life of Custer*, 206.

33. *OR*, 29, pt. 2: 38–39.

34. Ibid., 17–18. Pleasonton to GAC, Aug. 14, 1863, RG-393, pt. 2, E-1449, NA.

35. OR, 29, pt. 2: 63.

36. O'Neill, "Reprimanded—Custer, Humphrey and 'Bushwhackers'," [3].

37. Kilpatrick to GAC, Aug. 21, 1863, RG-393, pt. 2, E-1593, NA.

38. Circular, 3rd Cav. Div., Sept. 5, 1863, RG-393, pt. 2, E-1538, NA.

39. *OR*, 29, pt. 2: 38; C. R. Smith to Kilpatrick, Aug. 16, 17, 1863; GAC to Kilpatrick, Aug. 19, 1863; both, RG-393, pt. 2, E-1449.

40. *OR*, 29, pt. 2: 43; C. R. Smith to Kilpatrick, RG-393, pt. 2, E-1439.

41. Kilpatrick to A. J. Cohen, Aug. 17, 1863, C. R. Smith to Kilpatrick, Aug. 16, 1863, RG-393, pt. 2, E-1449; NA.

42. GAC to Kilpatrick, Aug. 17, 19, 20, 1863, RG-393, pt. 2, E-1449, NA; Kilpatrick to C. R. Smith, Sept. 12, 1863, RG-393, pt. 2, E-1593, ibid.; *OR*, 29, pt. 2: 61; O'Neill, "Custer for the Defense," 18–19; Stiles, *Custer's Trials*, 129. Information on. Col. Hill may be found in Krick, *Lee's Colonels*, 193.

43. Kilpatrick to C. R. Smith, Sept. 12, 1863, RG-393, pt. 2, E-1593, NA.

44. Urwin, *Custer Victorious*, 95, notes that the 1st Vermont was added to Custer's command "to keep the brigade combat-ready until a draft of recruits could be received from Michigan."

45. GAC to Kilpatrick, Aug. 26, 1863, RG-393, pt. 2, E-1449, NA; James I. Christiancy to Daniel S. Bacon, Aug. 27, 1863, EBCC; *OR*, 29, pt. 1: 78–79; *Detroit Free Press*, Sept. 2, 1863; *New York Times*, Sept. 17, 1863.

46. GAC to Kilpatrick, Aug. 26, 1863, RG-393, pt. 2, E-1449, NA; O'Neill, "Custer for the Defense," 19–24; *OR*, 29, pt. 2: 151, 153.

47. Wert, *General James Longstreet*, 300–03; Connelly, *Autumn of Glory*, 150–62, 211–29.

48. Lee had slipped across the Rapidan in the first week of August: *OR*, 29, pt. 2: 624.

49. Ibid., 167, 175.

50. Ibid., pt. 1: 111–12, 118, 131–32; Moore, *Kilpatrick and Our Cavalry*, 124–25.

51. Lyman, *Meade's Headquarters, 1863–1865*, 15–17; Trout, *Galloping Thunder*, 348–55; Henderson, *Road to Bristoe Station*, 36–38. McClellan, *Life and Campaigns of Stuart*, 372–73, notes that "neither Stuart nor any of his subordinates made [a] report of the operations of this day, and the forces engaged cannot be stated with certainty." He also relates that Stuart was warned of Pleasonton's advance by a former Confederate surgeon who lived in the vicinity. The man was thirsting for revenge as "his wife had recently died from fright caused by the conduct of some of Kilpatrick's men."

52. *OR*, 29, pt. 1: 118, 123–24; Hartley, *Stuart's Tarheels*, 258.

53. *OR*, 29, pt. 1: 118–21; Trout, *Galloping Thunder*, 350–51. A postwar copy of Custer's report, Nov. 13, 1865, is in ELRC, M-14.

54. Longacre, *Custer and His Wolverines*, 184.

55. *OR*, 29, pt. 1: 111, 119, 128–29; William Wells to his parents, Sept. 15, 1863, Wells MSS, Guy W. Bailey Library, University of Vermont; *New York Times*, Sept. 15, 17, 1863; Glazier, *Three Years in the Federal Cavalry*, 312–14; Kilpatrick to Henry E. Davies, Sr., Sept. 17, 1863, RG-393, pt. 2, E-1593, NA; Urwin, *Custer Victorious*, 97–98; Henderson, *Road to Bristoe Station*, 38–39. Van de Water, *Glory-Hunter*, 58, writes that in attacking the enemy batteries Custer "deserted his mired command" and "left his brigade to fend for itself in an attack." Such criticism seems unduly harsh especially since Custer was accompanied by a portion of the 1st Vermont, two of whose members—one being its commander, Maj. William Wells—were wounded by fragments of the shell that disabled their superior.

56. Lyman, *Meade's Headquarters, 1863–1865*, 17. Apparently Custer's wound was a soft tissue injury, the bone not being affected. Most accounts have it caused by a shell fragment; Stiles, *Custer's Trials*, 130, claims it was a bullet wound. Hatch, *Glorious War*, 190, dismisses dubious sources that have Custer remounting after his wounding and rejoining the attack.

57. GAC to E. B. Parsons, Sept. 5, 1863, GAC's Generals' Papers, RG-94, E-159, NA. Pleasonton's praise of Custer is in *OR*, 29, pt. 1: 112.

58. Annette Humphrey to GAC, Aug. 14, 1863, LAFC; Frost, *Custer's Libbie*, 75; Stiles, *Custer's Trials*, 131.

59. Leckie, *Elizabeth Bacon Custer*, 32–33; Stiles, *Custer's Trials*, 131; Merington, *Custer Story*, 64.
60. Reynolds, *Civil War Memories of Elizabeth Bacon Custer*, 6; Leckie, *Elizabeth Bacon Custer*, 33–36.

Bibliography

Unpublished Materials

Alger, Russell A. Battle and Campaign Reports. National Archives, Washington, DC.
_____. Papers. Bentley Historical Library, University of Michigan, Ann Arbor.
Appointment, Commission, and Personal Branch Files, Adjutant General's Office. Record Group 94, Microcopy 1395, National Archives.
Bachelder, John B. Papers. New Hampshire Historical Society, Concord.
Ball, William. Correspondence. Western Michigan University Library, Kalamazoo.
Barbour, George W. Diary, 1863. Bentley Historical Library, University of Michigan.
Biddle, James C. Letter of July 1, 1863. George Gordon Meade Papers, Historical Society of Pennsylvania, Philadelphia.
Blair, Austin. Correspondence, Burton Historical Collection, Detroit Public Library, Detroit, MI.
Buck, Andrew N. Correspondence. Bentley Historical Library, University of Michigan.
Christiancy, Henry C. Diary. Christiancy-Pickett Collection, U.S. Army Heritage and Education Center, Carlisle Barracks, PA.
Clark, Benjamin J. Correspondence. Clarke Historical Library, Central Michigan University, Mount Pleasant.
Clark, John A. Letter of July 30, 1863. Russell A. Alger Papers, Bentley Historical Library, University of Michigan.
Compiled Military Service Files. Record Group 94, Entry 519, National Archives.
Comte, Victor E. Correspondence. Bentley Historical Library, University of Michigan.
Corselius, Edward. Correspondence. Bentley Historical Library, University of Michigan.
Coxe, Charles B. Correspondence. Historical Society of Pennsylvania.
Custer, George Armstrong. Battle and Campaign Reports and Correspondence. Ellis Library and Reference Center, Monroe, MI.
_____. Cadet Application Papers. U.S. Military Academy Archives, West Point, NY.
_____. Cadet Delinquency Log. U.S. Military Academy Archives.
_____. Correspondence. Augusta Ward Frary Papers, Rochester Public Library, Rochester, NY.
_____. Correspondence. Austin Blair Papers, Burton Historical Collection, Detroit Public Library, Detroit, MI.

_____. Correspondence. Christiancy-Pickett Collection, U.S. Army Heritage and Education Center.

_____. Correspondence. Elizabeth Bacon Custer Collection, Little Bighorn Battlefield National Monument, Crow Agency, MT.

_____. Correspondence. George B. McClellan Papers, Library of Congress, Washington, DC.

_____. Correspondence. Gilder Lehrman Institute of American History, New York, NY.

_____. Correspondence. Henry E. Huntington Library, San Marino, CA.

_____. Correspondence. James H. Kidd Papers, Bentley Historical Library, University of Michigan.

_____. Correspondence. Joseph Hooker Papers, Henry E. Huntington Library.

_____. Correspondence. Lawrence A. Frost Collection of Custeriana, Monroe County Library System, Monroe, MI.

_____. Correspondence. L. Tom Perry Special Collections, Harold B. Lee Library, Brigham Young University, Provo, UT.

_____. Correspondence. Marguerite Merington Papers, New York Public Library, New York, NY.

_____. Correspondence. Monroe County Historical Museum and Archives, Monroe, MI.

_____. Correspondence. U.S. Military Academy Library, West Point, NY.

_____. Correspondence. Western Americana Collection, Beinecke Rare Book and Manuscript Library, Yale University, New Haven, CT.

Deloney, William G. Correspondence. Hargrett Library, University of Georgia, Athens.

Gamble, William. Letter of July 13, 1863. Gratz Collection, Historical Society of Pennsylvania.

Generals' Papers. Record Group 94, Entry 159, National Archives.

Gregg, J. Irvin. Correspondence. Gratz Collection, Historical Society of Pennsylvania.

Havens, Edwin R. Correspondence and Diary. Main Library, Michigan State University, East Lansing.

Headquarters Cavalry Corps, Army of the Potomac. Letters, Lists, Reports, and Telegrams Sent and Received, 1863–65. Record Group 393, Entries 1439, 1449, 1502, 1508, 1538, 1543, 1593, 1616, 1753, National Archives.

Hooker, Joseph. Papers. Henry E. Huntington Library.

Hurless, John W., Jr. "Where Was General Custer Really Born?" Ellis Library and Reference Center.

Kidd, James H. Correspondence. Bentley Historical Library, University of Michigan.

Litchfield, Allyne. Correspondence. Austin Blair Papers, Burton Historical Collection, Detroit Public Library.

_____. Correspondence. Litchfield-French Papers, William L. Clements Library, University of Michigan.

Macomber, Dexter M. Papers. Clarke Historical Library, Central Michigan University.

McClellan, George B. Papers. Library of Congress.

Merington, Marguerite. Correspondence. Walter L. Pforzheimer Collection, Beinecke Rare Book and Manuscript Library, Yale University.

Military Pension Files. Record Group 94, M-1064. National Archives.

Morey, John R. Papers. Bentley Historical Library, University of Michigan.

Pleasonton, Alfred. Battle and Campaign Reports. Joseph Hooker Papers, Henry E. Huntington Library.

_____. Letter of May 30, 1863. United States Military Academy Library.

_____. Papers. Library of Congress.

Rawle, William Brooke. Papers. Historical Society of Pennsylvania.

Rockwell, William H. Correspondence. Western Michigan University Library.

Smith, C. Ross. Correspondence. U.S. Army Heritage and Education Center.

Stahel, Julius. Letter of April 20, 1863. Austin Blair Papers, Burton Historical Collection, Detroit Public Library.

Stewart, Daniel. Correspondence. Western Michigan University Library.

Stuart, William V. Correspondence. Burton Historical Collection, Detroit Public Library.

Thompson, Henry E. Letter of September 30, 1863. James H. Kidd Papers, Bentley Historical Library, University of Michigan.

Trowbridge, Luther S. Correspondence. Bentley Historical Library, University of Michigan.

Wells, William. Correspondence. Guy W. Bailey Library, University of Vermont, Burlington.

Newspapers

Cadiz (Ohio) *Democratic Sentinel*
Cadiz (Ohio) *Republican*
Detroit Advertiser & Tribune
Detroit Free Press
Grand Rapids Daily Eagle
Indianapolis Journal
Monroe (Mich.) *Commercial*
New York Herald
New York Times
Richmond Whig
Woodstock (Ill.) *Sentinel*

Articles and Essays

Adams, William G., Jr. "Spencers at Gettysburg: Fact or Fiction?" *Military Affairs* 39 (1965): 41–42, 56.

Beauregard, Erving E. "The General and the Politician: Custer and Bingham." *The Harrisonian* 2 (1989): 2–7.

Bush, Gary L. "Sixth Michigan Cavalry at Falling Waters: The End of the Gettysburg Campaign." *Gettysburg Magazine* 9 (July 1993): 116–21.

Custer, Brice C. W. "Aunt Elizabeth as I Knew Her." *Little Big Horn Associates Newsletter* 2 (1968): 3–4.

Custer, G. A., IV. "The Hidden Flags . . . (Revisited)." *Research Review* 28 (2014): 19–26.

Custer, George Armstrong. "War Memoirs." *Galaxy* 21 (1876): 319–24, 448–60, 624–32, 909–18; 22 (1876): 293–99, 447–55, 684–94.

Davis, Daniel. "Brothers at Bassett Hall." https://emergingcivilwar.com.

Davis, George B. "From Gettysburg to Williamsport." *Papers of the Military Historical Society of Massachusetts* 3 (1903): 449–69.

_____. "The Operations of the Cavalry in the Gettysburg Campaign." *Journal of the United States Cavalry Association* 1 (1888): 325–48.

Hanson, Joseph Mills. "The Civil War Custer." *Cavalry Journal* 43 (1934): 24–31.

Havens, Edwin R. "How Mosby Destroyed Our Train." *Michigan History Magazine* 14 (1930): 294–98.

Heermance, W. L. "The Cavalry at Gettysburg." *Personal Recollections of the War of the Rebellion: Addresses Delivered Before the Commandery of the State of New York, Military Order of the Loyal Legion of the United States* 3 (1907): 196–206.

Isham, Asa B. "The Cavalry of the Army of the Potomac." *Sketches of War History, 1861–1865: Papers Prepared for the Ohio Commandery of the Military Order of the Loyal Legion of the United States* 5 (1903): 301–27.

Kempster, Walter. "The Cavalry at Gettysburg." *War Papers Read Before the Commandery of the State of Wisconsin, Military Order of the Loyal Legion of the United States* 4 (1914): 397–429.

Kidd, James H. "Address of General James H. Kidd, at the Dedication of Michigan Monuments Upon the Battle Field of Gettysburg, June 12, 1889." *Journal of the U. S. Cavalry Association* 4 (1891): 41–63.

Klement, Frank L., ed. "Edwin B. Bigelow, A Michigan Sergeant in the Civil War." *Michigan History* 38 (1954): 193–252.

Krolick, Marshall D. "Forgotten Field: The Cavalry Battle East of Gettysburg on July 3, 1863." *Gettysburg Magazine* 4 (1991): 75–88.

Leckie, Shirley A. "The Civil War Partnership of Elizabeth and George A. Custer." In Carol K. Bleser and Lesley J. Gordon, eds., *Intimate Strategies of the Civil War: Military Commanders and Their Wives* (New York: Oxford University Press, 2001): 178–98.

Lee, William O. "Michigan Cavalry Brigade at Gettysburg." *Gateway* 3 (1904): 45–50.

Longacre, Edward G. "Alfred Pleasonton, 'The Knight of Romance'." *Civil War Times Illustrated* 13 (December 1974): 10–23.

_____. "Judson Kilpatrick." *Civil War Times Illustrated* 10 (April 1971): 24–33.

McKinney, Francis F. "Michigan Cavalry in the Civil War." *Michigan Alumnus Quarterly Review* 43 (1957): 136–46.

McMahon, Thomas L. "The Flag of the 5th North Carolina, the First Southern Banner Captured in the East, Has Been Recovered." *America's Civil War* 15 (May 2002): 66–72.

Michie, Peter. "Reminiscences of Cadet and Army Service." In *Personal Recollections of the War of the Rebellion* (New York: G. P. Putnam's Sons, 1897): 183–97.

Miller, William E. "The Cavalry Battle Near Gettysburg." *Battles and Leaders of the Civil War* 3 (1887–88): 397–406.

Newhall, F. C. "The Battle of Beverly Ford." In *Annals of the War, Written by Leading Participants, North and South* (Philadelphia: *Times* Publishing, 1879): 134–46.

"Notes and Queries: Are the West Point Graduates Loyal?" *Historical Magazine* 7 (1863): 31–33.

Nye, Wilbur S. "The Affair at Hunterstown." *Civil War Times Illustrated* 9 (February 1971): 22–34.

O'Neill, Robert F. "Custer for the Defense: George Custer, Judson Kilpatrick and the Gunboat Raid of September 1863." *Research Review 2: The Journal of the Little Big Horn Association* 28 (2014): 16–24.

_____. "George Custer's Ascension to Command the Wolverines." *Blue & Gray* 26 (2009): 26–29.

_____. "'It is Horrible to Have Such a Man in Command of a Michigan Regiment': Col. William Mann and the 7th Michigan Cavalry During the Gettysburg Campaign." *Gettysburg Magazine* 48 (2013): 51–62.

_____. "Julius Stahel's Cavalry Division, June 1863." *North & South* 14 (2012): 52–62.

_____. "Reprimanded—Custer, Humphreys and 'Bushwhackers'." https://smallbutimportantpatriots.com/2016/04/27.

O'Neill, Tom. "Two Men of Ohio: Custer & Bingham." *Research Review: The Journal of the Little Big Horn Association* 8 (1994): 10–13.

Parsons, H. C. "Farnsworth's Charge and Death." *Battles and Leaders of the Civil War* 3 (1887–88): 393–96.

Phipps, Michael. "'They Too Fought Here': The Officer Corps of the Army of the Potomac's Cavalry During the Battle of Gettysburg." In *Mr. Lincoln's Army: The Army of the Potomac in the Gettysburg Campaign* (Gettysburg, PA: Gettysburg National Military Park, 1998): 92–135.

Pleasonton, Alfred. "The Campaign of Gettysburg." In *Annals of the War, Written by Leading Participants, North and South* (Philadelphia: *Times* Publishing, 1879): 447–59.

Rawle, William Brooke. "Further Remarks on the Cavalry Fight on the Right Flank at Gettysburg." *Journal of the United States Cavalry Association* 4 (1891): 157–60.

_____. "Gregg's Cavalry Fight at Gettysburg, July 3, 1863." *Journal of the United States Cavalry Association* 4 (1891): 257–75.

_____. "The Right Flank at Gettysburg," In *Annals of the War, Written by Leading Participants, North and South* (Philadelphia: *Times* Publishing, 1879): 467–84.

Ronemus, Nancy, ed. "A Letter from a Young Michigan Cavalryman. . . ." *America's Civil War* 10 (March 1997): 74–79.

Shevchuk, Paul M. "The Battle of Hunterstown, Pennsylvania, July 2, 1863." *Gettysburg Magazine* 1 (1980): 93–101.

Swift, Eben. "The Fifth Regiment of Cavalry." In Theophilus F. Rodenbough and William L. Haskin, eds., *The Army of the United States: Historical Sketches of Staff and Line* (New York: Merrill, 1896): 221–31.

Throckmorton, A. B. "Major-General Kilpatrick." *Northern Monthly* 2 (1868): 590–605.

Urwin, Gregory J. W. "Custer: The Civil War Years." In Paul Andrew Hutton, ed., *The Custer Reader* (Lincoln, NE: University of Nebraska Press, 1992): 7–32.

Weigley, Russell F. "David McMurtrie Gregg: A Personality Profile." *Civil War Times Illustrated* 1 (November 1962): 11–13, 28–30.

Wilson, James Harrison. "The Cavalry of the Army of the Potomac." *Papers of the Military Historical Society of Massachusetts* 13 (1913): 33–88.

Wright, J. M. "West Point Before the War." *Southern Bivouac* 4 (1885): 13–21.

Books and Pamphlets

Adams, Charles F., Jr., et al. *A Cycle of Adams Letters, 1861–1865*. Edited by Worthington Chauncey Ford. 2 vols. Boston: Houghton Mifflin, 1920.

Alberts, Don E. *Brandy Station to Manila Bay: A Biography of General Wesley Merritt*. Austin, TX: Presidial Press, 1981.

Ambrose, Stephen E. *Crazy Horse and Custer: The Parallel Lives of Two American Warriors*. Garden City, NY: Doubleday, 1975.

Averell, William W. *Ten Years in the Saddle: The Memoir of William Woods Averell, 1851–1862*. Edited by Edward K. Eckert and Nicholas J. Amato. San Rafael, CA: Presidio Press, 1978.

Avery, James H. *Under Custer's Command: The Civil War Journal of James Henry Avery*. Compiled by Karla Jean Husby; edited by Eric J. Wittenberg. Washington, DC: Brassey's, 2000.

Beauregard, Erving E. *Bingham of the Hills: Politician and Diplomat Extraordinary*. New York: Peter Lang, 1989.

Bigelow, John. *The Campaign of Chancellorsville*. New Haven, CT: Yale University Press, 1910.

Bilby, Joseph G., and William C. Goble. *"Remember You Are Jerseymen!": A Military History of New Jersey's Troops in the Civil War*. Hightstown, NJ: Longstreet House, 1998.

Boatner, Mark Mayo. *The Civil War Dictionary*. New York: David McKay, 1959.

Boudrye, Louis N. *Historic Records of the Fifth New York Cavalry*. Albany, NY: Munsell, 1865.

Bridges, David P. *Fighting with Jeb Stuart: Major James Breathed and the Confederate Horse Artillery*. Arlington, VA: privately issued, 2006.

Brown, Kent Masterson. *Retreat from Gettysburg: Lee, Logistics, and the Pennsylvania Campaign*. Chapel Hill, NC: University of North Carolina Press, 2005.

Bushong, Millard K., and Dean M. Bushong. *Fightin' Tom Rosser, C.S.A.* Shippensburg, PA: Beidel Printing House, 1983.

Carhart, Tom. *Lost Triumph: Lee's Real Plan at Gettysburg—and Why It Failed*. New York: Putnam's, 2005.

Carroll, John M., comp. *Custer in the Civil War: His Unfinished Memoirs*. San Rafael, CA: Presidio Press, 1977.

_____, ed. *General Custer and New Rumley, Ohio*. Bryan, TX: privately issued, 1978.

Catton, Bruce. *Glory Road: The Bloody Route from Fredericksburg to Gettysburg*. Garden City, NY: Doubleday, 1952.

Cleaves, Freeman. *Meade of Gettysburg*. Norman, OK: University of Oklahoma Press, 1960.

Coddington, Edwin B. *The Gettysburg Campaign: A Study in Command*. New York: Scribner's, 1968.

Collea, Joseph D., Jr. *The First Vermont Cavalry in the Civil War: A History*. Jefferson, NC: McFarland, 2010.

Connelly, Thomas L. *Autumn of Glory: The Army of Tennessee, 1862–1865*. Baton Rouge, LA: Louisiana State University Press, 1971.

Cooper, David M. *Obituary Discourse on Occasion of the Death of Noah Henry Ferry*. New York: John F. Trow, 1863.

Crackel, Theodore J. *The Illustrated History of West Point*. New York: Abrams, 1991.

Crowninshield, Benjamin W., and D. H. L. Gleason. *A History of the First Regiment of Massachusetts Cavalry Volunteers*. Boston: Houghton Mifflin, 1891.

Custer, Elizabeth Bacon. *The Civil War Memoirs of Elizabeth Bacon Custer, Reconstructed from Her Diaries and Notes*. Edited by Arlene Reynolds. Austin: University of Texas Press, 1994.

Department of Defense: Selected Manpower Statistics—Fiscal Year 1997. Washington, DC: Government Printing Office, 1998.

Downey Fairfax. *Clash of Cavalry: The Battle of Brandy Station, June 9, 1863*. New York: McKay, 1959.

Driver, Robert J., Jr. *First & Second Maryland Cavalry, C. S. A.* Charlottesville, VA: Rockbridge Publishing, 1999.

Dyer, Frederick H., comp. *A Compendium of the War of the Rebellion*. Des Moines, IA: privately issued, 1908.

Encounter at Hanover: Prelude to Gettysburg. Hanover, PA: Hanover Chamber of Commerce, 1963.

Evans, Charles M. *War of the Aeronauts: A History of Ballooning in the Civil War*. Mechanicsburg, PA: Stackpole, 2002.

Farley, Joseph Pearson. *West Point in the Early Sixties, with Incidents of the War.* Troy, NY: Pafraets Press, 1902.

Fordney, Ben F. *Stoneman at Chancellorsville: The Coming of Age of Union Cavalry.* Shippensburg, PA: White Mane, 1998.

Freeman, Douglas Southall. *Lee's Lieutenants: A Study in Command.* 3 vols. New York: Scribner's, 1942–44.

_____. *R. E. Lee: A Biography.* 4 vols. New York: Scribner's, 1934–35.

Freiheit, Laurence. *Boots and Saddles: Cavalry During the Maryland Campaign of September 1862.* Iowa City, IA: Camp Pope Bookshop, 2013.

Frost, Lawrence A. *The Custer Album: A Pictorial Biography of General George A. Custer.* Seattle: Superior, 1964.

_____. *Custer Legends.* Bowling Green, OH: Popular Press, 1981.

_____. *General Custer's Libbie.* Seattle: Superior, 1976.

Gallagher, Gary W. *Stephen Dodson Ramseur, Lee's Gallant General.* Chapel Hill, NC: University of North Carolina Press, 1985.

Gillespie, Samuel L. *A History of Company A, First Ohio Cavalry, 1861–1865.* Washington Court House, OH: Ohio State Register, 1898.

Glazier, Willard. *Three Years in the Federal Cavalry.* New York: R. H. Ferguson, 1870.

Gregg, David McMurtrie. *The Second Cavalry Division of the Army of the Potomac in the Gettysburg Campaign.* Philadelphia: privately issued, 1907.

Hamilton, Richard L. *"Oh, Hast Thou Forgotten": Michigan Cavalry in the Civil War— The Gettysburg Campaign.* n.p.: privately issued, 2008.

Hard, Abner. *History of the Eighth Cavalry Regiment, Illinois Volunteers, During the Great Rebellion.* Aurora, IL: privately issued, 1868.

Harris, Samuel A. *Major General George A. Custer: Stories Told Around the Camp Fire of the Michigan Brigade of Cavalry.* Chicago: privately issued, 1898.

_____. *Michigan Brigade of Cavalry at the Battle of Gettysburg, July, 1863.* Chicago: privately issued, 1894.

_____. *Personal Reminiscences of Samuel Harris.* Chicago: Rogerson Press, 1897.

Hartley, Chris J. *Stuart's Tarheels: James B. Gordon and His North Carolina Cavalry.* Baltimore: Butternut & Blue, 1996.

Hatch, Thom. *Clashes of Cavalry: The Civil War Careers of George Armstrong Custer and Jeb Stuart.* Mechanicsburg, PA: Stackpole, 2001.

_____. *Glorious War: The Civil War Adventures of George Armstrong Custer.* New York: St. Martin's Press, 2013.

Hebert, Walter H. *Fighting Joe Hooker.* Indianapolis, IN: Bobbs-Merrill, 1944.

Heitman, Francis B., comp. *Historical Register and Dictionary of the United States Army, from Its Organization, September 29, 1789, to March 2, 1903.* 2 vols. Washington, DC: Government Printing Office, 1903.

Henderson, William D. *The Road to Bristoe Station: Campaigning with Lee and Meade, August 1-October 20, 1863.* Lynchburg, VA: H. E. Howard, 1987.

Hennessy, John J. *Return to Bull Run: The Campaign and Battle of Second Manassas.* New York: Simon & Schuster, 1993.

Hewett, Janet, et al., eds. *Supplement to the Official Records of the Union and Confederate Armies*. 3 series, 99 vols. Wilmington, NC: Broadfoot, 1994–2001.

History of the Eighteenth Regiment of Cavalry, Pennsylvania Volunteers, 1862–1865. New York: Wynkoop-Hallenbeck-Crawford, 1909.

Hoke, Jacob. *The Great Invasion of 1863; or, General Lee in Pennsylvania*. Dayton, OH: W. J. Shuey, 1887.

Horn, W. Donald, ed. *"Skinned": The Delinquency Record of Cadet George Armstrong Custer, U.S.M.A. Class of 1861*. Short Hills, NJ: privately issued, 1980.

Howe, Henry. *Historical Collections of the State of Ohio: An Encyclopedia of the State*. 2 vols. Cincinnati, OH: C. J. Krehbiel, 1907.

Isham, Asa B. *An Historical Sketch of the Seventh Michigan Volunteer Cavalry from Its Organization in 1862, to Its Muster Out, in 1865*. New York: Town Topics Publishing, 1893.

Kelly, James Edward. *Generals in Bronze: Interviewing the Commanders of the Civil War*. Edited by William B. Styple. Kearny, NJ: Belle Grove Publishing, 2005.

Kidd, James Harvey. *One of Custer's Wolverines: The Civil War Letters of Brevet Brigadier General James H. Kidd, 6th Michigan Cavalry*. Edited by Eric J. Wittenberg. Kent, OH: Kent State University Press, 2000.

_____. *Personal Recollections of a Cavalryman with Custer's Michigan Cavalry Brigade in the Civil War*. Ionia, MI: *Sentinel* Printing, 1908.

Kirshner, Ralph. *The Class of 1861: Custer, Ames, and Their Classmates After West Point*. Carbondale, IL: Southern Illinois University Press, 1999.

Knight, Judson. *Scouting for Grant and Meade: The Reminiscences of Judson Knight, Chief of Scouts, Army of the Potomac*. Edited by Peter G. Tsouras. New York: Skyhorse, 2014.

Krepps, John T. *A Strong and Sudden Onslaught: The Cavalry Action at Hanover, Pennsylvania*. Orrtanna, PA: Colecraft, 2008.

Krick, Robert K. *Lee's Colonels: A Biographical Register of the Field Officers of the Army of Northern Virginia*. Dayton, OH: Morningside, 1992.

Lanman, Charles. *The Red Book of Michigan: A Civil, Military and Biographical History*. Detroit: E. B. Smith, 1871.

Leckie, Shirley A. *Elizabeth Bacon Custer and the Making of a Myth*. Norman, OK: University of Oklahoma Press, 1993.

Lee, William O., comp. *Personal and Historical Sketches and Facial History of and by Members of the Seventh Regiment Michigan Volunteer Cavalry*. Detroit: Ralston-Stroup Printing, 1904

Longacre, Edward G. *The Cavalry at Gettysburg: A Tactical Study of Mounted Operations during the Civil War's Pivotal Campaign, 9 June-14 July 1863*. Lincoln, NE: University of Nebraska Press, 1993.

_____. *Custer and His Wolverines: The Michigan Cavalry Brigade, 1861–1865*. Conshohocken, PA: Combined Publishing, 1997.

_____. *The Early Morning of War: Bull Run, 1861*. Norman, OK: University of Oklahoma Press, 2014.

_____. *Lincoln's Cavalrymen: A History of the Mounted Forces of the Army of the Potomac, 1861–1865*. Mechanicsburg, PA: Stackpole, 2000.

Long, E. B. *The Civil Way Day by Day: An Almanac, 1861–1865*. Garden City, NY: Doubleday, 1971.

Lyman, Theodore. *Meade's Headquarters, 1863–1865: Letters of Colonel Theodore Lyman from the Wilderness to Appomattox*. Edited by George R. Agassiz. Boston: Atlantic Monthly Press, 1922.

Martin, Samuel J. *Kill-Cavalry: The Life of Union General Hugh Judson Kilpatrick*. Mechanicsburg, PA: Stackpole, 2000.

McClellan, George B. *McClellan's Own Story: The War for the Union*. New York: Charles L. Webster, 1887.

_____. *Report on the Organization and Campaigns of the Army of the Potomac*. New York: Sheldon & Co., 1864.

McClellan, H. B. *The Life and Campaigns of Major-General J. E. B. Stuart, Commander of the Cavalry of the Army of Northern Virginia*. Boston: Houghton Mifflin, 1885.

McCrea, Tully. *Dear Belle: Letters from a Cadet & Officer to His Sweetheart, 1858–1865*. Edited by Catherine S. Crary. Middletown, CT: Wesleyan University Press, 1965.

McKinney, Joseph W. *Brandy Station, June 9, 1863, The Largest Cavalry Battle of the Civil War*. Jefferson, NC: McFarland, 2013.

McWhiney, Grady, and Perry D. Jamieson. *Attack and Die: Civil War Military Tactics and the Southern Heritage*. University, AL: University of Alabama Press, 1982.

Merington, Marguerite, ed. *The Custer Story: The Life and Intimate Letters of General Custer and His Wife Elizabeth*. New York: Devin-Adair, 1950.

Meyer, Henry C. *Civil War Experiences Under Bayard, Gregg, Kilpatrick, Custer, and Newberry, 1862, 1863, 1864*. New York: Knickerbocker Press, 1911.

Michigan at Gettysburg. Detroit: Winn & Hammond, 1889.

Monaghan, Jay. *Custer: The Life of General George Armstrong Custer*. New York: Little, Brown, 1959.

Moore, Frank, ed. *The Rebellion Record: A Diary of American Events*. 12 vols. New York: various publishers, 1861–68.

Moore, James. *Kilpatrick and Our Cavalry*. New York: W. J. Widdleton, 1865.

Morgan, James A., III. *Always Ready, Always Willing: A History of Battery M, Second United States Artillery from Its Organization Through the Civil War*. Gaithersburg, MD: Olde Soldier Books, n.d.

Morrison, James L., Jr. *"The Best School in the World": West Point, the Pre-Civil War Years, 1833–1866*. Kent, OH: Kent State University Press, 1986.

Nye, Wilbur S. *Here Come the Rebels!* Baton Rouge, LA: Louisiana State University Press, 1965.

Official Register of the Officers and Cadets of the U. S. Military Academy, West Point, New York. West Point, NY: privately issued, 1843–61.

O'Neill, Robert F., Jr. *The Cavalry Battles of Aldie, Middleburg and Upperville: Small But Important Riots, June 10–27, 1863*. Lynchburg, VA: H. E. Howard, 1993.

_____. *Chasing Jeb Stuart and John Mosby: The Union Cavalry in Northern Virginia from Second Manassas to Gettysburg.* Jefferson, NC: McFarland, 2012.

O'Sullivan, Richard. *55th Virginia Infantry.* Lynchburg, VA: H. E. Howard, 1989.

Patrick, Marsena R. *Inside Lincoln's Army: The Diary of Marsena Rudolph Patrick, Provost Marshal General, Army of the Potomac.* Edited by David S. Sparks. New York: Thomas Yoseloff, 1964.

Pennsylvania at Gettysburg. 2 vols. Lancaster, PA: B. Singerly, 1893.

Price, George F., comp. *Across the Continent with the Fifth Cavalry.* New York: D. Van Nostrand, 1883.

Rafuse, Ethan S. *McClellan's War: The Failure of Moderation in the Struggle for the Union.* Bloomington, IN: Indiana University Press, 2005.

Rawle, William Brooke. *The Right Flank at Gettysburg: An Account of the Operations of General Gregg's Cavalry Command.* Philadelphia: Allen, Lane & Scott, 1878.

_____. *With Gregg in the Gettysburg Campaign.* Philadelphia: McLaughlin Brothers, 1884.

Record Fifth Michigan Cavalry, Civil War, 1861–1865. Kalamazoo: Ihling Bros. & Everard, 1905.

Record First Michigan Cavalry, Civil War, 1861–1865. Kalamazoo: Ihling Bros. & Everard, 1905.

Record Seventh Michigan Cavalry, Civil War, 1861–1865. Kalamazoo: Ihling Bros. & Everard, 1905.

Record Sixth Michigan Cavalry, Civil War, 1861–1865. Kalamazoo: Ihling Bros. & Everard, 1905.

Rhodes, Charles D. *History of the Cavalry of the Army of the Potomac.* Kansas City: Hudson-Kimberley, 1900.

Robbins, James S. *Last in Their Class: Custer, Pickett and the Goats of West Point.* New York: Encounter Books, 2006.

Robertson, John, comp. *Michigan in the War.* Lansing, MI: W. S. George, 1882.

Ronsheim, L. Milton. *The Life of General Custer.* Cadiz, OH: *Cadiz Republican*, 1929.

Rummel, George A., III. *Cavalry on the Roads to Gettysburg: Kilpatrick at Hanover and Hunterstown.* Shippensburg, PA: White Mane, 2000.

Schaff, Morris. *The Spirit of Old West Point, 1858–1862.* Boston: Houghton, Mifflin, 1907.

Schultz, Duane. *Custer: Lessons in Leadership.* New York: Palgrave-Macmillan, 2010.

Scott, H. L. *Military Dictionary: Comprising Technical Definitions . . .* New York: D. Van Nostrand, 1861.

Sears, Stephen W. *Chancellorsville.* Boston: Houghton Mifflin, 1996.

_____. *Controversies & Commanders: Dispatches from the Army of the Potomac.* Boston: Houghton Mifflin, 1999.

_____. *Gettysburg.* Boston: Houghton Mifflin, 2003.

_____. *Landscape Turned Red: The Battle of Antietam.* New York: Ticknor & Fields, 1983.

_____. *Lincoln's Lieutenants: The High Command of the Army of the Potomac.* Boston: Houghton Mifflin Harcourt, 2017.

_____. *To the Gates of Richmond: The Peninsula Campaign.* New York: Ticknor & Fields, 1992.

Servacek, Robert. *Custer: His Promotion in Frederick, Maryland.* Frederick, MD: privately issued, 2002.

Starr, Stephen Z. *The Union Cavalry in the Civil War.* 3 vols. Baton Rouge: Louisiana State University Press, 1979–84.

Stiles, T. J. *Custer's Trials: A Life on the Frontier of a New America.* New York: Vintage Books, 2016.

Tap, Bruce. *Over Lincoln's Shoulder: The Committee on the Conduct of the War.* Lawrence, KS: University Press of Kansas, 1998.

Thian, Raphael P. *Notes Illustrating the Military Geography of the United States, 1813–1880.* Washington, DC: Government Printing Office, 1881.

Thomas, Hampton S. *Some Personal Reminiscences of Service in the Cavalry of the Army of the Potomac.* Philadelphia: L. R. Hammersly, 1889.

Tobie, Edward P. *History of the First Maine Cavalry, 1861–1865.* Boston: Emery & Hughes, 1887.

_____. *Service of the Cavalry in the Army of the Potomac.* Providence, RI: privately issued, 1882.

A Tour of Custer's New Rumley: Bus Tour of New Rumley and Harrison County, Ohio, June 5, 1998. New Rumley, OH: privately issued, 1998.

Trout, Robert J. *Galloping Thunder: The Story of the Stuart Horse Artillery Battalion.* Mechanicsburg, PA: Stackpole, 2002.

Trowbridge, Luther S. *The Operations of the Cavalry in the Gettysburg Campaign.* Detroit: privately issued, 1888.

Urwin, Gregory J. W. *Custer Victorious: The Civil War Battles of General George Armstrong Custer.* East Brunswick, NJ: Associated University Presses, 1983.

Utley, Robert M. *Cavalier in Buckskin: George Armstrong Custer and the Western Military Frontier.* Norman, OK: University of Oklahoma Press, 1988.

Van de Water, Frederic F. *Glory-Hunter: A Life of General Custer.* Indianapolis, IN: Bobbs-Merrill, 1934.

Walker, Paul D. *The Cavalry Battle That Saved the Union: Custer vs. Stuart at Gettysburg.* Gretna, LA: Pelican Publishing, 2002.

Wallace, Charles B. *Custer's Ohio Boyhood: A Brief Account of the Early Life of Major General George Armstrong Custer.* Freeport, OH: *Freeport Press,* 1978.

Warner, Ezra J. *Generals in Blue: Lives of the Union Commanders.* Baton Rouge, LA: Louisiana State University Press, 1964.

_____. *Generals in Gray: Lives of the Confederate Commanders.* Baton Rouge, LA: Louisiana State University Press, 1959.

The War of the Rebellion: A Compilation of the Official Records of the Union and Confederate Armies. 4 series, 128 vols. Washington, DC: Government Printing Office, 1880–1901.

Watson, William. *Letters of a Civil War Surgeon*. Edited by Paul Fatout. Lafayette, IN: Purdue University Studies, 1961.

Wert, Jeffry D. *Custer: The Controversial Life of George Armstrong Custer*. New York: Simon & Schuster, 1996.

_____. *General James Longstreet, the Confederacy's Most Controversial Soldier—A Biography*. New York: Simon & Schuster, 1993.

Whittaker, Frederick. *A Complete Life of Gen. George A. Custer*. New York: Sheldon, 1876.

Wilson, James Harrison. *Under the Old Flag: Recollections of Military Operations in the War for the Union, the Spanish War, the Boxer Rebellion, etc.* 2 vols. New York: D. Appleton, 1912.

Wing, Talcott E., ed. *History of Monroe County, Michigan*. New York: Munsell, 1890.

Wittenberg, Eric J., and J. David Petruzzi. *Plenty of Blame to Go Around: Jeb Stuart's Controversial Ride to Gettysburg*. El Dorado Hills, CA: Savas Beatie, 2011.

_____, J. David Petruzzi, and Michael F. Nugent. *One Continuous Fight: The Retreat from Gettysburg and the Pursuit of Lee's Army of Northern Virginia, July 4–14, 1863*. El Dorado Hills, CA: Savas Beatie, 2008.

Index